MONTE CASSINO

BY PETER CADDICK-ADAMS

Monty and Rommel: Parallel Lives

MONTE CASSINO

TEN ARMIES IN HELL

Peter Caddick-Adams

OXFORD
UNIVERSITY PRESS

Oxford University Press is a department of the University of Oxford.
It furthers the University's objective of excellence in research,
scholarship, and education by publishing worldwide.

Oxford   New York
Auckland   Cape Town   Dar es Salaam   Hong Kong   Karachi
Kuala Lumpur   Madrid   Melbourne   Mexico City   Nairobi
New Delhi   Shanghai   Taipei   Toronto

With offices in
Argentina   Austria   Brazil   Chile   Czech Republic   France   Greece
Guatemala   Hungary   Italy   Japan   Poland   Portugal   Singapore
South Korea   Switzerland   Thailand   Turkey   Ukraine   Vietnam

Oxford is a registered trade mark of Oxford University Press
in the UK and certain other countries.

First published in Great Britain in 2012 by Preface Publishing

Published in the United States of America by
Oxford University Press
198 Madison Avenue, New York, NY 10016

Library of Congress Cataloging-in-Publication Data
Caddick-Adams, Peter, 1960–
Monte Cassino : ten armies in Hell / Peter Caddick-Adams.
p. cm.
Originally published: London : Preface, 2012.
Includes bibliographical references and index.
ISBN 978-0-19-997464-1
1. Cassino, Battle of, Cassino, Italy, 1944. I. Title.
D763.I82C26257   2013
940.54′215622—dc23   2012030395

1 3 5 7 9 8 6 4 2

Printed in the United States of America
on acid-free paper

In memory of Richard Holmes CBE, TD, JP
friend, colleague and mentor
1946–2011

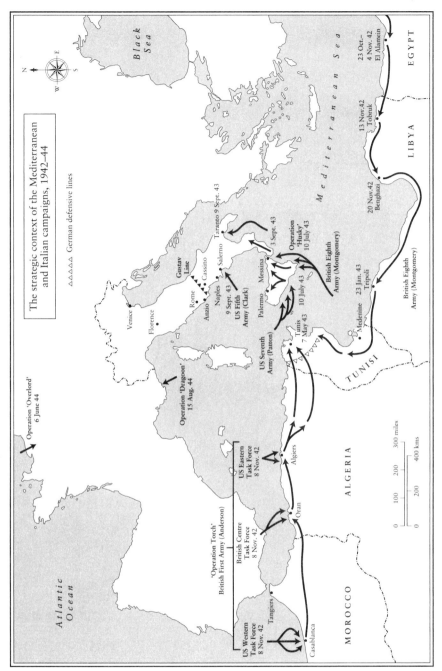

The strategic context of the Mediterranean and Italian campaigns, 1942–44

△△△△△ German defensive lines

Alexander's Army Group was the fusion of the Anglo–US forces that landed in Morocco and Algeria (Operation Torch) with Montgomery's Eighth Army advancing from El Alamein. While the invasion of Sicily (Husky) was a natural progression after the Allied conquest of Tunisia, future options were less clear, for Churchill and Roosevelt anticipated a simultaneous assault on France in 1944 from both the north (Overlord) and south (Dragoon). While Dragoon slipped by two months, all its resources came from the Italian theatre. The map also illustrates why Rommel's proposals to defend Italy from the north attracted Hitler initially. From there, he could counter any threatened invasions of southern France or the Balkans.

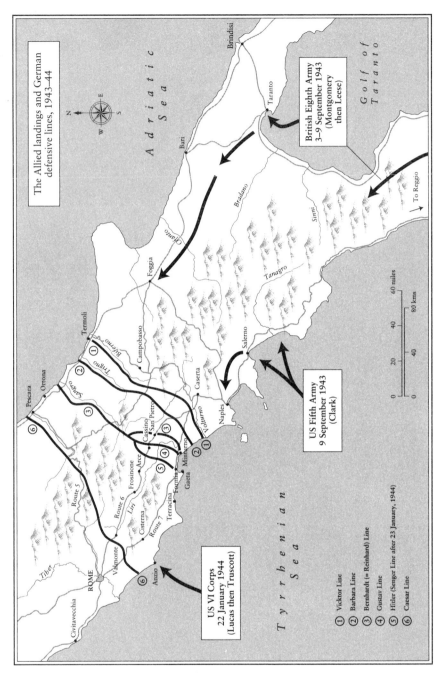

The Allied landings and German defensive lines, 1943–44

British Eighth Army
3–9 September 1943
(Montgomery
then Leese)

US Fifth Army
9 September 1943
(Clark)

US VI Corps
22 January 1944
(Lucas then Truscott)

① Vicktor Line
② Barbara Line
③ Bernhardt (= Reinhard) Line
④ Gustav Line
⑤ Hitler (Senger Line after 23 January, 1944)
⑥ Caesar Line

After the unexpected German success in holding Mark Clark's Fifth Army at Salerno for ten days, Hitler opted for Kesselring's plans of a southerly defence, rather than Rommel's based in the north. The result was various linear positions, strung across the waist of Italy, incorporating rivers and mountains wherever possible. The Victor and Barbara lines bought time whilst the most deadly, the Bernhardt, was constructed in depth by military engineers. The Bernhardt was at its strongest in the west, where a fall-back or switch position, the Gustav, was constructed around the natural bastion of Monte Cassino.

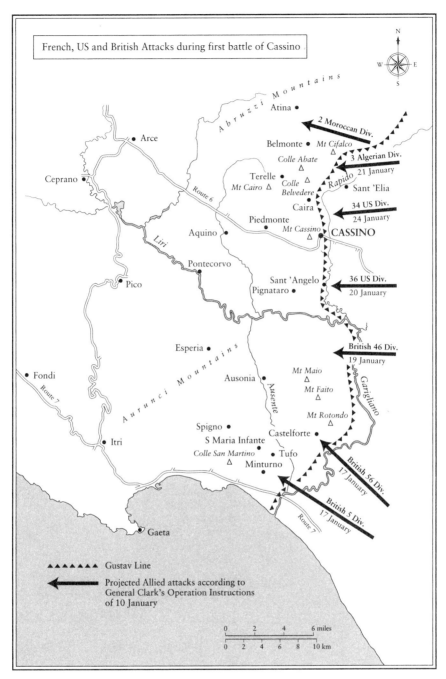

French, US and British Attacks during first battle of Cassino

N
W E
S

Abruzzi Mountains

Atina •

Arce •

Belmonte • Mt Cifalco △

2 Moroccan Div.

Colle Abate △

3 Algerian Div.
21 January

Ceprano •

Terelle • *Colle* △
Mt Cairo △ *Belvedere*

Route 6

Sant 'Elia •

Rapido

Caira •

34 US Div.
24 January

Aquino •

Piedmonte •

Mt Cassino △

CASSINO

Liri

Pontecorvo •

Pico •

Sant 'Angelo ▷
Pignataro •

36 US Div.
20 January

British 46 Div.
19 January

Esperia •

Aurunci Mountains

Mt Maio △

British 56 Div.
17 January

Fondi •

Ausonia •

Ausente

Mt Faito △

Mt Rotondo △

Garigliano

Route 7

Spigno •
S Maria Infante •

Castelforte •

Colle San Martino △

Tufo •
Minturno •

British 5 Div.
17 January

Itri •

Route 7

Gaeta •

▲▲▲▲▲▲▲▲ Gustav Line

⬅ Projected Allied attacks according to
General Clark's Operation Instructions
of 10 January

0   2   4   6 miles
0 2 4 6 8 10 km

The first battle of Cassino saw a series of Allied attacks between Cassino and the coast, which were sequential, and timed to coincide with the Anzio landings. After the war the local German corps commander, General Senger, criticised this approach, as he was able to switch his reserves to meet each assault. He argued that had the Allied thrusts been simultaneous, they would have broken through. Of the attacks, the French in the north showed most promise, but was halted through lack of reinforcements. Senger, though, was most worried by the British moves in the south, which he felt would have broken through had they been properly resourced.

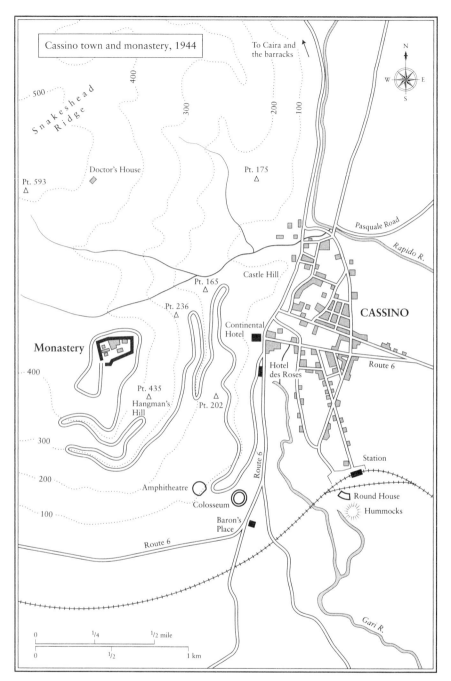

Cassino town and monastery, 1944

500

400

300

200

100

To Caira and
the barracks

N
W ☉ E
S

Snakeshead
Ridge

Doctor's House

Pt. 593
△

Pt. 175
△

Pasquale Road

Rapido R.

Pt. 165
△

Castle Hill

CASSINO

Pt. 236
△

Monastery

Continental
Hotel

400

Pt. 435
△
Hangman's
Hill

△
Pt. 202

Hotel
des Roses

Route 6

300

Route 6

Station

200

Amphitheatre

100

Colosseum

Round House

Hummocks

Baron's
Place

Route 6

Gari R.

0   1/4   1/2 mile

0   1/2   1 km

The second and third battles of Cassino were focussed on the town and monastery and overseen by
Lieutenant General Sir Bernard Freyberg. For reasons of geography, attacks on the monastery were
only possible from the north-west (Snakeshead Ridge) or up the sheer eastern face, leaping up the
hairpin bends. The main German centres of resistance were the Continental Hotel, Hotel des Roses,
Baron's Palace and Station area, all extremely well-built of local stone.

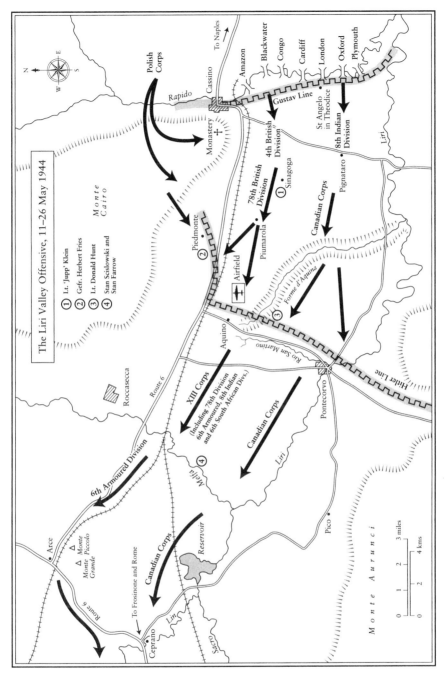

The Liri Valley Offensive, 11–26 May 1944

① Lt. 'Jupp' Klein
② Gefr. Herbert Fries
③ Lt. Donald Hunt
④ Stan Scislowski and
　 Stan Farrow

To Naples

Polish Corps

Rapido

Cassino

Monastery

Monte Cairo

Piedmonte ②

Airfield

Amazon

Blackwater

Congo

Cardiff

London

Oxford

Plymouth

Gustav Line

St Angelo in Theodice

4th British Division

78th British Division

① Sinagoga

Piumarola

Canadian Corps

Pignataro

8th Indian Division

Liri

③

Forme d'Aquina

Aquino

Rio San Martino

Hitler Line

Pontecorvo

XIII Corps
(Including 78th Division 6th Armoured, 8th Indian and 6th South African Divs.)

Canadian Corps

Liri

Pico

Roccasecca

Route 6

6th Armoured Division

Arce

Monte Piccolo

Monte Grande

To Frosinone and Rome

Canadian Corps

Melfa ④

Reservoir

Ceprano

Liri

Sacro

Route 6

Monte Aurunci

0　　1　　2　　3 miles

0　　2　　4 kms

Lieutenant General Sir Oliver Leese, commanding Eighth Army, oversaw the attack and pursuit up the Liri valley. Leese had huge resources available to him – comprising three corps (British XIII Corps, the Canadians and Poles), but made the mistake of cramming six Allied divisions into the valley (rarely more than five miles wide) in the final stages, slowing down the advance, rather than increasing it. This may have influenced Clark to strike for Rome, against Alexander's orders.

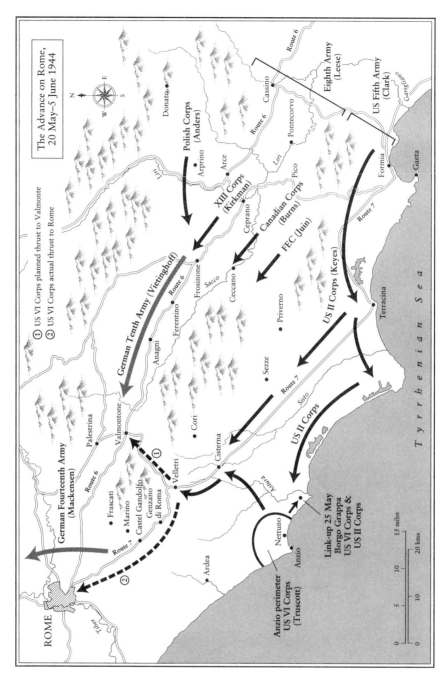

The Advance on Rome, 20 May–5 June 1944

① US VI Corps planned thrust to Valmonte
② US VI Corps actual thrust to Rome

Eighth Army (Leese)

US Fifth Army (Clark)

Polish Corps (Anders)

XIII Corps (Kirkman)

Canadian Corps (Burns)

FEC (Juin)

US II Corps (Keyes)

German Tenth Army (Vietinghoff)

German Fourteenth Army (Mackensen)

US II Corps

Link-up 25 May Borgo Grappa US VI Corps & US II Corps

Anzio perimeter US VI Corps (Truscott)

ROME

Tyrrhenian Sea

Donato
Cassino
Arprino
Arce
Pontecorvo
Pico
Formia
Gaeta
Ceprano
Route 6
Route 7
Frosinone
Sacco
Ceccano
Privemo
Terracina
Ferentino
Anagni
Sezze
Palestrina
Valmontone
Cori
Cisterna
Frascati
Marino
Castel Gandolfo
Genzano di Roma
Velletri
Route 6
Route 7
Route 7
Sisto
Astura
Ardea
Nettuno
Anzio
Tiber
Liri
Liri

15 miles
20 kms
10
10
5
0 0

Operation Diadem, devised by Alexander's talented chief of staff, John Harding, involved both the penetration of the Gustav and Hitler Lines and a breakout from Anzio. It is notable here that each corps in the fourth battle was attacking what had been a divisional objective in the first battle. The broad idea was for Truscott's Anzio force to prevent the escape of Vietinghoff's Tenth Army, but Mark Clark's switch of emphasis towards Rome allowed the Germans to escape. However, the Germans proved very disciplined in their withdrawal and there is no guarantee that Truscott's VI Corps (who suffered heavy losses at Cisterna) would have been able to stop them at Valmonte.

We are the D-Day Dodgers, out in Italy,
Always on the vino, always on the spree.
Eighth Army skivers and their tanks,
We go to war in ties like swanks.
For we're the D-Day Dodgers, in sunny Italy.

We landed at Salerno, a holiday with pay.
Jerry brought his bands out to cheer us on our way,
Showed us the sights and gave us tea,
We all sang songs, the beer was free.
For we're the D-Day Dodgers, the lads that D-Day dodged.

Palermo and Cassino were taken in our stride,
We did not go to fight there, we just went for the ride.
Anzio and Sangro are just names,
We only went to look for dames,
For we're the D-Day Dodgers, in sunny Italy.

On our way to Florence, we had a lovely time,
We drove a bus from Rimini, right through the Gothic Line,
Then to Bologna we did go,
And went bathing in the River Po,
For we're the D-Day Dodgers, the lads that D-Day dodged.

We hear the boys in France are going home on leave,
After six months' service such a shame they're not relieved.
And we're told to carry on a few more years,
Because our wives don't shed no tears.
For we're the D-Day Dodgers, out in sunny Italy.

Once we had a 'blue light' that we were going home,
Back to dear old Blighty, never more to roam.
Then someone whispered: 'In France we'll fight,'
We said: 'Not that, we'll just sit tight,'
For we're the D-Day Dodgers, the lads that D-Day dodged.

Dear Lady Astor, you think you know a lot,
Standing on a platform and talking Tommy-rot.
Dear England's sweetheart and her pride,
We think your mouth is much too wide –
From the D-Day Dodgers, out in sunny Italy.

Look around the hillsides, through the mist and rain,
See the scattered crosses, some that bear no name.
Heartbreak and toil and suffering gone,
The lads beneath, they slumber on.
They are the D-Day Dodgers, who'll stay in Italy.

Contents

Preface

THE MAN CURSED his tight-fitting clothing. Familiar friends, his woollen trousers and jacket nevertheless were scratchy and uncomfortable. Under his hat, the heat of the day was causing him to sweat, matting the golden locks of his hair and gluing his linen shirt to his chest. He dabbed at his forehead and neck with a handkerchief and swatted at the pulsing clouds of flies. Looking considerably younger than his thirty-two years, he wondered at the train of events which had caused him to leave London and come to central Italy. This was not the noble land of the caesars he had anticipated, but a landscape festooned with ruins and sullen, subdued people who possessed none of the sparkle he supposed the Mediterranean might have encouraged.

The only way up the hill was by a battered track, which zigzagged tortuously up the face of the rocky massif. Dominating all around him, unrelenting high ground: hard limestone with 6,000-foot jagged peaks and fifty-degree slopes. Too steep for any wheeled transport, the man made his way perched astride a donkey, slipping and swaying uncomfortably with its every stride. To one side loomed the rising massif: scree and dislodged stones of the broken hillside, razor-edged boulders and crags jutting out of the alpine grass like fangs. Every now and then a black smudge indicated a cave; those nearer the pilgrims' track held shrines, festooned with gaudily painted statues, rosary beads and freshly picked mountain flowers. To the man's other side, through the heat haze, a fantastic panorama: the River Gari gushing from the high hills to the north before merging with the wider Liri from the north-west and the great Garigliano, then feeding into the Tyrrhenian Sea some twenty miles distant. The silvery rivers snaked their way along the valley floors, past the tattered villages the traveller had explored hours before, and roads, no more than muddied, rutted tracks. All seemed billiard-table flat from his lofty vantage point, though, as he knew to his discomfort, the terrain was anything but level. As he gazed at the plain, he paused to take in the significance of the mountain he was ascending, and the huge building on top of it, named after the feature on which it perched, and why it had been so frequently and violently fought over.

His local guide, hidden under a vast straw hat, trudged on foot behind, humming a peasant song and urging the burro on lethargically. They moved slowly, at the pace of a funeral procession, the Englishman thought. Clouds of dust kicked up from the path. Apart from the rhythmic creaking of the animal's leather halter, all was incredibly quiet: there with none of the bustle of Rome or London that he was used to. Instead, a gentle background accompaniment of crickets, the scent of the bright mountain blooms and herbs – the tangled smells of fresh thyme, mint, juniper, eucalyptus and heather. Petals displaying lilac, pale yellow, cornflower blue, orange-red and endless shades of white dotted the hillside, around which multi-coloured bugs, bees and wasps competed for space. High above, the bells of the abbey boomed out periodically, echoing through the prehistoric landscape, as if to herald their arrival, as they had greeted countless others through the centuries.

Looking up, he hadn't been prepared for the abbey's vastness; it dominated the massif, the town of Cassino below and the entrances to the Rapido and Liri valleys; he thought it the largest building he had ever seen. His eyes took in the towering walls, made from massive cubes of light grey limestone, hewn many hundreds of years before from the surrounding mountains, and fitted together without a hint of mortar. The human effort of hauling them to this place was beyond his comprehension. The walls, in places over twenty feet thick, studded with rows of tiny windows, like gunports facing outwards, and silhouetted against a cloudless azure sky. Which is it, he thought; monastery or fortress?

The structure was gargantuan and undeniably impressive, but perhaps out of place in such a hidden setting. The peak it sat on had been terraced into submission: many tiers of earth and stones, some now crumbling, led down from the walls; some sprouted stunted olive trees, others vines, mostly now abandoned and overgrown. This was garden engineering on an impressive scale that had kept battalions of monks busy through the ages. As the traveller drew closer he noticed black-robed figures flitting about the grounds. A raven, perched high on the entrance gateway, watched his sorry approach and announced his arrival. He drank in the many floors and balconies, and the letters chiselled deep into the stone that spelt out the letters 'P A X' above the entrance – Peace.

There was, indeed, a sense of peace and quiet learning about the place, though torn apart by earthquakes and twice destroyed by invading armies. The traveller could see why a pre-Roman tribe, the Volsci, had established a fortified village up here, and why the Romans had moved the settlement to the foot of the hill, calling it Casinum. They left their shrine to Apollo on the hilltop, by a mountain spring, far away from the ordinary world of the valleys. Saint Benedict of Subiaco, seeking a refuge for contemplation, had decided to build his small retreat on the shrine's ruins in AD 529, craftily reusing the Volscian stone and Roman brick he found lying around. The visitor had read how Benedict – perched almost in the clouds – devised his *regula monachorum*, the rules for daily monastery life, here.

Once inside the cool, tall-ceilinged rooms, the man looked at a selection of leaves of illuminated vellum that had survived the upheavals of time and war, ornate robes of past abbots and other monastic treasures. He paused at the basilica, a baroque masterpiece, and admired the marble floors, delicate frescoes and ornate carved woodwork, and was lulled almost into a trance by the fresh incense and gentle rhythm of chanting monks. The library, one of the most important in the world, had grown steadily to contain tens of thousands of texts, including many works of Rome's earliest historians and philosophers. In the courtyard he saw the emblem of St Peter – the crossed keys – carved in stone and symbolising the gates of heaven, a reminder of the abbey's close associations with the papacy. In the eighth century, Abbot Desiderius, later Pope Victor III, had presided over more than two hundred monks here, and manuscripts produced in his *scriptorium* and by the whole Cassino school of illuminators became famous throughout Christendom. In 1066, Desiderius commissioned bronze doors, decorated with thirty-six panels detailing in silver damask lettering the possessions of the monastery and its surrounding territories. A later pope, Urban V, had underwritten the cost of rebuilding the monastery after the devastating earthquake of 1349.

But the wealth and lofty atmosphere of the abbey sat uncomfortably with the shockingly impoverished villages below, including Cassino itself, where, the traveller noted, 'there was not a single pane of glass to be seen, nor food to be had in any of the wretched hovels that passed for houses'. This was a journey of contrasts he would never forget. Shortly afterwards he devoted a few pages to the tour of Monte Cassino in his diary, and signed it: 'Mr Charles Dickens, January 1845'.

At 8.30 on the morning of Wednesday 15 March 1944, the town of Cassino was wiped from the map as Allied forces began Operation Dickens, named in honour of the writer's visit almost a century before. During that morning, almost five hundred US aircraft delivered a thousand tons of high explosive onto the little town, pulverising the centuries-old landscape familiar to Dickens, and countless other distinguished visitors, for ever. The Allied powers' crude assault heralded their third attack in as many months on the strongest point of the Gustav Line, Germany's defensive belt across the waist of Italy, constructed with elaborate care over the preceding months. But borrowing the writer's name brought the Allies no greater luck than their earlier assaults on the mountain bastion in January and February. By the end of the month, Operation Dickens, an attempt to seize both Cassino and the monastery above, fought in impossible terrain, hostile weather and against some of the best units of the German army, had ground to a halt, leaving the 2nd New Zealand and 4th Indian Divisions eroded and exhausted.

The New Zealanders and Indians were some of well over half a million Allied and Axis troops who poured into central and southern Italy during 1943–44. They comprised a mixture of men hardened by combat in Stalingrad, Leningrad, Tobruk and Tunis. Many of their number had battled across the wastes of Russia and deserts of North Africa, in Abyssinia and Sicily. Others, like the Poles, had escaped from captivity to fight their foes, while the Italians and some of the French had switched sides and were eager to prove their loyalty. The majority came from far distant lands, had no connection with Italy or even the Mediterranean, and would find the climate as much an enemy as the Germans. Many more were new to combat – green and anxious not to fail; a very few were reluctant conscripts looking for the moment to vanish altogether. This applied to Hitler's Wehrmacht also – though mostly German-Austrian, it also included a significant minority of waifs and strays from Eastern Europe, the Balkans and Russia, initially caught up in the euphoria of the Thousand-Year Reich. By 1944, most non-Germans wearing field grey, finding themselves stranded in Italy on the defensive against superior opponents, were eager to melt away. All of these men – and a few women – assembled to operate and enable the machinery of war, guided by a mixture of emotions, in the battle-ground of central Italy.

All had anticipated a land of sun, cherry blossom and grapes, but found something very different. If ever battlespace was dominated by geology and combat directed by climate and terrain, then Monte Cassino provided an extreme example. Here battle slid back to a medieval pace; hand-to-hand fighting was common; mules and horses were used in place of modern engines of war, as combatants on both sides quickly discovered that the ground around Cassino was unforgiving. An ankle-twisting loose scree, caused by the fracturing of limestone outcrops over the millennia, covered all gradients. The hard and brittle hills shattered like glass when hit by any projectile – shells, mortar rounds, hand grenades and even bullets sent splinters of rock in all directions, and causing a horrifically high number of head, face and eye injuries.

Confronted with bedrock everywhere, most troops found it totally impossible to dig foxholes and gun positions to protect themselves from enemy shelling or the elements. The infantry on all sides were issued with ridiculously small entrenching tools, or picks, which might have been useful for sandcastles on Salerno beach but made little impression on the rugged mountainsides encountered inland. The only shelter to be found was in the natural caves or fissures in the hillsides, enlarged by explosion, or by creating nests of rock rubble – termed *sangars* by British and Indian troops. Burying the human dead was all but impossible – a problem made worse the summer months, when the attendant flies, rats and wild dogs provided a health threat of their own.

The terrain also magnified artillery fire acoustically, which was nerve-wracking in the extreme and left speech impossible. One German commander in the hills wrote that 'the demoralising effect of the intense bombardment was increased tenfold by the echoes from the valleys'. There was a terrible sense of feeling trapped when caught on a narrow mountain track by shellfire, with nowhere to shelter. Additionally, much of the Italian landscape in the winter months was shrouded in an eerie freezing fog, crippling the ability of all armies to fight, disorientating individual soldiers, playing on their fears. 'Fog in front of the outposts, fog in front of the enemy, fog in front of the hotels, fog for taking away the wounded, fog for bringing up ammunition, fog, fog, fog,' remembered another soldier; 'there was no longer any day; there were only two species of night, one yellowish and full of clouds, that did not allow you to see and took you by the throat, the other full of flashes, of glimmers of light, of bursts of machine-gun fire, of fearful noises.'

Throughout history, from the Romans to modern times, armies of the northern hemisphere have tried to fight in the 'campaigning season', the period that extends from March to October. Outside those months, in Europe at least, poor weather degrades the wellbeing of soldiers and their ability to manoeuvre and sustain themselves. Wintry rain and snow turns gentle, fordable rivers into fierce torrents; unpaved roads become channels of thick, gooey mud. In such conditions, food, fodder and fuel for warmth become scarce; weapons malfunction and low temperatures sap the will to fight. Poor weather impedes land forces reliant on using motorised vehicles and even horses towing wheeled wagons laden with supplies and guns. As three Russian and two Italian winters during the Second World War would prove, such conditions could be complete show-stoppers, even to modern armies.

Apart from stunted olives, the area around Monte Cassino in 1944 was a grey, treeless landscape, with little vegetation for camouflage, and no wood for overhead cover or warmth-giving camp fires. Though rich and verdant today, this relentless lack of shelter proved corrosive to armies in winter, where temperatures in the high winds and blizzards remained well below freezing; healthy troops frequently died of exposure in such unforgiving conditions.

The battles of Monte Cassino would be fought over five months, through winter to the beginning of summer. Even at the height of the campaigning season, the beginning of a Mediterranean May would create other problems at Cassino, compounding the misery of already thirsty troops subsisting in a parched landscape. Life in the valleys varied dramatically between the rush of water from the mountains in mid-winter to the barren moonscapes of midsummer. Rivers subsided to a trickle; unless irrigated, the valley floors retained little water and soil baked in the sun turned to a fine dust – a powdered earth that hurt the eyes and nose, filled the mouth and clogged, jammed and eroded all the machinery of war – from engines and gun barrels to wristwatches.

Much of Cassino was fought along highways composed of crushed earth or stone, which deteriorated rapidly in the winter months. Even the surface of the few paved highways soon gave way under the incessant movement of vehicles. As many Italians still moved about the countryside by ox cart, none of these avenues had been designed to withstand the weight of a modern, mechanised, wheeled and caterpillar-tracked army on the move. Main routes were few; fewer still were paved. Hairpin bends, snaking up and down the mountains, had a lethality of their own in poor weather. 'We passed a burned-out American tank, rounded a curve and saw two trucks which had plunged down a ravine and were hanging almost perpendicularly against the side of the mountain,' wrote one observer.

The net effect of terrain, weather and shelling ground down some human beings with frightening results. Serving with the 5th Medium Regiment, RA, Captain Bill McLaren – later the famous rugby commentator – was investigating a farmhouse which had just had its roof blown off. Inside he discovered 'this guy sitting, or rather lying, in the corner, his knees tucked right up under his chin in an almost foetal position . . . He was shaking violently and had a disturbing, wild-eyed look about him. Talking to him had no effect whatsoever: he just carried on staring at the wall. Clearly he was shell-shocked. I felt so sorry for him – he'd obviously had a terrible experience of some kind – and made a point of arranging for him to be taken back to the "wagon lines".

No other campaign in Europe pulled in the same range of nationalities and cultures as that in Italy. The brutality and nature of the fighting at times reached the worst extremes of the Russian front, while the attrition rates often exceeded those of the Western Front. Failure to achieve a decisive result at Cassino for the first five months of 1944 condemned those in Italy to a further year of war. From the first landings of 3 September 1943 to the German surrender which took effect on 2 May 1945, the casualties in Italy were excessive, though balanced. The Allies suffered 312,000 killed, wounded and missing; over the same period, the Germans lost 435,000, an average loss to both sides of 1,233 personnel *every day*, almost one for every minute of the 606-day-long campaign. This attrition was most pronounced at Monte Cassino, where some 200,000 casualties were inflicted on Germans, Italians, French, Americans, British, Indians, New Zealanders, Poles, Canadians and South Africans during 129 days of hell. This is their story.

1

Roads to Cassino

UNLIKE MANY OF the Second World War's blood-soaked campaigns, there was, sadly, no inevitability about the grim series of battles fought across the Italian mainland. In 1942, Hitler had strategic visions of an unstoppable armoured steamroller advancing south from Stalingrad through the Caucasus and taking the Persian oilfields, while Rommel's Afrika Korps pushed beyond Egypt, over the Suez Canal into the Near East, in a vast pincer movement. By May 1943 these dreams were shattered with the Russian victory at Stalingrad and ejection of the Italo-German army from the North African littoral. Collectively, defeat on these two fronts deprived the Axis of nearly 1.5 million troops, while Tunisia significantly affected wider Italian morale and determination to resist.

By 1943 it was clear – even to Hitler's blinkered allies – that the Führer was on the defensive in the Russian and Mediterranean theatres and had no proactive plan to achieve his *endsieg* (final victory); he was by then relying on irrational hopes without positive foundations. In the east, he anticipated exhausting Russia with attritional campaigns to wear down the Red Army, seemingly unaware that his smaller Wehrmacht was being eroded faster by its larger rival. In the west, he put faith in tactical weapons whose potential had yet to be proven (rockets, missiles and jet aircraft), and a hope that disagreements between the Allies would bring about a change in the fortunes of war. Underlying this was a determination to hold on to every foot of conquered territory – in a world of diminishing human and material resources, this meant that one theatre could be reinforced only at the expense of another.

For the Allies, the campaign in Italy came about partly through a need, as Churchill saw it, *not* to embark on an ill-prepared, under-equipped invasion of France in 1943. More positively, the Allies sought to exploit their triumphs in Tunisia and Sicily, and continue the land offensive against Germany and Italy. There were mutterings about 'tying down' German divisions in Italy that might be deployed else-where, but the real prize was the conquest of an Axis capital, Rome, one of the most famous cities in the world. It was hoped that Italy would yield 'cheap' victories, in terms of time and lives, as the Germans were not expected to make a vigorous stand, while the Italian defence of their homeland was unlikely to be any more inspired that their performance in Libya, Tunisia or Sicily.

In mid-1943, the OKW (*Oberkommando der Wehrmacht*), the Supreme Command of the German armed forces, assessed several strategic options in the event that Italy left the Axis. Hitler considered two alternative courses of action, each proposed by a field marshal. Initially, Erwin Rommel – formerly the Desert Fox, now with no desert and no army, who was kicking his heels in northern Italy – advised his Führer that the Germans could and should hold only northern Italy along a geographic line that would prevent the loss of the Po Valley and its rich agricultural and industrial resources. Kesselring, already de facto Mediterranean theatre commander, argued the precise opposite – that a defence south of Rome was possible, advisable and highly desirable.

The OKW recognised the impending danger to German troops in Italy if the Italians defected and the Allies invaded mainland Italy: an Allied landing near Rome was assessed as likely, where local Italian troops might also help isolate German forces in southern Italy, though a full-scale invasion of the mainland was thought improbable except by prior agreement with the new government. The OKW contingency plan of August 1943 required Rommel to occupy all key roads and railways leading out of northern Italy, disarm Italian Army units, and secure the Apennine passes. Kesselring was to withdraw his forces towards Rommel, disarming Italian units on the way, crushing any resistance. Once complete, Rommel was to assume command over all German forces in Italy. Peeved at Hitler's disregard of his advice, and mindful of past tensions with Rommel, Kesselring submitted his resignation on 14 August. *SS-Obergruppenführer* Karl Wolff, the senior SS and Gestapo commander in Italy, intervened suggesting to his Führer that Kesselring's presence in southern Italy was vital to prevent an early Italian defection (which was nonsense); Hitler, however, refused to accept Kesselring's resignation.

Mussolini's premiership had been doomed from the moment the Allies launched Operation Husky, the invasion of Sicily by sea and air. When the Allies appeared to overwhelm the already reluctant Italian defenders on Sicily with ease, the Fascist Grand Council, as the only check on Mussolini's power, met fifteen days later on 24 July to pass a vote of no confidence in *Il Duce*, and bloodlessly deposed him from power. The Fascist salute was abolished, the Fascist militia was integrated into the regular forces and took an oath of loyalty to the King, Victor Emmanuel III. In August the new head of government, Marshal Pietro Badoglio, started secret peace negotiations and the Royal Italian Army would soon enter the war on the side of the Allies. The armistice, signed on 3 September in Sicily, was to be kept secret until the Allied invasion was well under way.

On 15 August 1943, Hitler activated his new Tenth Army, formed from the accumulation of German troops in Italy after Sicily. Leading them and promoted to the exalted rank of *Generaloberst* was the exceptionally capable fifty-five-year-old Heinrich von Vietinghoff, newly arrived from command of the Fifteenth Army in northern France. Vietinghoff was to coordinate XIV Panzer Corps with three divisions in the Gaeta-Naples-Salerno region and LXXVI Panzer Corps in Calabria and Apulia, and would personally influence the course of the campaign, being given enormous latitude by Kesselring, his superior. The German position in central and southern Italy stabilised as substantial numbers of combat troops arrived on the mainland; nevertheless, Hitler remained nervous that an Italo-Allied force could surround and destroy German troops in the south. In the event of an Allied landing on the mainland (and Wehrmacht intelligence assessed an Allied amphibious operation as being imminent), his plan was still to withdraw first to the Rome area, and thence towards Rommel's lair in the northern Apennines. The OKW directive of 18 August directed Tenth Army to repulse any invasion in the Naples and Salerno with at least three mobile divisions while all other forces withdrew towards Rome, disarming Italian units as they went.

Allied intentions were confirmed for Berlin on 3 September when Montgomery's Eighth Army crossed the Straits of Messina, landing in Calabria – by which time Kesselring had a strategy and troops in place to implement it. Vietinghoff's new Tenth Army was ordered to delay the British-Canadian force while withdrawing its troops slowly northwards. Five days later, the moment Berlin had most feared arrived: the armistice was formally announced as a second Allied force, Mark Clark's US Fifth Army, approached the beaches of Salerno. However, the prevarications and contingency planning of the previous months meant that Kesselring now knew exactly what to do, though faced with the dual task of resisting the Allied armies and rendering the Italian armed forces ineffective. Curious Italians would have witnessed long trains passing slowly south, flatcar after flatcar bearing tanks and half-tracks covered with camouflage netting and tree branches, and on every flatcar, seated at the rear, there was a steel-helmeted German soldier clutching his rifle watching for hostile aircraft.

After the September 1943 armistice, Hitler's anger at Italian 'open treachery' knew no bounds. German commanders throughout Italy triggered Operation *Asche*, the forcible disarmament and neutralisation of the Italian armed forces. Germany moved rapidly to take over the Italian zones of occupation in the Balkans and southern France, and 'neutralise' Italian forces in Italy. In an act of gross negligence, the muddled Italian high command had failed to issue orders to their subordinates specifying what to do in case of an armistice (which most in any case knew – or suspected – was just beyond the horizon). According to Tenth Army reports, very few units attempted to resist and most did nothing or faded away; in Rome, Kesselring persuaded the five Italian divisions based there to disarm and return home, while

Rommel did the same in northern Italy: the army which could have posed a threat and aided the Allies was neutralised overnight.

Some 720,000 Italian military personnel were immediately shipped north to German prison camps and all were obliged to work as slave labourers, a tenth of whom died in captivity. Other Italian garrisons in Albania, Slovenia, Yugoslavia, Croatia and the Aegean islands either surrendered to the Germans, joined partisan units, resisted or were shot. Between 15 and 22 September, 1,500 Italians died fighting the Germans on the Greek island of Cephalonia, but over 5,000 more, including the commander of Italian Acqui Division and some in hospital beds, were massacred by their former Axis partners. In total, in the aftermath of the armistice, German forces throughout the Mediterranean caused the deaths of over 35,000 Italians. There was also OKW concern about the presence of 80,000 Allied troops in Italian-run prison camps. It is estimated that perhaps 50,000 absconded immediately – often with the assistance of their former gaolers – before the arrival of new German guards, triggered by *Asche*. Of these some 36,000 were soon recaptured and sent north to the Reich, which left around 14,000 roaming the countryside, all reliant on the help of Italian civilians; most tried to regain the Allied lines or reach neutral Switzerland, while some joined partisan units. As the Allies pushed further north, the numbers of partisans would grow; by the end of the war, it was estimated there were as many as 232,000 partisans of all political persuasions, about half of whom were gun-toting activists.

Two months after Mussolini's dismissal and arrest, Hitler came to his rescue. *SS-Sturmbannführer* Otto Skorzeny received the mission – Operation Oak – of locating and liberating the Italian dictator, a task he would achieve spectacularly on 12 September. Skorzeny traced Mussolini to the Campo Imperatore Hotel, a ski resort on the Gran Sasso mountain, high in the Apennine range, eighty miles north of Rome. His men, elite SS-commandos, landed by glider, overwhelmed Mussolini's captors and flew *Il Duce* out by light aircraft. Thereafter, Mussolini was installed as head of the small puppet *Repubblica Sociale Italiana* or RSI (Italian Social Republic) and ruled from Salò, a small town on Lake Garda, until it was overwhelmed by partisans towards the end of the war. Considerable numbers of young Fascists stayed loyal to him and were reformed into combat units which fought the Allies alongside the Germans, including a brigade which fought at Anzio in May 1944, but operated later as a police and anti-partisan unit. By June 1944, it had grown into a full division, and was officially named the 29th Waffen-SS Grenadier Division.

General Alexander initiated the campaign that led directly to Monte Cassino on Friday 3 September 1943, the fourth anniversary of the declaration of war on Germany. A time for reflection and wonder for some: only a year earlier, any kind of victory against the Axis partners had seemed remote. But for the Desert Rats of Eighth Army, fresh from taking Sicily, there was no time to review the changes of fortune the intervening months had brought. Starting at 4.30 a.m. Britons and Canadians landed on the mainland near the tip of Italy's toe, in Calabria. Though Monty was loath to admit it, his invasion – codenamed Operation Baytown – had been merely a diversion from the main Allied effort.

There was every reason to expect that the subsequent Allied landings at Salerno (codenamed Avalanche) would create a seismic shift in Axis fortunes. For this main assault the Allies could call on an invasion force of 450 ships, and over 150,000 British and American troops. Though newspaper headlines boasted 'Landings at Naples Biggest of the War', they were in fact dwarfed by the invasion of Sicily earlier in July. The Italians had just surrendered, and the Germans could muster only 20,000 men. So when Clark's Anglo-American Fifth Army stormed ashore on the Italian mainland six days after Montgomery, there were high hopes of capturing Rome before the winter. Whereas Monty had encountered no opposition in the south, a series of violent German counterattacks forced a bitter ten-day battle for the Salerno beachhead. The Luftwaffe attacked each night and launched new, radio-controlled *Fritz-X* glider bombs against the fleet offshore, achieving notable successes. The British, landing in the north of the twenty-mile front, found themselves separated by a ten-mile gap from the nearest Americans to their south, terrain which the Germans soon filled.

Nothing escaped the attention of German artillery observers who could see every inch of the Salerno landing area, for the entire sector was overlooked by low hills, like an amphitheatre. However, they would not have been aware that Britain's only recorded mutiny of the Second World War occurred at Salerno, when 700 troops from many different units, including men returning from leave and some recently released from hospital, were rounded up and sent to the beachhead as urgently needed reinforcements, to be posted to strange units. None knew each other, but no one took the trouble to explain to them the gravity of the situation. Exhausted from three years' fighting in North Africa, where some had been decorated for bravery, they refused to go into battle. The rebellion was badly handled by officers who might have defused the ugly moment with good man management and patient explanation. A hardcore of ringleaders was sentenced to hard labour, those with rank or medals were stripped of them while the remainder were given the option of a rifle or court martial. This would turn out to be a mere precursor of a much wider discipline problem encountered by the Allies: the confluence of hostile weather, unfriendly terrain and determined opposition dented morale and encouraged desertion, which some claimed to have been on the verge of an epidemic.

For a while it seemed as though Avalanche might fail – on the fifth day ashore, Mark Clark was so discouraged that from his headquarters ashore he wrote, but did not issue, re-embarkation orders. At one stage Clark had to defend his own headquarters, fighting alongside his clerks and cooks, for which he would win a Distinguished Service Cross for personal gallantry. The arrival of Monty's force after an amazing march of 300 miles from the south, and the sheer exhaustion of the five German divisions who concentrated to eliminate the Salerno landings eventually enabled the Allies to break out and capture Naples on 1 October, but the price of victory was high: 7,811 Allied casualties. Eighth Army, led initially by Monty and subsequently by Oliver Leese, resumed their advance up Italy's eastern Adriatic seaboard. On their left, in the west, Fifth Army headed north along the narrow coastal strip and valleys that bordered the Tyrrhenian Sea.

Army commanders instinctively look for 'movement corridors', where terrain and enemy defences allow them the easiest passage: valleys are good; forests and low-level marshy ground or high, rocky hills tend to be bad. Italy offered very little in the way of easy routes. Hilly topography and rugged mountain peaks made up around eighty per cent of the Italian peninsula. Down its spine runs, for almost its entire length and roughly down the centre, the Apennine range. To east and west, like a ribcage, lesser hills and ridgelines span out to the coasts.

Italian geology dictated that most principal roads ran east–west, rather than north–south, which would always give the initiative to defenders and present any assailant with the problem of attacking against the grain of the landscape. Hugging the western coast between Naples and Rome lay the *Via Appia* (Appian Way), one of ancient Rome's oldest roads, continuing eventually to the port of Brindisi in south-east Italy. Known as Route 7, it struggled northwards along the narrow coastal plain and at several junctures is chiselled into the mountains which rise steeply almost directly from the Tyrrhenian Sea. Such a movement corridor, with its frequent bottlenecks, and dominated for all of its length by higher ground, was of little use to an advancing army, where relatively small defensive positions could impose a significant delay: a problem the Allies had already encountered in the jagged landscape of Sicily in July-August 1943.

If Route 7 was off-putting to the strategists, there was an alternative which, siren-like, beckoned. Roughly twelve miles inland, and parallel to the coast, lie a series of flat-bottomed river valleys, leading from just north of Naples, through Caserta and all the way to Rome – a distance of nearly 125 miles. For the most part these valleys had widths of between two and six miles, the most notable of which contained the River Liri. Along these geological features runs another old Roman road, the *Via Casilina*, or Route 6; although dominated by high ground on either side, it provided a better movement corridor for an army in a hurry than the coastal road – though was far from ideal. Using either road threw away any chance of surprising the defending Germans.

With the beachhead at Salerno now secure, Clark's US Fifth Army moved north-west towards Naples on 19 September. Meanwhile, the left wing of Montgomery's Eighth Army linked up with Clark's 36th Division and his right flank had captured the vital airfields around Foggia on 27 September. Thereafter the Allies advanced northwards through the Italian peninsula: Clark's Anglo-American forces to the west, with those of Montgomery to the east. With his opponents moving northwards

cautiously, Generaloberst Heinrich von Vietinghoff used his time effectively, fighting a clever series of delaying battles as German forces retreated
north from Salerno.

Behind them pioneers dug and drilled gun positions, machine-gun
nests and observation posts into the hillsides, laid minefields and flooded
valleys, creating defensive belts of awesome potential. The fortifications
were designed by the Third Reich's civil engineering group, the
Organisation Todt, and built by conscripted construction battalions and
civilian builders, including a 5,000-strong Slovak Engineer Division,
despatched from the Eastern Front for the purpose. In a letter home of
2 October, Captain Miles Hildyard MC of the Sherwood Rangers
Yeomanry described the systematic destruction as the Wehrmacht withdrew: they were 'destroying village water supplies, electricity . . . and
blocking streets with blown houses. Coupled with the effects of our
bombing, Italy is not prosperous. It makes our progress abominably
slow.'

The mauling of Clark's Fifth Army at Salerno revitalised the Germans,
no longer so keen to quit southern Italy. Rommel's pessimism and his
arguments for a northerly defence were beginning to lose their shine
and the Führer now leaned towards Kesselring's more optimistic slow
withdrawal northwards. On 13 October, Vietinghoff visited Generalmajor
Fries of 29th PanzerGrenadier Division and issued new instructions that
reflected Hitler's revised strategy. Fries was 'no longer to pull back in
long leaps. Instead, you need to fight in leapfrog fashion in the intervening terrain in all suitable locations. You must give the field army the
opportunity to expand the Bernhardt [Line] position [in central Italy].
It is intended for it to be the winter defensive line.' The issue was
concluded on 6 November, when Hitler appointed Kesselring
Oberbefehlshaber Südwest (Supreme Commander South-west), with
instructions that the Bernhardt Line 'will mark the end of withdrawals'.
Kesselring was to control his land forces through Army Group C, which
comprised Tenth and Fourteenth Armies. A bitter Rommel left Italy on
21 November, shortly after his fifty-second (and last) birthday, and was
soon assigned to inspect the Atlantic Wall in northern France.

Hitler's decision to back Kesselring would lead to the bloody
battles from January to May 1944 at Monte Cassino and the Anzio

beachhead. For these areas would otherwise have fallen to the Allies with minimal – if any – fighting. In so doing, the Führer, through his able nominee Kesselring, ensured that the Allies would not take Rome until 4 June 1944.

The quality of the German defences rested less on fixed lines and weapons and more on the men manning them and their leaders. German soldiers were a mix, as in any army, of the formidable, the passive and the inept. Their morale varied hugely. Growing disillusionment with Hitler and Berlin meant that many found they were 'fighting for the comrade on our right . . . or perhaps for our immediate commander, whom we respected or perhaps because we believed we were fighting for our honour, doing our duty as soldiers up until the last day', wrote one Wehrmacht colonel.

The most formidable formation was the Luftwaffe's 1st Fallschirmjäger Division. Following the battle for Crete in May 1941, Hitler refused to authorise any further large-scale airborne operations due to the high casualty rate. His paratroopers subsequently became élite infantry, serving in Russia, North Africa, Sicily, and Italy. From the start, they were a volunteer-only force, with a high drop-out rate in training. Leutnant Hermann Volk, who fought at Cassino, recalled how on the first day of training in Pomerania recruits had to stand to attention and fall forward towards a comrade standing opposite, but without stumbling: 'That was a true test of trust, for the many who put out their hands or legs to prevent injury were immediately rejected as unsuitable.'

Designed to land and fight in small groups, with limited prospects of resupply or reinforcement, Fallschirmjäger were trained to be highly resilient, resourceful, act without orders and to expect to tackle over-whelming odds. Though light in artillery, paratroops were reliant on large numbers of automatic weapons and grenades, and usually encountered as small, *kampfgruppen* (all-arms battle groups) organised from any available troops. They liked the nickname of '*Grüne Teufel*' (Green Devils) awarded to them by their Allied opponents in Tunisia and Sicily, on account of their distinctive three-quarter-length camouflaged parachute smocks. An excessive esprit de corps was encouraged, and a dispropor-tionate number of them gained high decorations, or fell in battle.

Apart from paratroops and specialised mountain soldiers (*Gebirgsjagers*), the German divisions in Italy comprised some mobile formations of PanzerGrenadiers, the equivalent of armoured infantry, designed to keep pace with tanks in armoured half-track vehicles and trucks, racing to trouble spots to plug holes torn in the defences. They proved their worth many times over, when for example at Salerno, 15th and 29th PanzerGrenadier Divisions fought in small, cobbled-together battlegroups, alongside tough Fallschirmjäger detachments, and nearly pushed the Allied attackers back into the sea. Other divisions were more static, such as Friedrich Franek's 44th Hoch und Deutschmeister Division, named after the senior regiment in the old Imperial Austrian army. Absorbed into the Wehrmacht in 1938, it was destroyed at Stalingrad. Because of its history, Hitler (himself an Austrian) decreed that it would be reformed immediately from the 2,000 men who were on leave or in hospital at the time of its annihilation, and it arrived in Italy in July 1943. To the Allies' disadvantage, other units destroyed at Stalingrad were also reformed and sent to Italy, and most senior battalion, regimental and divisional commanders had much Eastern Front experience behind them, giving them a hard edge that few Allied commanders could match.

The 1943–44 Wehrmacht in Italy was not exclusively Austro-German. As many as 300,000 *Volkdeutsch* 'ethnic Germans' living in Poland served on all fronts in the German army during the war; forcibly conscripted, they generally (sometimes only) spoke Polish and were, effectively, Poles. This produced the grim inevitability of 'German' Poles fighting the 'Allied' Poles led by Władysław Anders in the later stages of the campaign. Of those 'German' Poles captured, Anders's II Polish Corps would eventually screen, de-Nazify and recruit 35,000 to fight as Free Poles against Germany. Other *Volkdeutsch* encountered in Italy came from the Czech Republic, Slovakia, the Baltic States (Estonia, Latvia, Lithuania), even western Russia and Slovenia. Absorbed by deft changes of frontier into the Third Reich, they were conscripted when of adult age and inducted, willingly or not, into the Wehrmacht.

Another type of foreign national who wore Wehrmacht field grey but did not carry weapons in Italy were the *Hilfswillige* (usually abbreviated to *Hiwis*) – auxiliary helpers – who had volunteered their services in the 'glory days' (1940–42) of the Third Reich and were probably now regretting their rashness, but laboured as cooks, porters, pioneers, drivers, releasing other men for combat. One *Landser* (foot soldier) serving in Italy remembered: 'The entire kitchen help was Hiwis; we had a Russian cobbler who did a very good job of fixing boots and shoes; we had the luxury of a company barber, a Ukrainian . . . more than half of the repair platoon of the battalion were Ivans. As a matter of fact, none of them ever came close to ammunition or explosives. All of them deserted in October 1944 in Italy.'

There were also Armenians, Belorussians, Georgians, Russians, Tartars, Ukrainians and others who had volunteered in the early days of Operation Barbarossa, 1941–42, to fight the Soviet regime; they formed logistics units or eventually were allowed to bear arms as *Osttruppen*. By 1943 they formed up to fifteen per cent of many German divisions, totalling perhaps one million former Soviet citizens serving in Wehrmacht, Waffen-SS and other Nazi paramilitary organisations. After the tide turned against Germany in the east in October 1943, to avoid the pitfalls of mutiny or desertion, twenty-four fully armed battalions of these eastern volunteers (each of about 950 men commanded by a core of fifty German officers and NCOs) were assigned to Italy.

By far and away the most dangerous and efficient *individual* adversary faced by the Allies in Italy was fifty-eight-year-old Generalfeldmarschall Albert Kesselring. Known to his enemies as 'Smiling' Albert for his 'sunny' countenance (though you only crossed him once), Kesselring was by 1943 one of the Third Reich's most popular and accomplished generals. When he first arrived in Italy, he inherited as his headquarters the splendid Villa Falconieri overlooking Frascati, ten miles south-east of Rome. Belonging to the Italian Air Ministry in 1941, the fine sixteenth-century building had been owned by a pope and, later, Kaiser Wilhelm II. As his responsibilities grew, Kesselring's staff spilled over into the nearby – and equally grand – villas Aldobrandini and Grazioli, shared with Field Marshal Wolfram von Richthofen.

Kesselring was more decisive than most Wehrmacht colleagues – and many Allied ones – and managed well the difficult task of commanding at the highest levels of war, where grand strategy and politics meet. Though he wore the uniform of the Luftwaffe, he proved unusually adept at handling the many army formations under his command. As a theatre commander, he was answerable directly to Berlin, and, unusually for the Germans, who tended to run separate and competing land, air and maritime operations, Kesselring commanded all German forces in Italy. After the Sicilian campaign, he managed a remarkable evacuation from Messina under the noses of the Allies, amounting to 40,000 German and 62,000 Italian troops, 9,500 vehicles, 94 guns, 47 tanks, 17,000 tons of ammunition, fuel and stores. The Allies should have taken more note of this feat, which underlined Kesselring's operational brilliance in the way he achieved superb tri-service and multinational coordination. German losses were minimal and in every way, from their ingenuity to the over confidence of their Allied opponents, this episode resembled a miniature version of the 1940 Dunkirk rescue, and an achievement that did not bode well for the Allies in the months ahead.

Kesselring's headquarters was run by his brilliant chief of staff, General Siegfried Westphal. One of Hitler's youngest generals, he was forty-one when promoted Generalmajor in March 1943. In November of the same year, when Kesselring was appointed Commander-in-Chief South-west, Westphal joined him as his principal staff officer, serving until June 1944. Of him, Kesselring wrote: 'I could not have wished for a better chief of staff than Westphal, which whom I worked harmoniously in Italy. He knew my idiosyncrasies as I knew his.' Various accounts make it quite clear that Westphal was the architect of many of the victories attributed to Kesselring, and a reliable hand at turning commanders' whims into action. Westphal observed of Kesselring that 'he wore the uniform of the Luftwaffe, and was therefore in Hitler's eyes not so "prejudiced" as the Army leaders, and this made his task easier, although Göring missed no opportunity of blackening his name'.

Italy's departure from the Axis alliance had been preceded by an attempt by the Allies to kill 'Smiling Albert' and destroy his headquarters. At midday on 8 September 1943, using Ultra intelligence, Frascati was heavily bombed by 130 USAAF Flying Fortresses; much of the old town was destroyed and 700 people lost their lives, but Kesselring's three villas just outside the town survived intact. The Italian air force sent up some thirty fighters to intercept the raid in what proved to be their final sortie before the armistice. Kesselring recounted in his memoirs how a map found in a crashed B-17 accurately pinpointed his HQ. Within days, Kesselring (who assumed the raid was caused by an Italian traitor, not signals intelligence) had moved his entire staff to the safer ten-mile network of concrete passages and chambers excavated by the Italian Army on Monte Soratte, overlooking Sant'Oreste, twenty miles *north* of Rome. This functioned as Army Group C's command centre until May 1944.

Serving under Kesselring, but with equal rank as a fellow field marshal was Baron Wolfram von Richthofen, in charge of *Luftflotte 2* – comprising all German aircraft in Italy. It was his colourful cousins, Manfred (the Red Baron) and Lothar, who had acquired fame as air aces during the First World War; Wolfram in fact had served with them, claiming a modest eight victories, in the squadron commanded by Hermann Göring. Kesselring and Richthofen knew each other well, from staff jobs in the early days of the Luftwaffe, when Wolfram was chief of staff to the Condor Legion, operating alongside Italian officers of the *Regia Aeronautica* and developing close air support doctrine during the Spanish Civil War. He served in Russia, commanding *Luftflotte 4* assisting Army Group South, and was promoted to five-star rank in February 1943 before moving to Italy in June the same year.

Promoted in January 1944 to *General der Panzertuppen*, Fridolin von Senger und Etterlin would be the principal German corps commander on the Cassino front throughout the four battles, commanding a variety of divisions initially from 'a decrepit old Palazzo at Roccasecca', and later from Castell Massimo. With his receding forehead, hooded eyes, thin, angular face, bushy eyebrows and pointed chin, Senger had an unmilitary, professorial air. Born in 1891, Senger became a Rhodes Scholar, reading History and PPE at St John's College at Oxford in 1912, spoke fluent English, French and Italian, and had many interests outside the military. A lay member of the Benedictine Order (whose spiritual home was Monte Cassino monastery), with a deeply religious mother and family tradition of senior ministerial, legal and military service in the southern German states that preceded the Wilhelmine and Nazi eras, Senger was a practising Christian, who was known never to have subscribed to Nazism, yet managed to reconcile his own beliefs with service to his country as a talented leader and soldier. Senger thought the carnage and destruction wrought by all sides at Cassino mirrored the intensity of the Great War: 'Wandering along the path across this battlefield to reach a battalion command post reminded me of the Somme in 1916; the same surface all covered by clods or ploughed by shelling, no wall, no tree unhurt, no human being to be seen, but hell ablaze with the crack of explosions and that particular smell in the air of hot iron and newly turned soil', he mused in his diary: 'I wonder what will be the verdict of history concerning those of us who are discerning, unbiased, and strong enough to realise that defeat is inevitable and who nevertheless continue to fight and to contribute to the bloodshed.'

Hampered by a lack of real-time intelligence about their opponents that would astound military commanders today, German success in Italy relied greatly on the Wehrmacht's leadership training. Oberst Gerhardt Muhm, an officer in 29th PanzerGrenadier Division, recalled that from his first days as a cadet he was told always to '*Auftrag wiederholen*' ['repeat the mission'] assigned to him, to make sure he understood it. 'And so it was through the entire Italian campaign. I was always given an *Auftrag* [general task], never a *Befehl* [specific order].' Officers were trained to issue and receive clear and concise verbal orders, in preference to long-winded written ones. This proven doctrine, called 'mission-tactics' [*Auftrags-taktik*], was inherited by the Third Reich and taught to its junior leaders, and brought early triumphs in Poland, France and Russia.

By the time of the Italian campaign, leaders at every level had been trained to expect that they would carry out missions assigned to them, but were left free to use their own intelligence, enterprise and cunning in fulfilling them. The Germans knew that their opponents expected commanders to do the opposite (which they called 'orders-tactics', or *Befehls-taktik*), where leaders had to comply with an order issued by their superiors, with no chance to fall back on their own initiative or skill. However, by 1943 the Allied armies in Italy, too, were learning slowly that the man on the spot was often best placed to achieve a task, rather than his boss.

Kesselring, Vietinghoff, Mackensen and Senger had all been schooled in this wisdom throughout their professional careers, but increasingly found themselves at odds with Berlin – where orders were, not infre-quently, issued on a whim by Hitler, who having served only as a private and corporal in 1914–18, had no understanding of the advantages of 'mission-tactics' or anything else. For example, on 13 November 1943, the acting Tenth Army commander, General Joachim Lemelsen, wanted to withdraw a battered PanzerGrenadier regiment from San Pietro Infine, due to Allied pressure along the front. Understanding the value of mission-tactics, that the local commander knew best, Kesselring told Lemelsen that he would permit him 'to do anything that you convince me to be right'. Kesselring also checked with OKW in Berlin who agreed, and Lemelsen was instructed to let the regiment withdraw. Shortly afterwards this order was countermanded by Hitler personally, who wished to reserve for himself all decisions on withdrawals from the San Pietro area. The shattered PanzerGrenadiers had to stay at the front. The unit's fighting positions filled with water. 'Stone bunkers collapsed and had to be rebuilt, foxholes bailed out. Uniforms were sodden lumps of clay and filth. Beards were scraggly. It wasn't the days of heavy fighting that bothered them the most; it was more the horrible daily rain and the shortage of warm clothes and food.' Frido von Senger later wrote: 'how wrong it is to ignore battle exhaustion when assessing a situation. Only those who have seen the facial expressions of men grown apathetic through exhaustion . . . can form any idea of the loss of fighting power and physical strength involved.'

Hitler had bypassed both Kesselring and Lemelsen to interfere at regimental level, where the instructions issued in distant Berlin bore no relationship to the situation on the ground. Sadly for US 36th Division, all Texan National Guardsmen, and the Italians about to fight their first battle for the Allies, the result was Hitler's illogical determination to hold San Pietro Infine, the German defensive anchor at the western end of the Bernhardt Line. The ensuing bitter nine-day battle, from 8 to 17 December, would be brought to wider public attention in a documentary made by John Huston, then with the Army Signals Corps, but was considered too graphic in its depiction of the horrors of war – including dead GIs wrapped in blankets being loaded onto lorries – to be released to public audiences until after the war.

There were several other uniquely German aspects of leadership which commanders at every level would employ against the Allied advantages of air supremacy and material superiority. German leaders were trained always to be able to command at two levels up. A German eyewitness in 15th PanzerGrenadier Regiment remembered at San Peitro, 'the 5th Company was commanded by an *Oberfeldwebel* [staff sergeant] and the 7th Company by a *Feldwebel* [sergeant]'. Officers and NCOs were taught routinely to make this mental leap, as necessity dictated, which led to other doctrinal aspects of command. The need always for an immediate counterattack to restore lost positions, irrespective of orders, is one good example of this. Senger also observed that: 'In regard to the quick and accurate appreciation of a situation, the making of clear decisions and the framing of concise orders, our General Staff was probably superior to those of all other countries.'

Senior German commanders tended to come forward more often that their Allied counterparts, if necessary temporarily taking command of a company or battalion, which in itself raised morale – though the result was that 223 German generals died in combat or of wounds during the war, of whom 110 were divisional commanders and twenty-three corps commanders. General Alexander succinctly summed up the prevailing Allied view of their opponents in a February 1944 letter to his army commanders, Mark Clark and Oliver Leese: '[They are] quicker at regrouping forces, quicker at thinning out on a defensive front to provide troops to close gaps at decisive points, quicker in effecting reliefs, quicker at mounting attacks and counter-attacks, and above all quicker at reaching decisions on the battlefield. By comparison our methods are often slow and cumbersome.'

However, German commanders were unaware of a luxury their opposite numbers enjoyed: access to strategic intelligence gained by Ultra decrypts of their intercepted communications. Extracts with valuable tactical intelligence, and knowledge of orders of battle, were passed on to field commands. Such was the efficiency and security of this Allied strategic intelligence throughout the war that the Germans never guessed their minds were being read by such efficient electronic eavesdropping. Few were admitted to the secrets of Ultra, and Churchill made sure that those who knew were led to believe the source was a highly placed spy (Agent Boniface), not the massive application of brainpower at Bletchley Park.

This intelligence was pure gold dust: for example, in an April 1944 report from Field Marshal Kesselring to the OKW in Berlin, each of the twenty-two German divisions in Italy was combat rated on a one-to-four scale, ranging from 'capable of offensive action' to 'fit for static defence only'. Ultra decoding revealed that only two divisions were rated in the first category (1st Fallschirmjäger and 29th PanzerGrenadier), eight in the second, eight in the third ('fit for mobile defence') while four were fit only for static defence. In Italy, Ultra intelligence gained from Enigma was sometimes of limited tactical value to the Allies, as the Tenth Army tended to use landlines to relay coded orders, but Luftwaffe liaison officers with the Tenth transmitted frequent summaries of activities on their fronts, down to divisional level, and such knowledge helped the Allies plan the Anzio landings, then repel the German counterattacks, understanding when the assaults would be launched, by whom and where. Ultra was most useful for understanding troop movements by train and German intents: for example Hitler's interference with the PanzerGrenadiers at San Pietro, or Kesselring's determination to hold the Allies south of Rome for as long as possible. During the San Pietro battles a Kesselring-Lemelsen conversation deciphered at Bletchley Park went as follows:

> *Kesselring*: 'The enemy always comes on the boundaries.'
> *Lemelson*: 'The Devil knows how he always finds where we are.'

Key to the German scheme of defences were seven fortification lines stretching across the Italian peninsula. None of these were ever conceived of as solid lines in the manner of a castle wall, but rather a system of defended delaying obstacles, comprising fortified landmarks, echeloned in depth. Of these the Viktor Line was the most southerly, running from Termoli in the east, through the Apennine Mountains and along the Volturno River in the west. The Barbara Line was ten miles further north, and beyond that was the Bernhardt Line, crossing the narrowest sector of the Italian peninsula between Minturno and Ortona. Behind the western end of the Bernhardt was an even stronger switch position that exploited the rocky terrain to superb advantage – the Gustav Line, which would dominate the Cassino campaign. It followed the course of the Garigliano, Gari and Rapido rivers, and rejoined the Bernhardt Line just north of Cassino, which then reached the Adriatic coast at Tossacesia, a few miles north of the River Sangro – a total distance of eighty-five miles. Not only did the Gustav exploit some of Italy's most mountainous terrain, but by incorporating the river lines, it forced the Allied armies to mount river crossings in order to breach the German defences.

The Allied advance slowed in the terrain encountered beyond Salerno, especially after crossing the Volturno River on 12 October, some forty miles south of Cassino. Thereafter, the Anglo-American forces found themselves facing an endless range of mountains, fiercely defended by Germans, entrenched and sheltered in their hilltop positions. The Viktor and Barbara lines were soon breached, but their purpose had been mainly to buy time while the Bernhardt and Gustav lines were completed. Constructed under the able direction of Army Group C's Chief Engineer, Generalmajor Hans Bessel, these latter positions were a completely different affair: observation posts, machine-gun and artillery posts were blasted into the mountain sides or dug into fields, guarding obstacle belts, which included anti-tank ditches, minefields and barbed wire entanglements. Deep shelters to protect crew, mortar pits and protective positions for tanks and self-propelled artillery were excavated on reverse slopes and carefully camouflaged. The Germans also constructed a hundred shelters from pre-fabricated steel parts and seventy-six pillboxes around Cassino. The latter housed a two-man machine-gun crew and were known to the Germans as MG *Panzernester* or 'armoured crabs'.

Existing houses were strengthened with cellars for defenders and most stone buildings were 'mouseholed' to enable their garrison to rush from one point to another, under cover. Many settlements around Monte Cassino were built on outcrops of travertine limestone, a stone charac-terised by small pitted holes and troughs in its surface: the hard-wearing travertine was a favourite and cheap building material throughout the region. More resilient than brick, in using local stone Cassino's builders had unwittingly turned every house into a bullet-proof fortress. Much of old Cassino was built of travertine blocks – the Roman amphitheatre and town baths (which still functioned in 1943–44) were of local marble – while south of Cassino town, the much smaller settlement of Sant'Angelo in Theodice is built on an outcrop of travertine, overlooking the Rapido River. Settlements built on hilltops, clustered around a church, provided the Germans with a defender's paradise of strong, stone-built positions with covered approaches, and excellent observation posts.

The whole German defensive concept was not linear as such, but a network of mutually supporting resistance nests, laid out in depth and capable of conducting all-round defence. The Gustav Line was at its most formidable around the town of Cassino, and on the hill overlooking it. The massif of Monte Cassino itself was one of the strongest natural defensive positions in military history, with the monastery, like some great all-seeing eye, peering down on everything. 'Its size and location were surprising,' wrote Lt Harold Bond of the Texan Division, 'for one does not expect to find a huge building perched high on the top of a steep mountain . . . Like a lion it crouched, dominating all approaches, watching every move made by the armies down below . . . It was a strange feeling to know that men up there, watching our movements through field glasses, could, if they thought us worth the trouble, bring down terrible artillery fire on our heads.'

Beyond the forward lines at Cassino, the Germans sowed more than 23,000 anti-personnel mines, most of them either the *Schü*-mine, a small box-like fragmentation device (made mostly of wood, it was almost impossible to find with a mine detector), which went off under only 10lb of pressure, blowing off a man's foot. The dreaded S-mine was even more frightening; the size of a tin can and called a 'Bouncing Betty' by the Americans (though, more accurately, a 'de-bollocker' by the British), these devices were buried with just the igniters protruding above ground or connected to trip wires; when triggered, a small cylinder jumped into the air and detonated after three feet, projecting a lethal spray of ball bearings in all directions at groin height. Both fiendish types were designed to maim rather than kill, the logic being that it took other soldiers to convey casualties back to aid posts, depriving attackers of vital manpower in the assault. The American combat soldier turned scholar Paul Fussell observed that attacking infantry feared the *Schü*- (shoe mine) almost as much as shelling. 'Artillery and mortar fire was deafening, caused frightening damage – sometimes total disappearance or atomisation into tiny red bits – and was considered worse than bullets: to be killed by bullets seemed "clean and surgical", whereas shells would not only tear and rip the body, they tortured one's mind almost beyond the brink of sanity.' The lasting effect of the shoe mine was that 'for years after the war ex-soldiers seized up when confronted by patches of grass and felt safe only when walking on asphalt or concrete'.

Other obstacles were more natural: rivers were included in the defensive scheme wherever possible, whose banks were mined, and nearby fields deliberately flooded. Each German division at Cassino held a sector of about four to five miles in length, deploying forward only a couple of infantry battalions (about 1,200 men), arrayed to a depth of at least 500 yards in three phases of defence. Forward positions overlooking obstacle belts acted as a screen, to prevent Allied infiltrations, especially at night. Behind them were small groups deployed in strongpoints, equipped with machine guns and mortars. Lack of numbers was compensated by mobility wherever possible, so that reinforcements could be rushed from crisis to crisis, in the manner of a fire brigade – the Germans fought the Cassino campaign with six divisions that had varying degrees of mobility – the rest remained fairly static, glued by lack of transport to their positions, but rotated when possible. Most ground not occupied physically by infantry was covered by machine-gun and/or artillery fire.

While to the Germans there were clearly separate, established lines of defence, each with its own name, it did not seem that way to the Allies, who were merely aware of fighting through continuous depth positions, with the whole Bernhardt-Gustav complex simply called the 'Winter Line'. In December 1943, the Germans also began to build another reserve position eight miles to the rear of the Gustav Line, the Hitler Line, which ran from the slopes north of Cassino, via Pontecorvo in the Liri valley westwards towards the sea at Terracina. On 23 January 1944, it was retitled the Senger Line (after the local corps commander General von Senger und Etterlin), to minimise the propaganda effect of defences named after the Führer being defeated.

The Hitler Line was not a naturally strong position, so relied on mobile defence provided by armour and a quick-fix solution of revolving tank turrets set into concrete bunkers. Across the Liri valley its defences were more systematic and well documented: forward minefields were enclosed by barbed wire, behind which was an anti-tank ditch, which had been made with explosives placed at five-yard intervals. Covering the wire and anti-tank ditch were slit trenches and foxholes housing machine guns. Further back were tank-turret bunkers, sited in a series of spearheads; at the tip of each was a turret, with each flank covered by towed anti-tank guns, operating in pairs, usually concealed behind houses or in dense cover. Fields of fire were created by demolishing buildings, felling trees and undergrowth. Some self-propelled anti-tank guns were also positioned even further to the rear to give real depth to the defences, and add weight to any counterattack. The Hitler Line's western end was also protected by another planned mini-defence, the Dora Line. Finally, about fifty miles behind the main Bernhardt-Gustav defences, lay the Caesar Line, just to the south of Rome; however, with most time, resources and manpower committed to the other defences, the Caesar did little to slow the Allies when they broke through – if they even noticed it.

2

An Italian Winter

THE WINTER OF 1943–44 was literally a killer. From mid-October to the end of December 1943, very heavy rain fell in central Italy for fifty days out of seventy-three, turning all low ground into oceans of freezing mud, swamping airfields and roads. On high ground, rain turned to sleet and snow, creating drifts of up to twenty-three feet which smothered unfortunate outposts. Allied and Axis field hospitals were inundated with three times the number of exposure and frostbite cases to combat casualties. Temperatures were so low that vehicle steering columns and engine components froze and fractured, immobilising vital transport. Conditions were merciless. Allied commanders found, much to their surprise, that the only reliable form of transport in these conditions was horse or mule, but in the inventory of their vast, modern, mechanised army, replete with tanks, half-tracks and vehicles of every description, of quadrupeds they possessed virtually none.

The war diary of US 2nd Chemical Mortar Battalion, whose task was to project concealing smoke for infantry advances, recorded of November 1943: 'it was only the beginning of a time in which living conditions reached their lowest ebb. There was absolutely no shelter except for caves and slit trenches – it rained or snowed constantly – and cold reigned over all. During the next three-month period, an average of a hundred men of the battalion were sick in the hospital. Fully ten per cent of the command was rendered inoperative by weather conditions and poor food . . . Supplies of winter clothing went first to the infantry, which is as it should be, but no one in Fifth Army seemed to realise that our men suffered the same rigorous hardships in the miserable weather and without benefit of proper clothing. Many boys felt that they would be better off in the infantry where they could be issued parkas or combat jackets and overshoes.'

A 'driving torrent of rain' turned roads, tracks and paths into mud on the slopes and lower ground. 'If we had only known,' said British artilleryman James Murray of the 23rd Field Regiment, 'that this was only the beginning of the mud bath.' The rain fell steadily and insistently; a truck driver of the 2nd New Zealand Division, who, with his mates had anticipated endless sunshine, remembered despondently 'the trucks drawn up in a circle with their tailboards facing the centre. The gong was an old shell case; a bedraggled tent drawn over the lot to ensure that even dramatic whispers will be heard accurately; the glow of the swinging charcoal braziers, and every now and then the roar of a plane fumbling its way through the rain and the darkness.' The Volturno River, normally about six feet deep, rose by a further fifteen feet and was in full spate by 5 December, sweeping away rafts, boats and pontoon bridges which had been established since its first crossing in October, and threatened lines of communication; water and mud had conspired to bring Allied military logistics to a complete and unexpected halt.

The winter season also precluded the effective use of airpower in support of the land campaign, though there were aspirations to outflank the Germans by sea. Apart from enough craft being made available to enable the planned landing at Anzio in January, the remaining landing craft fleet has been withdrawn to England in advance of Operation Overlord. Thereafter, preparations for the invasion of Normandy would take priority over resources for Italy, and throughout 1944 there was a steady trickle of men and resources away from Italy to support the invasion of France from the north and south. As 1944 dawned, in Italy Allied air superiority was just that – superior, but not omnipotent. Though the Allies ruled the skies, overhead

Luftwaffe fighter aces still managed to ply their trade. Piloting his Messerschmitt 109G, *Leutnant* Ernst-Wilhelm Reinert had shot down a Supermarine Spitfire over Monte Cassino as his 165th victory on 7 December and would continue to plague Allied aircraft over Cassino and Anzio until he fell ill with malaria in March; by then he had downed fifty-one Allied aircraft over Tunisia, Sicily, Salerno and Monte Cassino, of an eventual 174 'kills'. Small numbers of intrepid German flyers could, and did, venture out – but usually at night, when they were more of a night-time irritant than a major threat. Meanwhile the USAAF and RAF attacked German logistics and made daytime movement of military formations hazardous. When the weather permitted the use of tactical air support, the results were usually unimpressive because of the proximity of friendly troops to the enemy: amidst a myriad of mountains and valleys, all looked remarkably similar to a fighter pilot flashing past at 350mph.

Artilleryman Sergeant James Murray and his comrades, who, since Operation Torch in November 1942, had dragged their 25-pounders through Tunisia and landed at Salerno in September 1943, found the mud of Cassino 'much more uncomfortable than anything we had encountered in North Africa. The mosquitoes were having a field day. We lived off and on with the Italian mud for a very long time. Where we did move, it meant digging and winching the heavy vehicles through that Italian mud . . . You did your job as best you could, then, when you did have some time off, there was always the urge to clean up and try to keep some sanity. If you lost that urge you were in trouble and the mud did not help.' An ambulance driver with the American Field Service wrote home: 'Our camp is one of the muddiest spots in all of Italy and it has been raining now for three weeks and we just spend our time while in camp wading around up to our ankles in mud. I have hardly seen my shoes thru the cake of mud for weeks.'

Despite the onset of the Italian winter, and the efficacy of the German defences, Allied commanders still hoped for a reasonably rapid advance and quick capture of Rome. But these hopes were to be dashed in the last weeks of 1943, which would see the Allies, including Italian troops in their first action with Mark Clark's Fifth US Army, suffer 16,000 casualties in breaching the Bernhardt Line, on their way to the Cassino defences, and the next row of determined opponents manning the Gustav Line.

It was clear with the onset of winter that the fully mechanised Allied armies had been humbled by nature and would need to cast back to older days of warfare. In their haste to reach Rome by Christmas, the technology-dependent armies had not quite appreciated the advantages of mules over motorised vehicles on tracks and off-road in the unforgiving mountains of Italy.

Technically mules are the product of a donkey jack mated with a horse mare, and a hinny the opposite – a stallion horse crossed to a donkey jennet, but the military doesn't differentiate – they are all mules, sterile and unable to reproduce, with those distinctive donkey ears and behaviours. Their virtue is that they are generally stronger than horses, have the endurance of a donkey – carrying up to approximately 200lb for distances of up to sixteen miles without resting – and require less food than either. Generally more patient when heavily laden than horses or donkeys, a mule's skin is harder and less sensitive than that of their parents, making them better at coping with the extremes of sun and rain encountered in Italy, while they also show a natural resistance to disease and insects; their hooves, too, are smaller, but harder than those of horses. In Italy, they could wade through mud that would stop a jeep, were perfectly balanced to negotiate tiny, narrow winding trails that were everywhere chiselled into the mountainsides, and seemed to have the ability to just keep going at a steady pace, deaf to distractions. In terms of their ability to haul everything from food, water and medicine to ammunition, batteries and weapons up – and the dead and wounded down – the phrase 'stubborn as a mule' acquired a new, comforting meaning.

A need for the lumbering quadrupeds had already been identified during the Sicilian campaign of July and August, where US 3rd Division had acquired a pack unit of 349 mules and 143 horses. Their performance had impressed Mark Clark who, in looking at the map of mainland Italy, had foreseen the need for many more. At his request a study was made that showed that 1,300 mules would be required for Fifth Army alone, but only a few animals could be found immediately in southern

Italy, Sicily and Sardinia. Accordingly, stock was bought from as far afield as Lebanon, Palestine, Cyprus and North Africa, and by early 1944, the American forces were buying 900 mules a month. Fifth Army had decided against bringing over American mules because they would require large amounts of hay and grain that could not be procured locally, whereas local animals were accustomed to a mixture of home-grown hay and tibben (chopped straw).

In any case, the forage problem for Italian mules soon became acute enough for the Allied Joint Purchasing Forage Board to be established, but horseshoes, nails, and pack saddles were also difficult to source for the growing number of animals, a quantity that increased steadily throughout the winter months. The quickest solution to the new logistics challenge was to use existing pack mule units of the newest ally, that of Italy herself. Although they had served Mussolini, most of the Italian Royal Army (*Regio Esercito*) were desperate to help drive the Germans from their own lands and prove themselves to their newfound comrades-in-arms of the Allied coalition. They eagerly offered units of *Salmerie* – experienced pack-mule handlers, working to the command of Allied officers. These became the first Italians to fight formally under Allied command.

Initially the mule handlers came from the mountain artillery regiment of the Italian Calabria Division, which had surrendered to the Allies on Sardinia; the first detachment deployed on 18 October 1943 with five officers, 321 men and 250 mules, led by *Captaino* Corrado Galli, formerly commander of an artillery battery; a second, far larger, unit followed in November from the Friuli Division, which had earlier fought against the Germans on Corsica. Both units were transported to the mainland to provide pack transport for the British 46th and 56th Divisions of X Corps, advancing towards the Gustav Line at Cassino with US Fifth Army. They were experienced muleteers, and by 24 December four Italian Army pack mule detachments with 1,572 NCOs and men, 28 officers and 1,214 mules were already in action. The number of mules in active service would reach 14,500 a year later. These Italian mule units would prove vital to sustaining the Cassino operations, and comprised an array of volunteers from infantry and artillery regiments, from widely differing backgrounds who were not trained 'muleskinners' (muleteers), but keen to play their part. US commanders were careful to praise their high *esprit de corps*. Both Galli and his sergeant major, thirty-one-year-old Oberto Pellegrini from Pisa, were awarded US Bronze Stars, Galli's citation acknowledging that 'his untiring efforts and capable leadership reflected the finest traditions of the Italian Army'.

Private Jo Kindlarski, a US 3rd Division rifleman, witnessed the typical lot of a mule train. On 8 November he escorted an animal resupply column train for seven miles at night up Monte Cesima, south-east of Mignano. Loaded with badly needed ammunition, the group were rarely less than 400 yards away from the enemy, and constantly under fire. The handlers, the mules and their escorts kept going and delivered the supplies, despite the loads and mules being struck by shrapnel, but missed Kindlarski; his courage that night was soon recognised with a Bronze Star.

Soon a veterinary hospital was established to supervise the mule stock and tend injured or overworked animals; they also de-brayed (silenced) new animals with a simple operation on their vocal chords. By November 1943, Italian officers and men had begun a school to instruct Fifth Army troops in the handling of mules, and muleteers were already clothed in British battledress dyed dark green. In all, six Italian, seven Indian, five Cypriot and eight French North African mule transport companies, with more than 15,000 animals, would support the campaign.

In December 1943, US war reporter Ernie Pyle wrote one of his most famous reports of a mule train winding down from Mount Sammucro, bearing Allied dead, including the corpse of a popular, twenty-five-year-old commander in 143rd Infantry Regiment of 36th Division. 'I was at the foot of the mule trail the night they brought Captain Waskow's body down. The moon was nearly full at the time, and you could see far up the trail, and even part way across the valley below. Soldiers made shadows in the moonlight as they walked. Dead men had been coming down the mountain all evening, lashed onto the backs of mules. They came lying belly down across the wooden pack saddles, their heads hanging down on the left side of the mule, their stiffened legs sticking out awkwardly from the other side, bobbing up and down as the mule walked. The Italian muleskinners were afraid to walk beside dead men, so Americans had to lead the mules down that night. Even the Americans were reluctant to unlash and lift off the bodies at the bottom, so an officer had to do it himself, and ask others to help.'

George Groom, serving in the King's Shropshire Light Infantry, was knocked unconscious during hand-to-hand fighting on the Cassino front and temporarily paralysed. Writing home, he described how some time later, he came to, tied to a mule. The mules 'struggled down the mountain along a narrow track, but some of the wounded fell to their deaths as the mules tumbled off the mountain when they lost their footings'. Even with professional handlers, mules were an inexact science. Until February 1944, when relieved by the 4th Indian Division muleteers, the 5th Italian Salmerie Company supporting the US 34th and 36th Divisions operated under cover of darkness, in all weathers, usually rain or snow, but especially under the constant threat of German artillery. One of its officers later recalled how 'we gritted our teeth against water, mud, snow and especially against loneliness, armed with our moral strength and our mules. We needed a lot of patience and tenacity to prove that the past had not broken our firmness of nerves; that the honour of the Italian soldier was left intact.'

German artillery observers were aware of the use of mules (they used them also) and searched for likely locations for mule parks. The resultant shelling killed and wounded many animals, whose distress played on the nerves of muleteers and soldiers alike. One American doctor described an attack where the entire mule train was destroyed. 'The Italian muleskinners are hysterical . . . To treat them is impossible. None of them will hold still long enough to be bandaged. They scramble off the mountain, leaving a trail of blood behind them.' Meanwhile a British soldier, Victor Donald Delves, recalled that mule handlers looked after their animals 'in the same way we would look after our cat or dog'. After a shell burst on the mountainside, he recalled hearing someone 'shouting and crying quite loudly, I looked round and saw one of the mules with its intestines coming out of its stomach. The mule was desperately trying to get to its feet, but was losing the battle because it was so badly injured. I will never ever forget the mule handler, calling out the mule's name and as it got weaker and could struggle no more, the poor soldier had both arms around the mule's neck and kept shouting its name as the tears rolled down his cheeks . . . after about three minutes, I heard a rifle shot. The poor mule had been put out of its misery.'

Others recalled night-time mule trains halting at the sound of gunshots or German voices, and noticing that the mules paused in mid-stride, alert, with one leg raised, and would not continue until their Italian handler motioned them on. Trooper Kenneth Hall with the 17/21st Lancers was seconded to a pack train, remembering that he 'could hang onto the tail of a mule to help pull me up. It could not kick out at me as long as I had hold of the tail, but I was warned that as soon as I let go I had to jump clear fast.' The historian of the US 45th Division summarised their value: 'Without mules our winter campaign in Italy would have been impossible. On the flats, motor vehicles could churn through the mud; on the worst slopes, only men, climbing upward a few inches at a time with a case of rations or a can of water on their pack-boards, could make the ascent. Between these two extremes were miles of trails where the mule became an exasperating necessity.'

The officers in the 5th Salmerie Company demonstrated real leadership. Equipped with an old Fiat truck of First World War vintage, antiquated Carcano model 1891 rifles, the ten officers of the company managed 370 men, six horses and 258 mules. Eventually the 5th Salmerie would be awarded the honorary title of *Monte Cassino*. Lieutenant Maiocchi led his mule teams for twenty hours over impossible ground at night, carrying ammunition and rations, resting for just five hours before continuing; Second Lieutenant Marco Tangerini was commended for twice coaxing his column of mules under fire, stumbling along razor-sharp precipices at night, with heavily laden, frightened animals, which might easily tumble to their deaths, pulling their handlers over as well. Ernie Pyle observed that 'the Italian method of saying "giddap" to a mule is to go "*brrrr*" like we do when we are cold. When I stand along the pack trail and listen to the skinners "*brrr*-ing" their mules upward, it sounds like the whole population is freezing to death.'

Combat units of the Italian Royal Army saw action against the Germans as a limited ground force in the approach to Cassino over the winter of 1943. Fighting alongside the Allies, they were known, for political reasons, as the 'Italian Co-Belligerent Army' (*Esercito Cobelligerante Italiano*), a grudging half-complement to those Italians who chose to fight and die liberating their own country. The first formations to assemble and train under the Allies were not volunteers, but a few pre-existing sub-units who had demonstrated their loyalty by helping the Allies or militarily hindering the Germans, either in Sicily or the invasion of the mainland. By April 1944, with their ranks swelled by volunteers and others who had escaped capture and internment by the Germans, they were reformed into the *Corpo Italiano di Liberazione* (CIL).

Allied policy towards the Italian military was not clear because two factions at Allied Force Headquarters (AFHQ) held opposing views: left-wing sympathisers wanted a new force, purged of Fascists *and* monarchists, to operate in conjunction with the predominantly pro-Communist partisans in the north, while others feared a Communist takeover and preferred to use the existing Royal Army, cleansed of Fascists, as the basis of an ongoing Italian military contribution. Richard Lamb, a British liaison officer with the Italians, observed that 'volunteers were plentiful . . . some lorry-loads arrived carrying Communist banners and singing the "Red Flag". But few were true Communists. All they wanted to do was to liberate their country from the Germans, and they were pro-Russian because they knew Russia was fighting the Germans. Once they were told firmly they were in the King's army the majority became nominal if not enthusiastic monarchists.' After Cassino, in late September 1944, equipped and mentored by the British, the CIL reorganised into six separate, division-sized 'Combat Groups' of 12,000 each, and fought with success at the Gothic Line against Kesselring's last major defence in the spring of 1945.

Besides the combat units, by the time of the fourth Allied offensive of Monte Cassino in spring 1944, half a million Italians also served formally and informally in uniform alongside the Allies, performing essential tasks as mine clearers, drivers of vehicles and mules; engineers, mechanics and labourers repairing roads, machinery and equipment; builders, cooks, porters in hospitals, and working for the hugely bureaucratic civil affairs activities of AMGOT (Allied Military Government of Occupied Territories), which released many trained soldiers of the US Fifth and British Eighth Armies for combat. *Sottotenente* (Second

Lieutenant) Livio Messina was a typical example of Italians who came to work for the Allies. As a newly minted officer he was in command of a signals platoon in the Livorno Division on Sicily when the Allies invaded in July 1943. Mussolini had been in power for his entire life and Livio saw no reason to question *Il Duce's* greatness or wisdom of going to war. His view changed when his division took part in the counterattack against the US 1st Infantry Division landing at Gela, which destroyed two-thirds of the poorly trained, ill-equipped Livorno Division.

When Mussolini was first deposed, Livio didn't know what to think: 'it seemed impossible that a system so deeply entrenched in Italian society as Fascism could collapse after two decades with the abruptness of a ripe pear dropping from a tree'. As Italian units disintegrated around him, Livio made his way to Messina, caught the last ferry to the main-land, then travelled home to Naples. On hearing of Italy's armistice, Livio's reaction was probably similar to many who had once believed in Mussolini: the news brought tears to his eyes. He cried 'not only because of frustration and anger at what he had been through, but also because of the shame he felt at his country's humiliation. He was afraid of what might happen now' – of the Germans' reaction. His world turned upside down, the twenty-one-year-old hid while the Germans rounded up young men for deportation, and welcomed his former opponents as friends when they liberated Naples in October 1943. As the breadwinner for his mother and two sisters, Livio then worked in uniform for AMGOT as an official interpreter for over three years until the post-war Allied Commission departed in 1947.

Immediately after the September 1943 armistice, there were Italian aspirations to raise a mountain division, and form new units from troops captured in Sicily, Sardinia and southern Italy, but these were met by a general Allied reluctance to commit co-belligerent troops to combat. It was also felt that their doctrine and equipment was outdated, their motivation questionable, and that it was only the Italian navy who could make a worthwhile contribution. The prevailing political view was prejudiced against closer cooperation, and undoubtedly based on the experience of three years of fighting an opponent who had declared war on the Allies first. Captured Italian clothing and equipment stores were allocated to Tito's partisans (who were credited with tying down many good German formations), and so the British Eighth Army had to equip the Italians who had been given limited roles in rear area lines of communication.

After Montgomery (who was violently opposed to harnessing local talent in the form of special forces) left for England in December 1943, the British formed the 120-strong F Reconnaissance Squadron of the SAS. These were Italians clothed, paid and equipped as British soldiers, to prevent them from being shot as *franc-tireurs*. They were mostly ex-*Folgore* Division paratroopers and raised by Major Kym Isolani, a British-Italian intelligence officer attached to 1st Canadian Division. F Recce Squadron operated behind enemy lines on reconnaissance tasks and escorted groups of escaped POWs through the Allied defences. General John Harding, then XIII Corps commander, later paid tribute to them as 'the first Italian unit to take up arms against our common enemy and to show by its spirit and deeds that Italy would fight alongside the Allies to regain its liberty'.

One of the earliest recorded interactions between the Allies and an Italian resistance movement was 'Wigforce', a small British/Italian partisan unit commanded by Major Lionel Wigram of the Royal West Kents, which worked with 36th Brigade of 78th Division in the Sangro sector in January–February 1944. Their activities never went beyond the scope of patrols or small raids and were terminated when Wigram was killed in a raid on Pizzoferrato on 3 February 1944. Apart from Wigforce, one of the first active resistance units (though not necessarily working to Allied command) was the *Brigarta Maiella*, formed in the Abruzzi mountains from young, hot-headed anti-Fascists. They were among the first partisan brigades to take up arms, often linked with a political party or cause, of which there were legion, and usually mentored and supplied by the American OSS or British SOE.

The most significant formation of the Co-Belligerent Army was the all-volunteer First Motorised Group (*Primo Raggruppamento Motorizzato*), a brigade-sized formation comprising 295 officers and 5,387 men. This came about as the result of significant lobbying by the Badoglio government, who pressed after the armistice for the immediate deployment of Italian forces using their own weaponry and equipment. On their Italian uniforms they wore a distinctive small red shield with a white cross, the symbol of the House of Savoy – emphasising their loyalty not to Fascism, but to their King, Victor Emmanuel III. Authorised by Eisenhower on 23 September 1943, the very much experimental First Motorised Group – even the lack of standard military terminology betrayed Allied suspicions as to its value – was assembled in a hurry under canvas at Lecce, in southern Italy, on 28 September.

Largely because of Allied bureaucracy, but also the chaos imposed by the armistice and German reaction to it, the group was initially short of footwear, rations, rifles and ammunition, and had no winter clothing. Despite the Fifth Army's abundance of American-manufactured vehicles, the Italians had to find their own trucks – the resulting 'museum collection' of transport mocked the 'Motorised' part of their title. Command was given to fifty-two-year-old *Comandante di Brigata* Vincenzo Cesare Dapino, who had led an Alpini regiment in 1941 and, more recently, the *Legnano* Infantry Division. Dapino was chosen because his division was only one of two that had remained intact, resisted the Germans and made contact with the Canadians advancing towards Brindisi from the Straits of Messina. Instead of being permitted to select the best junior leaders available for his showcase formation, tragically Dapino possessed only a motley collection of poorly trained junior officers and an inadequate number of experienced NCOs; when he deployed, his engineer company had only just joined the formation.

In early December, Fifth Army's Mark Clark, unaware of any shortages among the Italians, was told that First Motorised were ready, and that their training had been assessed as satisfactory, even though Dapino's three infantry battalions, motorised artillery regiment, anti-tank battalion, engineer, medical, supply and *Carbinieri* (military police) detachments had managed only to conduct minimal training and none as a brigade. Clark sent word via General Geoffrey Keyes, II Corps commander, to whom the First Motorised were attached, that he was to commit the Italians to combat. He and Keyes knew that a forthcoming attack by US 36th Texan Division on the Bernhardt Line defences at Monte Sammucro, San Pietro and Monte Lungo, flanking both sides of the Via Casilina (Route 6) about ten miles south of

Cassino, would be a good opportunity to blood them. Keyes and Fred Walker, commanding 36th Division, hoped to brush aside the German defenders in the hills around the so-called Mignano Gap with a determined attack, and clear the road to Cassino. Beyond, the Liri valley beckoned, with a route virtually all the way to Rome. There was still a slender hope, that first week of December 1943, that the momentum of a powerful punch through the German defences might just allow the Allies through in sufficient strength to celebrate Christmas in the Italian capital. The Italians knew this and had arrived at the Cassino front in cattle trucks with '*ROMA O MORTE*' chalked on the sides, their new government sensing it needed a presence in the front lines if there was even a remote possibility of a breakthrough. The First Motorised Group thus became the unwitting agent for the desires of a whole nation to prove itself a worthy ally.

Far less prepared than it should have been, on 7 December 1943, First Motorised's infantry deployed forward to relieve a US battalion on Hill 253, the Allied toe-hold on the southern edge of the Monte Lungo complex of hills, overlooking the town of San Pietro Infine. These hills and the town itself formed part of the German Bernhardt Line. The whole area was riddled with mines, wire entanglements, foxholes, extremely well-camouflaged machine-gun nests, while every inch was covered by mortar and artillery batteries, able to launch an endless series of pre-set defensive fire concentrations on receipt of simple codewords.

There is no such thing as a gentle stroll over Monte Lungo even today. Seemingly dumped by nature in the middle of the valley that leads from Cassino towards Naples, the three-and-a-half-mile-long whaleback feature of Monte Lungo is surrounded to the east by Route 6, while to the south-west a railway on an embankment runs alongside the Peccia, a narrow fordable stream. Towering over the north-west edge of Mignano, Lungo is an intimidating, oblong-shaped mountain, a flattened oval, the sides of which are made of razor-sharp limestone, and overlooked by all the surrounding hills. Its long spine is in fact a ridge which leads from Point 343 in the south, to its peak, Point 355, overlooking Route 6, half a mile to the north-east, and San Pietro Infine another half-mile beyond that. German truck drivers named the fork off the Route 6 leading to San Pietro, 'dead man's curve', as the road was patterned with shell craters and registered by US artillery observers. On the top of Monte Lungo there remain obvious gaps in the rocks, once blown by German engineers to create observation posts and fighting positions, which were then reinforced with railway sleepers and plundered building materials that they dragged up the hillside.

Early intelligence from the Fifth Army was that Monte Lungo itself was lightly held, though in the weeks before the Italians attacked, III (*Jäger*) Battalion of the tough and resourceful 15th PanzerGrenadier Regiment had taken over the position. However, with the Allies ruling the skies and a general shortage of petrol, by late 1943 PanzerGrenadiers moved as often by foot as by truck, and their transport – when available – was more usually a lorry rather than an armour-plated half-track. Nevertheless they were thoroughly battle-hardened and had been giving the Allies a hard time ever since Salerno, when – with the rest of their comrades of 29th PanzerGrenadier Division – they had nearly pushed the Allied attackers back into the sea. Some, like the III Battalion commander, *Rittmeister* Freiherr Ernst-Georg von Heyking, a highly decorated Prussian cavalry officer, were veterans of Poland, France and Stalingrad: not the sort of opponents against which to throw the battle-innocent Italian soldiers.

Under the watchful eye of 36th Division's Fred Walker, at 6.20 a.m. on 8 December 1943, in thick mist, and while it was still dark, First Motorised Group launched a two-battalion (1,200 men) attack on Monte Lungo. They formed the centre formation of a three-brigade attack, with US 142nd Infantry Regiment assaulting Mount Maggiore to the left, and US 143rd Regiment attacking San Pietro and Mount Sammucro on the right. The first battalion of Dapino's 67th Regiment were to take Lungo itself, while on their left, 350 men of the 51st Bersaglieri Battalion would clear the railway line in the low ground, to the south-west. The 67th were unfamiliar with the ankle-twisting rising ground, and in the dark soon fell behind their supporting artillery barrage, owing to the gradient. The overkeen young Italians, in their first fight, began yelling in exhilaration as they charged up the steep hillside, reaching Point 343. This attracted heavy machine-gun and mortar fire from the

German defenders, entrenched in depth, which further artillery concentrations fired on the hill could not suppress.

On the peak at Point 355, among the 9th Company of von Heyking's PanzerGrenadiers, Obergefreiter Ewald Scherling, number one on an MG-42 machine gun, heard the attackers' shouts. Despite resting under cover from a slight wound, Scherling leapt out and, though blinded by the dark and fog, firing from the hip, aimed at their voices. The Italians had bunched together in the mist and were immediately felled by Scherling's spandau 'like corn cut by a scythe'. Soon, all officers in the two leading companies had become casualties, along with many of the attacking soldiers. Leaderless, the remnants paused, then fled downhill, pursued by Scherling leading a counterattack, wielding his machine gun while two comrades handed him ammunition belts; others fired rifle grenades, which burst among the rocks showering the Italians with lethal stone and grenade splinters. The Bersaglieri Battalion fared no better, being sliced up in their valley by hostile crossfire from neighbouring hills. Attempts to deploy the 67th's second battalion suffered at the sight of their comrades pulling back in disorder, wounded and under shellfire.

Apart from the thick morning fog, the weather was appalling: rain and sleet alternated with a cutting wind, which only added to the plight of the Italian First Motorised who were without any winter clothing. Their misery would have been shared by many of their German opponents, such as Rittmeister von Heyking's neighbours on the Camino-Lungo massif, the 15th PanzerGrenadier Division, who were likewise still wearing summer kit. Generally, conditions were so poor that even the Texan 143rd Infantry Regiment in Walker's 36th Division, attacking on the Italians' right that day, had just requested supplies of shoelaces, as theirs had rotted in the incessant freezing wind, rain and snow.

During the morning attack, 36th Division's Fred Walker was having a 'difficult time', managing the battle while having to greet a host of dignitaries at his command post, presumably there to witness Italy's triumphant entry into land combat on the Allied side. While First Motorised reorganised for defence, guarding against counterattack, US artillery was employed in sweeping the crests, keeping the PanzerGrenadiers at bay – but the Italian attack had ground to a halt.

Reports of casualties from the assault on Monte Lungo – the first counter-blow struck by Italians fighting with the Allied armies – must have hit Brigadier Dapino like a sledgehammer. His Bersaglieri had attacked again, but without result, and by nightfall, he'd lost over 300 for no gain: 178 killed or missing and 131 wounded. Dapino's first casualty, Alfredo Aguzzi, a twenty-two-year-old native of Rome serving with the Bersaglieri motorcycle company, confirmed the lethality of indirect fire in the jagged hills. He had been talking with friends behind the front when he was caught by shrapnel from a mortar bomb fired from Monte Lungo before the assault had even begun, on 7 December. Vincenzo Dapino knew these were 'not excessive' casualty figures for a US regi-ment or British brigade fighting in mid-winter in these hills, but he also understood they would come as a blow to Italian pride and prestige, the more so with most of the Allied top brass literally looking over his shoulder at Walker's command post.

Had Dapino talked to German eyewitnesses of the Italian attack, he might have been more heartened, for in German eyes, the Italians had demonstrated nothing but bravery and determination. After the war, von Heyking himself stressed that the Italians had almost succeeded in overrunning the PanzerGrenadiers: 'the Italian battalion had come to within breakthrough distance. Its attack stalled in the face of hand grenades and MG-42, machine pistol and pistol fire, but more soldiers came on behind them. Within a few minutes our weak positions . . . had been overrun. The majority of our soldiers had been killed, and the enemy poured on, certain of victory. Nothing seemed to be able to stop him any more. But there was one last machine-gun crew . . . Scherling's.'

While the Allies were musing over the failure of the day's activities, that night, Rittmeister von Heyking removed his own Iron Cross and pinned it to the chest of Obergefreiter Scherling. In his battalion commander's eyes, Scherling had saved the day. Heyking then recom-mended Scherling for the higher Knight's Cross, which was later awarded, three days after Ewald Scherling was killed in combat.

If even mentioned, most Allied histories unfairly dismiss the First Motorised Group's attack in a few lines, implying it was amateurish, almost as if they were expected to fail, reinforcing the prevailing view of Italy's poor military reputation. Yet, other units attacking the area at the same time did no better. The US 36th Texas Division suffered 2,235 combat casualties and 2,186 sick after forty-three days in the Mignano-San Pietro area during November and December 1943, while the newly formed US-Canadian First Special Service Force (the Black Devils) suffered 77 per cent casualties in this their first combat. The truth was that the 3–9 December series of battles for the Camino Hill feature, including Monte La Defensa and Monte Lungo, west of and dominating Via Casilina (Route 6), were an attritional slog for all the Allied participants.

Among them, serving as a signaller in 56th Heavy Regiment RA, was Gunner Spike Milligan, who described the build-up before the Camino Hill battle: 'A string of mules accompanied by Cypriot attendants come from the left and pass slowly by . . . ammunition is being dumped by the guns, through the day the pile of mustard-coloured shells mounts up. Mud is everywhere . . . the fire plan takes over and we just sit and wait for targets from the OP. There are nearly a thousand guns savaging the night'. In a passage that applied equally well to the German PanzerGrenadiers and the Italians of First Motorised Group, Ernie Pyle wrote: 'Thousands of men have not been dry for weeks. Other thousands lay at night in the high mountains with the temperatures below freezing and thin snow shuffling over them . . . They lived like men in prehistoric times, and a club would have become them more than a machine gun'.

Perhaps reinforcing the prevailing Allied view of the Italians, Major General Fred Walker of the 36th then approached Dapino with a request that his soldiers act as porters to supplement the existing mule trains. An enraged Dapino responded that his men had come to fight for themselves and their country, not carry for someone else, and the matter was dropped. The US 36th Division planned a further effort to clear the area on 15 December, with attacks on Monte Sammucro, dominating Route 6 from the east, and on San Pietro itself. It was hoped that this pressure would allow the First Motorised Group to complete their original mission of capturing Mount Lungo. The US troops on Sammucro were sustained by Dapino's fellow Italians leading mule trains. Each night they plodded up the stony paths with dry clothing, bandages, ammunition, rations and water, and hurried down before daybreak, bringing the dead and broken with them, following trails marked with white mine tape.

The Italian 67th Regiment climbed Monte Lungo's slopes again on 16 December at 9.15 a.m. This time there was no mist, they knew the ground and adopted disciplined fire-and-manoeuvre tactics. After a sharp fight, Rittmeister von Heyking's III Battalion was pushed off Monte Lungo and his counterattacks destroyed by well-aimed artillery fire. In contrast to a week before, Comandante Dapino's casualties amounted to just forty-eight, while von Heyking lost over 200 PanzerGrenadiers, and was forced to pull back from San Pietro, since the dominating ground on both flanks – Mount Lungo in the west, and Monte Sammucro to the east – had fallen.

Some of 36th Division's battalions were also involved in clearing Monte Lungo, but while the official history suggests the Texans took the summit, the achievement was – wisely – awarded to the Italians. Having walked the slopes of Monte Lungo, it is difficult to see how several battalions could have been attacking the same geographically confined area at the same time. Given the day's losses suffered by the Italians, the surmise is that the second Italian assault was *enabled* by 36th Division, which has translated through time into an American tactical victory. The PanzerGrenadiers, meanwhile, fell back two miles to the next hillside village, San Vittore, which they would hold until after Christmas.

The Italians were warmly congratulated on their achievements by generals Clark and Keyes, but the American part of the assault had not been easy. Starting on 15 December, 36th Texan Division had launched round-the-clock attacks on the Germans in and around San Pietro; despite employing tactical air support, twelve of sixteen tanks supporting the assault were disabled. As 36th Division entered San Pietro itself on 17 December, 500 of the 800 villagers who had sheltered from the fighting in nearby caves emerged to greet their liberators – the rest had died and their thousand-year-old village was not merely in ruins, but indistinguishable from the surrounding rocky terrain (as it remains today). San Pietro is one of the better-known battles of the Cassino campaign, for it was filmed by Major John Huston of the US Signal Corps, on release from Hollywood (where his first movie, *The Maltese Falcon*, was enjoying huge success) and commanding Fifth Army's Photographic Unit. The resultant documentary, *The Battle of San Pietro*, released as a training film in 1945, blended actual battle footage and re-staged assaults by the 36th Division. The sad, roofless ruins of the old medieval settlement, built on the lower slopes of Monte Sammucro, with its caves, the sixteenth-century church of San Michele (with its separate entrances for men and women), and winding, steep lanes, have been preserved – and a new town has sprung up nearby. The civilian casualties and destruction inflicted on San Pietro serves as a metaphor for the suffering of every Italian town and village in 1943–44.

In forcing the Germans out and capturing the settlement, the American infantry battalions lost up to 70 per cent of their strength and a disproportionate number of officers. For Italy, the two attacks cost the Italian First Motorised Group 57 killed, 132 wounded and 139 missing, but they had more than retrieved their honour, and, learning the lessons of their hasty formation, in future would more carefully select and train their personnel. Numbers soon doubled to 10,000 men, and on 22 January 1944, Dapino was succeeded by Umberto Utili, an artilleryman who had been a corps chief of staff in Russia, head of Italy's military mission to the Fifth Army, and altogether a more experienced commander. Belatedly it was realised that Dapino, while a good general, was also commanding a national contingent of troops, and far away from his boss in Brindisi, Giovani Messe, Chief of Staff of the Co-Belligerent Army. Messe had recognised that the setbacks of 8 December 1943 were due to Dapino allowing himself to be pushed into deploying his First Motorised Group before they were ready. A strong commander with more gravitas and able to represent the best interests of the Italian Army – if necessary standing up to Allied pressure – was needed: Utili, also, had visions of a much larger Italian force.

In fact, almost immediately Utili arrived, the First Motorised was threatened with erosion. Umberto Utili was obliged to use his strength of character to turn down two orders from Fifth Army requesting the detachment of Italian battalions for work (not combat) elsewhere along the front. First Motorised was eventually attached to British Eighth Army and, while expanding in size, patrolled with the French and Poles. Under

General Utili the force was retitled the *Corpo Italiano di Liberazione* (CIL) on 18 April 1944, embracing both the First Motorised and what was available of Nembo Parachute Division. As numbers rose to 25,000, the CIL would fight again on the Cassino front at Monte Marrone on 31 March. Utili went on to become one of the heroes of Italy's war of liberation, and when he died in 1952, asked to be buried at Monte Lungo with those of his old formation who still lay at the foot of their first battlefield.

3

France Fights On

THE DRAMAS PLAYED out at Monte Cassino from January would be intrinsically linked to a second Allied strategy, further north, at Anzio, a small fishing village on the coast just over thirty miles from Rome. The Allied plan for breaching the Gustav Line was devised in conjunction with an amphibious left hook round the German flank, to be launched quickly before the remaining landing craft in the Mediterranean were withdrawn for the Normandy invasion. While the US Fifth Army was to assault along the Gustav Line at Cassino on 17 January, drawing German reserves southwards, a second Anglo-American force, US VI Corps, would land at Anzio five days later. It was hoped that the shock and threat of a corps-sized force arriving behind German lines from the sea would provoke a hasty withdrawal from the Cassino position on the Gustav Line and a retreat north. Kesselring had been given a play to act – the question was: would he perform according to the Allied script?

The origins of the Anzio operation lay with a small British amphibious landing behind German lines on the Adriatic front at Termoli on 2–3 October 1943. It inspired hopes that a similar, larger assault on the western coast, somewhere south of Rome, could outflank the Gustav Line. On 8 November, General Alexander, commander of the 15th Army

Group, sent Clark at US Fifth Army a directive to plan a landing at Anzio for 20 December 1943. However, a shortage of both troops and landing craft made the initial date impossible. That the operation was revived was due to Winston Churchill, recovering that same month from a bout of pneumonia in Marrakesh. He envisioned landing two divisions at Anzio, bypassing German forces at Cassino and cutting off their line of retreat south of Rome – and began badgering both Alexander and Clark for detailed plans. Churchill's logic was that if Kesselring pulled troops out of the Gustav Line to attack Anzio, then Allied forces would be able to break through the line at Cassino; conversely, if German troops stayed put at Cassino, the Anzio operation could capture Rome and cut off the German line of retreat. This landing was designed to hold 'the shingle' for only about a week, while the Germans reacted and withdrew, and so was named 'Operation Shingle'.

The success of an amphibious landing on a geological basin of reclaimed marshland, dried-out water courses (which Allied soldiers, fresh from North Africa, christened *wadis*), surrounded by a ring of high hills, would depend on complete surprise and the swiftness with which the invaders could exploit their success and break for Rome. It required a Patton-esque commander, able to weigh risks and strike boldly. Alas, Major General John P. Lucas, commanding the scheme, was not that man. The two men who *might* have breathed fire into the operation and produced a different result had both followed the redirected landing craft and infantry divisions back to southern England in December 1943; generals Dwight D. Eisenhower and Bernard Montgomery had in any case by then turned their attention to the challenge of invading Normandy, not Anzio.

Mark Clark, remembering how close the Germans came to defeating him personally at Salerno the previous September, told Lucas not 'to stick your neck out'. The unfortunate general had conflicting advice: be bold, but don't take any risks. Lucas's orders were not clear: there was talk of advancing to the Alban hills surrounding the Anzio beachhead, with the intention of threatening the rear of General von Senger's XIV Panzer Corps, and 'being prepared' for an advance on Rome. The timing, however, was left to Lucas.

Incredibly the initial landing itself would succeed beyond expectations, achieving complete surprise: an Allied reconnaissance jeep reached the outskirts of Rome with no resistance. But rather than maintain the momentum, Lucas made the decision to hold the limited beachhead seized on Day One, and build up men and materiel. By midnight on 22 January, 36,000 soldiers and 3,200 vehicles were ashore; thirteen of his troops had been killed and ninety-seven wounded, while about 200 Germans had been captured. Afterwards Churchill venomously attacked Lucas's lack of nerve: 'Instead of hurling a wildcat onto the shore all we got was a stranded whale.' At the heart of Shingle was the Allied surmise that Lucas would seize Rome from a secure logistics base. A more dispassionate observer might have noted that the moment the Germans decided against withdrawal from Cassino, they would rush reserves from all over Europe to destroy the Anzio beachhead. Thus, while Lucas consolidated, Kesselring ringed the beachhead, just as he had done at Salerno. For weeks a deluge of shells rained on the two invasion beaches, the plains inland, and anything else observable from the hills. Churchill was incandescent when he learned of Lucas's inactivity: the more so when he heard there were 18,000 vehicles in the small beachhead: 'we have a great superiority of chauffeurs' was his accurate retort.

A hallmark of the Wehrmacht's activities in 1939–45 was the incredible speed with which they consistently reacted to operational-level crises by the swift employment of massive reserves. Although surprised, Kesselring had contingency plans to deal with landings at all likely locations. These required divisions to have motorised, quick reaction units to deploy ahead of the main body and attack the seaborne invaders. Accordingly, the first two battlegroups he sent towards Anzio were also his most powerful: by 5 a.m. on 22 January, elements of the 4th Fallschirmjäger and Hermann Göring Panzer Divisions would both be on their way, a mere three hours after the first Allied troops had waded ashore. It was certainly Lucas's lack of offensive action that convinced Kesselring he could contain and crush the landings, and by 24 January he had assembled a very creditable 40,000 troops around Lucas's positions. With deft juggling of his available troops, Kesselring merely kept Vietinghoff's Tenth Army on the Gustav Line, and rolled everything else into Mackensen's Fourteenth Army, which bottled up Lucas at Anzio. By early February the ratios read: 100,000 German troops (1st

Fallschirmjäger Corps and LXXVI Panzer Corps) to Lucas's total manpower of 76,400. Far from 'holding the shingle for a week', over the next month and into February, the Allies would be forced to draw reinforcements for Anzio from those previously allocated to Cassino. Attacks on the Gustav Line would have to be launched to take the pressure off the landing. The Anzio tail would begin to wag the Cassino dog.

Mark Clark's US Fifth Army anticipated a busy January, including several assaults across the river valleys extending in front of them, which in turn were dictated by the one firm date on Clark's calendar, the attack by VI Corps from the sea at Anzio on the 22nd.

First into the fray at Cassino, on the night of 11–12 January 1944, was a force that has been almost forgotten, not least by the nation under whose banner it fought: France. When it comes to the 1944 Allied victories achieved in Italy, the army led by Général Alphonse Juin has been written out of most French history books, never mind Allied ones.

On 18 June 1940, Général de Gaulle had broadcast an appeal from London to his fellow Frenchmen asking them to carry on the fight; however, just 35,000 rallied to his cause. Not only did France have to build the army that fought in Italy almost from scratch, but she also had to resurrect a military reputation lost in May 1940. French military stock had tumbled far since the days of 1918, which saw France on the winning side, or 23 March 1933, when Winston Churchill had summed up the popular world view in his statement to the House of Commons, 'Thank God for the French army.' Both generals Alexander and Montgomery as relatively junior divisional commanders had witnessed the collapse of French units during the 1940 campaign, and when the first French troops landed in Italy on 25 November 1943 they found Montgomery in charge of British Eighth Army and Alexander as Army Group commander; both had to be convinced of the French as an effective and loyal force.

It was only after Operation Torch – the Allied invasion of Morocco and Algeria, commenced on 8 November 1942 – that a sizeable French army fighting with the Allies was even a possibility. Beforehand, as deputy commander (under Eisenhower) of Allied forces in the North African theatre, Mark Clark had landed secretly by submarine on the Algerian coast between 21 and 24 October 1942 (in Operation Flagpole) to nego-tiate the surrender or cooperation of the Vichy French. An early convert to the Allied cause was the French-Algerian Alphonse Juin, whom Clark first met on 10 November: he was immediately taken with Juin's effi-ciency, energy and enthusiasm. The Frenchman was soon leading his North Africans troops against the Axis forces in Tunisia, and Clark's request that Juin lead the French force in Italy evidenced their mutual regard and growing friendship; Clark would later describe Juin as 'one of the finest soldiers'.

Nevertheless Juin's position was not as straightforward as other senior commanders in General Alexander's coalition army in Italy. Juin, like the Italians, had been part of the Axis, and had to demonstrate not only that he was a trustworthy disciple of the Allied cause, but also that he was loyal to Free France. This requirement was all the more complicated as some of his men had been loyal to de Gaulle since 1940: to them Juin was a mere turncoat and *arriviste*. Assurances of loyalty were not accepted readily by the prickly Charles de Gaulle in the early 1940s: he was suspi-cious of most officers, having been let down by the one he trusted most, his mentor, now commanding Vichy, Maréchal Philippe Pétain.

Short and stocky, with a cheerful face and smiling eyes that concealed a legendary brain, Alphonse Juin understood how to motivate and lead his predominantly North African troops. Born in Algeria and the son of a gendarme, he was a classmate of Charles de Gaulle at the St Cyr Military Academy, from which he graduated first in 1912. Known among his colleagues as *L'Africain*, he had led the 15th Moroccan Motorised Infantry Division in May 1940, when he was taken prisoner by the Germans. In November 1941, he was released and became overall commander of Pétain's Vichy French land forces in North Africa, total-ling 137,000 men.

Juin would invariably inspect his mountain corps on the back of a hardy pony, his general's kepi perched on the back of his head and a cigar clamped between his teeth. He had lost the use of his right hand and arm on the Western Front in 1915, and therefore saluted with his left. His bonhomie was genuine and infectious with his troops and other Allies alike – in contrast to the unsmiling Clark – and most spontaneous photographs of Juin capture a rosy-cheeked, cheery grin in an otherwise depressing landscape. When Général André Dody's 2nd Moroccan Division brought with them female ambulance drivers, Mark Clark voiced his opposition, but Juin was firm: 'The women of France, like the men, are proud to die for their country' – and they remained at the front.

In 1940, France operated three separate armies: the largely white *Armée Métropolitaine*, which defended the homeland, *L'Armée d'Afrique*, which recruited in French North Africa (Algeria, Morocco and Tunisia) and *La Coloniale*, which included soldiers from France's other territories. With the *Métropolitaine* defeated, discredited and imprisoned in 1940, it was Juin's very un-European *Armée d'Afrique* and *La Coloniale*, the all-volunteer *Legion Etrangère* (Foreign Legion) of non-French mercenary soldiers, and Berbers from Morocco who would fight in Italy and then go on to help liberate France. While many troops in the *Armée d'Afrique* were familiar with Western ways, many soldiers in *La Coloniale* were illiterate, spoke only in their own dialect and were unfamiliar with trappings of the modern world such as shoes, motor transport, automatic weapons, medicine and even clocks or time-keeping. Both armies were staffed by volunteer white officers and NCOs, but those of the *Armée d'Afrique* (who were often talented colonial settlers, including some North African Jews) tended to be closer to their men – indigenous conscript soldiers – and led from the front.

French colonial units consisted of indigenous, conscripted soldiers recruited by tribe, ethnicity or region, led by a handful of white officers and NCOs; while the white officer class were very good (and suffered casualties in higher numbers than their Allied counterparts), the maintenance of this racial hierarchy, in denying command positions to native soldiers, would have ramifications for France's post-war colonial policies in French Indo-China (Vietnam) and Algeria. There was also a French tendency to 'spend' African lives more readily than European ones, and the overall percentage of the Juin's casualties would be excessively high, more than any other Allied unit in Italy. Overall, the French Expeditionary Corps (FEC) was 60 per cent African in ethnicity, although Juin's Africans would suffer 80 per cent of the casualties.

In January 1944, Juin's FEC was only two divisions strong: André Dody's 2nd Moroccan and Joseph de Monsabert's 3rd Algerian, both newcomers to Italy. Later arrivals, who missed the first battle for Cassino, but took part in the fourth battle in May were François Sevez's 4th Moroccan Mountain Division, who appeared in February 1944 equipped with mules, and Diego Brosset's 1st Free French Division, a composite unit that was nearly 60 per cent European, had allied itself with de Gaulle in 1940, fought as part of British Eighth Army in North Africa, and were reluctant to serve under Juin (because of his previous loyalty to Pétain and Vichy); they eventually arrived in April 1944. Totalling 112,000 men, all of these units would fight at first or fourth Cassino, before being withdrawn to invade southern France as part of Operation Dragoon in August 1944. Then the FEC was officially dissolved and absorbed into the First French Army under General de Lattre de Tassigny, though initially still retaining its North African flavour.

Though most Expeditionary Corps troops wore French helmets with American uniforms and equipment, the Berbers, or *Goumiers*, were instantly recognisable by their odd assortment of British helmets, US webbing and long, striped, blanket-like tunics which reached to their ankles. As soldiers, the *Goumiers* were considered 'robust, very hardy, tireless marchers' and 'excellent marksmen'. They were organised into company-strength *Goums*, three of which (plus a heavy weapons *Goum*) made a *Tabor* (similar in size to a large battalion). Juin's FEC included two *Groupements des Tabors Marocains* (GTM), each equating to a brigade (or regiment), on its arrival in November 1943, and three by April 1944. *Général* Augustin Guillaume's three GTM were effectively Juin's fifth division. They totalled 240 officers, 840 NCOs (all French), 12,900 men, including some Berber NCOs, 1,230 mules and 1,025 horses.

Most of the troops of the French Expeditionary Corps had grown up in the hills and Atlas Mountains of North Africa: high hills were their playground, and they were the Allies' only units skilled and equipped for mountain warfare. With training that emphasised small unit autonomy and infiltration, and logistics that rested on expert mule handling, none of the Expeditionary Corps regarded the mountains surrounding Cassino as a barrier, but more of an opportunity to test their unique military skills. There was a strong element of psychology attached to the Corps' way of war. Most of Juin's men possessed short, traditional, curved daggers, the *koummya*, which added the same element of fear that Axis forces already associated with the Gurkhas and their *kukris*. This most Arab-looking of knives – generally worn visibly on the left side, with its intricately worked wooden handle, excessively curved, doubled-edged blade, carried in a silver sheath – was usually a family heirloom and added practicality to the favourite Corps tactic of silent, fast-moving night attacks. Rumours soon circulated in German lines that the Berbers specialised in assembling collections of specific body parts, often ears – not all were false.

Not long after the FEC landed in Italy, concern was expressed by Italian civilians that the Corps' Goumiers, in particular, were sexual predators who regarded women as part of their booty of war. A young girl was reported raped by three 'arab soldiers of the French army'; the regiment concerned identified the trio. North of Naples, another French soldier was shot in front of his unit after the discovery of child who had been raped and strangled. French military records, now declassified, suggest that initially these were isolated acts committed by single individuals or small groups, which also included theft, armed robbery, and plunder, and were punished by the Allied authorities. Later in the campaign, however, such crimes were certainly more prevalent and there was undoubtedly extensive physical abuse of Italian civilians by members of the FEC. Analysis of French military archives suggests that some 360 Expeditionary Corps soldiers were brought before the military courts for violent crimes committed against many thousands of civilians during the Italian campaign; some were executed, the rest imprisoned.

However, such crimes reignited a deep-seated Italian fear of the Arab North African littoral, and resulted in a prejudice which lingers to this day. In 1944, this expressed itself, over on the Adriatic front, when a British Eighth Army Basuto cook was killed by a farmer's wife: the unfortunate soldier had merely knocked at her door wishing to buy eggs, but was mistaken for a *Goumier* bent on trouble and, for his politeness, received an axe in his skull.

The initial enterprise for which Clark required the FEC was preparatory to a three-corps attack on 11–12 January along the line of the Garigliano–Gari and Rapido rivers. Initially the two French divisions were to advance on the extreme Allied right flank, across defended mountain terrain and close up to the Gustav Line in the areas of Atina and Belmonte-Castello, north of Cassino itself. Once there, they would execute an anti-clockwise right hook, slicing through the Gustav Line, in the hills, far beyond Cassino, and reach the Liri valley in the region of Roccasecca. This would bypass the Cassino area altogether, putting Juin beyond, some ten miles up the Liri valley.

Meanwhile, Dick McCreery's British X Corps was to cross the Garigliano, surging through the Aurunci Mountains south of Cassino, while Geoffrey Keyes's US II Corps bridged the Gari and Rapido rivers to make contact with Juin's forces in the Liri valley. Clark's overall plan was both ambitious and in the best traditions of modern warfare, with sequential, corps-sized sweeping flanking movements to the left (Operation Shingle) and right (the French) and a frontal attack with his remaining two corps. Although the terrain restricted the mobility of his highly motorised forces, Clark hoped his plan would restore the element of manoeuvre to hard-pressed troops.

Opposite Juin's Moroccans was the 2nd Company/95th Gebirgsjäger Artillery Regiment – tough German mountain troops, assigned to the most difficult theatres, and part of the 5th Gebirgsjagers, known as the Gämsbock Division because of their chamois (mountain goat) badge. Among their ranks was a twenty-nine-year-old *Unteroffizier* (NCO), Anton Auggenthaler, who had previously spent a gruelling twenty months on the Leningrad front. In November 1943, the entire 5th Gebirgsjäger Division, led by the goatee-bearded Generalleutnant Julius Ringel, had been deployed to Italy, taking over a twelve-mile sector of the front on 22 December. Their battle honours already included Poland, France, Crete, Serbia, Yugoslavia, and Russia. Auggenthaler had served in them all, and been awarded the Iron Cross 2nd Class and a Crete campaign 'cuff title'.

A mere four days after arriving in Italy, the Moroccan 8th Infantry Regiment had attacked them; Auggenthaler's protecting infantry managed to push the Moroccans back a number of times but on the fourth attempt, reserves from 115th PanzerGrenadier Regiment had to be summoned, supported by Auggenthaler's guns, and shunted the Moroccans back to their own lines, sealing the breach. The next day, with the Moroccans in pursuit, they pulled back to the Gustav Line to await the French again.

Juin's Moroccans had proved their mettle and Clark hoped they would continue to roll back the Germans. On the night of 11/12 January 1944, in filthy weather, and before any of the other attacks went in, the Moroccans and Algerians moved off from start lines secured by the US 34th Division. Juin's Corps attacked without a preliminary barrage and in line abreast, their forays initially achieving great surprise against the 5th Gebirgsjäger Division north of Cassino, who had not expected *any* attack, and certainly not by mountain troops. The Moroccans were thrifty and had equipped themselves with additional Italian machine guns, mortars and copious quantities of ammunition; they pushed into the night and having despatched the outpost troops with their knives, dealt with larger positions and trenches with grenades. One German unit war diary recorded 'a relentless tide of hellish giants that surged all around them'. American officers following observed 'there were no [French] stragglers; nor were any weapons or equipment abandoned. I was able to see numerous dead Germans; many showed signs of bayonet wounds; some had their skulls caved in. Morale excellent; very few prisoners taken.'

Whereas Dody's Moroccans had already been bloodied during the previous month in Italy, Général de Monsabert's 3rd Algerian Division had not. Monsabert had served in the First World War as a battalion commander, and afterwards mostly in North Africa. He led a formation of indigenous volunteers against the Germans in Tunisia over 1942–43, before being given command of his division on its creation on 1 May 1943. Attacking on Dody's left, from an area held by US 45th Division, the Algerians had more challenging terrain and tripped over Ringel's 5th Gebirgsjäger Division relieving the 305th Division, so had to contend with double the expected opposition. They were also unlucky, for almost immediately a German shell hit an orders group of the 3rd Battalion/7th Algerian Regiment, removing the battalion's command element in an instant. The French battled to the peak of their main objective, the 4,576ft Monna Casale, which changed hands all day. Eventually the Algerians were left in possession, Ringel's troops having suffered up to 80 per cent casualties in some units.

With the Gebirgsjäger shunted back over the Rapido River and surrounding heights to the main Gustav Line positions, this first French assault ground to a halt in sleet and snow on 17 January. Juin's force had sustained high casualties (including 300 frostbite and exposure cases), but he appealed to Clark that, with another division, he could break through the crumbling German lines, outflank Cassino to the north and north-west, and enter the Liri valley as planned. This was probably true, but the only reinforcements available were American, and US Fifth Army had already earmarked them for other attacks. Reluctantly, Juin was obliged to cancel further assaults on the Cassino massif, and consolidate the ground they had won against counterattack.

US Fifth Army planned to launch its main attack in the Cassino area on the night of 17/18 January, initiating what later would be known as the first battle for Cassino. Closest to the sea, two British divisions of X Corps would force their way across the Garigliano: British 46th Division would cross overnight on 19/20 January, followed by 36th Division of US II Corps crossing upstream over the Rapido the following night. The idea was to pull the German reserves in different directions, while building up the pressure. Simultaneously, the French were to renew their attacks, having recovered from their first encounters in the heights. US VI Corps would then, on 22 January, land at Anzio.

On 21 January, therefore, the French went in again, with both divisions initially continuing along their original axis, heading north-west towards Atina. The Moroccan 2nd Division struggled in the teeth of a howling gale to scale and take the 3,700ft Monte Santa Croce, ten miles to the north-east of Cassino. This was a considerable achievement for soldiers without the sort of specialist clothing climbers are used to today, in hobnailed boots that slipped on icy rock, having to contend with German snipers who could pick off men dangling on ropes, while machine-gun, mortar and artillery fire projected potentially fatal rock splinters at crazy angles. Impact fissures, where hot metal struck rock, can still be seen on cliffs in the region, as can the long, deadly shards of stone, lying on the ground, that killed as efficiently as shrapnel.

The main target for the French was the mighty Monte Cifalco, the summit of which provided an ideal location for Anton Auggenthaler's artillery, with natural shelter from aerial bombardment and artillery fire. Auggenthaler's company was equipped with four 75mm mountain guns that weighed 1700lb each and had a maximum range of 10,000 yards (five and half miles). He and his men were trained to strip these down into ten loads for transport by mule and reassemble them quickly. His Gämsbock Division had very few motor vehicles, but 4,300 mules and 550 mountain horses on strength, and were trained to carrying everything uphill by mule or soldier: each high explosive or smoke shell weighed 13lb.

However, two days into the new attack, and without prior warning, on 23 January Fifth Army HQ ordered Juin instead to shift his axis of advance to the left. His new orders were to seize the impossibly steep Colle Belvedere ridge, Monte Abate and the village of Terelle, all about five miles north of Monte Cassino, dominating the head of the Rapido River valley. This required them to completely change direction, and reorientate towards the south-west, though both divisions and their logistics were orientated north-west. They were also expected to launch the new attack in just forty-eight hours. When Juin selected Général Joseph de Monsabert to lead the new assault, he responded: 'Storm Belvedere? Who's dreamed up that one? Have they looked at it? You'd have to first cross two rivers, the Rapido and the Secco, then smash through the Gustav Line in the valley, and finally, all the time attacking the Bosche, climb more than 2,000 feet over a bare rock pile, itself heavily fortified, that can be fired on from Cifalco and the rest of the summits round that. It's pure wishful thinking! It's a crazy gamble!'

Part of the reason for the switch was that II US Corps and X Corps had failed to cross the Rapido and Garigliano rivers. If the French reached the Liri valley via Atina, there would now be no one there to meet them. Also, these new objectives were at the end of the Rapido River valley, overlooking the little villages of Sant'Elia, Caira – and Cassino itself. With excellent observation over the Rapido plain and rivers, any German crew-served weapon systems guided by good optics on these hills – like Auggenthaler's 75mm mountain guns – would cause serious damage to an Allied attack towards Cassino town. With the Belvedere and Abate heights in Allied hands, Clark hoped the Germans would then withdraw reserves from Cassino to counterattack these vital positions. More importantly, the Anzio landing has just gone in and Clark wanted to be in a position to advance and link up with Lucas whenever he moved out from his perimeter.

Of course Kesselring soon solved this problem for him, but the decision to shift axis on 23 January threw away Juin's perfectly feasible indirect approach and committed Clark (who seems, with the short notice, to have acted with a degree of uncalled-for panic) to the series of frontal assaults now commonly associated with Cassino. Alphonse Juin considered it 'a mission which in other circumstances I would have deemed impossible. It was not at all to my taste, involving as it did an attempt to outflank the enemy at close range rather than on a much wider arc of manoeuvre.' But he obeyed nevertheless.

It took time to reorientate the French advance and dump supplies in new locations for a major attack, there being only a few mountain tracks, and little ability for wheeled transport to get to the new start lines. It also meant leaving the threatening bulk of Monte Cifalco with Auggenthaler and his comrades unconquered in the rear. Colonel Jacques Roux's *Régiment de Tirailleurs Tunisiens*, of the 3rd Algerian Division (4/RTT), was selected to launch the new assault, with much French and American artillery on call. French-manned US 155mm 'Long Tom' heavy guns in particular would make a big difference here: they could hurl a 99lb shell up to fourteen miles, often at high trajectory over the mountain peaks, whereas Allied field artillery or armour could not get close enough to help. En route for Sant'Elia 'which used to be a town and is now a mass of blown-up masonry', war correspondent Martha Gellhorn described 'in a hollow below the climbing road, Italian women washing clothes at an old stone trough, and six-wheeled trucks ploughing somehow up the hill through the mud that looks like churned brown cement. The echo of shell explosions bangs crazily against the mountains. You pass through a mudflat, where nothing grows except guns, and two French batteries of 155s open up against the Germans, who are on a mountain you cannot see, and everyone on the road is briefly deafened. If you are right under the guns, you open your mouth and breathe hard.'

Though German artillery was very good, it was not available in the same quantities, and was often molested by Allied aircraft, though less so in the winter fog, sleet and snow. Many of the defenders were artillerymen like Auggenthaler, spotting for or serving guns, but there were numerous Gebirgsjäger, Fallschirmjäger, PanzerGrenadier infantry detachments and Friedrich Franek's 44th Hoch und Deutschmeister Division. Several accounts talk of pillboxes, machine-gun bunkers and mortar emplacements covering likely approach routes in the mountains.

These were not great prefabricated concrete affairs as found along the Atlantic Wall in northern France, but camouflaged shelters usually made of piled stones that had been 'topped-off' or strengthened with concrete, often (for the machine guns) with overhead cover. Barbed wire had been strewn wherever possible and anti-personnel mines liberally sown about – particularly on the mule tracks.

Both sides realised that the capture or retention of the Colle Belvedere – indeed most high ground in the Cassino area – would be down to old-fashioned infantry tactics, where technology would be no substitute for human skill, determination and endurance: this is where training and leadership would count. Sustaining the fight for either side was a constant headache. Everything had to be carried up by hand or mule: German infantrymen typically dragged uphill two boxes (eight fifty-round belts) of machine-gun ammunition weighing in at 30lb. The French in their turn took their 0.30-inch Browning machine guns, which also weighed 30lb, without ammunition or tripod; hand grenades weighed a pound each: infantrymen usually carried four; every round for a 60mm mortar was another 4lb. In addition to their own weapons and their ammunition needs, all of Roux's men were required to carry several grenades and mortar rounds each: no wonder knives were an attractive option.

Roux briefed his officers on 24 January with the assistance of a few aerial photographs, but they had been taken in far from ideal conditions, and no one had seen the ground beforehand. He chose his 3rd Battalion under *Commandant* (Major) Paul Gandoët to storm the positions on the Belvedere, working in concert with Major Berne's 2nd Battalion. Roux's Tunisians had an approach march of nearly twenty-four hours just to reach their line of departure. They had to descend from high ground, ford the Secco River by Sant'Elia, wading up to their waists in icy cold water, then ascend again first the series of summits that comprised the Belvedere ridge, then the higher Monte Abate peak beyond. Before they started off at 7 a.m. on 25 January, they had soon walked a considerable distance across the mountains and were soon tired and hungry. Worse was to follow: the speed with which Clark required the new assault meant that Juin's mule trains had not yet arrived; therefore the men had to carry all that was required.

In the event, the Tunisians elected to take ammunition but little food or water.

This would have serious consequences, for the men were not only heavily laden, but would have to combat cold, hunger and thirst. Although he had entrusted the Belvedere mission to Général Monsabert, Juin was sufficiently aware of all this Clausewitzian friction to elect to remain at his subordinate's side, in avuncular fashion, for the entire week's fighting, beyond the left bank of the Rapido on the slopes of Hill 784, where Monsabert had his HQ. Roux and Monsabert also knew that any assault on the Belvedere would be observed and shelled by German artillery at Monte Cifalco – Anton Auggenthaler and his Gebirgsjäger guns – to their rear. There was German artillery ahead, also. Twenty-three-year-old Leutnant Karl Gruner was an officer with a battery of four 75mm Skoda guns belonging to the II Battalion, 96th Artillery Regiment (44th HuD Division), stationed on a hillside position below the Colle Abate; he later recalled the early hours of 25 January when, 'fire spat from the mouth of every enemy gun'.

Preceded by an artillery barrage and four squadrons of USAAF Marauder bombers trying to suppress the defenders, during a day that stayed misty and rainy, men from both of Roux's Tunisian battalions crept forward. Major Gandoët, CO of the Tunisian 3rd Battalion, had previously identified a long, upwards rock funnel which offered a hidden approach to the German positions on the Belvedere and Colle Abate, but was a perilously steep 2,000ft climb. It also offered cover from fire and view of the German units behind, on Mount Cifalco. Starting to climb at ten in the morning in wet clothing (from the river crossing) that would freeze as they ascended, Captain Raymond Jordy and his 11th Company led the way up the fissure, the base of which was covered with damp vegetation, slippery stones and boulders, easily dislodged; in some places it was thirty feet deep, with towering rock walls either side. Jordy and his men toiled up this rocky scar in the mountainside as quietly as possible, yet laden with mortars and machine guns, rifles and grenades, water in their canteens and K-rations (small tins and packets of high-energy combat rations sufficient for a day) and medical supplies stuffed into spare pockets and packs. Ice and sleet didn't help, but the fog shrouded their movements.

After four hours, Lieutenant Tumelaire's platoon with two 60mm mortars had reached the halfway point, overcoming a surprised German post in the mist; the main height, 2,234ft, was only reached and taken at nightfall as Jordy's exhausted men swamped bewildered German defenders from an unexpected direction. In tough hand-to-hand fighting, Roux's Tunisians had taken the Colle Belvedere by the evening, but been driven off the summit and were occupying the upper slopes. One of Gandoët's 9th Company officers, Lieutenant El Hadi, had one arm torn off by shrapnel when leading the advance, but he carried on, plunging into bayonet fighting with his good arm and only succumbing nearer the summit when riddled with bullets. Throughout, Auggenthaler and his fellow gunners on Monte Cifalco to the rear fired blindly through the mist at the Belvedere and Abate, wounding many unlucky attackers.

To the front, Karl Gruner's gunfire was directed by radio, but he could see North African troops creeping up the mountainsides. It left him feeling very exposed, for he could not see any trace of his own protecting infantry, and the proximity of the French eventually drove him back to other positions. 'The last reserves from our infantry regiment, a platoon of infantry and pioneers arrived to help us entrench our field pieces in new positions,' he remembered. 'With our guns and artillery of the 5th Mountain Division on our left we were then able to inflict serious losses on our opponents.' Both sides paused to lick their wounds before the Tunisian battalions resumed the fight on 26 January, forcing the Germans off the Belvedere by eight that evening. Underlining the fierce tribal loyalty that bound many of these troops together, *Sous-Lieutenant* Bouakkaz had publicly sworn he would be the first to the summit, but the young officer was killed by a bullet to the forehead, whereupon three of his men carried his body all the way to the top to fulfil his sacred oath. Two of his *Tirailleurs* sat the corpse on a rifle which they carried horizontally, while a third braced his shoulders, the macabre quartet leading the rest of their platoon to the summit.

Some men went on to take Monte Abate at 2.30 a.m. on 27 January, but were dislodged at about eleven the same morning. Major Berne's 2nd Battalion was encircled and he was captured; Captain Léoni, his jaw smashed by a bullet and his revolver empty, continued to lead using his cane to point out tasks and missions, but at 11.30 a.m. a German officer approached, and taking the remnants prisoner, declared – full of admiration – '*Tapfere Soldaten!*' (brave soldiers). Throughout the day, strong German counterattacks gradually forced the French to relinquish some of the heights, but the latter were also now feeling the effects of having run out of food and water. Colonel Roux was killed during the day, trying to escape after being ambushed on the Belvedere and taken prisoner.

A train of eighty mules was sent out to resupply the desperate Tunisians after dark on 28 January; however, all but two were felled by German mortar and machine-gun fire. Both sides were as badly off as each other. Long after the battle a natural spring, high in the saddle between the Belvedere and Monte Abate, was found to be ringed by dead soldiers – Germans and French – who had risked all to slake their thirst. Meanwhile, Leutnant Gruner's 75mm battery remained vulnerable until 28 January, when just before dawn, German reinforcements finally arrived. 'I warned an officer that the North African contingent on top of Colle Abate, a very short distance from us, could easily carry our position,' Gruner recalled, 'so again we moved our guns and opened fire at close range. Our concentrated fire surprised and defeated the Tunisian detachments; a patrol of our infantry meanwhile managed to win back the Colle Abate, taking many prisoners.' Later on the 28th, more French reinforcements arrived and were able to start to push the Germans back off the heights on 29 January, though the Colle Belvedere changed hands twice more before nightfall, which saw the French finally in possession. Another twenty-nine mules arrived with supplies at seven that evening and though the counterattacks did not halt immediately, both sides had fought themselves to a standstill.

Juin thereupon sent Clark a signal that his men had 'accomplished the mission you entrusted to them' but could do no more. By the time the 4/RTT descended the Colle Belvedere on 3 February, they had endured four full days of close combat (26–29 January) and lost over half of their number: 1,481 killed, wounded or missing. Among the last to die was

Captain Raymond Jordy, commanding the 11th Company of Gandoët's 3rd Battalion. He had already won the *Légion d'honneur* in Tunisia and had taken and retaken the Belvedere; his 11th Company had started with 185 men: only thirty-five survived unwounded. On 29 January, Gandoët had asked Jordy to stay close to him, to command if he were killed. Somehow they both survived the fighting but as the two descended, a fluke German shell fired from Monte Cifalco killed Jordy while he walked down with his boss.

Karl Gruner remembered the setback: 'On 29 January, the Tunisians took a hill from which they could train their guns on us. Then it was no longer possible to maintain our position, which we abandoned on the night of 29/30th and took our guns along the twisting road towards Terelle.' The town marked Leutnant Gruner's fourth or fifth change of location, by which time the French seemed to be perched on the mountains all around. At this point his CO, Hauptmann Rudi Heger, awarded a Knight's Cross in January 1943 at Stalingrad, was hit by a shell and killed instantly; it was a loss that Gruner felt keenly. Shortly afterwards he encountered an American prisoner, who was 'frightened and sitting on the bare ground, holding a rosary along with a booklet of prayers. He had a German name, but did not speak any words of German.' Gruner chatted to him, offered him a cigarette and chocolate, 'while in my mind I was thinking of my cousin, Carl Gruner, also an artilleryman, who was serving in a US battalion. He was then twenty-two years old, a year younger than me. Our mutual grandfather lived in Würzburg.'

It was later calculated that seventeen of the forty-four available German battalions facing the US Fifth Army and French Expeditionary Corps on the Cassino front in January 1944 were involved in trying to prevent the French from gaining the Belvedere and Monte Abate. A measure of the fighting was that each of the heights that made up the ridge changed hands at least three times, and on one, the French repulsed twelve separate counterattacks. The 90th PanzerGrenadier, 1st Fallschirmjäger, 5th Gebirgsjäger and 44th Hoch und Deutschmeister Divisions lost 1,200 prisoners to the French and suffered a similar number of killed and wounded – experienced soldiers they could ill afford to lose and had no means of replacing. Among them was Anton Auggenthaler, killed on Monte Cifalco on 27 January. He is buried, with Gruner's CO, Rudi Heger, killed on 1 February, and 20,047 other comrades in the German military cemetery on the Colle Marino, near Caira.

Martha Gellhorn visited the French Expeditionary Corps in early February, just after they had seized the Belvedere heights. Although overlooking the fact that most of the Corps came not from France, but Africa, she nonetheless observed for her world readership that: 'A sizeable unit went into the attack and hardly more than twenty per cent were able to walk off the mountain, but the French hold it, and that is what they want. Because each mountain they take, at whatever cost, is a mountain nearer home ... The French are earning their way home and they do not complain ... They are fighting for the honour of France, which is not just a phrase, as you might think, but the personal, undying pride of every one of them. And they are fighting to get home to a country cleansed of Germans.'

The road to the Colle Belvedere today remains a nerve-wracking serpentine affair of ten hairpin bends during the ascent out of Caira village. Looking out from the open plateau above it is immediately clear why this terrain was so fought over. The view down the Rapido valley towards the Monte Cassino abbey stretches for miles, and encompasses everything from Monte Trocchio, then behind Allied lines, the Rapido River plain, to the town and abbey. The Belvedere summit, from where paragliders now launch themselves, is an incredibly peaceful, lush meadow, dotted with brightly coloured alpine flowers. However, scattered everywhere are low stone walls built in semi-circles – the remains of French and German defensive positions made from the only protective material available. The treacherous rocky route to the Belvedere summit (still considered beyond the skill of many experienced mountaineers today) followed by some of the 3rd Tunisian battalion in 1944 is still known as the Ravine *Gandoët*.

The FEC would continue to hold the Colle Belvedere area through the next battles and were transferred to the far side of the Liri valley for the fourth battle, Operation Diadem, in May, where they would play a leading role in bursting open the Gustav Line. Through January into February, the FEC won great admiration for their tenacity in these hills and the special qualities they had demonstrated as mountain troops. However, their achievement came at a high price: the Corps would continue to take consistently higher casualties than other Allied units to achieve their missions. This is borne out by the statistics from the first Cassino battles. Of all the Allied armies the FEC left proportionally more of their blood in the soil of Italy: for a force that peaked at about 112,000 they suffered 7,836 casualties from mid-December 1943 to mid-February 1944. This was partly due to the French tendency to push African units harder, but they also cared less about the resultant cost in lives. Although this was a culture over which the Corps commander had no individual control, the success on the Belvedere was a personal triumph for Alphonse Juin. He had won his men's trust and they had earned great respect from their fellow Allies. In six months, Juin had taken a widely disparate group of tribesmen from different countries, colonial settlers and exiled Frenchmen, and forged them into an awesomely impressive formation capable of taking and giving out extreme punishment. Regardless of casualties, the French now controlled the heights at the northern end of the Rapido valley, overlooking the town and monastery of Cassino.

4

A Very British Way of War

B Y JANUARY 1944, one man stood in charge of the entire Allied presence on the Italian mainland: Harold Rupert Leofric George Alexander. As commander of 15th Army Group, now called the Allied Armies in Italy (AAI) to reflect its growing multinational character, Alexander coordinated the actions of his two subordinate armies, one British, one American, while reporting to the Supreme Allied Commander Mediterranean, his fellow Briton, Sir Henry 'Jumbo' Maitland Wilson. Alexander's hand would guide and shape Allied military fortunes throughout the period of the four Cassino battles.

As one of Britain's highest-achieving commanders, Alexander was in every way the Allied counterpart to Kesselring, who was six years his senior. Alex was educated at Harrow and Sandhurst and commissioned into the Irish Guards in 1911. He had experienced a relatively 'good' First War, leading a Guards battalion at Cambrai as an acting lieutenant colonel and commanding a brigade during the surprise German offensive of March 1918. He was wounded twice in four years of fighting, winning an MC, DSO and *Légion d'honneur*. He had the unusual, even unique, British experience of commanding German troops in combat: when the new republic of Latvia was attacked by the Red Army on 1 December 1919, he led a battalion of the Baltic German *Landeswehr* (militia) in

Latvia's war for independence. This instilled in him an admiration for the fighting qualities of the Germans, which he never quite lost, and would resurface, particularly at Cassino.

In the inter-war years, Alex spent some time in India and at the Imperial Defence College before being promoted to major general, making him the youngest general in the British Army. In September 1939, he took his 1st Infantry Division to France, and after overseeing its safe withdrawal to the coast on the sands of Dunkirk, was placed in command of I Corps. Alexander was likeable, cheerful, tall, patrician and – crucially for Churchill – looked every inch a general. He was not prone to self-advertisement (unlike Montgomery or Mark Clark) and tended towards the taciturn, which some have mistaken for a lack of intelligence. He was considered a safe pair of hands by Churchill who, during his August 1942 'Cairo purge', appointed Alex as Commander-in-Chief, Middle East. This led naturally to his army group commands, first in Tunisia, then Sicily and finally, Italy.

The British Minister in the Mediterranean, Harold Macmillan, witnessed Alex's methods and was impressed. In Tunisia 'we stopped at the headquarters of General Omar Bradley . . . He showed upon the map how the battle was progressing, and there were certain dispositions of which I could see General Alexander did not altogether approve. By a brilliant piece of diplomacy, he suggested to his subordinate commander some moves which he might well make. He did not issue an order. He sold the American the idea, and made him think he had thought of it all himself. [This system] made Alexander particularly fit to command an Allied army. Later, when he found himself in the Italian campaign controlling the troops of many countries, he developed this method into a remarkable technique.'

Alexander also had the good fortune to have been supported by two exceptionally able chiefs of staff, initially Dick McCreery, followed by Lieutenant General John Harding, from January 1944, both of whom he treated as intimate friends. Harding was an excellent battlefield tactician who had already won three DSOs and was badly wounded in the hand by a shell while commanding 7th Armoured Division in North Africa. He presided over Alexander's headquarters at Caserta, forty-seven miles south of Cassino, the former royal palace of the Neapolitan monarchs, built by the Bourbon King Charles III in the 1750s. Caserta was logistically a sensible location for Alex's army group headquarters; psychologically too it gave the impression of the powerful and resource-rich Allies who were in 1944 running the liberated portion of Italy.

Unlike most senior British officers in Italy, who were protégés of Montgomery, the young British X Corps commander Dick McCreery was also much favoured by the Chief of the Imperial Staff, Sir Alan Brooke. The bright but shy McCreery had found himself between posts in Cairo in 1942 at the moment of Alexander's arrival in the Middle East: 'He and I saw eye to eye on military matters,' wrote Alex; 'he was, too, my trusted friend and companion whose wise advice and companionship meant much to me . . . Events were to prove that I had chosen wisely.' McCreery's abilities in command were characterised by 'attention to detail, careful planning and a strategic flair that had few superiors'. Aged forty-five at the time of the first battle for Cassino, McCreery had ceased to work for Alexander and become by far the youngest corps commander in the British Army.

The failure of assaults so far had shown that the Allied leaders, military and political, had completely misjudged the severity of the Italian landscape, and were over-optimistic about their chances of success. Sir Alan Brooke lunching with Harold Nicolson privately admitted that 'the terrain defies description. It is like the North West Frontier; a single destroyed culvert can hold up an army for a day.' Brooke then went on to laud their opponents: 'they are fighting magnificently. Marvellous it is, perfectly marvellous . . . The morale of their troops is still admirable and only a slight change can be seen in the quality of the prisoners captured.'

He might have already compared notes with the *Daily Telegraph*'s war correspondent Christopher Buckley, who on reaching Sicily described the 'sinking of my heart. It seemed so terribly reminiscent of 1916, of a war fought in terms of advance of a few hundred yards over shell-torn ground, every yard purchased with a man's life. There had been so little of this in [North] Africa.'

As the Allies came up to the Garigliano-Gari-Rapido River barrier in January, their next move was obvious: geography dictated that US Fifth

Army would launch its main attack towards the Liri valley, initiating what would become known as the first battle for Cassino. Major Fred Majdalany of the Lancashire Fusiliers later wrote: 'it was not a prepared offensive against the Gustav Line, but a hurried resumption of a weary advance that had battered its way to a standstill . . . A plan was devised which looked coherent on paper. But the fact remains that the first assault on one of the most powerful defensive systems of the war was an *ad hoc* affair, hastily undertaken without anything like proper preparation.'

Once the French Expeditionary Force had made their move through the mountains on the extreme right, a whole series of sequenced attacks would follow: the assault on the river lines overnight on 17/18 January by two British divisions of X Corps, who were to force their way across the Garigliano; a day later, a third British division would cross; on 20/21 January both divisions of US II Corps were to bounce the Gari-Rapido upstream; and eventually, on 22 January, US VI Corps would land at Anzio. The idea was to dislocate the Germans (in this case, Senger) as much as possible.

For the British part of first Cassino, codenamed Operation Panther, McCreery envisaged three concentrated punches through the Gustav Line, and then to find and exploit the weak spots. McCreery's X Corps had borrowed Major General Gerard Bucknall's battle-hardened 5th Infantry Division from Eighth Army for the occasion, all of whom had been in continuous action since landing in Sicily. This division, reinforced by 201st Guards Brigade, was to push across the Garigliano astride Route 7 at Minturno on the coast, turn right, and join 56th (London) Division in forming a wide bridgehead, then thrust down the Ausente River valley to Ausonia, nine miles beyond the Garigliano. They would then advance beyond, via San Giorgio and into the Liri valley, where they would link up with two divisions, one British, the other American, who would, meanwhile, have crossed upstream, broken through the Gustav Line and charged along the valley.

The 56th Division were originally a Territorial formation, recruited in London, and known as the 'Black Cats', after their uniform and vehicle insignia, the outline of a black cat on a red background; the feline was associated with Dick Whittington, a much fabled early Mayor of London.

Led by the exceptionally able forty-five-year-old Major General Gerald Templer, the Black Cats had seen action in Tunisia, and had stormed ashore at Salerno as part of X Corps in September. They were to force the Garigliano opposite Castelforte at the same time as 5th Division made their crossing downriver. Upstream, McCreery's third formation, 46th Division, was to follow later by crossing opposite Sant'Ambrogio, guarding the left flank of the 36th Texan National Guard Division, the victors at San Pietro.

Major General John 'Ginger' Hawkesworth's 46th (North Midland) Division was another old Territorial outfit, which had likewise landed at Salerno with X Corps and were often referred to as the 'Oak Trees', on account of their divisional badge, an oak, signifying both the Sherwood Forest, their original area of recruitment, and a symbol of 'strength and reliability'. The capable Hawkesworth, in his fiftieth year, would eventually take over X Corps when McCreery was promoted to Eighth Army command at the end of the year. Crucially, after forcing the river, the Oak Trees were to push on to Sant'Apollinare, securing the high ground overlooking the Americans' crossing areas near Sant'Angelo. The assaults of British 46th were very much interlinked with those of US 36th Division; the failure of one would impact on the other.

Although 5th Division was an old regular formation, and 46th and 56th were Territorials, these designations had become meaningless by 1944. Most British soldiers in 1944 were conscripts, and all were known as 'national servicemen' in an effort to sweep away the divisive distinctions between different kinds of unit seen in the First World War. It illustrated (as had the Salerno mutiny) that Britain's military recruitment and reinforcement system had broken down due to the already excessive casualties incurred in the Mediterranean theatre. Before one attack, a battalion in Templer's Black Cats received replacements from *fourteen* different regiments, causing its commanding officer to urgently request a supply of cap badges, 'so that at least men could have familiarity with the badge of the regiment in which they had to be prepared to die'. Indeed, the most statistically likely to be killed or injured were the newest arrivals, who were at their most vulnerable in their first three weeks, with no 'buddy' to look after them and show them how to live, fight and survive in the field. Infantry divisions were no longer permanent fixtures, but had become holding units for brigades that were shuffled around according to manpower needs. Gone were the closely knit, locally recruited battalions of the First World War – which blighted whole communities when military disaster occurred.

Logistically, although McCreery's three divisions were equipped with small four-wheel-drive jeeps, these were limiting, and could only carry three stretchers at a time; so pack animals remained the main means of conveyance through the treacly mud around the rivers and stony tracks in the hills. The 1st and 4th Italian Pack Companies and the horse handlers of the 14th Italian Cavalry Group, totalling 1,000 quadrupeds, were responsible for moving the entire X Corps' combat supplies forward. Later, they would convey the empties, the dead and the wounded, back to hard standing, several miles away beyond sight of the German guns. The 5th Division's history noted that it took, on average, six hours to get the wounded down by mule from the heights to a regimental aid post, and another one and a half hours to waiting ambulances at the foot of the hills. Where the terrain was too poor even for mules, as Staff Sergeant Bill Quirk of 184 Field Ambulance remembered, human stretcher-bearers took over: 'We had a stretcher chain reaching over three mountains with about a thousand men (Indian, British, Italian and any others that could be brought in). They were spread out four to a stretcher with varying distances between each team according to the difficulty of terrain. Each group brought a loaded stretcher anything from fifty yards to quarter of a mile each and handed it over to the next group and took an empty one back with them . . . it was very uncomfortable as the chain worked well into darkness in pouring rain and even snow and ice on the higher reaches. In places the paths were so narrow and steep it was a two-man job, and quite a few were killed by the constant shelling.'

The penny had only just dropped for all Allied commanders that mules and human porters were henceforth to be the main driver in successful logistics, but a thousand mules were too few to supply the combat needs of three infantry divisions, including all infantry, mortar and artillery ammunition, rations, water, petrol, wireless batteries, tools and medical equipment. The work was exhausting: muleteers often reported having to follow their white-taped paths through muddy mine-fields and icy mountain trails for twelve-hour return journeys. McCreery was soon obliged to supplement his jeeps and mules with human porters, Basutos, Cypriots and Palestinians of the Royal Pioneer Corps, to sustain his gains. George Pringle, serving in 175th Pioneer Company, which supported Hawkesworth's North Midland Division, recalled that portering made a 'change' from his company's other tasks, which had included working as infantry at Salerno, probing for mines on the banks of the Garigliano, building sangars or constructing roads under fire. Pringle observed that mules brought pack loads forward from motor transport until tracks petered out: 'then our company took over carrying the 50lb loads on our backs, securely fastened to avoid us overbalancing into the valley below. We had also given up our rifles so that our hands would be free for climbing. We moved steadily and almost breathlessly, lest we made our presence known to an enemy patrol. Each time a loose rock was dislodged and fell noisily we froze in our tracks as the Germans or our own forces fired an inquisitive flare into the sky, illuminating the mountainside. We clung there until word was passed back that we could proceed and we made our way to the RV point.' On their descent, Pringle and his mates acted as stretcher-bearers 'bringing down from the mountain ledges the soldiers who were too badly wounded to make their own way. Usually four men would handle a stretcher case, but it was often only two, due to the narrowness of the track, slipping and stumbling over the rocks while the wounded soldier would be groaning. On a few occasions it would be only one man in the wind and darkness who would have to carry his burden across his shoulders, because a stretcher could not be used'.

The porters of the Royal Pioneer Corps were frequently the unsung heroes of the Cassino campaign, managing to evacuate casualties and sustain troops in remote mountains positions that wheeled transport and even mules could not reach. They were often older conscripts, the youngsters having been pre-selected for combat. By December 1943 there were thirty pioneer companies, each of nearly 300 men, supporting the British on the Cassino front. By April 1944 this would rise to forty-three companies, totalling 12,000, including Indian, Mauritian, Basuto, Bechuana and Swaziland units. Pioneers were not immune from casualties themselves, as 187 Company reported: 'Private Tancred, forty-two years of age, was carrying a wounded officer down Monastery Hill. This took him sixteen hours and when he had completed the job he collapsed and died from exhaustion.' Meanwhile, Captain Robert Cain commanded his company of Basuto porters so ably in shocking weather conditions, that 'although aged fifty-three, he repeatedly struggled up the mountain tracks leading his men and rallied them under fire, thereby holding a wavering company to their duty under extremely difficult circumstances'. This leadership brought Cain a Military Cross. Cain's age and that of his commanding officer, a First World War VC winner, aged forty-six, illustrated the relative seniority of the Royal Pioneer Corps, when infantry company commanders were in their early twenties and COs usually under thirty. Behind the lines, British RPC officers and NCOs managed 150 companies (45,000) of Italian pioneers and 230,000 Italians on civil labouring duties, reinforcing the fact that for every Allied serviceman at the Cassino front, there were fifteen to twenty working in some capacity to sustain him there. The Pioneers' work was unglamorous, rarely acknowledged, yet vital to the success of the campaign.

Facing 5th and 56th Divisions and X Corps were battalions from Generalmajor Bernard Steinmetz's 94th Infantry Division. Although he had only taken over command on 2 January, Steinmetz was a highly regarded old warhorse. He had been one of the last commanders flown out of Stalingrad a year previously, where the old 94th Division had been destroyed. Steinmetz's division was therefore a newly raised unit, formed in April 1943, but posted to Italy in September before its training was complete. His superior, Senger, considered it the weakest of all his formations, though he rated Steinmetz and his divisional staff highly. Both Vietinghoff and Senger 'had nightmares' about the 94th's lack of experience, limited equipment and general vulnerability along a key sector of the Gustav Line. To ease their fears, they arranged for 24,000 mines to be laid along the divisional front. Steinmetz, Senger and Kesselring may also have found temporary comfort in the mid-January assessment from German military intelligence that there was 'not the slightest sign that a new landing will be undertaken in the near future'.

Two of Steinmetz's battalions lay dug-in under a series of twelve-foot shelters, between the old Roman settlement of Minturno on the coast and the Ausente River, and a further pair of battalions from 276 Regiment guarded the river line between the Ausente and Castelforte; each pair could call on a third battalion for support. Steinmetz also guarded thirty miles of coast north of the Garigliano River against amphibious attack. This part of the Gustav Line followed the high ground a mile beyond the Garigliano, over which all bridges had been blown, while both banks were targeted by artillery and machine guns, and the surrounding terrain covered with obstacle belts of wire and mines.

The X Corps attackers would also have to drag their plywood, canvas or rubber assault boats across several drainage ditches before reaching the main river, which was deep, fast flowing and over 100ft wide in places. The assault wave in their boats were clad in thick woollen battle-dress, ankle boots and the distinctive British helmets of the day. Clutching rifles, they carried minimal webbing, but enough to contain bayonets, 0.303-inch rifle or Bren ammunition, a few hand grenades or mortar bombs, water bottle and iron rations. NCOs tended to sport a 9mm Sten or .45-calibre Tommy gun, and officers binoculars, a map case and Webley pistol; all carried a field dressing and were trained in basic first aid, while extra ammunition was carried in bandoliers over the shoulders. With a uniform weighing in at 20lb and equipment at 40–60lb, this mocked the idea of 'minimal webbing' to keep the weight down. Their load was not dissimilar to that carried by Roman Legionaries, Wellington's Redcoats or troops on the Somme, belying the notion that technology enables troops to carry less.

Only once bridges were up would the heavy paraphernalia of war – motorcycles, Jeeps, trucks, artillery and tanks – be able to support them. Soldiers over the centuries had come to grief here. In November 1503, during the Second Italian War, the Spanish tried and failed repeatedly to cross the Garigliano to fight the French on the other side. Eventually they succeeded, using makeshift bridges made out of boats and barrels strapped together, and within hours 4,000 Spanish troops led by Gonzala de Cordoba were able to surge across.

Preceded by an artillery barrage, Templer's Black Cats, attacking with two brigades at 9 p.m. on Monday evening, 17 January, were rapidly across the Garigliano at several points, and soon laid down Bailey bridges. A recent innovation by British War Office civil servant, Donald Bailey, Bailey bridges revolutionised military logistics by reducing the components to interchangeable sections, capable of being lifted by a six-man team, so no cranes were necessary. All the modular parts were transportable in a standard 3-ton lorry and, Lego-like, capable of producing multiple designs of different spans and loading capacities. Each ten-foot steel length was manually pinned, bolted or clamped together to span gaps of varying lengths, or were launched across rivers, usually by Bailey-designed pontoons, to form rafts or floating bridges. Thus the only tools required were a few wrenches, and a trained 115-man team could build a five-span bridge in thirty-two minutes, though in daylight and without interference from the Germans. During the Italian campaign the Allies would build over 3,000 Bailey bridges, the Garigliano and Rapido assaults particularly relying on Donald Bailey's genius.

Once the Bailey bridges were across, Templer's Black Cats and Bucknall's 5th Divisions could be supported by the armour of 40/Royal Tank Regiment (about sixty Shermans). Armour and infantry had a symbiotic relationship in Italy, characterised by mutual need, occasional distrust, and admiration. Rifleman Alex Bowlby recalled his battalion marching up an Italian lane lined with Sherman tanks and armoured cars which could not advance until the infantry had opened the way. He recalled: 'I never felt so conscious of my regiment as I was then. This was the way to risk one's life. There was no King or Country about it – it was the regiment. And I wouldn't have changed places with anyone,' due to the spontaneous applause they received from the armour crews.

Nevertheless, Bucknall's two-brigade assault at the same time at the coast ran into early trouble. Within 5th Division, odds of five to one were being offered against the crossing being achieved (which cost at least one senior officer a small fortune). To assist the attack, two companies of the 2/Royal Scots Fusiliers set out to bypass the defenders by sea in six-wheeled amphibious trucks (DUKWs), accompanied by tanks in landing craft. En route one wandered as far out to sea as a cruiser providing naval gunfire support, and was then concerned by the sudden appearance of a strange submarine. There was nothing to be done but sink it; as the Fusiliers aimed their PIATs (an early form of the bazooka) expecting to be the first infantrymen to sink a U-boat with anti-tank weapons, a sailor emerged from the conning tower and accosted them:

'Who the hell are you?'

'Royal Scots Fusiliers.'

'Never 'eard of you,' responded the RN matelot, whereupon his submarine submerged and disappeared.

The overnight amphibious landing foundered when some troops were beached south of the Garigliano (on the 'home' side), others landed on the correct side, but were dispersed, and landing craft became disorientated and returned with their cargoes of tanks and artillery. This left too few on the beaches, their weapons clogged with muck, and under mortar fire; the operation cost the Royal Scots Fusiliers 140 casualties. This whole sector had been quiet for some time (officers of the Scots Guards recorded duck-shooting across the river earlier in January), and Bucknall had decided to forego artillery preparation in the hope of achieving surprise – which largely worked. His infantry paddled furiously in tiny assault boats across the Garigliano overnight, while the rest of the division built bridges and rafts, and overran many of Steinmetz's forward positions, dug laboriously over the preceding months.

To deceive, as well as surprise, before the attack, Bucknall even had his distinctive divisional insignia (the letter 'Y', standing for York, their home depot) removed from vehicles and signposts, and replaced with the anonymous number '7', leading sharp-eyed German patrols to believe a new, untested, division had taken over that sector. An ex-Cambridge oarsman, now major, commanding a gunner battery and a battalion commander leapt into a rubber assault boat, and in best boat race fashion, started to power their way across the water, the major calling the time, 'In – Out.' Puzzled to find they had made no progress, they discovered in their adrenalin-fuelled moment they had neglected to untie their craft from the river bank.

Most of 5th Division's objectives were on high ground – Tufo and Point 156 changed hands several times – or overlooked by elevated terrain, from which the German artillery exacted its toll, while the attackers picked their way through the minefields: daylight soon exposed the vulnerable bridging sites and narrow, muddy tracks marked by white tape through the obstacles, mines and ditches. On Point 156, led by shouts in best battle-comic style of '*Schweinhunde Englander!*', German troops were cajoled forward in their counterattacks by one zealous officer, who got close enough to the 2/Royal Inniskilling Fusiliers ('the Skins') to seize one of their Vickers machine guns. Nonetheless, both 5th and 56th had gained shallow bridgeheads and pushed Steinmetz's weak 94th Division out of their forward lines, occupying the defenders' bunkers – one British unit even captured a ready-cooked breakfast – while fending off counterattacks by their former owners, aided by artillery and naval gunfire from two cruisers and five destroyers.

Broadcaster Frank Gillard of the BBC was on hand to make a recording under fire of the assault, on fragile bakelite discs which found their way back to London, and the wireless news service announced to the world on 18 January: 'in an new attack by British troops in Italy, the crossing of the Garigliano River has been made, an entry into the main defences of the Gustav Line'. It would take Radio Berlin until the 21st to comment on the British assault. Early on 19 January, both divisions injected more battalions across the Garigliano by raft, ferry and Bailey bridge, protected by smoke, to enable the capture of Minturno, three miles beyond the river, by 1/Green Howards of 15th Infantry Brigade.

Meanwhile, Major General Hawkesworth's 46th North Midlanders were due to launch their attack over the river and opposite the entrance to the Liri valley on 18–19 January. To the Americans it was crucial that Hawkesworth not only made it across the river, but captured the high ground near San'Apollinare, overlooking the proposed US crossing sites. The violent German reaction to his other divisions' activities may well have induced in Dick McCreery a sense that his X Corps was spread too wide, and a reluctance to commit 46th Division on their own, seven miles upstream from 56th Division, two days ahead of the Texans. This was in case his remaining formation got stuck on the wrong side of a river, the target of focused German counterattacks, with few reserves to call on. So, not unsurprisingly, McCreery delayed Hawkesworth's start by a day, aware that this would probably infuriate his boss, Mark Clark at Fifth Army. Clark was indeed unimpressed and remained convinced the 'Oak Trees' would need two days to seize the high ground so that the Texans could cross safely. Alas, Clark could not now delay the 36th's own assault across the Rapido, as it was synchronised with the Anzio landings, due to take place overnight on 21/22 January. In his view, the Texan assault across the Rapido needed enough time to work through the German chain of command, ensuring that Kesselring would draw his reserves away from Rome and Anzio.

While a sophisticated air support package was being delivered to assist X Corps at this stage, Clark actually had the opportunity to cancel the North Midland's and Texans' upstream assault altogether and could have chosen instead to reinforce McCreery's X Corps bridgeheads down-river, which would have been in line with American doctrine. However, the American general had been stung by the perception that Salerno had been promoted as a British – or an Allied – success, whereas he firmly believed it to be a US (and a personal) victory. Like Montgomery, Clark possessed a pathological need for his own publicity, and was therefore unwilling to surrender any opportunity of an American break-through to assist a British one. It may have been this clash of nationalities as much as a need to support the Anzio operation (and perhaps an outside chance of a breakthrough into the Liri valley) that resulted in Clark's decision to proceed as planned with the upstream thrust, which would have catastrophic results for the Texan Division.

At 8.30 p.m. on Wednesday 19 January, in thick fog, British 46th Division's attack went in with US field artillery in support. At the same moment they witnessed the level of the Rapido rise suddenly by six feet and the speed of its current increase. The Germans had opened the sluice gates of the San Giovanni Incarico irrigation dam, twenty-five miles upstream in the Liri valley, in an attempt to disrupt the earlier activities of 5th and 56th Divisions. Deploying just the 128th (Hampshire) Brigade, all attempts to cross at several points met with failure, with men and boats being swept away in the torrent, as well as the unwelcome attentions of the now-awake defenders, a battalion of 15th PanzerGrenadier Division. Born out of the old 15th Panzer Division (mostly captured in Tunisia), Generalmajor Eberhardt Rodt's 15th PanzerGrenadiers were no easy opponents and had already defended Sicily and Salerno with aplomb and damaged the 36th Texan Division at San Pietro Infine in December. His men were responding to a vicious teleprinter message sent personally from Hitler to Kesselring anticipating the forthcoming battle, and passed down to the defenders. 'It is not sufficient to give clear and tactically correct orders,' the Führer's missive read. 'All officers and men of the Army, the Air Force and the Naval forces must be penetrated by a fanatical will to end the battle victoriously, and never to relax until the last enemy soldier has been destroyed or thrown back. The battle must be fought in a spirit of holy hatred.'

Just one company (of 2/Hampshires) managed a lodgement on the far bank out of two battalions attempting the task. Well-sited German positions on high ground were able to direct fire onto bridging equipment, boats, engineer stores and vehicles on the far banks, while protective smoke was blown away by the wind. The diary for 20 January of one British officer reflected philosophically on the day's events: 'So, as often happens in war, the plan went awry; the 128 Brigade attack was a failure, a failure not so much due to the enemy as to nature. The river, at the points selected for the crossing, was too fast-running, and the boats were swept away, and ropes broken.' Only a few men managed to get across on the left; 'on the right about three-quarters of a company succeeded. Then the Boche got wind of it, poured small arms fire and threw grenades onto the boats as they struggled to get across. It was a heroic effort, which had to be called off. Let us hope that some of them manage to get back under cover of darkness tonight. I cannot help feeling that the attack in this particular area was based on faulty appreciation, especially as all patrol reports had stressed the difficulties of crossing the river here. However, such is the confusion of war.'

Neither of the other two brigades attempted crossings, and were eventually redirected to assist 56th Division, while Hawkesworth's 128th Brigade made no further efforts to force a bridgehead. There were accusations that 46th Division's crossing was half-hearted: US II Corps commander Geoffrey Keyes later noted bitterly that 'the Germans had little difficulty in turning back . . . a less than forceful effort'. Other assessments blamed 46th Division's inability to cross on equipment shortages, including forty amphibious DUKWs, originally intended to help X Corps cross the Garigliano, which had been diverted to Anzio to replace others lost at sea.

With the failure of his division's attempt to cross the river, and ease the forthcoming attack of the Texans, Hawkesworth at least had the decency to go over to 36th Division's HQ and apologise in person for the failure, offering to provide one of his battalions to support the Texans' attack. Their commander was unmoved: 'The British are the world's greatest diplomats,' he wrote in his diary; 'but you can't count on them for anything but words.'

Some Americans, however, appreciated other aspects of the British attitude to combat. A US volunteer ambulance driver attached to 23 Field Regiment's aid post wrote: 'I was glad to be with Englishmen like these in action. Their casualness helps to calm jumpy nerves. Typical was the comment, when Jerry was dropping a number of shells in the neighbourhood, "The cheeky bastard! I suppose he'll be drawing his rum ration from us tomorrow."'

Generalmajor Bernard Steinmetz soon realised his 94th Division was in danger, having identified two entire divisions attacking his four battalions. Senger, his commander at XIV Panzer Corps, with a nose for trouble, soon visited him and hastily despatched battalions from the neighbouring 15th Panzer Grenadier, 44th and Hermann Göring divisions, and persuaded Kesselring to release part of 29th and 90th PanzerGrenadier Divisions – which would otherwise have been on hand to crush the Anzio landings. Senger reckoned with hindsight that the thrust against Steinmetz 'had special significance, for if it had led to a breakthrough, the entire German front would have been rolled up from the south. Compared to this, the subsequent attacks [of the Americans and French] . . . would have been of secondary importance.' Thus, Mark Clark's objective of distracting German attention from the Anzio area had already been achieved on the coast by X Corps, and the upriver crossings by Hawkesworth and, subsequently, the Texans, may have been unnecessary. The reinforcements rushing to Steinmetz's aid had problems of their own, and for logistical reasons arrived at the front only in piecemeal battalions, without concentrated force, while the 90th

PanzerGrenadiers were held up due to Allied air interdiction and lack of fuel. Nonetheless, Senger attacked the bridgeheads hard on 20 and 21 January, contesting Castelforte and the heights to its south, Monte Rotondo and the Damiano Ridge.

On Saturday 22 January the Allies landed at Anzio, necessitating some hard decision-making by Kesselring, Vietinghoff and Senger. While they had sent two divisions of reserves south to block the X Corps breakout, they did not immediately recall those formations, but sent others to Anzio instead. On the eve of the Anzio invasion, Radio Berlin was able to announce with more truth than usual that 'on the southern Italian front superior enemy forces attacked and after heavy fighting succeeded in breaking through south-west of Castelforte. In a methodical counterattack they have been driven back to their initial positions.' For most Germans, their only source of news was the wireless, with propaganda information broadcast through *Volksempfänger* (literally 'the people's receiver') – Nazi Germany's cheap radio sets with dials marked only with German stations.

By contrast, the reality for the Reich's soldiers near Castelforte appears in the entry for 22 January, found in the captured diary of a German NCO in 276 Regiment (of Steinmetz's division): 'I am done. The artillery fire is driving me crazy. I am frightened as never before . . . cold. During the night one cannot leave one's hole. The last days have finished me off . . . to every one of our shells the enemy sends ten or twenty.' With 25-pounders firing up to 700 rounds per day, the 5th Division's historian agreed that most credit was due 'to the solid steel wall of defensive artillery fire that was invariably put round our positions when they were being counterattacked. No infantrymen in the division need feel ashamed or would be unprepared to acknowledge that the gunners probably held the small Garigliano bridgehead.'

One of those doing the shelling was Lance Bombardier Spike Milligan of 19 Battery, 56 (Heavy) Regiment, RA – equipped with massive 7.2-inch calibre guns, capable of hurling a 202lb shell over nine miles. Milligan recalled heading towards the Damiano Ridge on 20 January, 'passing a steady stream of ambulances; one I noticed had shrapnel holes in the sides', and making his way to his battery's observation post, 'all around are dead Jerries. MG bullets are whistling overhead as we duck and run inside.' The next day he and his comrades started to climb up the ridge: first 'we pass a Sherman tank, a neat hole punched in the turret; a tank man is removing kit from inside. Lying on a groundsheet is the mangled figure of one of the crew. "What a mess," says the tankman in the same tones as though there was mud on the carpet.'

As he ascended the terraced hillside, Milligan's party was targeted by mortars. 'We hit the deck. A rain of them fall around us. I cling to the ground. The mortars rain down on us. I'll have a fag, that's what. I am holding a packet of Woodbines, then there is a noise like thunder. It's right on my head, there's a high-pitched whistle in my ears, at first I black out and then I see red, I am strangely dazed. I was on my front, now I'm on my back, the red was opening my eyes straight into the sun. I know if we stay here we'll all die . . . I start to scramble down the hill. There's shouting, I can't recall anything clearly. Next I was at the bottom on the mountain, next I'm speaking to Major Jenkins, I am crying, I don't know why, he's saying, "Get that wound dressed."'

Like Milligan, most combat casualties in Italy – around seventy-five per cent – were caused by mortar rounds or artillery, the injuries made worse by the hard rocky ground, where quite small fragments could rip and tear fatally. Bullets caused surprisingly few wounds. Over a seven-month period during the Cassino fighting, Captain H. Morus Jones, medical officer with the Durham Light Infantry, analysed the injuries he treated: sixty-four per cent of 285 casualties were caused by shells or mortar bombs; the remainder were from gunshots, mines and grenade wounds. In the same timeframe he also treated 675 non-battle casualties: the Italian campaign saw unusually high sickness rates, chiefly malaria and venereal diseases, many of which were a testament to poor discipline.

Another issue in Italy was desertion. This could take extreme forms: Surgeon Lieutenant Colonel Johnny Watts RAMC encountered a pair of 'private soldiers who had deserted, and equipping themselves with home-made badges of rank and police armbands, had made tracks for this village, away up in the Apennines'. Arriving as the first British to visit the village they 'had settled down as the virtual tyrants of the place, helping themselves to anything they wanted and ruling by terror.

It was only after some weeks that the absence of any contact with the Allied forces had made the Italians complain by letter sent at night by a young boy.' The deserters' undoing came about by their staging rogue roadblocks, where they were apprehended, one being shot, but 'five days after his operation, the man stole an RAF sergeant's battle-dress blouse, and in pyjama trousers, with his stitches still in his leg, deserted again. Up to the time of our leaving Salerno he had not been recaptured, and had presumably managed to join the "Free English", as the bands of deserters in the hills were called.' Americans reported British officers patrolling the Cassino area with drawn pistols to prevent men from sloping off to the rear. In British battalions, it was hinted at, if not explicitly mentioned, as in the Operations Orders for 2/Cameronians (of 5th Division), prior to the attack on Minturno, 'No one except a stretcher-bearer or a wounded man helps a wounded man out of action.'

Morale was to some extent maintained by proximity to Italian civilians, on whom many Allied troops were billeted with beneficial results for both parties. These were mostly farming communities, caught in the war zones and reluctant to move – and troops inevitably bartered for luxuries beyond the NAAFI-issued basics. The staple items included 'ninety cigarettes, a bar of chocolate and a bar of soap per man (we also had a free issue of fifty cigarettes or a tin of tobacco, and a bar of doubtful "vitamin" chocolate). Tobacco wasn't rationed. Beer was. The Eighth Army in Italy's war-cry "One bottle per man per month perhaps" was pretty accurate.' British troops were billeted under cover whenever possible, often on Italian farms, and troops soon learned some very basic Italian, even if only the 'Three Dov'é's – *Dov'é casa, dov'é vino, dov'é signorina*'. Soldiers discovered that apart from soap, chocolates and cigarettes, trousers fetched the highest barter price among farmers (tens of thousands of pairs were written off as 'Lost in Battle'), and were exchanged for wine, fruit and eggs – while young warriors unused to exotic alcohols were sometimes found senseless, having lost the occasional tussle with bottles of brandy or vermouth, under the impression they were drinking wine.

Elsewhere, in Naples (and later on, in Rome) and even moderately sized towns, there were bars and brothels where soldiers could relax – or hide and live. In February 1944, Captain David Cole of 2/Royal Inniskilling Fusiliers visited Naples with a brother officer and recalled being 'at once surrounded by little boys trying to sell us their mothers or their sisters. Any speculation as to what attractions their mothers and sisters might have to offer us was, however, strangled at birth by lurid signs on every wall, pillar and post, saying "Danger. VD".' Sergeant Norman Lewis of the Field Security Police working in the same city noted in his diary that the Allied 'Bureau of Psychological Warfare has just stated in its bulletin that there are 42,000 women in Naples engaged either on a regular or occasional basis in prostitution. This out of a nubile female population of perhaps 150,000 . . . Nine out of ten Italian girls have lost their menfolk, who have either disappeared in battles, into prisoner-of-war camps, or been cut off in the North . . . How else are they to live?'

Katsugo Miho, born in Hawaii in 1922, was a Japanese-American who served in an all-Nisei combat unit with his brother. He remembered a 1944 visit to Naples where sanitation was so bad that after returning, 'all of us had to be doused with DDT because of the problem with lice in the town'. More irritating Katsugo felt were the 'little raggedy-rag kids all over the streets of Naples. Not begging but approaching the GIs. They would come up to us, "Joe, Joe, Joe, cigarette? Chocolate? No chocolate? *Mangiare.* [eat] Come my house, *mangiare.*" Invariably they would end up with, "*signorina*, my sister, young, young". There were no restaurants, so most of us accepted to go and eat spaghetti in private homes, paying for our meals with cigarettes or chocolate.'

In February 1944, Alexander and his theatre commander Jumbo Wilson corresponded about the desertion rate, the former writing that he favoured the reintroduction of the death penalty when the time was right: 'It was a great mistake to have done away with the death penalty for desertion . . . it will be a difficult thing to get it through the House, and as it is a political question, I won't advise when this should be tried.' Army-wide, between October 1943 and September 1944, some 16,892 British soldiers deserted (6 per 1,000), which was broadly in line with the experience of 1916–18. Of these, 2,237 were Eighth Army men sentenced for desertion, while 840 were convicted for absence – and of course, many were never caught. Eighth Army suffered easily the highest desertion rates within the British forces, which were also the highest of any Western Allied army.

The problem was a real concern because most deserters came from the infantry, and though their numbers were small, represented a much larger percentage of the combat arm who were, in any case, in short supply. This was exacerbated by the fact that on several occasions British numbers in Italy were reduced when divisions were withdrawn for Operations Overlord and Dragoon, while the total casualty rate (combat plus sickness) for 1944 was 647 per 1,000 among British troops, which made the additional impact of desertion very great. Among officers, attrition rates from battle casualties were an even greater problem. Inniskilling Fusilier officer David Cole calculated: 'the arithmetic was not encouraging. Of the thirty-six or so fellow officers who had landed with me in Sicily, fourteen had been killed and sixteen wounded, some of them twice and some so badly as never to return.'

The fear of 'being next' weighed heavily in the minds of many, particularly officers and NCOs, who had more responsibilities. Denis Healey, the future Labour Defence Secretary, had bicycled through Hitler's Germany in 1936 and graduated just before the war from Balliol College, Oxford. He volunteered for the army in September 1939 but was not called up for a year. By 1944 he was a twenty-six-year-old major in the Royal Engineers, and had served in First Army's North African campaign, then with Eighth Army in Sicily and Italy. The war, he reckoned, taught him two lessons: 'The first is interdependence – we all depended on one another – and the second is the importance of planning.' Not impressed by Monty ('though a brilliant fighting general, he wore his vanity like a foulard scarf'), his landing in Porto Santa Venere in Calabria, on Italy's toe, 'was exceptionally bloody'. Later Principal Beachmaster at Anzio ('a piece of cake by comparison, we even captured a couple of German officers in a cottage in their pyjamas'), Healey found he was able cope with the stress of combat: 'Unfashionable though it is to admit it, I enjoyed my five years in the wartime army . . . Long periods of boredom were broken by short bursts of excitement . . . To my great relief, I found I did not get frightened in action – not that I enjoyed being shelled or dive-bombed any more than the next man; but fear never paralysed me or even pushed me off my stroke. On the other hand I was never called on to show the sort of active courage which wins men the VC. A dumb, animal endurance is the sort of courage most men need in war. I was constantly amazed by the ability of the average soldier, and civilian, to exhibit this under stress.'

Many, though were not so lucky in wrestling with stress and fear, personal demons that had nothing to do with cowardice. Allied military authorities in Italy initially struggled to understand what was politely termed 'bomb-happiness'. In addition to a wound caused by mortar shrapnel to his right leg, Spike Milligan was diagnosed with shellshock, which resulted (to the great benefit of his future fans) in him leaving the front line and serving with an entertainment troop, where he became the central figure of a musical comedy act. He only discovered his diagnosis when he awoke to find himself labelled 'Battle Fatigue'. Captain Morus Jones had encountered seventy-five such cases of 'exhaustion', observing that they formed three groups: those who soon recovered after rest and returned to their companies; the 'bomb-happy' who needed to be confined to safer jobs in the rear; and lastly those suffering acute attacks of 'nerves', who were going irretrievably downhill, and knew it: for them the unit Medical Officer, such as Jones, was frequently the only chance of an 'honourable escape'. Such soldiers are not merely frightened and capable of being helped 'they are ill: ill in the same sense that they would be if they had influenza or malaria', wrote one historian. However, some battlefield commanders were not so aware of the varying degrees of this medical problem. Milligan's battery commander originally misread his symptoms and told him that the noise of the guns will 'boost your morale', which only exacerbated his illness. After Italy, Milligan became a lifelong sufferer with manic depression/bi-polar disorder and had multiple nervous breakdowns, conditions it is thought were triggered by his shellshock.

George S. Patton famously scotched his chances of leading the Normandy invasion when he twice visited evacuation hospitals during the July–August 1943 Sicilian campaign and encountered GIs who were suffering from psychiatric problems. On 3 August he manhandled a soldier out of a medical tent who, when asked his injury, told the general, 'I guess I can't take it.' A week later he encountered another soldier lying on his hospital bed shivering, diagnosed with shellshock, and accused him of being 'a God-damned coward, a yellow son of a bitch!' He slapped him and waved a pistol in his face; today we might wonder if it wasn't George Patton who was the more damaged of the pair, but both – much reported – incidents underlined that Patton, like many of his generation, simply did not believe in shellshock, 'nerves', exhaustion, bomb-happiness, battle fatigue and other non-medical euphemisms for what we today understand as Post Traumatic Stress Disorder (PTSD). The Patton incident generally pushed Anglo-American military opinion towards accepting that PTSD existed and could be treated.

By the end of 1943, the British had created a Psychiatric Military Hospital, the US Army established a School of Military Neuro-Psychology and psychiatrists were listed in the US Army's order of battle. Around sixteen per cent of Allied battle casualties in Italy in 1944 were estimated to have been from some form of battle exhaustion or shellshock. It was concluded that sleep deprivation was often an underlying cause, and found that up to seventy per cent of men could be returned to duty after forty-eight hours complete rest. Nevertheless, as one British officer looking back, observed: 'Men wear out in battle like clothes.' It was generally acknowledged that troops 'lasted' longer in combat if their sub-units were rotated and/or rested every twenty to thirty days, but there was never agreement as to how long soldiers should remain serving at the front, not necessarily under fire, though by 1944 most medical experts reckoned it was around 150–200 days before a period of individual leave or unit R&R was needed.

On 23 January, 1st Battalion London Scottish and 10th Royal Berkshires, 56th Division tried to seize the Damiano Ridge but without success. British medics were sent up under Red Cross flags to retrieve the wounded. To their surprise, a German officer appeared silhouetted on the ridge line and shouted in English, 'Gentlemen, will you please stop firing while we bring in our wounded?' The subsequent ceasefire lasted long enough for both sides to retrieve their casualties. Elsewhere, a rifleman remembered that 'the day after their night battle, their stretcher-bearers had teamed up with the enemy's, and after picking up the wounded they had all sat down together for a smoke'. The (largely unwritten) codes of decency between combatants that had evolved in the Western Desert between the British and Germans did find some echo in Italy, but as the campaign ground on in unforgiving terrain and weather (the 10th Royal Berkshires attacked and held the Damiano Ridge without greatcoats or blankets), much of this bonhomie evaporated. One British soldier recalled, after beating off a counter-attack at Minturno: 'After the battle there were several wounded Germans waiting for treatment at an aid post and among them was a young German, grey faced, and badly hurt, waiting for attention. I remember him clearly: he had a light green scarf around his neck. This young German was in great pain and it showed on the poor devil's face. Nearby were three of our Tommies, and all at once one of them went berserk, and in an insane and terrible rage, swearing and cursing, he went for this young German. He got hold of his scarf and throttled him with it, all the while screaming with anger. His mates grabbed him and tried desperately to drag him away, but he shook them off, and I am sure he killed him.'

Overnight on 23/24 January, the 1/London Scottish tried again for the Damiano Ridge. They came under sustained fire from several machine-gun nests firing at point-blank range, killing or wounding all of one company's officers and senior NCOs; whereupon thirty-one-year-old Londoner Private George Mitchell, dropping his mortar, charged alone up the hill through intense Spandau fire, jumped into the weapon pit, killed the crew and silenced the gun. The advance then continued, but shortly afterwards was again held up. This time Private Mitchell's assault on the position resulted in six of the enemy killed and twelve taken prisoner. He led two more successful attacks before falling dead, shot by one of the enemy who had surrendered. Though he died in the attempt, Mitchell and his company seized and held their portion of the ridge, for which he was awarded a posthumous Victoria Cross. Up on the ridge, wearing field grey, a German diarist from 276 Regiment (94th Division) wrote: 'There are at least twenty German dead . . . One tries not to look at them . . . The Tommies creep stealthily around. Their snipers shoot only too well. Again and again head wounds. The mortars fire and the whistle and explosion of shells go on, day and night. Sometimes, for a moment or two only, there is peace, and then I think of home. Sunlight by day, the night spent on cold stones.'

Dick McCreery was ultimately able to sustain his attacks only by bringing down the rest of Hawkesworth's 46th Division from the abandoned crossing attempt at Sant'Ambrogio. His X Corps engineers had become well experienced in bridging Italian rivers, and had learned lessons from the Volturno crossings of October 1943. Now fed by two substantial Bailey bridges, codenamed Skipton and Pateley, during 26–27 January, Templer's 56th Division was able to snuff out a useful corner of the German defences, overlooking the bend northwards of the Garigliano River, and dominated by the 2,300-foot Monte Ornito and Monte Valle Martina. As resistance stiffened, with Senger's reinforcements making their presence felt, even the application of 43 Royal Marine Commando and 9 (Army) Commando could not progress the penetration further beyond Castelforte. Over the same period further south, 5th Division (now led by Coldstream Guardsman Philip Gregson-Ellis, Bucknall having departed, mid-battle, for England, from where he would lead XXX Corps into Normandy), with their extra Guards Brigade and due to their early occupation of good German positions, were able to push out to the heights overlooking Minturno, including the Tremensuoli Ridge and Monte Natale. Here one subaltern of 3/Coldstream Guards noted that his officers' mess 'was swarming with hibernating flies and starving fleas. Our plates of food became black . . . as the flies descended in hundreds from the rafters.'

At this stage, however, McCreery was forced to wind down his attacks; and having already lost one brigade of 56th Division to the Anzio beachhead on 30 January, the rest of Templer's Black Cats followed suit on 6 February. Thus all offensive activity beyond the Garigliano had ceased by 9 February, and Templer's sector was shared between Hawkesworth and Gregson-Ellis. Within a month, 5th Division would also follow on to Anzio, where it relieved the Black Cats, the latter by then much exhausted and reduced in numbers. Between 23 January and 13 February, X Corps suffered 4,145 casualties. The cost to 5th Division (who had lost an average of 150 men per battalion) was high, and although these gains were not in line with X Corps' original hopes, they had secured the high ground beyond the Garigliano, and more importantly, learned that the Germans, despite the speedy deployment of operational reserves from further north, were now no longer strong enough to throw them out. Though X Corps was relieved by US troops at the end of February, and McCreery may have discovered the secret of how to break into the Gustav Line, he had yet to understand how to apply his resources to break out: the first attempt to outflank Cassino along the coast had failed.

5

Blood and Guts

THE THIRD ASPECT of General Mark Clark's opening assault on the Cassino front involved his fellow countrymen. At the time when Dick McCreery's X Corps were trying to force their way beyond the Garigliano, and Alphonse Juin's Frenchmen were battling in the mountains to the north of Cassino, Mark Clark assigned two of his most experienced divisions the task of attacking Cassino and breaking into the Liri valley itself. The instruments of his boldness were to be to the US 34th and 36th National Guard Divisions. Appropriately they were attacking upriver from two of their British equivalents, the 46th and 56th Territorial Divisions.

When mobilised in 1940, the National Guard had immediately doubled the size of the US Army, contributing nineteen divisions and numerous other units. In April 1943, wearing the distinctive shoulder patch of a 'T' (for Texas), its 36th Division sailed overseas, landing in North Africa, where they conducted amphibious training. On 9 September 1943, as the first US combat division to land on continental Europe, they hit the beach amidst the old Roman ruins of Paestum as part of the Salerno landings. The 34th Division, also National Guardsmen, recruited from North Dakota, South Dakota, Iowa and Minnesota, could, like the 36th Division, trace their lineage back to a regiment that had fought in the

Civil War and to the First World War. Their shoulder badge of a red bull's skull surmounted by two curved horns on a black background gave rise to their nickname, the 'Red Bulls'.

Inter-war politicians had allowed the US military to run down in size and capability, so that on 30 June 1939 the regular force numbered just 188,000 personnel (including 22,000 in the US Army Air Corps), 400 tanks and 800 aircraft. In size it ranked nineteenth in the world, ahead of Bulgaria and after Portugal; of its nine infantry divisions, only three had any structure beyond that of separate regiments, the purchase of modern equipment had been neglected, and training was uninspiring. The extraordinary (Churchill called it 'remarkable') expansion of the US military-industrial complex, overseen by General George C. Marshall, was initially gradual; the guard's mobilisation and first peacetime draft in US history was only approved by Congress (and only for one year) in September 1940, but extended indefinitely (with a majority of a single vote) in August 1941. By the time of the Japanese strike at Pearl Harbor, the US Army had grown nearly tenfold to 1.7 million (including 275,000 in the Air Corps alone) in twenty-nine infantry, five armour, and two cavalry divisions. Over the next few years, it expanded again to an astonishing 8.3 million, including 100,000 women, comprising eighty-nine divisions, of which sixty-eight eventually served in Europe and Mediterranean, and twenty-one in the Pacific. This was matched by harnessing American industry to supply the required clothing, weapons and equipment in mind-boggling quantities: 47 billion rounds of small-arms ammunition, 87 million hand grenades, over 30 million 20-litre Jerrycans; 22 million steel helmets; 6 million M1 carbines; 4 million .30-06 Garand rifles; 676,000 two-and-a-half-ton trucks; 38,000 half-tracks, and 30,000 four-wheel-drive ambulances were produced in the USA during the war. Each GI was backed, on average, by twelve tons of equipment. The original 213-division army (the 'Victory Program' of September 1941) proved an impossible dream, as fierce competition developed for the finite manpower pool between the US Army and industry, farming, the US Navy, US Marine Corps, Coast Guard and Merchant Marine. This rapid ballooning of military capability is unmatched in military history. Only the Soviet Union achieved similar force sizes and production during the war, but they had started with a large army, and a centralised (if inefficient) economy.

Within this huge organisation sat the 36th National Guard Division, with, in addition to its three infantry regiments (each of three battalions), four artillery battalions, a cavalry reconnaissance troop, engineers, medics and divisional support units. The 36th was commanded by General Frederick Livingwood Walker, with a brigadier general as assistant division commander and a second brigadier as his divisional artillery commander; colonels commanded the three infantry regiments and lieutenant colonels the battalions. Walker was born in 1887, making him the same age as Montgomery and, at fifty-six, but nearly a decade older than most US division commanders. He took over 36th Division in September 1941, and his career path suggests he was under the patronage of Marshall, the outstanding US Army Chief of Staff from 1939 to 1945, American counterpart to Sir Alan Brooke, trusted military adviser to Roosevelt, and very much the architect of victory in the way he shaped war policy and oversaw America's huge military expansion. Walker was closer in age (seven years younger) than most other senior officers to Marshall, neither were West Point graduates, and both had commanded the 15th Infantry in China at different times. Fred Walker's age would create significant tensions with his two immediate superiors, Geoffrey Keyes, commanding US II Corps, and General Mark Clark, commanding US Fifth Army. Keyes was a bright, daring and impulsive cavalryman who graduated from US Army War College in 1937 (with future generals Mark Clark, Matthew Ridgway and Walter Bedell Smith), where Walker was their instructor. Keyes was ambitious for his II Corps, fiercely loyal to Clark, his boss, and inclined to Anglophobia, much to the detriment of Dick McCreery and British X Corps.

Mark Clark's astonishing ten-year rise from major in 1933 to lieutenant general in 1943 was outpaced only by Eisenhower himself, whose protégé he was. Though journalists and war correspondents were always instructed to label his command as 'General Mark Clark's Fifth Army', he liked to be addressed as Wayne – his middle name – by friends. In June 1942, when Ike departed to England to command US forces in Europe, he took the nimble and politically savvy Clark as his deputy, commanding the embryo US II Corps. That October, Clark became deputy commander of Allied Forces in the Mediterranean theatre, again under Eisenhower, when he made his secret submarine trip (Operation Flagpole) to negotiate the surrender or cooperation of the Vichy French, ahead of Operation Torch.

Robert Murphy, the senor US diplomat in the Mediterranean, observed that Mark Clark was 'one of those romantic generals destined to move always in an atmosphere of high drama', and unlike the other Torch commanders whose arrivals in Algiers after Torch were undramatic, 'Clark arrived in the midst of a German bombing raid with a Messerschmitt flaming down dangerously close to his Flying Fortress'. Sharp-minded, tall and angular in appearance – almost gaunt – Clark had already been appointed to command Fifth Army in early 1943, which was initially the American training organisation in the Mediterranean theatre, while US Third Army fought the Sicilian campaign under Patton. Although Eisenhower was promoted as fast as Clark, the former was an unusually gifted and tactful diplomat and genuinely very well liked by colleagues and contemporaries. Clark was more difficult, and the view of some who knew him was 'aggressive, impatient, imperious in bearing, and inclined to be sharp of tongue, although he could be elegantly charming'. He possessed a flair for publicising himself and his activities. Alan Whicker remembered of him: 'His vanity was remarkable – he could have given lessons to any Hollywood prima donna. Even during the desperate days of the war when we were hard-pressed to hold our ground he kept a publicity machine of some fifty men around him and insisted his permanent cameraman only took pictures from the left – his best side, he believed.' These characteristics, plus his swift rise in rank and title, prompted some resentment among his colleagues.

The personalities of the three – Walker, Keyes and Clark – were contrasting, and these differences would be brought to a head in a crisis, and there would be many in Italy. Throughout operations at Cassino, Clark's mind was actually focused on Anzio, from which he expected great, career-enhancing results – and perhaps the lack of a firm hand for the first three battles at Cassino may be explained by Clark's preoccupation with his amphibious operation. The context of Overlord – the Normandy landings – is important here, for Clark (aware of the plans for D-Day) knew that any defeat of his assault from the sea would have a profoundly depressing effect on the morale of the Allied invaders of northern France, and would provide a much-needed boost for the Germans, who had already exceeded their own expectations of delay and damage against the Salerno invasion the previous September. Thus, Anzio *had* to succeed, for any hint of failure would reverberate beyond measure in Berlin, London and Washington DC.

Unfortunately, the exact purpose of Anzio was open to interpretation. Alexander at 15th Army Group (under pressure from Churchill) had issued a directive to Clark on 3 January which read that his Fifth Army was 'to carry out an assault landing [in the] vicinity of Rome with the object of cutting the enemy lines of communication and threatening the rear of German 14 Corps'. Clear and simple; or was it? Clark immediately interpreted this with a different emphasis, recording: 'I intend to attack in greatest possible strength in the Liri valley several days in advance of Shingle with the object of drawing maximum number of enemy reserves to that front and fixing them there. In that way and in that way only can the Shingle force exercise a decisive influence in the operation to capture Rome.'

The altered emphasis towards Rome was important – though Alexander let this pass – for Clark knew that once D-Day was under way, whatever his Fifth Army achieved in Italy would no longer be front-page news: all were aware that the deciding event in the European war would be a landing and offensive against the main German stronghold in the west. With the nose of a politician, Clark therefore hoped to be in Rome before his friend Eisenhower invaded Normandy as a way of achieving some prominence before Operation Overlord began. So as early as 2 January in Clark's mind (if in no one else's), the operation to dislodge the Germans on the Gustav Line by threatening their rear had morphed into an attempt to seize Rome.

There were many limitations, not least the short timeframe in which the necessary landing craft would be available before recall to England, but Clark was determined to overcome all such constraints, noting on 4 January: 'We are supposed to go up there, dump two divisions ashore with what corps troops we can get in, and wait for the rest of the Army to join up. I am trying to find ways to do it, not ways in which we cannot do it. I am convinced that we are going to do it, and that it is going to be a success.' He knew that sending his other major formation, US VI Corps under Major General John P. Lucas, seventy-five miles up the coast to land at Anzio was risky in the extreme. They needed to be supported on land, not merely by an umbilical cord of shipping from Naples. The closer Clark could get his land forces, US II Corps, British X Corps and the French, to Anzio – he assessed the town of Frosinone (forty miles) within reach of both – the quicker a link-up would be made, spelling success for the high-risk venture. Clark was thus hedging his bets: while he wanted to draw any defenders known to be lurking in the Rome area away from intervention at Anzio and down to the Cassino front, he was also hoping to bridge the Rapido and surge up the Liri valley. Explicitly he wanted one or other, preferably both, elements of US Fifth Army to capture Rome.

Opening the way into the Liri was a lot to ask of any division, let alone the battle-weary 36th Division. Unaware of much of the bigger picture, as far as Major General Fred Walker was concerned his task was to get his division across the Rapido River, downstream of Cassino, and opposite the village of Sant'Angelo in Theodice, in order to punch their way into the Liri valley. Behind him lay Major General Ernest N. Harmon's US 1st Armoured Division to rapidly exploit any opportunity.

Fred Walker's final operation before drawing breath for the Cassino battles was to storm Monte Trocchio on the night of 15/16 January, an isolated 1,300-foot hill opposite Cassino, with a distinctive sugar-loaf profile. To everyone's surprise the 36th's patrols found all the German positions abandoned, but they reported back that the view across the Rapido-Gari valley to Cassino, some three miles distant, was staggering. Once cleared of mines and booby-traps, the 'bare outcrop of rock, like a whale's back and razor-pointed along the crest', surmounted by a small, ruined castle, became home to literally hundreds of allied artillery observation posts.

General Walker was a worried man. He had turned his 36th Division, acknowledged as a peacetime social club for well-connected Texans, into a tough fighting formation that had been bloodied at Salerno, where two battalions had been destroyed and his assistant division commander collapsed under the strain. The fighting through San Pietro and awful winter conditions had cost him more, when he had confided in his diary: 'I regret the hardships they must suffer tonight . . . wet, cold, muddy, hungry, going into camp in the mud and rain, no sleep, no rest . . . How they endure their hardships, I do not understand . . . they are still cheerful. All honour to them. I do not understand how the men continue to keep going under their existing conditions of hardship.' War reporter Martha Gellhorn, 'holding a tin hat in front of my face as a shield against the rain', remembered travelling up to the front at this time: 'The windshield and the top of the jeep were down and the snow had changed to hail . . . There you were, on a roller-coaster road freezing to death, and if the enemy couldn't see you, he was blind; he was sitting right across there, on that other snow mountain . . . It was colder here than anywhere else – though it was cold everywhere – and no one believed this wind would ever blow at less than gale force.'

By now the 36th had lost over a third of its combat strength to enemy action and the weather, and although these numbers were soon made up, the division had been deprived of its old look and feel. Despite wearing the 'T' patch, the truth was that many of the Texas Division were not Guardsmen and no longer hailed from the Lone Star State. In some ways this was a blessing, meaning quite small communities would not be so hard hit when the casualty bill was high; but some of the glue that held men together had been loosened. All felt it, in the alien, rugged landscape of Italy, especially in weather that few Americans had ever experienced (least of all in Texas), and particularly at Christmas. Many of the replacements, wild-eyed and fearful, had yet to be integrated into their units: Infantryman Ralph Schaps, a National Guardsman with the neighbouring Red Bulls Division, observed that sometimes these would have 'very little training, but if he was a survivor he learned quickly to discipline himself or he fell by the wayside. The poor conditions made them tough, physically and mentally, in a hurry or they just did not survive . . . Coming off the line after weeks of tension, lack of sleep, and exposure to death, we often had the staring look of zombies – a numbness and indifference to anything.'

There is evidence, from his diary entries, that their gloom was shared by Fred Walker, whose inclination towards pessimism increased when he realised the magnitude of the task Clark and Keyes had set him. *Every*

senior officer in the Italian campaign, of whatever nation, had witnessed
– and survived – the First World War as a junior officer, and had lost
friends in it; therefore we should not be surprised how the attritional
campaigns of 1914–18 dominated, almost obsessed, the minds of most
generals in Italy – and their political masters. Cassino reminded Senger
and Hitler of the Somme; Churchill was known to be haunted by
Gallipoli, while Alexander and his contemporaries were desperate not
to be seen to be fighting another version of Passchendaele; or Alphonse
Juin, of Verdun. Walker had been wounded while serving with the US
3rd Division in France, where, as a battalion commander he won the
Distinguished Service Cross in repelling the major German attack across
the Marne River in July 1918. In Fred Walker's mind, the Rapido of
January 1944 became the Marne, but his men would now have to play
the role of the Germans he had slaughtered on 15 July, floundering in
the current.

Opposite the 'T-patchers', on a slight rocky outcrop midway between
Monte Trocchio and Cassino on the western banks of the Rapido River,
lay the village of Sant'Angelo. The village's population of 400 had fled
as the Germans demolished houses and turned the stone-built settlement
into a bristling fortress. Its elevated position overlooking the river had
condemned it to destruction, even before Allied bombs and shells had
started raining down in the area, and its gap-toothed, powdered ruins
anticipated how the monastery at the top of the hill, which in turn
dominated the village, would look in the coming months. Whereas the
Bernhardt Line further forward had largely been improvised, at
Sant'Angelo the Germans had plenty of time to exercise their defensive
ingenuity: the position was too good an opportunity to miss. While
Walker's men had been battling through the hills, the engineers of
Organisation Todt had turned Sant'Angelo into a warren of dugouts,
bunkers, and machine-gun nests, which enfiladed the many bends in
the river, and were manned by the 15th PanzerGrenadiers of Generalmajor
Eberhardt Rodt – the same division who had caused so much trouble
downstream to the British 46th (Oak Trees) Division. Senger, who had
known Rodt from pre-war service in the cavalry, and his performance
in Sicily, thought the forty-eight-year-old Rodt 'quiet and confident' and
felt he could rely on his division. 'The regimental commanders whom

I visited confirmed this impression of reliability.' Opposite the crossing points lay Major Burkholtz's battle-hardened II Battalion/104th Panzer Grenadier Regiment, supported by the 71st Artillery Regiment, and the 115th Panzer Reconnaissance Battalion.

Both banks of the river were waterlogged and mined, bridges had been blown, and barbed wire added to the forbidding nature of this corner of the Cassino plain, and one of the strongest sectors of the Gustav Line. Very little would escape the attention of German observers on the slopes of Monte Cassino, of which the Allies, now firmly lodged on the opposing scree of Monte Trocchio, were painfully aware.

The lack of enthusiasm with which Walker entered his fight on the Rapido was shared by Major General John P. Lucas. The US VI Corps commander was preparing to assault Anzio in Operation Shingle, and both men confided their misgivings in private diaries. Lucas wrote of the Anzio plans on 4 January: 'Unless we can get what we want, the operation becomes such a desperate undertaking that it should not, in my opinion, be attempted.' Echoing this pessimism, on 8 January, Walker had written of his own forthcoming mission: 'Have been giving a lot of thought to plan for crossing Rapido River some time soon. I'll swear I do not see how we can possibly succeed in crossing the river near Angelo when that stream is the MLR [Main Line of Resistance] of the main German positions.' Walker had put some of his concerns to Keyes and Clark, but did not push them, as he probably feared immediate replacement as the older man, if he did. Walker was also unaware of the broader issues that accompanied the Shingle operation, with its implications for the future invasion of Normandy. Meanwhile, Clark's Anzio commander, Lucas, had kept his concerns to himself, but privately scribbled in his journal on 14 January: 'They will end up putting me ashore with inadequate forces and get me in a serious jam. Then, who will take the blame?'

Both men seemed to have expected defeat, though claimed victory was possible. The 3,000-ton cruiser USS *Biscayne* had already served as a flagship for Operations Torch, Husky (Sicily) and Avalanche (Salerno); 20 January 1944 saw her en route to Anzio in the same role, this time carrying the depressive Lucas, who committed mixed emotions to paper, though not ones that exuded any sense of victory: 'I have many misgivings . . . but am also optimistic,' while hours before starting the Rapido crossing on the same day, Walker found time to observe: 'Tonight the 36th Division will attempt to cross the Rapido River opposite Sant'Angelo. Everything had been done to ensure success. We might succeed but I do not see how we can . . . So I am prepared for defeat. The mission should never have been assigned to any troops with flanks exposed. Clark sent me his best wishes; said he was worried about our success. I think he is worried over the fact that he made an unwise decision when he gave us the job of crossing the river under such adverse tactical conditions. However, if we get some breaks we may succeed.'

Haunted by the Marne, and now the Rapido, Walker knew, as soldiers throughout military history have known, that assault river crossings are one of the most difficult and risky military manoeuvres to achieve – and any complications multiply if the venture is undertaken at night. As early as AD 390 the Roman general Vegetius had written of them in his military handbook, *Epitoma rei militaris*: 'As the enemy generally endeavour to fall upon an army at the passage of a river, either by surprise or ambuscade, it is necessary to secure both sides . . . by strong detachments, so that the troops may not be attacked and defeated, while separated by the channel of the river.' Just as the Allies did in 1944, even the Romans in their marching columns carried pontoon bridges, 'small boats hollowed out of one piece of timber and very light, both by their make and the quality of the wood. The army always has a number of these boats upon carriages, together with a sufficient quantity of planks and iron nails. Thus with the help of cables to lash the boats together, a bridge is instantly constructed.' Thus, although Walker possessed fifteen centuries' worth of distilled wisdom of how, when and where to assault a river, his task was by no means easy: what he also needed was luck.

Coordination of the attacking arms would be vital – in this case, engineers and infantry, and although a rehearsal had taken place on the relatively placid, wide and gentle-banked Volturno, its characteristics were vastly different. The approaches to the Rapido were flat and muddy, the river banks high, and the current lived up to its name. During planning and rehearsals, the division's engineers felt their advice was politely ignored and were amazed to discover that the final crossing sites were different from those they had helped select, while only one of the infantry regiments which had participated in the dry run were to take part in the action. The assault would become the defining event of Walker's career.

Throughout the day over a hundred sorties of single-engined P-40 Kittyhawks and twin-engined A-20 Havocs bombed German positions in the vicinity, while sixteen battalions of field artillery threw in a barrage thirty minutes prior to the assault. Advancing with two of his three regimental combat teams, Walker's division left their assembly areas on 20 January at six in the evening, but due to darkness, general confusion and slow going in mud, were very late in attacking – long after their scheduled start of 8 p.m., which negated the effect of their supporting barrage. Colonel Aaron A. Wyatt's 141st brigade-sized regimental combat team (RCT) was to cross at an S-bend in the river north of Sant'Angelo and Colonel William H. Martin's 143rd RCT at two points south of the village. As there were no tracks suitable to get trucks carrying assault craft and bridging equipment to the crossing sites, Walker's infantry had to carry their boats to the river banks (in addition to extra loads of ammunition); many of the rubber dinghies and wooden pontoons were found to be unusable, already damaged by German artillery and mortar defensive fire missions. Under the shelling, exhausted and in dense fog, men strayed into the minefields, the white marker tape indicating cleared paths having been trampled into the mud, and many men fell before reaching the river. As boats were launched into the water, full of combat equipment, some just sank with their cargos, damaged by shell holes they hadn't noticed; others capsized heavily laden with men and kit; a few floated away when their crews took cover from hostile shelling.

Besides the damage to assault craft, much of the engineer bridging equipment was also wrecked, 141st RCT losing a quarter of theirs. They managed to erect four floating duckboard footbridges, and all but one was rapidly destroyed. By daybreak on 21 January, troops could only gingerly pick their way across one remaining, damaged bridging structure. Under heavy fire, about a hundred men had managed to stake a small claim on the far bank, but found themselves hemmed in by mines, booby-traps, barbed wire, and under machine-gun fire while shells knocked out phone cables. Brigadier General Wilbur, the assistant divisional commander, ordered those men on the near bank to retire to their assembly areas and the men on the far shore were told by a messenger to dig in and hold until relieved. Downriver, Colonel Martin's 143rd RCT experienced much the same, with bridges destroyed and boats sunk, though most of the regiment's 1st/Battalion had made it across by daybreak. Several observers recall one boat swamping with water as it was launched, then, full of troops and equipment, being swept downstream and eventually flipping over, men yelling and screaming as they drowned in the icy current, weighed down by kit and wet uniforms. By 7 a.m., under accurate observed fire and counterattack, the battalion was forced back into a tiny pocket, their backs to the river. After requesting (and initially being denied) permission to retire, on his own initiative, the battalion CO withdrew his survivors back across the Rapido by mid-morning.

At the same hour, Walker in his headquarters had the unpleasant experience of a dressing-down from his former student, Keyes, who was keen to resume the offensive as soon as possible. By obtaining new engineer stores and rounding up stragglers, the assault was renewed at four that afternoon, but using the same crossing points – which the Germans, of course, had now mapped and registered. Artificial smoke laid down by the 36th Division's artillery and engineer smoke-pots nearly suffocated the Guardsmen, disorientating them, and causing as much confusion as the darkness of the previous night. Nevertheless, during the evening of 21 January, 141st RCT managed to reinforce their tiny bridgehead with another battalion, but as their bridges and boats were again destroyed overnight, and unable to be resupplied, those of the RCT on the far bank were gradually surrounded and captured. Likewise, the 143rd RCT managed to throw a second battalion across, but had to withdraw everyone in the face of growing overnight resistance.

By first light on 22 January, it was clear to everyone that the mission had failed, and the Germans were simply too strong to overcome at this location. At the end of the affair, Walker, ever-faithful to his diary, confided: 'January 22 will long stand out in my memory . . . Yesterday two regiments of this division were wrecked on the west bank of the Rapido.' Lieutenant Colonel Wyatt's 141st RCT had lost over half its riflemen and company officers, killed, captured or wounded. Over all, the 36th Division lost more: 1,681 – 143 killed, 663 wounded and 875 missing, most of whom were known to have been captured. The recriminations of this particular failed assault continue to this day, with whole books devoted to this single action – partly, perhaps, a reflection of the Lone Star State's antipathy towards the federal government in Washington DC. Shortly afterwards, on 2 March 1944 – Texas Independence Day – a group of twenty-five officers of the division, alumni of the University of Texas, met and vowed to call for a public investigation of the Rapido crossings. Reflecting post-war public concern in Texas, the Military Affairs Committee of the House of Representatives held two days of hearings in March 1946 into the circumstances of the action. Thirty witnesses appeared, including Walker and Colonel William Martin, commander of the 143rd RCT, who saw the affair in terms of 'a fine National Guard Division being destroyed by faulty orders from a West Point commander'. The committee on Capitol Hill upheld the army view that 'the attempt to cross the Rapido was a legitimate if difficult operation' where Clark 'exercised sound judgment in ordering the attack'.

In retrospect, Clark's optimism about the Rapido and Anzio missions reflected some uniquely American attitudes to combat in 1944. The USA had fewer of the cultural misgivings about military violence that stayed the hand of most European commanders. The American experience of mass casualties in battle was eighty years earlier, in the 1861–65 Civil War, not the more recent world war, where America had arrived late and suffered 116,000 military fatalities – a fraction of the millions of dead suffered by Britain, France and Germany. There was a belief held privately by some American commanders that Britain and other Allied nations shied away from potentially attritional frontal assaults, even if necessary, because of 1914–18, and the massive British artillery barrages employed from Alamein onwards supported this notion – Montgomery's 'metal, *not* flesh'. By contrast, the way America had survived the 1929–39 Great Depression, which had overcome some European states, gave rise to national self-confidence and a belief that this war was going to be won by US brawn and muscle alone, that the application of technology somehow came second. This belief may have been misapplied in January 1944 on the Rapido, but would surface again the following June, for the American assault on Omaha Beach.

Ironically the German forces around Sant'Angelo had no idea until much later of the significance of their actions. Generalmajor Rodt's PanzerGrenadiers captured 500 Americans, but lost 64 killed and 179 wounded of their own. Their report up to Senger's IV Panzer Corps read simply that they had 'prevented enemy troops from crossing the river at S. Angelo'; no reserves were required.

First light on 22 January had seen the Anzio landings under way (assisted by Beachmaster Denis Healey), and, with his eyes still fixed on Rome, Clark became ever more determined to link up with Lucas's VI Corps as soon as possible. Extreme uncertainty on the Anzio front would affect Clark's decision-making throughout the first battle for Cassino, and play out during the whole January–May campaign. Essentially Lucas, cautious by nature, badly misjudged the speed and determination of the Germans to bottle him up. He was unwilling to advance immediately without building up his forces first, while von Mackensen's Fourteenth Army reinforced quicker and tried to drive a wedge in the shallow Anzio-Nettuno beachhead between 1st British and 3rd US Divisions. Lucas's VI Corps attempted their breakout on 31 January but found the German defenders – now five divisions – well prepared, waiting, and too strong. The German counterattack with four divisions on 16 February (Operation *Fischfang*) was vicious and would have reached the coast were it not for massive Allied air support and naval gunfire. The beachhead remained under constant artillery fire, requiring nearly 3,000 tons per day just to sustain it, while casualties from battle and sickness (the area was one big malaria-ridden swamp) rose. One month into the Anzio campaign Lucas was replaced. Thereafter VI Corps under its new commander, Lucian K. Truscott (formerly commanding US 3rd Division in the assault), was obliged to endure daily bombing and shelling for no gain until the breakout in May, coinciding with the fourth Cassino battle.

While Lucas was gingerly stepping ashore at Anzio, Clark was trying to roll up the Cassino front, needing to quickly punch his way into the Liri valley and charge up it like a US cavalry squadron racing to the rescue of besieged homesteaders at Anzio, surrounded by hostile native Americans. On 23 January, he reorientated the French axis of advance. With the failure of X Corps and the 36th Division, Clark also decided to keep up the pressure along the river line and tasked Keyes's other II Corps division, the 34th – Major General Charles Ryder's Red Bulls – to also cross the Rapido plain further north, where the river was narrower and fordable, and seize Cassino via a right hook through the hills. In a two-pronged attack, the Red Bulls' 133rd Regiment would attack on the right, with 756th Tank Battalion in support, capture the village of Caira and an old Carabinieri training school known as 'the Barracks' north of Cassino, before ascending to seize the hills above. To its left, 135th Regiment would also cross the Rapido and, turning south, attack Cassino from the flank. The division's third regiment, 168th, was to pass through the gains of the first wave, climb the heights and wheel round inside the French, over the ridges to outflank the town and monastery.

Clark was unable to wait for spring and dry weather, so the attacks had to commence straight away. For the Americans in the valley, this meant 10 p.m. on the night of 24 January. Senger, writing after the war, was very critical of this sequential approach – first the French Corps, then X Corps, then the British 46th, after them the US 36th, followed by the US 34th Divisions. 'When I look at the Allied plan for a break-through, from the point of view of the defender,' he wrote, 'I cannot refrain from criticism. According to the original plan, which was tacti-cally well thought out, there was to be an attack against the right wing of my corps, followed by a number of blows against the Cassino front. But after the first attack failed, the original plan was followed too rigidly. This gave me the chance to draw reserves from the sectors where the attacks had failed, to constantly change the operational boundaries of the divisions, and to parry the blows one by one. Nor did I understand why the enemy attempted to break through at so many points of the front. It seemed to me that in doing so he was dissipating his forces.'

Into this sector of the valley floor, the Germans had emptied the Rapido, turning the surrounding meadows into 'morasses whose surface was about the colour and consistency of a thick lentil soup', cut down all vegetation, and built a row of concrete and steel pillboxes along the base of the hills, some cut into rock, others installed in the ruins of buildings, providing German machine-gunners with perfect fields of fire. Above them observers could direct accurate artillery and mortar concentrations into any corner, while attackers would also be hemmed in by barbed wire obstacles and a 300-yard-deep belt of mines – the approaches to Point 213 were surrounded by fifteen yards of defensive wire. From a distance, the foothills beyond the Rapido marsh, which eventually led up to the monastery and beyond to Monte Cairo, looked deceptively smooth, but up close were rough and broken with minor ridges, knolls and hollows all jumbled together. Inclined to the poetic, war correspondent Christopher Buckley, who observed all four Cassino battles, thought 'there was something titanic' about the setting in which it was waged. 'The grandeur of the backcloth never palled . . . I can still shut my eyes and recall every detail of that dreadfully majestic scene. Always I see it as the painted backcloth of a stage set. It is far too theatrically improbable for nature . . . The words were noble and theatrical. I do not divorce the words. And none was more noble than Cassino.'

During the first night of the Red Bulls' attack, supported by armour and copious quantities of artillery, the three battalions of 133rd Regiment managed to force their way across the boggy Rapido plain as far as the old barracks – about twenty rectangular single-storey barrack blocks, shelled to ruins. However, from their well-hidden bunkers, the defenders ripped into the American battalions toiling across the fields, and in the daylight hours pushed them back. Initially the tanks could find no way across, and many bogged in the Rapido marsh on the home side of the river. On the night of 25 January they attacked again, having cleared paths through the minefields, with much the same result. One of the 133rd's battalions was the 100th Nisei, recruited from Japanese-Americans in the Hawaii Army National Guard, who had landed at Salerno and were anxious to demonstrate their loyalty. After the River Volturno crossing, they had made the division's first bayonet charge. Not only was their gallantry in their first battle without question, but their hardiness in tackling combat in the depths of an unforgiving Italian winter also drew much admiration.

Sergeant Takashi Kitaoka was typical of those serving in the 100th Nisei battalion. Born in 1912 on the Hawaiian island of Maui, he was the youngest of four, born to parents who had migrated from Kumamoto, Japan. He grew up in conditions of relative poverty and, with anti-Japanese prejudice evident in his schooldays, stopped speaking Japanese or assimilating his parents' culture. Bright, hard-working and industrious, he left his local school, boarded at the Mid-Pacific Institute in Honolulu, graduated at the University of Hawaii and went on to Baylor Law School in Texas, graduating with a law degree in 1940; shortly afterwards he returned to Hawaii when he was drafted. 'I didn't like getting a draft notice at all,' Takashi observed. 'I was completely disappointed because I didn't know what was going to happen. It was a shock, really, to me because I had absolutely no connection with the army, military or anything.' Newly married, on 7 December 1941, Takashi was woken by the noises of battle. 'We went out of the house and saw all the planes flying.' This was the Japanese raid on Pearl Harbor, which brought a new focus and tension to his military life. Eventually AJA troops ('Americans of Japanese Ancestry') were moved to Wisconsin, where Takashi was promoted to staff sergeant in charge of a squad of a dozen men in Baker Company of his battalion.

By September 1943 the Nisei had arrived at Salerno, and experienced hostile fire for the first time. 'In plain language, we were scared shitless,' Takashi recalled. 'You talk about fighting when you're back in training but this is the real thing . . . We were dumbfounded.' Takashi had not had any experience in prior combat: 'You can imagine how we felt. We keep on going, that's all.' On the way to Cassino, he remembered following tracks cleared by US engineers through a German minefield. The path was marked by toilet paper left under rocks, which soon blew away. 'Every time you take a step, you didn't know whether you were going to hit a mine or what.' Then came their attack on 26 January, at dawn. Takashi remembered approaching Cassino down a small hill and having to descend into an anti-tank ditch via a makeshift ladder. 'The craziest damn thing is, each man in the company had to go down that ladder . . . backwards.' Once down, they found themselves pinned down by fire and unable to move until nightfall because the whole area was mined. 'The very next morning, one of my jobs as the first sergeant was to check the number of men we had. We went into that valley with 187 men; that's a full complement of a company. In twenty-four hours, when I checked our company, there were only twenty-eight men left and I was one of the twenty-eight. That's how much hell we caught.'

Overnight on 26/27 January, the Red Bulls tried a third time, with 168th Regiment (originally Ryder's reserve) attempting to link up with, and pass through, 133rd Regiment, who by now had a slender hold on the far side

Why both sides wanted Monte Cassino. This post-battle view looks back east across the Rapido valley, towards Allied lines and Monte Trocchio (centre right), captured on 16 January 1944. Taken from outside the abbey, in the foreground (left) lies the Castle on its own little hill, below which is Cassino town. Into it runs Route 6, from Naples (centre), and the curved railway (right).

Cassino was a sleepy town of about 25,000 before the war, famous for its abbey. Just below the abbey is Hangman's Hill, named after the cable car pylon which brought up tourists and pilgrims. The hill in the centre is Point 593 and the castle is just visible to the extreme right. This pre-war view looks straight down Route 6, at the end of which was the Continental Hotel.

It rained heavily for fifty of the last seventy-three days of 1943, which brought the Allied advance through central Italy slithering to an unanticipated halt. Rivers (here the Volturno) rose, aircraft were grounded, but the wet sapped morale, too, as men struggled with immobility in below-zero temperatures.

Around Cassino, mud was 'the colour and consistency of a thick lentil soup'. Whilst US engineers wearing waders struggle in the thick mire to improve a mountain track, a mule train led by an Indian soldier picks its way past.

(*Above left*) The Italian Winter of 1943–44 was literally a killer. It smothered outposts and the metal components of some engines froze and fractured. Across the Allied armies very few troops were issued with specialised winter clothing, and there were more casualties from exposure and frost-bite, than combat. (*Above right*) Mules could wade through mud that would stop a jeep, and were perfectly balanced to negotiate the inches-wide long, winding trails that were chiselled into the mountain sides. They seemed to have the ability to just keep going at a steady pace, deaf to distractions. In such conditions, the phrase 'stubborn as a mule' acquired a new, comforting meaning.

When Donald Coleman Bailey devised his Meccano-like bridge in 1940, he had no idea it would prove a war-winner. Capable of assembly into rafts, pontoon bridges, and endless variations to suit different obstacle widths and vehicle loads, every piece could be manhandled by a team of six men, with no cranes or welding required. Bailey's structures were crucial at Cassino, the confluence of several rivers, and in the Italian campaign over 3,000 Bailey bridges were constructed by all the Allied armies.

Albert Kesselring, much-decorated and supremely able, was appointed *Oberbefelshaber Südwest* by Hitler on 21 November 1943. Despite the fifty-eight-year-old field marshal's nickname of 'Smiling Albert' (for his 'sunny' countenance), he was a dangerous adversary. After the Allies attacked his villa in Frascati on 8 September, he moved his HQ to an underground complex 20 miles north of Rome.

The efficient Fridolin von Senger und Etterlin commanded XIV Panzer Corps throughout the campaign. A practising Christian and lay member of the Benedictine Order (whose spiritual home was Monte Cassino), he somehow managed to reconcile his own beliefs with service to his country as a soldier.

On 15 August 1943, the German Tenth Army was activated under Generaloberst Heinrich von Vietinghoff, newly-arrived from the Fifteenth Army in northern France. He commanded with zeal and professionalism throughout the Cassino campaign, and eventually succeeded Kesselring as theatre commander.

A Mountain soldier – *Gebirgsjäger* – guards his charges from aerial attack. His weapons, such as the M-34 (seen here), generally had high rates of fire and when mounted on a tripod were especially useful as heavy machine guns – they could reach across the valleys with Zeiss optics, to ranges of nearly two miles.

German paratroops – *Fallschirmjäger* – were the chief adversaries in Cassino town and abbey. Part of the Luftwaffe, whose insignia is sported here, they were trained to fight in small groups without leaders, lavishly equipped with automatic weapons, and above all, were physically very fit.

Nebelwerfers were highly-mobile 6-barrelled mortars operated by specially-trained crews, which could send a concentration very accurately over the mountains for 7,500 yards. Allied soldiers recalled the bombs were heralded by a high-pitched scream – hence its nickname of 'Moaning Minnie'.

Huge numbers of S-mines (*Schrapnellmine* or *Springmine* in German) were scattered around Cassino as part of the Gustav Line defences. The size of a tin can, and called a 'Bouncing Betty' by the Americans and, more accurately, a 'de-bollocker' by the British, S-mines jumped into the air when triggered and detonated after three feet, projecting a lethal spray of ball bearings in all directions at groin height.

(*Above*) Italian and German soldiers gather round a field kitchen on Sicily in July 1943. By September some of these Italians had joined Brigadier Vincenzo Dapino's Italian First Motorised Group to attack Monte Lungo with the US 36th Division. Their assaults were the first retaliatory blows struck against the Germans by the Royal Italian Army. (*Right*) When Montgomery's Eighth Army landed in Calabria on 3 September 1943 and Clark's Fifth Army invaded Salerno six days later, curious Italians would have witnessed flatcars bearing tanks and half tracks covered with camouflage netting and tree branches, flooding into northern Italy. Here troops pause in Pisa on their way south.

Commanding the Allied Armies in Italy, or 15th Army Group, as it was also known, was the fifty-two-year-old Honourable Harold Alexander, universally known as Alex, who was both extremely popular and a great diplomat with the many nations under him. Leading a battalion of Baltic Germans in 1919–20, he never lost his admiration for their fighting qualities, and cabled Churchill on 20 March 1944, 'The tenacity of these German paratroops is quite remarkable … I doubt if there are any other troops in the world who could have stood up to the bombing and gone on fighting with the ferocity they have.'

Alphonse Juin (left), the popular head of the French Expeditionary Corps, with Alexander (centre) and Mark Clark, head of the Fifth Army, in Sienna on Bastille Day, after the Cassino campaign. Juin salutes with his left hand because of the First World War injury to his right.

Churchill being briefed by Eighth Army commander Oliver Leese (left). Alexander looks on. Leese had succeeded his old chief Montgomery as GOC of the Eighth Army in December 1943, but many felt he lacked Monty's flair with his men. Yet Leese had an agile brain, tremendous energy, and a powerful personality.

In 1944, Sir Bernard Freyberg was already a living legend. The fearless commander of the New Zealand Corps had won a VC and three DSOs in the First World War, but Mark Clark found him intimidating. Yet Freyberg himself would be under strain in the second and third battles, as his son had been posted missing at Anzio. A leader of great determination, at Cassino Freyberg soon found he was up against his old adversaries from Crete, the *Fallschirmjäger*.

of the Rapido. Early on 27 January, two companies of tanks supported 168th Infantry's attack; most slid into the marsh, removing the only means of suppressing the deadly German pillboxes, but four tanks managed to wade across and began detonating anti-personnel mines and shredding barbed wire obstacles, clearing paths for the infantry. Though there were no anti-tank guns in this sector, all four were eventually rendered *hors-de-combat* by quick-thinking German troops using mines and *panzerfausts* (a forerunner of the modern rocket-propelled grenades).

Despite their losses, the 756th Tank Battalion had enabled 168th Regiment to reach the base of Point 213 early on 28 January. They were soon running out of serviceable vehicles so called on 760th Tank Battalion's armour to help push on to Caira, using the stony river bed as a road, rather than the impenetrable swamp either side, and by the quick-thinking employment of metal matting (designed for temporary airstrip runways) to absorb the weight of armoured vehicles. Late on 29 January, the surviving tanks slithered through the minefields, and forced out German machine-gunners, who had no immediate antidote to the appearance of armour. The 168th Regiment had captured Caira, head-quarters of Oberst Willy Nagel's 131st Grenadier Regiment (of Franek's Hoch-und-Deutschmeister Division), a warren of ruined buildings concealing several huge concrete bunkers, each built to house a platoon, with bunks, food, ammunition, and even heating.

The tanks had done well, but their potential was not always realised. They suffered from the terrain because engineers couldn't quickly lay bridging or adequate 'corduroy roads' (made from tree trunks), and they were immobilised by intrepid German infantry who crept quite close with anti-tank mines or *panzerfausts*, the latter with the recommended distance for a 'kill' a mere thirty to sixty yards. Against threats such as these, Allied tanks thrived when there was intimate infantry support, able to beat off tank-hunting parties, while the armour, in turn, was adept at destroying bunkers, machine-gun nests, barbed wire and anti-personnel minefields – the enemies of all infantrymen. Allied armour suffered at Cassino time and time again because of the lack of infantry–tank cooperation; neither fully understood each other's capabilities, or needs.

The tank battalions supporting the Red Bulls were equipped – as nearly all Allied armour units, whether British, Canadian, Polish, New

Zealander, South African, Indian, French or American – with the M4 Sherman tank, which had first arrived on the battlefields just in time to save Montgomery's bacon at El Alamein in October 1942. Though much criticised at the time – and more, subsequently – for its seeming inability to compete with the best contemporary German tanks, the Sherman's production quantities had a quality of their own, which the Third Reich could not match. By the time manufacture had finished at the American Locomotive Company, Baldwin Locomotive Works, Detroit Tank Arsenal, Lima Locomotive Works, Pressed Steel Car Company, Pacific Car and Foundry Company and the Pullman Standard Car Company, among others, a staggering 62,312 Sherman hulls had been assembled. The greatest proportion of these were tanks, but a bewildering variety of superstructures for self-propelled artillery, tank destroyers, mine-clearing, bridge-laying, rocket-launching, flame-throwing, armoured recovery and other engineer and amphibious requirements were also devised. Like the Panzer IV (the main German tank), the Sherman (named after Ulysses S. Grant's able lieutenant in the American Civil War) weighed thirty tons, was crewed by five and mounted a 75mm gun. As neither tank could fire with accuracy on the move, manoeuvre in combat represented instinctive teamwork between the commander, driver and gunner, as vehicles of both sides had to stop and shoot, often at multiple targets, and suddenly. At nine feet, it was a tall tank, meaning it was easy to spot in combat, and used a similar engine, gearbox, tracks and suspension system as its predecessors in order to cut down on time and retooling.

The tank's gunner used a telescopic sight to confirm targets and aim, also controlling the electric turret traverse, which operated far quicker than the manual equipment fitted in German tanks – a significant advantage over the Panzer IVs, Panthers and Tigers encountered in 1944 Italy. He could also use his 0.30-inch Browning machine gun for ranging, and operated the main gun by floor pedal. The loader sat or stood to the left of the gun, reaching for armour-piercing, high-explosive, white phosphorus or smoke shells. Shermans were supplied with ninety rounds, at Cassino mostly high explosive for blasting caves and bunkers. Tank crews in Italy found that ammunition racks also snugly accommodated bottles of vino, and some crewmen recalled that at Cassino live chickens were kept in the turrets to ensure a constant supply of fresh eggs. Good loaders would anticipate the type of ammunition required, before any order was given, and usually wore a large padded glove to punch rounds into the breech and handle hot shell cases.

Inside a tank, sleep was almost impossible, for each member of the crew was required to be constantly on the alert. The frequent smack of bullets, shrapnel, and debris on the outside armour always held the threat of something larger and more penetrating. Several commanders had their periscopes sniped and snatched away from their eyes when the glass above splintered and the device on its ball joint swung violently upwards; some received nasty face wounds this way. The air inside the cramped conditions, though foul, could get icy cold, especially in the early mornings or when the engine had been stopped for a long period.

At Cassino, squadrons of Shermans were often used as artillery to supplement the field guns, when rapid fire of their 75mm high-explosive shells was needed. Then the turret became a vomit-inducing hell of cordite fumes and hot brass shell casings. Leaving the hatches open in Italian weather brought problems of its own: with that affectation that comes to the cavalry around the world naturally, one British tank officer in Italy concluded that the only personal weapon he needed was an umbrella. Infantry–armour cooperation in Italy was so important that many Shermans had tank telephones installed on their rear mudguards, or an infantry wireless set, enabling the two arms to talk direct. Other armour units deployed captains moving on foot with the infantry to liaise in person, while it was not unknown for some tank officers to carry deckchairs on their engine decks on which local infantry commanders could perch, in order to discuss tactics face to face.

Sherman drivers and co-drivers climbed up the forty-five-degree sloping armour plate on the front, grasping the main gun barrel to lever themselves up and into their separate hatches, forward of the turret. The driver, a product of over six months' training at an armour school, sat forward left in the hull, alongside the bow machine-gunner/co-driver, who perched alongside on his right. The white-painted interiors were boiling in Italian summers, freezing in the Apennine winters, and the driver had the warmest corner. Sprung seats enabled both forward crew members to sit with their heads poking out, but they battened down for combat. If the driver was incapacitated for any reason, the bow gunner was trained to take his place.

Between them ran the huge drive shaft which led to the engine at the rear; they could look forwards through periscopes, and over their shoulders at the three-man turret crew behind. In the event of trouble, exit was via hatches over their heads which opened upwards; however, the barrel of the main gun frequently obstructed this escape route, so they could choose to wriggle backwards into the turret, or out via a small escape hatch in the floor. Both these options took time, which was in short supply if the tank was on fire. A disproportionate number of drivers died in their seats, usually burned to death, unable to escape.

It was the number of Shermans that caught fire when struck by German shells or mines, often killing their crews, which created most concern. Crews blamed the efficacy of German weapons, inadequate armour (nowhere did the Sherman have more than three inches of armour plate), but most often the petrol engines, for the violent explosions that consumed the crew and sometimes ripped turrets off the hulls. So much so that the Germans with grim humour called Shermans 'Tommy-cookers', while the British dubbed them 'Ronsons' (after the cigarette lighter of the era, which 'never failed to light first time'). In fact it was usually turret ammunition that was ignited to cause the fatal explosions, rather than fuel. Either way, the infantry's view was: 'Our tanks did not fare very well against tank mines. They would explode and catch fire and the poor bastards inside had little chance of getting out. It's a pretty horrible sight and the screaming is blood-curdling. I thanked the good Lord I was not a tanker.' On the Rapido plains, though, the worry was more the 'lentil soup' marsh than the Germans – and for this the narrow tracks of the Sherman had no answer.

Ryder's Red Bulls had broken into a very small fragment of the Gustav Line at Caira, and his 168th Regiment moved beyond, scaling the foothills of Points 156 and 213 – but it took him the better part of two regiments (brigades) and two tank battalions to achieve this, over five days. On 1 February, Ryder, reinforced with 142nd Regiment, renewed his attack by throwing half of his men onto the hills south of Caira, Monte Castellone and Colle Maiola, and the remainder south, to Cassino town, advancing via the old barracks, which they cleared on 2 February. The attack on the high ground went well, despite thick fog and freezing rain, both peaks being taken, and were never subsequently yielded, in spite of fierce counterattacks over the succeeding days. The Americans, trying to consolidate their gains, found all they could do was to build little sangars, first making small hollows and then piling stones around them by hand. Soldiers on both sides were issued with small steel entrenching tools as part of their personal issue infantry kit, but these could make no impression on the stony ground. 'It was brutal country to fight in,' reflected twenty-nine-year-old First Sergeant Don Hoagland, a Minnesota National Guardsman, like Ralph Schaps in the Red Bulls Division. 'You'd lay down at night in your shallow hole, and if you had a couple of blankets, you would put one down in the wet hole, lie down, and pull a wet blanket over you. That's the way you slept.'

The German defenders, now including the resourceful 90th PanzerGrenadier Division, were particularly adept at setting ambushes in the ruins of the barracks and Cassino itself, combining quite small teams of tank-hunting infantry and lone panzers. The PanzerGrenadiers were led by the forty-six-year-old Generalmajor Ernst-Günther Baade, an Afrika Korps veteran, great favourite of Senger's and fellow cavalryman, who had been in charge of air defences during the evacuation from Sicily. With a Knight's Cross swinging at his throat, in December he had been promoted to divisional command, and was, by nature, one of life's eccentrics, but his men worshipped him. As Senger recalled: 'Over his riding breeches Baade used to wear a Scottish khaki kilt. In place of the large leather sporran worn by Scotsmen he had a pistol, suspended in a holster from his neck.' Known as a dynamic leader, and one of very few senior commanders awarded a special decoration for single-handedly destroying a tank at close range, Baade spent much of his time at the front, 'smelling the battle', but also carried around a monk's cowl as a disguise in order to evade potential capture. Senger soon gave Baade control over the sector, no matter who actually 'owned' the sub-units there.

After destroying several Shermans trundling past the barracks and into Cassino, on 2 February, Oberleutnant Metzger and his comrades let five American tanks drive into the ruins of Cassino, picked off the fifth to block their escape route, lured the four ahead into a small square, surrounded them and persuaded the crews to surrender with threats of magnetic mines, hand grenades and *panzerfausts*; three tanks were promptly driven off and reused against their former owners. This was the first recorded attack on Cassino town itself, though it had already been damaged by misdirected shells and bombs. Above them, US 135th Infantry made promising progress through the hills towards the abbey. The following day, more American tank and infantry groups from Ryder's division tried to work their way into Cassino town, but were frustrated by anti-tank gun ambushes from the PanzerGrenadiers who could also call on supporting fire from above, on Castle Hill. Aerial photographs from 1944 show that the northern suburbs of Cassino resembled a graveyard of Sherman tanks – and some of their crews.

On 4 February, Ryder's Red Bulls made significant progress through the hills, sufficiently so for XIV Panzer Corps commander Senger to request a disengagement from Cassino altogether and redeployment to Anzio. Instead of agreeing to Senger's request to withdraw, Kesselring decided to redeploy Heidrich's 1st Fallschirmjäger (Parachute) Division from the Adriatic front, opposite Eighth Army, to Cassino, and over-ruling Senger's objections, use them to augment Baade's 90th PanzerGrenadiers. He felt that their small-team focus and skill in adapting to difficult terrain would prove a winning combination. He initially threw into the Cassino area the 1st Parachute Regiment, a battalion from 3rd Parachute Regiment, and the Parachute Machine-Gun Battalion. Strategically, by pulling in reserves from France, Germany, and the Balkans, Kesselring was conforming to the Allied strategy of getting the Germans to denude other fronts. The trouble was that the Germans were becoming so efficient at redeploying troops quickly (despite an alleged Allied air superiority) and adept at using the Italian terrain as a force multiplier, that it was the Allies who needed reinforcing as much as their opponents. Although Clark was aware of the information generated by the Ultra intercepts (although not their provenance), the Americans had no idea how much damage and anxiety they were causing.

Baade's PanzerGrenadiers bitterly contested the hills, refusing to yield Point 445 or the critical Point 593, key heights that overlooked Cassino abbey, though it had only just occurred to Ryder that these were far more significant features than the abbey or town. On 5 and 6 February, the Americans edged forward above the town, 2nd Battalion, 168th Regiment managed to take Point 593, were driven off it, then retook the feature, while a platoon managed to reach a German-garrisoned cave under the walls of the abbey, took fourteen prisoners and withdrew.

Another battalion tried and failed to take Castle Hill, while vicious street fighting erupted in the town. Every building had been sandbagged or reinforced to become a strongpoint, concealed amidst piles of rubble. Under the protective fire of American shelling, including eight-inch howitzers, Ryder's 133rd Regiment found they had to rely on bazookas to blast open holes in buildings (ten rounds at point-blank range per strongpoint was about the norm to 'silence' a German position), while the 100th Nisei Battalion proved themselves adept at subduing their opponents with well-lobbed hand grenades – a skill attributed to the Japanese-Americans' prowess at baseball.

The 7th of February saw inconclusive fighting for the hills, and Baade's PanzerGrenadiers had now been reinforced by the Fallschirmjägers in the town. Each US advance was met by stout resistance, the result being that the Americans – who could 'afford' the casualties – were been worn down quicker by the Germans, who could not: Senger reckoned he was losing a battalion a day at this stage of the defence. General Ryder measured some of his progress from the morale of captured prisoners, and also by translating their personal letters. Outgoing mail found on a 90th PanzerGrenadier read: 'For two weeks we have been in action. The few days were enough to make me sick and tired of it. In all that time, we've had nothing to sleep in but foxholes, and the artillery fire kept us with our noses in the dirt all day long. During the first few days I felt very odd and . . . didn't eat anything at all. I lost my appetite when I saw that . . . not a single man from my original squad is left, all of them missing. And it seems to be the same in the entire company.'

But the PanzerGrenadiers' opponents, too, were running out of men: casualties from battle and sickness in US forces were appalling, with some companies down to just thirty men. The strain imposed by continuous fighting in the mountains was exaggerated by mud, rain, cold, and unhygienic living conditions; only the fittest, hardiest, and those with extreme stamina could resist these multiple assaults on the body. One of the issues facing Ryder and Walker was company-level leadership. As the more experienced officers became casualties, they were replaced by youngsters, who were not National Guardsmen, had no affinity with their troops, and were fresh out of the Infantry Officer Candidate School at Fort Benning, Georgia. To create the huge numbers of junior leaders required, over 100,000 potential officers were processed through seventeen-week courses, each of about 200 candidates, of whom 67 per cent were commissioned. Added to this, the intense combat and heavy losses since the start of the Italy campaign the previous year meant that many divisions still training in the United States were stripped of trained officers and men to build up the replacement pool.

Reinforcements (or 'repple-depples') arrived from replacement depots, and it was to here also that recovered sick personnel were shipped, meaning that those wounded rarely rejoined their old units. Green, newly arrived officers relied heavily on their sergeants, who were the lynchpin of the infantry companies in 34th and 36th Divisions. Thus, there were too few good junior leaders to control the high numbers of non-battle casualties resulting from exhaustion and physical breakdown which trickled to the rear. Twenty-three-year-old Second Lieutenant Harold Bond of 141st Regiment, 36th Texan Division, remembered his bewilderment at finding a fellow officer in the foothills with a drawn pistol, sending back soldiers who were moving to the rear on the slightest of excuses. A fellow officer in the same regiment, Captain Red Morgan, agreed: 'the walking wounded were carefully screened. We could not spare a man that could still throw a grenade or fire a rifle.' Ryder of 34th Division knew that at one stage for his division's casualty evacuation chain 'over 1,100 mules and 700 litter bearers were required over and above the normal transportation and medical personnel', some of whom were Italian Army volunteers.

Ryder was under pressure to continue from both his corps commander, Keyes, and Mark Clark, who in turn was aware that Alexander was preparing to send in the Indian Army and New Zealander troops to relieve the 34th Division if Cassino was not soon cleared. In Clark's mind American prestige was under threat. However, the truth, as always, was different: Alexander had heard mutterings that American morale was plummeting as fast as their casualties were rising, and despatched his own (American) deputy chief of staff, Lyman Lemnitzer, to investigate behind Clark's back. Lemnitzer found 'morale progressively worse . . . [the troops] disheartened, almost mutinous'. Therefore, Clark was given until 12 February to clear Cassino, when the New Zealanders would be deployed. Clark knew their impossibly well-decorated commander, General Sir Bernard Freyberg, VC, DSO and *two* bars, was a prickly soldier of immense experience, who would require handling with kid gloves and would not sit easy in the role of subordinate.

Senior Allied commanders were also making a rod for their own backs, as generals are wont to do with politicians, by talking up their chances of victory. On 2 February, Clark had signalled to Alexander that 'present indications are that the Cassino heights will be captured very soon', while six days later Alexander told Churchill: 'I have high hopes of a breakthrough in this sector and if it looks promising I shall reinforce.' Although the evidence already suggested that Cassino was a far tougher nut to crack than anticipated and that the resources available might be insufficient to triumph, Churchill and Brooke, Roosevelt and Marshall were still being told what they wanted to hear. And reading it, too, it seems. Allied newspapers reflected the 'spin' they were given.

The Times, among many, was upbeat all week in its reports. On 2 February it claimed 'the Fifth Army is exerting the strongest possible pressure on its southern front. Resistance in the village of Caira, which had been enveloped, has been finally stifled. Cassino itself, one of the strongest places in the whole line of defence, has been imperilled by the turning movement from the north, and the enemy may be compelled to abandon it without the Americans having to resort to a frontal assault, which would be very costly.' This news reflected information given to Allied war correspondents on 30–31 January and was manifestly at odds with the truth. Within two days, on Friday 4 February, *The Times* was heralding: 'The drama of Cassino is drawing to a close. As the Americans extend their hold on the heights above the village of Caira, and the French close in on Terelle, the German hold on the mountain mass which blocks the valley is gradually being prised open.' Correspondents would have been briefed by officers on Clark's or Alexander's staff, who must have known that the move on Terelle had already been abandoned by Clark the previous month. This misplaced optimism continued on 5 February with *The Times* repeating: 'The battle for Cassino on the main Fifth Army front is drawing to a close.' Reality only started to reassert itself on Tuesday 8 February (the day of Alexander's buoyant signal to Churchill) with the paper admitting 'the grim struggle, the key-point in the German defence of the road to Rome, is not yet over . . . Fierce and bitter fighting continues all round the town, and the enemy recaptured one hill about 500 foot west of the town during one violent counterattack.'

On 8 February, too, the Nisei Battalion was switched to the heights and had almost reached Castle Hill, but at the last minute wind blew away their protective smoke screen and German crossfire cut into their ranks from above; although Private Masao Awakuni managed to destroy a self-propelled gun, the Nisei Battalion had to go to ground, and remained pinned down until 12 February. They had arrived with a strength of nearly 1,500, but would lose around 700 casualties in these attacks. On the German side, a captured order of the day underlined the reason for their stiffening resistance: 'The Gustav Line must be held at all costs for the sake of the political consequences which would follow a completely successful defence. The Führer expects the bitterest struggle for every day.' Ever since the winter of 1941, when he had issued harsh instructions for the Wehrmacht to stand fast and not retreat in Russia, Hitler had sent similar diktats to his troops, which were often inappropriate, and by 1944 had become a deluge. They had little effect, except to promote fear among senior commanders of blame and a summary execution if a military reverse was to occur – whether or not such was their fault.

Over the next four days, the heights beyond Cassino witnessed a whole series of sub-unit actions as the Americans contested each hill, ridge and peak; the vital feature of Point 593 changed hands several times, before falling to the Fallschirmjäger on the 11th. Ralph Schaps of Company H in 135th Regiment remembered capturing it initially after close hand-to-hand combat. 'Our attack up the last few yards of Hill 593 to the summit was one of those story-book happenings. We actually stormed up the hill double-time, firing our weapons from the hip. Some riflemen even had their bayonets fixed. [The CO] had scraped up any service personnel which included cooks, supply people, truck drivers. He also sent up the regimental recon and intelligence platoon as replacements . . . I had some teeth knocked out by a Jerry rifle butt during the melee but hardly felt it. There was a lot of screaming and cursing as we were not going to let the goddam Krauts push us off the hill.'

The weather was freezing: temperatures hovered around minus ten (worse with wind chill) by day and as low as minus thirty overnight. 'It either rained or snowed every day,' Schaps remembered of his time on

Point 593; 'in spite of the cold, the stench from rotting bodies was becoming overpowering. There was no way we could bury any of the corpses that littered the whole area.' Ryder's eroded division was now reinforced by the arrival of Walker's 36th Texans who, having recovered from the Rapido, moved up onto the heights to the Redbulls' right, and both renewed the assault on 11 February. Clark wished this to be choreographed with simultaneous attacks by the British X Corps and Juin's Expeditionary Corps, but both of these formations were already spent, so the effort fell on the Texan National Guardsmen. Shortly before the men could advance, a blizzard blew up and obliterated visibility for the Allied artillery observers, making tactical fire support in the hills impossible.

Walker nevertheless attacked. He was now using clerks, drivers and anti-tank gunners as infantry, so depleted were his ranks. But they could make no headway against the PanzerGrenadiers and Fallschirmjäger based around the most important stone dwelling in the hills beyond Cassino monastery, that of Albaneta Farm, used variously as an aid post and regimental HQ. Neither did Ryder have any success against the dominant Point 593, so slid left, aiming for the monastery itself. Launched in sub-zero conditions, with alternating rain, sleet and snow, the offensive soon slithered to a complete halt. New Zealander Howard Kippenberger sadly observed the reality at US II Corps headquarters: 'There was heavy rain all day, the attack failed as almost everyone expected.' Schaps wrote: 'We were filthy, unwashed, unshaved and slept on the ground without any blankets or covers. We were cold, wet and miserable.' The simple act of relieving oneself was 'almost an impossibility during daylight hours unless one was prepared to defecate in the confines of the slit trench, as often times was the case'.

One captain of US 141st Regiment observed that the two battalions in his vicinity should have totalled 70 officers and 1,600 enlisted men, but their combined strength was now about twenty officers and 150 men. A stalemate had now been reached with both sides, although reinforced, approaching exhaustion; any German attempts to counterattack were met with a wall of Allied artillery, while German fire from the peaks prevented any American progress. During the first two weeks of February alone, US II Corps heavy guns (eight-inch howitzers) had fired more than 10,000 rounds, while the two divisions' 105mm field artillery fired nearly 100,000 shells supporting the countless infantry attacks. Reluctantly, Clark and Keyes allowed the remaining GIs from 34th and 36th Divisions to trickle down from the hills and out of the town, where progress had been equally snail-like and costly. Among them, in heavy rain, were infantrymen Don Hoagland and Schaps. Hoagland wrote that he couldn't imagine men being in any worse shape: 'They were like zombies shuffling along. It was just continual lack of sleep, continual pounding, continual attrition. It was a nasty, nasty battle in a nasty, nasty war.' For Schaps the descent was 'a nightmare'. 'We had to almost carry some of the men down the hill as they had trench foot and were hardly able to walk. We marched ten miles to an assembly area where we were given our first hot meal in two weeks.'

Schaps's platoon has started with forty-two men; just he and six others walked down. The next day, while they were still in their assembly area, they were bombed by their own air force. As they shuffled past, on their way to food and rest, the famous photojournalist Margaret Bourke-White remembered graphically: 'I knew from the divisional emblem on their sleeves that those men had been up in the mountains around Cassino . . . I thought I had never seen such tired faces. It was more than the stubble of beard that told the story; it was the blank staring eyes. The men were so tired that it was like a living death. They had come from such a depth of weariness that I wondered if they would ever be able quite to make the return to the lives and thoughts they had known.' Also watching was Brigadier Kippenberger: 'The Americans had battled since January with a stubbornness and gallantry beyond all praise, but they were fought out . . . utterly exhausted. When relieved, fifty men had to be carried out on stretchers.'

The cost to the 34th National Guard Division was nearly a third of its infantry: 318 killed, 1,641 wounded, and 392 missing or taken prisoner. Just as the destruction reminded many British and German officers of the Somme, Verdun or Passchendaele, the casualties were similar in number. Several battalions in 34th and 36th Divisions suffered casualties of fifty per cent in the hills and street-fighting, while all lost at least a couple of hundred. However, the Germans, too, had taken a hammering. Senger's XIV Corps headquarters calculated on 4 February that the effective strength of twelve of their battalions in the Cassino sector amounted to just 1,500 men, a tenth of their numbers on paper; they were holding their own, though at an irreplaceable price.

For a brief while, humanity returned: an uneasy truce was arranged over two hours on 14 February – St Valentine's Day – for both sides to collect their dead on Monte Castellone. Lieutenant Colonel Hal Reese of 143rd Regiment was chosen to oversee it for the Americans, on account of his rusty German from occupation duty in Koblenz during 1919. One of his German counterparts told Reese that he was from that city and remembered the US soldiers on the streets; Reese produced an old photograph of him at the time, and within minutes all – Americans and Germans alike – were fishing out photographs of loved ones, and posing for new photographs. There was a noticeable lull across the battlefield as both sides licked their wounds. The first battle for Cassino had ended.

6

How to Destroy a Monastery

Oh bury me at Cassino
My duty to England is done
And when you get back to Blighty
And you are drinking your whisky and rum
Remember the old Indian soldier
When the war he fought has been won!

War song of the Indian 8th Infantry Division

THE NEXT ARMY to engage the Germans at Cassino came from India. In his 1992 prize-winning novel, *The English Patient*, set in Second World War Italy, Michael Ondaatje introduced readers to the character of Kirpal Singh, known as 'Kip', a Sikh in the British Indian Army. Originally from Punjab, the fictional Kip worked as a bomb disposal expert in the Royal Indian Engineers, detecting and defusing devices left by the retreating Germans in war-torn Italy.

Kip may also have been a subliminal tribute to the first Indian to win the coveted VC in the Second World War: Premindra Singh Bhagat, second lieutenant with the Royal Indian Engineers, was a Sikh bomb disposal and mine clearance expert, who cleared fifty-five miles of road over four days in 1941. To this day, few realise that the Indian subcontinent contributed the largest volunteer army of any in the Second World War. Over 2.5 million Indian men and women volunteered for service in the Allied forces. Over 100,000 served in Italy, the fourth largest contingent, after British, French and US forces, in three complete infantry groups, the 4th, 8th and 10th Indian Infantry Divisions and the 43rd Gurkha Independent Infantry Brigade. Of that number 5,782 would rest for ever in Italian soil, and over half the remainder, mostly aged between nineteen and twenty-two, would be casualties.

Though very large, the Indian Army at the start of the Second World War was a very dated force, with poor mobility, antiquated artillery, no mortars or anti-tank weaponry, outmoded signalling equipment (much of it still based on flags and heliograph rather than wireless), while all its cavalry were still mounted. Many of its young volunteers were illiterate and had to be educated as well as trained. The army had to modernise as well as expand rapidly, and politics ruled out any resort to conscription. In 1940, when it appeared that an invasion of Britain was not only likely, but inevitable, and the French believed 'in three weeks England will have her neck wrung like a chicken' (Churchill's later witty response: 'Some chicken; some neck'), Gandhi published an open letter urging cessation of hostilities, yet also wept at the thought of Westminster Abbey destroyed by bombs. Jinnah, on the other hand, believed that if Britain lost, the Muslims were likely to suffer, and declared for the Allies, hoping (correctly) that such devotion might help 'buy' an all-Muslim state after the war – the eventual Pakistan.

This prompted Leo Amery, Churchill's Secretary of State for India, to confide in his belief that India's effective war contribution would rely on Muslim effort. Churchill (once a young subaltern in India) believed that Britain should not break with the 100-million-strong Muslim community, who represented an immediate manpower pool on which he would rely. In the event the Indian Army embraced many faiths. With his beard and turban, Michael Ondaatje's fictional Kip was a Sikh, whose homeland was the Punjab, a province of northern India which furnished around 20 per cent of all recruits, although they comprised less than 2 per cent of the total population. Even in combat they wore their turbans rather than steel helmets. The first Indian troops arriving on the Cassino front in February 1944 sported an impressive shoulder badge depicting a red-coloured eagle on a black background, with huge wings outstretched and claws extended – hence the divisional nickname of the Red Eagles. Badges and insignia matter to soldiers, the bolder, the better – and the red eagle was one of the best.

The Red Eagles were, in microcosm, a reflection of the whole Indian force. Their infantry battalions were mostly British-officered and within each brigade one of the three battalions was entirely British, hence the 1st Battalion of the Royal Sussex Regiment, 2nd Cameron Highlanders, and the 1/4th Essex, fighting alongside Rajputanas, Punjabis and Gurkhas. In theory, the mix was to 'stiffen' Indian troops, but in practice the latter often out-performed their European colleagues – in fitness and in valour. British officers were expected to master the language and culture of their Indian charges, which in no small way accounts for the continuing British culinary love affair with curry. The rank structure mirrored that of the British, with its *sepoys* (privates), *naiks* (corporals), *havildars* (sergeants), *jemadars* (lieutenants), *subedars* (captains) and *subedar-majors* (majors), and the full range of intermediate grades. Several Gurkha regiments (including 1st Battalion of the 2nd Gurkha Regiment, 2/7th and 1/9th) would fight with the Red Eagles at Cassino, but each regiment had its own distinct identity. The Indian and Gurkha units, far from home, realised that regimental pride and battalion spirit would have to make up for a lack of warmth, ammunition, medicine and food on the slopes of Cassino, and this sense of loyalty would prove vitally important in the trials ahead.

All Gurkha regiments had acquired a fearsome reputation even before the Second World War. Generally short and stocky, the Gurkhas, exceptionally tough warriors from the mountainous Gorkha district of Nepal, would shave their heads before combat. An officer with 4th Gurkhas and later novelist, John Masters, wrote of a Gurkha patrol in the vicinity of Cassino who, 'after slipping by two enemy sentries in the dark of the night . . . found the other four Germans of the post asleep in a row in a barn. They beheaded the two men on the inside, but left the two on the outside to sleep – to wake up, to try to rouse their comrades . . . It was a brilliant improvisation, which went straight to the unlovely heart of psychological warfare.'

By 1944 the most experienced division in Eighth Army – having fought against the Italians in the Western Desert in Operation Compass; Mussolini's men in Abyssinia and Eritrea; French Vichy forces in Syria;

and with Eighth Army in Egypt, Libya and Tunisia – was the 4th Indian Division. They arrived in Italy from Egypt in January 1944 and deployed in the midst of a particularly treacherous winter to Eighth Army's front in the east. This cannot have been pleasant for those used to the hot climes of India and the Middle East, where the division had served since the outbreak of the war, via the 1941 Abyssinian campaign against the Italians. It included men like Nila Kantan, who was brought up in Andra Pradesh, on India's east coast, the fourth largest state. Nila, a Brahmin, had volunteered for the Indian Army in 1940 at the age of nineteen. His village, which he had not left before, consisted of poor, mud-walled houses with thatched roofs, on the banks of the Godavari River. 'Being very lean, thin and puny, I was not fit, so they rejected me for the infantry. I did not mind; every job in the army is useful, you see. The infantry is the Queen of Battle, they take all the credit; but I doubt very much if the infantry can do anything without the support of the other services.' So Nila joined the Royal Indian Army Service Corps as a driver, serving in Eritrea, Syria and North Africa, where he was wounded on his first day in Egypt during an air raid and hospitalised for a month. He then moved on to Italy with the rest of the Red Eagles. As well as its three infantry brigades all the division's support units were Indian-recruited, like its reconnaissance regiment, an old, revered cavalry unit who had also served in the Great War, the Central India Horse. Normally equipped with armoured cars and light tanks, at Cassino they reverted to invaluable supply duties, happily reunited with horses and mules.

The 4th Indian Division had been led since December 1941 by Major General Francis Tuker – known as 'Gertie' to his friends: a bright, scholarly former commander of 1/2nd Gurkhas. Said to possess a 'vigorous' though 'sometimes unorthodox mind', Tuker could be outspoken to the point of irritation. He published articles on innovation, new tactics and doctrine in the military press, and had a profound understanding of modern armed warfare, from artillery to air power. He was generally adored by his men, if not his peers or contemporaries. The forty-nine-year-old Tuker had one particular misfortune which would directly affect the second battle for Cassino: he suffered periodically from chronic rheumatoid arthritis, which forced him to his sickbed.

*   *   *

With Lucas's VI Corps under heavy threat at Anzio, and US II Corps spent at Cassino, Clark ordered Leese to transfer three divisions from the Adriatic across to the Cassino front, initially New Zealand 2nd Division and 4th Indian, to maintain the pressure. British 78th Division followed on 17 February. The New Zealanders were pleased to work alongside the 4th Indian, for they had operated together during the Libyan campaign of 1941; they were highly regarded by their Allies as 'a veteran fighting force with a first-class reputation'. The three divisions required a corps commander to coordinate their activities, but instead of promoting the able Tuker (who had been trained in mountain warfare), Alexander chose to elevate the New Zealand commander, Lieutenant General Freyberg, instead. Freyberg had already served as a temporary corps commander in Tunisia, was a First World War VC-winner and a living legend.

Among the reasons for Freyberg to continue chipping away at Cassino, rather than switching over to the defensive and waiting for better weather, was the need to distract Kesselring from hurling all his resources at Anzio, Clark's bullish optimism that he was about to break through, and the progress Keyes's II Corps had made up to 11 February – many of the heights to the north and north-east of Cassino had been gained, and there was a sense (actually self-delusion) that one more push might reach Route 6 and isolate any Germans left at Cassino. Thus, on 3 February, Freyberg was a busy man, having to hand over command of his own division, reset his mind to attacking Cassino at corps level, and plan a 'relief-in-place' of the US 34th and 36th Divisions on the heights, who would be replaced by the 4th Indian Division. American Harold Bond, controlling the mortars with 36th Division, remembered the incomers: 'We saw their officers on their way up to make their reconnaissance . . . They were clean and sprightly, rested and strong. They seemed to be in good humour as they hiked up the trail carrying their swagger sticks or, in some cases, walking sticks. It was a sunny, clear morning, in sharp contrast to the snow and rain which had greeted us. They were experienced and well-trained men and knew exactly what they were doing. I noticed that some of the officers did not even wear their steel helmets. The officers went on past our positions towards the battalion command post, after asking us a few questions about the battle conditions up here. My men [were] dirty, unshaven, and weary . . . but none of us envied them.'

So constrained was the terrain that the Red Eagles Division's plan was to establish the three battalions of its 7th Indian Brigade on to the high ground first, then to feed into them the 5th Brigade, while the third brigade, the 11th, would be used as porters, labourers and carriers to sustain the other two. Signalman B. Smith, attached to the 4/16th Punjabis of 7th Indian Brigade, remembered the move into the hills, using mules to carry his radio equipment: 'Animals and men picked their way carefully between the water-filled shell holes with many a halt. The night was still and very dark. The column made its own character-istic noises: a mule snorting, the clang of an iron hoof on a stone, the jingle of harness, the creak of leather and the soft murmuring of men; and all the time we listened, ears attuned, senses alert even when talking to a comrade, like wild animals alive to danger.'

Just getting Lieutenant Colonel Jack Glennie's 1/Royal Sussex up into the hills proved a nightmare. The Red Eagles had to borrow almost 300 American six-wheeled trucks to bring all their supplies forward to dumps, then cross-load to mules, of which there were a hopelessly inadequate number. En route, two of the lorries carrying the Royal Sussex's spare mortar ammunition and hand grenades skidded into a ravine, losing the lot. Once there, the Sussex men were told to occupy Snakeshead Ridge, and its south-west tip, Point 593, which tired American staff officers assured them was in the hands of the Red Bulls Division. It was not, and it was soon clear that US II Corps headquar-ters had only the vaguest of notions as to where their men actually were.

On the ground, Glennie discovered in his sector the survivors of four battalions, from three different regiments, of two US divisions. John Buckeridge, lieutenant with 1/Royal Sussex, returning to the positions his C Company had inherited from the outgoing American 34th Division on Snakeshead Ridge, in the lee of the building that came to be known as the Doctor's House, recalled: 'They were exhausted, they had nothing left in them. There was no handover as such; they simply left everything – all their maps and equipment, weapons, machine guns, ammunition, rations – and stumbled off, half-asleep.' The positions they took over were little stone sangars no more than twelve to eighteen inches high. 'We soon found that during the hours of daylight we were prisoners up there, unable to put our heads over the top without being shot; I only realised this when soon after first light one of my corporals was shot in the head by a sniper, and during the morning my batman was shot and killed next to me while I was shaving.'

Signalman Smith and his section passed groups of 'American infantrymen slithering back down the hillside'. He reached his destination, 'a battered white farmhouse on a terraced hillside. The two Indian bearers quickly doffed their packs, bid us goodnight and disappeared. Just below the farm on a small terrace we could discern a line of sleeping figures with room to spare at the end. So we joined them, unrolled our waterproof bags and, dog tired, we promptly fell asleep.' Smith and his chums woke to laughter and 'looked to our left at the recumbent forms. They were all on stretchers with blankets over their faces and with their boots sticking out uncovered. We had slept with the dead, poor fellows. American dead.'

Once the Germans discovered the presence of the Indians, they devised and unleashed crude propaganda, in the form of printed leaflets, trying to split the cohesion of the Allied coalition effort. Often these featured a picture, such as a cartoon Churchill pushing a reluctant Indian soldier towards the front; Sahibs back in Raj mistreating Indians; the 'comfortable' life awaiting Indian POWs who deserted to the Germans; Britons 'robbing' India of its national wealth; or details of Subhas Chandra Bose and his Indian National Army. Given the assemblage of races, language and illiteracy was a problem. One typical accompanying text, available in Hundi, Urdu or Hindustani, read:

SOLDIERS OF THE 4TH INDIAN DIVISION! You have seen in the last attack on Cassino how many Indians have gone to permanent sleep. Looking at these miserable deaths, every human cries. This is the same place where the American forces attacked earlier and got a bloody nose. Where the American and British forces fail, the voiceless Indians are put in the front to be cannon fodder. Think a bit, what business have you got in Italy? Why are you unnecessarily making thousands of Indian children orphans and Indian women widows? Take advantage of the chance to quickly cross over to the German side. Spend your time in a German prisoner-of-war camp and at the end of the war go home safely. Your brothers are present here in the thousands.

Note: You can cross over to the Germans safely by showing this paper.

Another, blunter, leaflet threatened, 'Indian 4th Division – you are a target of our bullets. The Indians are led by Subhas Chandra Bose, who has formed an Indian Army in Germany to fight against the British.' The Germans were at a disadvantage because of the sheer number of ethnic opponents; besides the Indians, they had special leaflets for Poles, the French (with Moroccan and Algerian versions), South Africans, Canadians, Americans, New Zealanders and Britons. The 4th Indian Division's history noted of the German propaganda efforts: 'Often the Urdu leaflets reached the Royal Sussex and the English leaflets the 4/16th Punjabis; or else they both reached 1/2nd Gurkhas who could read neither.' The New Zealand Official History likewise observed how its troops 'often received leaflets in Urdu or Polish, or addressed to the "depressed lower classes of England".' An officer of the 3/Welsh Guards recalled that his men 'spoke in Welsh over the wireless on their arrival in Cassino; after about a week, the Germans showered us with leaflets, in Hundustani'.

This form of propaganda only had a chance of working on a static front like Cassino, but there is no evidence that any Indians deserted, as encouraged: the traffic was one way. Most nights, Wehrmacht soldiers trickled through the lines, a few (usually Russians and other East Europeans) responding to Allied air-dropped propaganda leaflets guaranteeing them safe passage. These were printed in English and German and labelled 'Passierschein [safe conduct pass]: The German soldier who carries this Safe Conduct is using it as a sign of his genuine wish to give himself up. He is to be disarmed, to be well looked after, to receive food and medical attention as required and to be removed from the danger zone as soon as possible. Signed, Alexander, Supreme Allied Commander, Mediterranean Theatre.' The Germans later countered these with identical leaflets, but aimed at their own troops, which read: 'The German soldier who carries this Safe Conduct is using it as a sign of his genuine wish to go into captivity for the next ten years, to betray his Fatherland, to return home a broken old man, and very probably never to see his parents, wife or children again.' Few were fooled.

At Anzio and Cassino the two sides fired huge volumes of paper (leaflets and pseudo-newspapers, printed by local psychological warfare units) at one another in specially adapted mortar and artillery shells, aerial leaflet 'bombs' and even hollowed-out rifle grenades. Though artillery-fired propaganda was often singed, leaflets of either side were eagerly sought, but for latrine purposes, not their literary content.

Deserters provided valuable insights into German morale, like the letter found on Austrian Hansi Rettensteiner of the 44th Hoch und Deutchmeister Division, written on 13 February, but never posted home. The Indian Division's intelligence officers quickly translated the pencilled scribbles on scraps of paper that young Comrade Rettensteiner (as he described himself) addressed to his family:

> I have had no post from you or anyone else for three weeks now. We are up on a mountain again with our mortars in a position 2km from the Americans. Yesterday I was over with the Americans . . . The infantry launched an attack the day before yesterday and suffered a lot of wounded and dead, and today we collected them with the Red Cross flag. We were very close to the American positions. The American soldiers gave us cigarettes and chocolate.
>
> Dear parents, I sent you a bar of chocolate. Did you get it ok?

Within days of their arrival, 4th Indian Division suffered an unforeseen setback when Major General Gertie Tuker succumbed to his recurrent rheumatoid arthritis, which no amount of penicillin could alleviate, and on 6 February he handed over command of his beloved division and retired to a base hospital at Caserta, near Alex's HQ. Ordinarily, forty-year-old Brigadier Harry Kenneth Dimoline, a Territorial officer, would never have expected to take command, even temporarily, of a division in combat, but there was no time to find a replacement. American divisions had assistant divisional commanders for situations such as these; the British did not, so Tuker handed over to the senior brigadier, his CRA (Commander, Royal Artillery). Although 'Dimo' Dimoline may have experienced as little as a two-week course on staff duties and higher command, he had commanded the divisional artillery from 1942, and been awarded a CBE and DSO – a sure mark of approval in an Eighth Army under Montgomery's command. Though 'poor Dimoline was having a dreadful time getting his division into position' up on the heights, there is plenty of evidence to suggest that Brigadier H. K. Dimoline was a perfectly competent and safe pair of hands for the Red Eagles at Cassino.

Tuker's replacement by Dimoline, and the string-and-sealing-wax nature of Freyberg's New Zealand Corps (with no dedicated corps staff) were two added pressures on Mark Clark, for whom the whole Italian campaign seemed to be unravelling, with Lucas making no headway at Anzio. Lucas's own breakout attempt had failed on 31 January, while at the same time two battalions of US Rangers were surrounded, killed or captured, at Anzio; a third Ranger battalion sent to rescue them also lost heavily. This seems to have sent more shockwaves around Allied headquarters than the general gloom about Lucas, for the Rangers were America's elite special forces, and half the total force had been destroyed in a day. Clark took this badly, as another blow to American prestige. Poor weather also negated effective air cover over Anzio and Cassino, reducing the campaigns to purely land-based affairs, in which the Germans appeared to have the upper hand. Mark Clark, with his eyes firmly on Anzio, and little rapport with the British or their Empire forces, left the details of how to continue the Cassino offensive to his new corps commander, Freyberg. For the Allies, there was a distinct pause while Freyberg worked through his options.

Before he departed for hospital, Tuker feared that Clark, Keyes, their staffs, and possibly Alexander and Freyberg, might have lost sight of the main aim (of forcing a withdrawal of the Germans, best achieved by encircling Cassino, via breakthroughs elsewhere) and that they had all become fixated with attacking and capturing Cassino and its abbey by frontal assault if necessary. Beforehand, Tuker had taken time out to discuss mountain warfare with Alphonse Juin, realising that the German defences were likely to be less formidable up on the higher ground around Monte Cairo because of the limitations of logistics. In fact, beyond Monte Cassino the general rule was the higher the terrain, the kinder it became, with fewer of the ferocious gullies and jagged ridges than there were around the abbey. Tuker, with his experience of mountain warfare in Waziristan and along the North West Frontier, firmly believed that the key to Allied success was a wide, anti-clockwise sweep through this less well-defended ground – the classic 'indirect approach', which would play to the strengths of his warriors, many of whom had been brought up in the Indian mountains. With three divisions on hand (the Indians, New Zealanders and British 78th) to push through the hills and charge up the Liri valley, this would have been a logical continuation of the previous American activity. Tucker had also envisaged a simultaneous attack across the Garigliano River to the south of Cassino, supported by the massed firepower of the Allies, concentrated on a single point.

Freyberg was initially very supportive, but his confidence began to wain the moment Tuker departed for hospital in Caserta, even though 'Gertie' was still sending missives from his sickbed. Freyberg was concerned (correctly) that the operation might come unstuck logistically, for sustainment in the hills was possible only by mule or human porter, and there were not enough for the proposed operation. In Tuker's absence, Freyberg backtracked, aware also that Clark had ordered a *direct* attack. This is where the lack of a corps staff really counted: with a dedicated chief of staff and good planning team, Freyberg's officers could have lobbied for Tuker's plan effectively to the prickly and hostile Clark.

Tuker was already in hospital when, on 9 February, General Freyberg, having deliberated his options, issued his tasks for the forthcoming attack. 'NZ Corps Operational Instruction No. 4' ordered 4th Division to 'attack and capture Monastery Hill and Point 593; exploit south to cut Route 6 and capture Cassino from the west'. This was the day the US 34th Division were battling hard for Point 593; while Freyberg could not have foretold the outcome, his plan bizarrely ignored any benefits that ownership of Point 593 might have conferred on the victors. For Freyberg had opted for a frontal assault of Cassino town and the monastery, something Tuker insisted should only be considered as a *last* resort. Tuker's plan called for an attack on the abbey itself from the north along the mountain ridges, coupled with another on the town from the south-east, over the Rapido and along the railway line. After the Cassino offensives Tuker would write: 'men were hurled time and time again against a mountain which had for centuries defied attack from the south and which in 1944 was not only the strongest position in Italy, but was held by the pick of the German troops in that theatre of war'. These 'were military sins, no less'.

As his beloved Red Eagles were to mount an unsubtle direct attack, Tuker felt obliged to prepare them as best he could, from afar, in his hospitable bed at Caserta. With Dimoline's full support he requested all information on the terrain and abbey from Keyes at II Corps and Fifth Army headquarters. He was perturbed to find they knew nothing. Any intercourse with Italian officials would have been deemed a breach of security, so Tuker despatched a subaltern to Naples to search the bookshops and libraries. He returned with two key books, among others, the *Baedeker Guide to Central Italy*, published in 1879, and another from 1920 that described up close the awesome dimensions of the monastery in depressing detail.

Made entirely of giant cubes of locally quarried limestone, in places the exterior walls of the abbey peaked at a hundred feet, were over thirty feet thick at the base, tapering to twelve feet higher up. Built on top of a warren of underground crypts and chapels, inside were four courtyards, the main church (basilica), a seminary, a boys' school, refectory, a huge library running the length of one side, workshops, a cemetery, kitchen garden and stone outbuildings for animals. The site included earlier Volscian and Roman structures, and had become the model for Benedictine abbeys, albeit on a smaller scale, around the world. Every day of the year, the monks gathered eight times a day in the carved walnut choir stalls of the basilica to observe their prayers and readings with Gregorian chant, beginning with Matins at midnight and Lauds at three in the morning, ending with Vespers at six in the evening, and Compline at nine.

Tuker opined that *if* his division had to make a direct assault on the abbey, the area needed to be flattened first, a view shared by Dimoline and his other brigadiers. Responding to Freyberg's orders of 9 February, Dimoline submitted a formal request to his corps commander on 11 February that the abbey be bombed. The following day, Tuker himself met Freyberg to support Dimoline's request, and let fly with two written memoranda, stating that *if* the direct assault was to go ahead then the entire Monte Cassino terrain, including Point 593, required to be 'roughed up' first by aircraft and land-based artillery, followed by immediate, coordinated infantry attacks. Significantly, he also reiterated the advantages of his original envelopment plan, bypassing the monastery altogether and obviating the need for any aerial bombardment. 'It is apparent that the enemy are in concrete and steel emplacements on Monastery Hill,' he wrote. 'From a wide experience of attacks in mountain areas I know that infantry cannot "jump" strong defences of this sort in the mountains. These defences have to be "softened up" either by being cut off on *all* sides and starved out or else by continuous and heavy bombardment over a period of days. Even with the latter preparation, success will only be achieved in my opinion if a thorough and prolonged air bombardment is undertaken with really heavy bombs a good deal larger than "Kitty-bomber" missiles.'

Tuker was referring to the American-built Curtiss P-40, known when in RAF service as the Kittyhawk. While they were in theory fighters, Kittyhawks were better suited to their other role of close air support, being slower and less manoeuvrable than Messerschmitt 109s or Focke-Wulf 190s. In Sicily a 'cab rank' tactic had been developed whereby fighters would loiter until directed onto a specific target, using map coordinates, by a Forward Air Controller based with the ground troops. Several twelve-plane Kittyhawk squadrons operated from Italy, including 3 Squadron, Royal Australian Air Force (RAAF), based on a temporary airstrip at Cutella, near Termoli on the Adriatic coast, 'a very pleasant strip built on the sand dunes and about half a mile inland from the sea which enabled the crews to go swimming in warm weather', remembered one pilot. In the summer months, 'crews slept on camp beds under mosquito nets draped over the wings of their aircraft'. It was at Cutella that 3 Squadron RAAF began experimenting with heavy bomb loads. Kittyhawks were able to carry one 500lb bomb or two 250lb bombs, but found that the central drop tank they carried for long-range missions could be substituted for a 1000lb bomb, which the fighter could carry for short distances, and the idea of the 'Kitty-bomber' was born.

For the air attack on the monastery, Tuker, as a scholarly student of ancient and modern warfare, knew precisely what was needed: blockbuster bombs 'applied directly from the air', concluding the 1,000lb bomb would be next to useless to effect this. What Tuker meant by a 'blockbuster' was the RAF's 4,000lb high-capacity bomb, otherwise known as 'cookies'. Ten feet long, blockbusters had no fins and were basically cylinders full of explosive. Accuracy was not important, as they were designed to create blast damage to buildings on a huge scale

– consequently they had to be dropped from above 5,000 feet. Tuker had already argued: 'Today, in Italy . . . the Boche is in steel and concrete: he has anti-tank and anti-personnel mines and plenty of anti-tank guns. Virtually the whole breakthrough of his positions must be done by infantry . . . If we intend to put infantry through we have only one means to do it and that is by the surprising weight of our fire. 1914–18 proved that artillery weapons will not give this effect. The only effect left to us is the weight of our air power and that *must* be used in its *fullest* weight and concentrated and coordinated with artillery and ground small arms. The blow *must* be in depth, division following division, armoured and infantry, and carried through *fast* by this great fire power, for the enemy has position after position on which to fall back.'

Angry and ill, Tuker's second memo to Freyberg concluded: 'When a formation is called upon to reduce such a place [as Monte Cassino abbey], it should be apparent that the place is reducible by the means at the disposal of that division or that the means are ready for it, without having to go to the bookstalls of Naples to find out what should have been fully considered many weeks ago.'

Once Tuker, Dimoline and Bernard Freyberg had between them determined on the military necessity of destroying the abbey, there arose the entirely fatuous debate as to whether the Germans were occupying the buildings, or not. Royal Sussex lieutenant John Buckeridge remains convinced to this day that he and his colleagues saw German troops moving in and out of the abbey. For Buckeridge – as for the tens of thousands of Allied soldiers in the neighbourhood – the sacred buildings had become sinister and malevolent; with its rows of small windows, wherever you went, 'there was the monastery watching you'. US Lieutenant General Ira C. Eaker, commander of the Mediterranean Allied Air Force, flew with his friend Jacob L. Devers (Jumbo Wilson's deputy) over the abbey on 14 February and reported that he did not see any German soldiers, though supposed they would have taken cover anyway. But in a subsequent interview, he claimed to have observed on the same flight 'a radio mast . . . German uniforms hanging on a clothesline in the abbey courtyard; machine-gun emplacements fifty yards from the abbey walls'.

The weather precluded much day-to-day accurate observation by the Allies, and while 14 and 15 February were clear days, the 13th had witnessed a blinding blizzard all day (in fact, rain, sleet or snow, depending on altitude), so that close understanding of the German positions was – at best – patchy. Signals intercepts, too, did not help: parent units and area locations cropped up in wireless transmissions, but not the detail of weapon types and numbers at specific grid references.

Perhaps Eaker and Devers had begun to believe their own propaganda, for on 10 February *The Times*, briefed by Caserta, had stated: 'The Americans are still stuck within a few hundred yards on the monastery. Their guns are careful not to make it a target. The Army command is mindful not only of the historical associations of the place, but of the precious manuscripts and art treasures from the university, library and museums of Naples which are believed still to be stored there. The Germans trade on this discrimination and our men can see wireless aerials established on the roofs and telescopes at the windows.'

The briefing from Allied Forces HQ that led to this article was blatantly misleading and demonstrably false. For the Allies already knew the art treasures of Cassino had long gone.

On 14 October 1943, two German officers had turned up separately at Monte Cassino abbey with the same goal, though probably differently motivated. Hauptmann Maximilian Becker, a Berlin doctor serving in the Hermann Göring Division, realised that the conflict erupting across Italy would soon engulf the peaceful valleys around Cassino, and that the cultural artefacts he knew to be stored in the historic abbey were in danger. He had realised there was simply nowhere else in the West where, over the centuries, some of the world's most important *objets d'art* had been accumulated as gifts, relatively unmolested, secure and away from the envious gaze of many. The library that Dickens admired had grown by 1943 to include over 40,000 books, illuminated manuscripts and ancient vellum scrolls with seals, including many secular works of Rome's earliest historians and philosophers. Priceless items were sent there for safekeeping from elsewhere, including the Neapolitan Royal collection of coins and medals – ranked one of the most significant in the world – and locks of hair and other treasures associated with the romantic poet John Keats, whose house in Rome, then preserved as a museum, was felt to be more at risk than the isolated abbey. Becker had observed the warning signs of the approaching battle; twice Allied bombs had hit the town, while the abbey's electricity and telephones had been cut by stray munitions and a thousand refugees had claimed sanctuary within the monastery's walls.

Days earlier, while setting up an aid post, Becker had discovered over 200 crates containing the archives of Naples Library hidden in a lesser Benedictine monastery in the area, and had them moved further out of harm's way. As Becker strode towards Abbot Gregorio Diamare's office, he was surprised to encounter Oberstleutnant Julius Schlegel, Hermann Goring's divisional transport maintenance officer, apparently there on the same mission. Both officers appealed separately to the abbot. The abbey's treasures needed to be evacuated, they said; the division's transport could be used to get the artworks and artefacts to safety. But the seventy-nine-year-old priest, who had overseen the Cassino community for thirty-four years, was adamant. The Allies would respect his domain, he was sure of it. Besides, he suspected the officers' motives. He feared they might seize the artworks and cart them off to the Fatherland to be presented as booty to their division's patron, Reichsmarschall Hermann Göring, a known hoarder of illegally seized art from across Europe. The answer was no.

Becker and Schlegel returned together the next day and, aided by a German monk, Father Emmanuel Munding, eventually overcame the abbot's scepticism. The German officers promised to deliver the abbey's treasures to Benedictine monasteries in Rome, and to the Italian government the Neapolitan art collection, hundreds of paintings from the *Museo Nazionale*, Naples – including works by Leonardo da Vinci, Raphael, Titian, Tintoretto, and Bruegel's *The Blind Leading the Blind*. Schlegel's motivation may have been the propaganda value of the act, or plain loot, but Becker, a north German Protestant, seems to have been more deeply attached to the idea of saving the artworks from destruction; both might have regarded their humane activities as an insurance policy against a future, non-Nazi, post-war world. After consulting with his monks, at a third meeting on 18 October, the abbot agreed to the evacuation of as many artefacts and artworks as possible, and most of the community's priests.

It was arranged that Schlegel's trucks – which each day brought loads to the front from the divisional supply depot at Spoleto, north of Rome, and usually returned empty – would drive back via Cassino and the Italian capital loaded with crates containing Monte Cassino's treasures. As time began to run out and the battle moved closer, Schlegel set up a crate-making workshop in the abbey, using his own men and some of the Italian refugees camping in the cloisters (the rest departed when invited by Schlegel to help with the evacuation or leave), whom he paid with food and cigarettes, while paintings and books were wrapped in the community's valuable tapestries and vestments. To assuage Abbot Diamare's concerns, Becker and Schlegel agreed for the first few trucks to include monks, who would send back receipts confirming their safe arrival. Subsequently, monks, Benedictine nuns from neighbouring convents and orphans in their care, also rode the eighty miles to Rome in each lorry. A Reich propaganda crew was employed to film and photograph every stage of this remarkable event – in case anyone mistook their activities for looting – and the 696th edition of Germany's weekly propaganda newsreel, *Die Deutsche Wochenschau*, in February 1944 was almost completely devoted to the heroic act, a gift from the Fatherland. It took less than three weeks and over a hundred lorry-loads to remove most of Monte Cassino's library, fine art and the Neapolitan paintings, and the abbey's most treasured relics: the remains of St Benedict himself.

Abbot Diamare was grateful and later presented the division's commander, Becker and Schlegel with illuminated Latin texts written on vellum as thanks. However, it took some diplomatic pressure from the timid wartime papacy to ensure that the most of the 180 cases of Neapolitan art removed to Spoleto eventually found their way into safekeeping at the Vatican. Even this did not stop fifteen crates of art treasures, perhaps a forgotten present for Goring, the division's honorary chief, finding their way into a Nazi cache where they were discovered deep in a salt mine in Austria in 1946.

As if preparing their readers for the worst, on 11 February *The Times* noted: German machine-gunners are 'known to be manning the road to the abbey of Monte Cassino, and men of the Fifth Army, groping their way up the slopes, have seen German machine-gunners along the abbey walls'. Days later the paper authoritatively informed its readers: 'On Monte Cassino, known to the army as Abbey Hill, above the town, enemy resistance is extremely stubborn. It is disclosed today that the Vatican authorities asked that the monastery at the crest of the hill, the cradle of the Benedictine order, should be spared. The Allies have complied with the request as far as possible, but the Germans are using the monastery as a fortress, its large buildings and massive walls forming an important part of their defences dominating the road to Rome below. The monastery has hitherto not been a target for the Allies' guns or bombers.'

German radio, while not mentioning the abbey, agreed that 'the situation in the last twenty-four hours has been dominated by the battle for Cassino, which is continuing with the utmost ferocity'. Hostile to any bombing was General Keyes of US II Corps, who also flew over the monastery several times, each time reporting he had seen 'no evidence of any Germans in the grounds'; furthermore, when informed of those who claimed to have seen Germans there, he stated, 'they've been looking so long they're seeing things'. Brigadier General J. A. Butler, deputy commander of the Red Bulls Division, likewise ventured: 'I don't believe the enemy is in the convent. All the fire has been from the slopes of the hill below the wall.' However, another argument in favour of destruction ran: 'If not occupied today, it might be tomorrow and it did not appear it would be difficult for the enemy to bring reserves into it during an attack or for troops to take shelter there if driven from positions outside. It was impossible to ask troops to storm a hill surmounted by an intact building such as this, capable of sheltering several hundred infantry in perfect security from shellfire and ready at the critical moment to emerge and counterattack ... Undamaged it was a perfect shelter but with its narrow windows and level profiles an unsatisfactory fighting position.'

Below Monte Cassino, an American artillery commander summed up the mood of his men: 'I don't give a damn about the monastery. I have Catholic gunners in this battery and they've already asked me for permission to fire on it, but I haven't been able to give it to them. They don't like it.' Freyberg was initially reluctant to forward Dimoline's request for the abbey's destruction, until pressurised by Tuker. When he did so at 7 p.m. on 12 February, Freyberg was seemingly unaware of the blast effect Tuker required, and requested a mission of an entirely different nature, asking for a strike by thirty-six P-40 Kittyhawks, in three waves of twelve, carrying 500lb bombs, a misreading of Tuker's memo earlier that same day, when the latter had stated specifically that 'Kitty-bombers' would be inadequate. This certainly underlines a fault either in Freyberg's own understanding or, more likely, a misunderstanding within his double-hatted and overworked staff. Many historians have subsequently laid the blame for the monastery's demise on Dimoline, Tuker or Freyberg, but this is an unfair judgement of the situation in which they found themselves: by insisting on an aerial attack against the abbey, Tuker (ironically still hoping for the direct assault to be cancelled and his indirect approach substituted) unwittingly opened up a controversy that has raged ever since.

To the troops on the ground the mission was entirely justified. Major Luther Wolff, a surgeon with the US 11th Field Hospital, summed up the view of most Allied troops at the time in his diary entry: 'The infantry boys that come in wounded tell us they are taking a terrific beating trying to save the monastery at Cassino and it makes everybody angry that the big boys insist on saving this building. We simply have to get over this sentimental fair-play, save-the-building attitude . . . the wounded GIs are universally in favour of knocking down the monastery.' The destruction-to-be was debated at the time in the world's press; the *Daily Telegraph*'s Christopher Buckley observed that beforehand, 'day after day the fullest publicity was given to the pros and cons of the bombing. It was widely discussed in press and radio. There was a good deal to be said on either side of the case, and publicists in Britain and America saw to it that nothing was left unsaid.' Despite Tuker's specific request for 'blockbusters', and Freyberg's for Kittyhawks, Ira C. Eaker's Mediterranean Allied Air Force (MAAF) had their own ideas. This was the air command organisa-tion for the Mediterranean, established on 10 December 1943, to ensure cooperation between the USAAF and the RAF, and coordinate the theatre's long-range strategic bombers (US Fifteenth Air Force), and tactical close air support aircraft of the US Twelfth Air Force. Both possessed bombers, and the two commands would contribute aircraft to the raid on Cassino abbey on the morning of 15 February. The forty-nine-year-old commander of the Twelfth, John K. Cannon, had pleaded with Alexander for the opportunity: 'If you let me use the whole of our bomber force against Cassino we will whip it out like a dead tooth.'

Recent military history is awash with the siren voices of air force commanders offering similar 'magic' solutions, but campaigns are never so simple. Even the timing was controversial. The raid was not coordinated with Freyberg's HQ, the MAAF considering it an independent mission to be undertaken when the weather permitted and aircraft could be released from supporting Anzio. Freyberg's HQ waited for details of the raid to coordinate it with an immediate attack by 1/Royal Sussex of the 4th Indian Division, who themselves were still toiling up the hills and into position. Consequently, the operation took place two days before the Sussex were ready to launch their ground assault.

For the first-ever mission of an Allied strategic bombing force supporting a tactical mission on land, Eaker, for his own reasons, laid on a raid of epic scale, by way of demonstration. In one of the most-advertised aerial bombing missions in history, Freyberg's thirty-six Kittyhawks with 18 tons of bombs had become 256 heavy and medium bombers (B-17 Flying Fortresses, B-25 Mitchells and B-26 Marauders) in fifteen waves, dropping 576 tons of munitions throughout the day. Not a single 'blockbuster' was included, but over 250 tons of irrelevant 500lb bombs (of which each B-17 could carry twelve), and 100lb incendiaries were also released, which had no effect on the abbey but killed Italian civilians and Allied soldiers in the vicinity. Troops and war correspondents had no inkling of this as they cheered, observing the spectacle, while between the raids, Allied artillery pounded the mountain.

More bombs were dropped the following day, but as correspondent Alan Whicker noted caustically, 'after the bombing the US Army Air Support Group reported enthusiastically, "A remarkable spectacle for many ground observers who were able to see that precision bombing is a fact, not merely an expression." Some 230 Italians died following this precision, but no monks and no Germans. At the same time the Allies received an early but bitter taste of American "friendly fire" which was to become notorious in later wars: the Eighth Army commander [Oliver Leese] lost his caravan headquarters three miles from Cassino, and the French Corps HQ [Alphonse Juin] twelve miles away was heavily bombed . . . Mark Clark was at his command post seventeen miles away when sixteen bombs exploded nearby.'

Such 'precision' bombing was already a private joke within the US Army: when Colonel Mark W. Boatner, commanding the US 168th Regiment, was warned beforehand that the monastery was to be hit by the USAAF, 'this caused him to push his cap to the back of his head, bite his cigar and with his hands on his knees regard us sympathetically over his steel-rimmed spectacles. "Waal" he said, "If it is incumbent arn you to depend on our barmers, and I wuz in your shoes, I'd hie me back to dear old Pittsburgh."'

This ridiculous overkill seems to have been the result of the Allied land and air forces failing to understand one another's capabilities and what each was trying to do. The air arm assumed the land component wanted the abbey removed from the map, as though a large and irritating enemy outpost, but instituted a raid as much to advertise their own capabilities. The ground forces needed their opponents suppressed by blast bombs and any shelter denied to the Germans, so they could mount an instant assault against their objectives. The real problem was that although the danger posed by the abbey to Mark Clark's forces had been foreseen for a long time, no decisions had been taken in advance. Indeed, throughout most of the inadequate decision-making process, the Roman Catholic Mark Clark and his chief of staff, forty-three-year-old Major General Al Gruenther, remained opposed to the concept. As early as 10 June 1943, the Combined US-UK Chiefs of Staff had reminded the then theatre commander, Eisenhower: 'Consistent with military necessity, the position of the church and of all religious institutions shall be respected and all efforts made to preserve the local archives, historical and classical monuments and objects of art,' while on 25 October 1943, Fifth Army HQ signalled to the Commander of Mediterranean Air Command, 'all possible precautions to be taken to avoid bombing abbey on Monte Cassino, due west of Cassino.' On 1 January 1944, Fifth Army told Alexander's HQ that 'our artillery commanders understand that neither churches nor houses of worship are to be fired on'.

The eventual operation was agreed via hurried telephone calls between commanders, rather than considered written orders. When Freyberg called Fifth Army with his request on the evening of 12 February,

Gruenther (the chief of staff) would not authorise anything in Clark's absence; neither would Alexander's chief of staff, John Harding, who was also consulted. Clark was eventually contacted and reiterated his opposition, but this was overridden by Alexander who stated through Harding that while he regretted the necessity for its destruction, he had confidence in Freyberg's judgement. Freyberg, however, was no ordinary corps commander; he carried additional clout as a national contingent commander of the other division (the New Zealanders) in his corps going into battle, and in his last phone conversation with Gruenther late on 12 February had issued a veiled threat. He did not believe that it would be 'sound to give an order to capture Monastery Hill and at the same time deny the commander the right to remove an important obstacle to the success of the mission . . . He stated that any higher commander who refused to authorise the bombing would have to be prepared to take the responsibility for a failure of the attack.'

Freyberg could get away with such blackmail not only on account of his dominating personality but because of this political power, which made him Clark's equal as the leader of a coalition military force. According to their various phone logs, Clark, Gruenther, Harding and Alexander discussed the issue again on the morning of 13 February, essentially arriving at the same conclusion, while Freyberg stuck to his view that the monastery needed to be bombed. Clark – clearly troubled – again discussed his concerns with Alexander on 14 February, where-upon Alex, possibly himself in need of reassurance, contacted the Supreme Commander, Mediterranean, Jumbo Wilson. Once Wilson approved Alex's request, the die was cast, but it is clear that Allied commanders at every level had misgivings – even, initially, Freyberg. However, once Freyberg's view had altered from reluctance to enthu-siasm for the demise of the abbey, he clung to his beliefs with dogged determination. Clark felt ill at ease in his presence and found him obstinate; Alex was probably in awe of his highly decorated First World War contemporary.

Thus, on the afternoon of 14 February, Allied artillery shells scattered leaflets containing a printed warning in Italian and English of the abbey's impending destruction. These were produced by the same US Fifth Army propaganda unit that normally peddled surrender leaflets and devised psychological warfare messages. The monks negotiated a safe passage through the German lines for 16 February – too late, as it turned out. American Harold Bond, of the 36th Texan Division, remembered the texture of the 'honey-coloured Travertine stone' of the abbey that fine Tuesday morning, and how 'the Germans seemed to sense that something important was about to happen for they were strangely quiet'. Journalist Christopher Buckley wrote of 'the cold blue on that late winter morning' as formations of Flying Fortresses 'flew in perfect formation with that arrogant dignity which distinguishes bomber aircraft as they set out upon a sortie'. John Buckeridge of 1/Royal Sussex, up on Snakeshead, recalled his surprise as the air filled with the drone of engines and waves of silver bombers, the sun glinting off their bellies, hove into view. His surprise turned to concern when he saw their bomb doors open – as far as his battalion was concerned the raid was not due for at least another day.

Brigadier Lovett of 7th Indian Brigade was furious at the lack of warning: 'I was called on the blower and told that the bombers would be over in fifteen minutes . . . even as I spoke the roar [of aircraft] drowned my voice as the first shower of eggs [bombs] came down.' At the HQ of the 4/16th Punjabis, the adjutant wrote: 'We went to the door of the command post and gazed up . . . There we saw the white trails of many high-level bombers. Our first thought was that they were the enemy. Then somebody said, "Flying Fortresses." There followed the whistle, swish and blast as the first flights struck at the monastery.' The first formation released their cargo over the abbey. 'We could see them fall, looking at this distance like little black stones, and then the ground all around us shook with gigantic shocks as they exploded,' wrote Harold Bond. 'Where the abbey had been there was only a huge cloud of smoke and dust which concealed the entire hilltop.'

The aircraft which committed the deed came from the massive resources of the US Fifteenth and Twelfth Air Forces (3,876 planes, including transports and those of the RAF in theatre), whose heavy and medium bombardment wings were based predominantly on two dozen temporary airstrips around Foggia in southern Italy (by comparison, a Luftwaffe return of aircraft numbers in Italy on 31 January revealed 474 fighters, bombers and reconnaissance aircraft in theatre, of which 224 were serviceable). Less than an hour's flying time from Cassino, the Foggia airfields were primitive, mostly grass affairs, covered with Pierced Steel Planking runways, with all offices, accommodation and other facilities under canvas, or quickly constructed out of wood. In mid-winter the buildings and tents were wet and freezing, and often the runways were swamped with oceans of mud which inhibited flying. Among the personnel stationed there was Joseph Heller, whose famous novel *Catch-22* was based on the surreal no-win-situation chaos of Heller's 488th Bombardment Squadron, 340th Bomb Group, Twelfth Air Force, with whom he flew sixty combat missions as a bombardier (bomb-aimer) in B-25 Mitchells.

After the first wave of aircraft struck Cassino monastery, a Sikh company of 4/16th Punjabis fell back, understandably, and a German wireless message was heard to announce: 'Indian troops with turbans are retiring'. Bond and his friends were astonished when, 'now and again, between the waves of bombers, a wind would blow the smoke away, and to our surprise we saw the gigantic walls of the abbey still stood'. Captain Rupert Clarke, Alexander's ADC, was watching with his boss. 'Alex and I were lying out on the ground about 3,000 yards from Cassino. As I watched the bombers, I saw bomb doors open and bombs began to fall well short of the target.' Back at the 4/16th Punjabis, 'almost before the ground ceased to shake the telephones were ringing. One of our companies was within 300 yards of the target and the others within 800 yards; all had received a plastering and were asking questions with some asperity.' Later, when a formation of B-25 medium bombers passed over, Buckley noticed, 'a bright flame, such as a giant might have produced by striking titanic matches on the mountain-side, spurted swiftly upwards at half a dozen points. Then a pillar of smoke 500 feet high broke upwards into the blue. For nearly five minutes it hung around the building, thinning gradually upwards.'

Nila Kantan of the Royal Indian Army Service Corps was no longer driving trucks, as no vehicles could get up to the 4th Indian Division's positions overlooking the abbey, so he found himself portering instead. 'On our shoulders we carried all the things up the hill; the gradient was one in three, and we had to go almost on all fours. I was watching from our hill as all the bombers went in and unloaded their bombs; soon after, our guns blasted the hill, and ruined the monastery.' For Harold Bond, the end was the strangest, 'then nothing happened. The smoke and dust slowly drifted away, showing the crumbled masonry with fragments of walls still standing, and men in their foxholes talked with each other about the show they had just seen, but the battlefield remained relatively quiet.'

The abbey had been literally ruined, not obliterated as Freyberg had required, and was now one vast mountain of rubble with many walls still remaining up to a height of forty or more feet, resembling the 'dead teeth' General John K. Cannon of the USAAF wanted to remove; ironically those of the north-west corner (the future target of all ground assaults through the hills) remained intact. These the Germans, sheltering from the smaller bombs, immediately occupied and turned into excellent defensive positions, ready to slaughter the 4th Indian Division when they belatedly attacked. As Brigadier Kippenberger observed: 'Whatever had been the position before, there was no doubt that the enemy was now entitled to garrison the ruins, the breaches in the fifteen-foot-thick walls were nowhere complete, and we wondered whether we had gained anything.'

The bombing was headline news around the world. While the never-forceful Pope Pius XII in the Vatican was strangely silent for three full days, Berlin was not slow to exploit the propaganda opportunities. 'According to information, the Benedictine abbey of Cassino has been in flames since the American attack this morning,' German radio swiftly reported. 'As there were no German troops in the monastery or its vicinity at the time of the bombardment,' the broadcast continued, 'there was no one available to fight the fire, and the venerable building could not be saved.' Despite their worldwide campaign of sacking and plundering, the Germans wasted no time decrying the Allies as 'desecrators of European culture', while propaganda leaflets describing the Allied 'War Against Art' were widely distributed by the War Department of Mussolini's minuscule republic in Salò. Iris Origo, an Anglo-American writer married to an Italian nobleman in Tuscany, recalled hearing Abbot Diamare's broadcast: 'quietly, in a tired and saddened tone, he told the story as if it had happened a hundred years ago. It was terribly moving and I can hardly imagine what the Benedictines from the monastery now scattered all over the world must have felt in hearing that quiet, heartfelt account of the end of that source of civilisation – now, after fourteen centuries of religious life, buried for ever.'

Were the Germans ever in the abbey? Two days after the bombing at first light Abbot Diamare led the surviving monks and civilian refugees who had sought sanctuary with him down to a German first-aid post. On 18 February, he was interviewed personally by one of his lay brethren, Fridolin von Senger – commander of XIV Panzer Corps – at the latter's new HQ in Castelmassimo, near Frosinone, twenty-eight miles up the Liri valley from Cassino. During the meeting, recorded for German radio, Diamare confirmed that the abbey had been declared by Senger 'a protected zone', from which German troops, weapons, and observation posts were banned. Diamare concluded: 'Until the moment of the destruction of the Monte Cassino abbey there was within the area . . . neither a German soldier, nor any German weapon, nor any German military installation.' Two abbey officials later signed declarations to the same effect.

Kesselring and Senger had indeed stipulated a 300-yard neutral zone around the abbey in December 1943, but this alone did not protect the religious complex from misdirected random shells (Allied and German), of which several hundred had fallen in and around the abbey even before the battle commenced. Recent research suggests that two caves and other locations within the military-free zone (but not inside the abbey) were used to store munitions, as headquarters and observation posts. The monks' own records indicate the neutral zone was abolished by the Germans on 5 January, but that they continued to respect the abbey buildings, from which troops, weapons and military equipment were banned with a *Feldgendarmerie* guard at the gate. This only ended with the bombing of 15 February.

Alex's ADC, Captain Rupert Clarke, writing in 2000, believed that 'Senger was a very devout Catholic and would never have breached' the protected zone, but more significantly cited evidence gained from Alex's GSO1 (Intelligence), Colonel David Hunt, of a misinterpreted radio intercept. A parachute commander had been heard to ask, '*Ist Abt in Kloster?*' and was answered, '*Ja in Kloster mit Mönchen.*' The intelligence officer who received the intercept only recorded the answer 'Yes' from the enemy. The translation then produced was 'Is the HQ in the abbey?' the word '*Abt*' being taken as an abbreviation for '*Abteil*' (a battalion or unit) rather than abbot. It was only when Colonel Hunt questioned the translation and the whole intercept that it transpired that the correct reply to the question was, in fact '*Ja, Abt in Kloster mit Mönchen*' – 'Yes. The Abbot is in the monastery with the monks.' Tragically this discovery was made too late.

Nevertheless, there had been a widespread and sincere belief among the Allies at the time that the Germans had occupied the monastery. For instance, Hermione, Countess of Ranfurly, private secretary to Jumbo Wilson, Supreme Commander in the Mediterranean, recorded in her diary on the day of the bombing: 'Today, after dropping leaflets warning Italian civilians to evacuate, we have blitzed the old Benedictine monastery at Monte Cassino. It stands high above the town of Cassino and the Germans installed there can see every movement on the plain below and rake our advance with terrible fire.' She did, however, acknowledge, in a footnote when her diary was eventually published after the war, 'as we later discovered, there were no Germans at Cassino before it was bombed'. The real truth of the matter is that the debate as to whether the Germans actually occupied the abbey is irrelevant: the moment the Allies decided to attack Cassino, whatever their tactics, the religious settlement was doomed.

The Allies quickly felt under pressure to justify their actions and senior politicians were rolled out to brief the press in the days after the bombings. *The Times* reported: 'As an indication of the reluctance with which the Allied command ordered the bombing of the Benedictine abbey at Cassino, President Roosevelt read at his press conference today two orders issued by General Eisenhower on 29 December last, concerning the protection of historic monuments.' Radio Berlin seized on this report the next day, 17 February, broadcasting of 'a senseless lust of destruction . . . The monastery has been destroyed several times, but then it was by barbarians . . . Today these barbarians are called British and Americans. One cannot help asking how Roosevelt will explain the destruction of such sacred religious places to his Catholic electorate.' That the Allied justifications were swallowed at the time is evidenced by 'Mr Richard Brown', an 'ordinary member of the public' on Britain's home front, who kept a private diary throughout the war and recorded on 18 February: 'at Cassino on the Fifth Army front, a Benedictine monastery stands on a hilltop, literally. Jerry used it for OP and for light artillery to our discomfort as it commanded the road to the north-west. We objected and tried to ignore it, then sent leaflets warning any Italians there that we would have to shell it. Next day lots of Fortresses bombed it. It's a big pity as the interior was a wonderful example of marble and ornamentation but couldn't be helped. Naturally it created worldwide interest.'

It must have been gut-wrenching for all concerned to read in *The Times* the following day that after the first phase of the subsequent attack involving the Indian and New Zealand divisions units, and after heavy enemy counterattack, 'the position remains unchanged'.

7

The Empire Strikes Back

W ITH THE GERMAN defenders temporarily disorientated, dazed and most likely shellshocked in the moonscape of craters that had been the abbey, Brigadier Dimoline, under pressure from Freyberg, was adamant that his 4th Indian Division – though unprepared – should still attack as soon as possible afterwards. Freyberg had put his moral authority on the line and was appalled that the area had not yet been molested. The nearest battalion, 1/Royal Sussex, were ordered to throw something together for that night, 15/16 February, not against the monastery as originally planned but at the dominating Point 593, from their positions a mere seventy yards away on Snakeshead Ridge. Only one company was in a position to assault, and, unable to reconnoitre the ground beforehand, this attack, though boldly executed, failed, losing two officers and eighteen men.

The failure was nobody's fault, except the early arrival of the bombers. As their CO Jack Glennie noted later: 'We needed forty-eight hours for recce, planning, building up our ammunition supply . . . oblique aerial photos of the objective were a real necessity but were not available. However, we got on with it because we were told we must do something to take the pressure off the Anzio beachhead . . . and we had so far always been successful.' The following night they tried again, this time in battalion strength, but due to the complicated topography of the area, some of the Sussex men were hit by their own supporting artillery as they formed up. Perhaps the international dimension of the huge Allied artillery resources available created the conditions for such friendly-fire confusion, as one of the Indian Division's gunners noted: 'From battery to battery I heard every conceivable accent – American, British, New Zealand. Elsewhere orders cackled in Polish and French. Then like the opening phrase of a colossal symphony the guns roared in unison. The night was pricked with belching flames; across the valley stabs of light against the mountainside showed where the shells struck.'

Terrain dictated an advance on a single company front, and they soon ran into Fallschirmjäger on and around Point 593, who were alert and prepared. The Sussex reached the heights but in the dark, the defenders had the advantage and drove them off: over the two nights, 1/Royal Sussex lost twelve out of fifteen officers and 162 out of 313 men – a casualty rate of nearly fifty-four per cent of their fighting element.

Preparations for another attack over much the same ground, this time by the rest of 7th Indian Brigade, on a third consecutive night were hampered logistically. Of 200 mules that set out from Caira village to supply the assault wave, only twenty animals survived the gauntlet of German harassing fire on the approach routes. Having lost the element of surprise, the 4/6th Rajputana Rifles hit Point 593, while the 1/2nd Gurkhas moved forward on their left, over the ground now largely occupied by the Polish cemetery – a series of appalling slopes and ravines overlooked by the monastery. In combat, the cultural differences between British and Indian melted away: their respective lives were, after all, equally threatened by the same bullets and shells. Lance Corporal F. S. Simons, on sentry duty supporting the Indian Division as they collected for their next assault, recalled the extreme tension of the moment: 'The night was pitch black, not a light anywhere, and certainly no cigarette-ends burning red like an inviting target. I was on sentry duty, alone, afraid and numb. All feeling lost from the freezing cold and the thin icy driving rain. Then a tap on my shoulder – it was my mate Baz, one of the Indian soldiers with a cup of his special *chai* [tea]. Not a word spoken except through his eyes, understanding, caring, knowing. We probably couldn't have talked to each other anyway: just me and Baz, in his turban with his special *chai*.'

Both battalions, though slowed by the terrain, thorn bush, barbed wire and devilish anti-personnel mines scattered liberally about, counter-attacked. The 1/9th Gurkhas of 5th Indian Brigade were also called forward and managed to get as far as the area of the present-day Polish cemetery, almost under the walls of the abbey, but found themselves marooned there at daybreak, withdrawing at dusk on 18 February. Terrain prevented the deployment of large units and the Indian Division's tactics of small attacks against single positions exposed them to enfilading fire from others. It also allowed the Germans to work out the likely Allied objectives, using their well-sited observation posts from the ruins of the abbey – and move in reinforcements accordingly.

Despite the fact that the Gurkhas had been brought up in mountainous terrain, the three actions had brought Dimoline no closer to success. He might have conferred with Juin on this point, whose Algerians, Moroccans and Tunisians had found the going just as tough. Altogether, for no progress, 4th Indian Division had suffered 603 casualties, badly smashing up four good battalions. While the Indians had been attacking the heights, the New Zealanders had moved against Cassino town. Freyberg paused to devise a new stratagem. Although the Germans detected little pause (and consider the second and third battles as one), for the Allies this welcome breather marked the end of the second battle for Cassino.

At this stage, the struggle at Anzio was reaching a climax, for on 16 February the Germans launched a new offensive, Operation *Fischfang*, and for two days it seemed they would break through. By throwing all reserves into their defence, US VI Corps managed to halt the German thrust at a cost of 3,500 casualties, to the Germans' 5,400. Both sides paused, exhausted. Offshore, the light cruiser HMS *Penelope* was sunk with a loss of 417 lives.

Against this backdrop, and even though Alexander's chief of staff John Harding had begun to put together the seeds of Operation Diadem, which would become the fourth battle for Cassino, there was great pressure all the way from Churchill, whose idea Anzio was, via Alexander and Clark, for Freyberg to continue to push at Cassino. At the same time another pressure on Clark was removed, for he had also been earmarked to command the Allied landings in southern France, originally code-named Operation Anvil, scheduled to take place simultaneously with Normandy. Initially southern France was to take priority over operations in Italy, and troops transferred from the latter campaign to enable the former. But on 29 February, Clark was told that he would stay in Italy, and no longer had to concern himself with the Anvil plans. By mid-March, the US-UK Combined Chiefs of Staff also conceded that there was no advantage to be gained in denuding the Italian front, and the timings for Anvil were allowed to slip. Renamed Operation Dragoon, the landings would eventually take place on 15 August, commanded by Jumbo Wilson's deputy, Jacob. L. Devers.

For the renewed effort at Cassino, Freyberg came up with the code-name Operation Dickens, after the Englishman who had visited the area a hundred years before. The new offensive recognised the extreme diffi-culty of attacking the monastery from the heights, so the axis of assault was shifted to a two-pronged effort against the town itself, orientated from the north. Freyberg's two divisions (4th Indian and 2nd New Zealand) were to withdraw while the town was attacked from the air, then 5th Indian Brigade were to advance from Caira against the lower heights overlooking the town, take Castle Hill and the zigzag bends in the road leading to the abbey, while 6th New Zealand Brigade were to move against the northern edge of the town itself. The Indians were to provide fire support for the New Zealanders from their elevated positions, and then to assault and capture the monastery itself (assessed by Freyberg less important) from Hangman's Hill (Point 435). In peace-time a funicular cable car had run from the town to a pylon just outside the abbey; its cable had been accidentally severed before the fighting by a German aircraft and now the upper pylon, in the grim humour of the troops in the valley, seemed to beckon like an executioner's gibbet – hence Hangman's Hill. Operation Dickens optimistically also extended to plans for the US 1st Armoured Division to capture objectives far up the Liri valley.

On 19 February, Freyberg briefed his army commander, Mark Clark, on Operation Dickens. Clark was 'shocked' that Freyberg intended an exploitation down the Liri valley without either flank secured. This throws light on Bernard Freyberg in two respects: it underlines the poverty of his corps planning without a dedicated staff, and it suggests limitations in his own tactical and operational abilities. The upshot was that Freyberg modified his plan to include the capture of the abbey. Given the lack of success in using such methods to date, it is surprising that Freyberg again opted for another aerial bombing programme – this time against Cassino town. USAAF officers had advised him that the likely effect of flattening the town would be to enable his infantry to advance through its wrecked streets only with extreme difficulty, and that armour would not be able to operate in it 'for at least a couple of days'. Freyberg's attitude was dismissive, while he also expected bull-dozers to open movement corridors through the rubble.

Freyberg issued his orders for Operation Dickens on 22 February, envisaging a start two days hence; however, the weather intervened constantly, forcing repeated postponement of Dickens. Three days of good weather were required for the ground to dry out enough to bear armoured vehicles, and the start day had to be clear enough for the vast airfleet to operate from Foggia. On 23 February it began to pour down, and did not stop for most of the next three weeks, meaning sleet and snow for shivering troops in the heights. Freyberg, a passionate sportsman, chose the surname of the most famous cricketer of the day, Australian Don Bradman, as his codeword to initiate Dickens. Each afternoon at 4 p.m., Freyberg's troops waited for the signal 'Bradman is batting tomorrow', but for twenty-one successive afternoons, until 14 March, they received only 'Bradman not batting' messages. Troops in the 19th NZ Armoured Regiment remembered that security suffered so much that even the local Italians were soon asking, 'Dickens tomorrow?' There were poor jokes about the weather, which was invariably either as 'cold as the Dickens' or as 'wet as the Dickens', 'but every bambino knew that an assault on Cassino was brewing and that Dickens was the codename for it'. Other Italian labourers working around British bases got to know of the codeword and began to joke that '*Signore* Bradman would not be batting today.'

Despite the lull in offensives, sniper activity, patrols, shelling and sickness continued daily and eroded the waiting troops (an average daily toll of forty to fifty casualties, noted the Indian divisional history), while 7th Indian Brigade were forced to remain in their sangars, alongside the dead up on Snakeshead Ridge. Modern troops in adverse conditions have the advantage of scientifically designed warm, windproof and waterproof clothing, but at Cassino in 1944 there was none of this: the only protection against the elements was a sleeveless leather jerkin issued to British and Indian soldiers, blankets and greatcoats. The greatcoats, which became heavy when wet and froze in the cold, were often left behind, especially if the choice was between bearing the weight of a sodden coat or extra ammunition. Scraps of soldiers' greatcoats – identifiable by their buttons – can still be found wedged in the rocks around Cassino, evidence of last desperate attempts to stay warm in those hellish winter months of 1944.

The pause enabled 4th Indian Division to achieve a lasting monument to their presence at Cassino. During February, the Royal Indian Engineers of 4th Field Company upgraded a five-mile mule track leading from Caira village steeply uphill through the heights to the north-east and north, out of sight and beyond the abbey. This recognised that the umbilical cord of vital logistics to sustain Allied formations in the hills could not rely on an old, precipitous mountain path, which had greatly constrained the offensive activities of previous divisions. Named 'Cavendish Road', after an earlier Royal Engineers commander, the track was reworked from a few inches to a width of eight feet, with hardcore and drainage, so it could take jeeps. With the continued delay of Operation Dickens, at the end of the month Freyberg's HQ directed the path be widened to take armour and heavily laden trucks. The 6th New Zealand Engineer Company joined three Indian ones in the work, cutting into the mountainsides with bulldozers, explosives and compressed-air drills, and building culverts over several streams that coursed downhill. The very creditable (and lasting) result was a road twelve feet wide.

Meanwhile, the Germans had taken advantage of the lull to complete a relief of units in the sector, bringing in all of 1st Fallschirmjäger Division, led by forty-five-year-old Generalleutnant Richard Heidrich. Whereas various sub-units of 1st Fallschirmjäger had previously been trickled into the Cassino sector, supporting 90th PanzerGrenadier Division under Senger's friend, Ernst-Günther Baade, the entire Fallschirmjäger Division was now committed, with the monastery and town under a single, unified headquarters. This takeover was gradual, allowing the incomers to familiarise themselves with the terrain. Formally in command of Cassino from 26 February, Heidrich had a glowing record and many decorations; he had seen action in the First World War, and had risen faster than many in the inter-war period. He commanded the German Army's first parachute battalion and, transferring to the Luftwaffe, landed on Crete in May 1941, before serving on the Leningrad front.

There were changes afoot in the Allied camp, also. On 9 March, Brigadier Dimoline (only temporarily commanding the Red Eagles) returned to his duties as Commander, Royal Artillery, and was relieved by Major General Alexander 'Sandy' Galloway, a forty-eight-year-old Scot, former Staff College student of Montgomery's and lieutenant colonel commanding the 1/Cameronians in 1939. He had commanded a brigade in North Africa and was 'on loan' from 1st Armoured Division in Tunisia, whom he was training for combat, when the call came to take over 4th Indian Division. The need to steal a commander from another active division illustrates the small pool available of suitable divisional commanders in the British Army at that precise moment; the most able candidates were being pinched by Montgomery in preparation for Overlord, three months hence. Meanwhile, the ground at Cassino remained too saturated for either armour or any form of meaningful logistics; the airfields around Foggia, too, were waterlogged. In the event, Freyberg's second aerial attack – this time focused on the town – erupted on 15 March.

The bombing was also the trigger for the 5th Indian Brigade of the Red Eagles to attack the heights overlooking the town. Although Freyberg planned for the two divisions to act in concert with one another, because of the terrain and German resistance, the Indians' battle on the hill was fought completely independently from that of the New Zealanders, a few hundred yards away, down in the town. The key, in Galloway's mind, to getting his 5th Indian Brigade up the hillside to the abbey was the small foothill overlooking Cassino town known as Rocca Janula (Point 193), on which sat an old castle. A hairpin bend of the zigzag road leading to the monastery was cut into the rock nearby. Sandy Galloway reasoned that if he could use the castle as a base, he could feed battalions up the hillside, leapfrogging via the hairpins, each of which offered some cover. His objective was to feed a striking force up to Hangman's Hill, using the castle as a stepping stone, sufficient to seize the abbey, and in concert with a surprise tank attack on the far side of the building on 19 March, making use of the newly enlarged Cavendish Road.

Thus on 15 March, hard on the heels of the aircraft tasked to bomb Cassino town into extinction, came the Kiwi infantry companies, one of whom was to take Castle Hill. Following them in the vanguard of the Indian Division was one of its British battalions, 1/4th Essex, who would garrison the castle and the first hairpin bend beyond, Point 165. While the 1/4th Essex secured their patch of hill, the 1/6th Rajputana Rifles had been assigned to pass through and take the next two hairpin bends, Points 202 and 236; the third battalion of the Indian Brigade, 1/9th Gurkha Rifles, were then to move beyond to capture Hangman's Hill and the abbey.

Although the day had been clear enough for the bombing, at dusk the downpour began again, turning the town, through which the Indians had to navigate, into a sticky mass of rubble, wood and metal, while the slopes became a treacly morass of mudslides and wet rocks. The poor weather and inky night sky made for zero visibility, unless one side or the other sent up signal flares. For the Indians this made any progress up the hillside agonisingly snail-like. Major George Nangle had just turned thirty-eight and was the fourth generation of his family to serve in the Indian Army. Born in India but schooled in England, he had graduated from Sandhurst in 1925, where he won the Quetta Cup awarded to the best cadet going into the Indian Army. Now as CO of 1/9th Gurkhas he had to get his battalion up to Hangman's Hill, but recalled the nightmare of just getting through the town. 'The place was an unbelievable mess after the bombing. There was no vestige of a road or a track, only vast heaps of rubble out of which peered the jagged edges of wall. The whole of this mess was covered by huge, deep craters that needed hand and foot climbing to get in and out of . . . we could only make for that part of the jumble that seemed to be nearest to the castle.'

The 1/4th Essex managed to reach the castle by 5 p.m., taking over from the New Zealand company who had secured it. However, given an over-ambitious plan and the ferocity of the terrain and the defence, the Rajputana Rifles ('the Raj Rifs') were not able to secure either of their hairpin object-ives: German artillery caught their two rear companies, leaving the remainder of the battalion to struggle as far as the castle. The 1/9th Gurkhas, behind the Raj Rifs, had to wait for those ahead to ascend, so that by dawn on 16 March they found them strung out across the hillside on their way up to Hangman's Hill, but with C Company under Captain Michael Drinkall, *Jemadar* (Lieutenant) Manbahadar Adhikari and *Subedar* (Captain) Jaibahadar Chand having reached their objective, despite being under mortar fire. They would remain there for the next nine days.

Daylight brought unwanted attention from Fallschirmjäger snipers to all three battalions, and when the 1/6th Rajputana Rifles broke cover to launch a second attack on the third hairpin (Point 236), they came under withering fire, and an unlucky mortar round caught the battalion HQ, wounding their commanding officer. Later on a New Zealand platoon managed to seize the second hairpin, Point 202 (later joined by some Rajputanas and stray Essex), while another Raj Rif attack finally secured the third hairpin at 7 p.m., but lost it the following morning, retreating to the castle. It was only late in the afternoon of 16 March that C Company of the 1/9th Gurkhas were able to advise Major Nangle, now back down in the town, of their position at Hangman's, and the rest of the battalion then hurried to reinforce them. Lieutenant Jack Miles of the 1/9th Gurkhas recalled at this stage that his company commander, Major Paddy Radcliffe, simply 'went missing. I was with him in B Company HQ when he left to traverse no more than fifty yards of ruined streets and buildings for a CO's conference in Battalion HQ. He never arrived. Nobody saw him fall, nobody heard anything to indicate what had happened and his disappearance was one of the mysteries of the war to my mind. It was later presumed that he had been killed by a sniper. It led to my taking command of B Company.'

The Gurkhas joined the Essex in the castle at 4 a.m. on 17 March, then pushed up to Hangman's Hill, just in time to repulse a Fallschirmjäger attack, then secure their prize. Although Galloway was under pressure (from Freyberg and Clark) to use his Gurkhas to assault the monastery, he knew they needed access to reinforcements and supplies to have a hope of taking and keeping such a strong position. He was adamant that a supply route be opened to Hangman's Hill, which required the town to be secured. To supplement whatever ammunition and rations could be carried up to Hangman's, in the first of many similar missions aircraft dropped parachute supply containers onto the Gurkhas' position, guided by coloured smoke. A fair proportion of these landed on target, but slithered down the slope out of reach. To retrieve them in daylight invited certain death, but similar supply drops continued over the next few days, prompting the Germans to fire coloured smoke flares all over the slopes to confuse the Allied planes. All the troops marooned on Hangman's recall the shortage of food and water. Some canteens were filled in nearby shell craters – there was no shortage of rain – but the practice ceased when dead bodies were discovered below the water level.

On the night of 17/18 March, two companies of 4/6th Rajputanas managed to carry up more supplies (the ascent between the castle and Hangman's Hill took them three hours) but were unable to return in daylight. With them, commanding D Company, was Tom Simpson who recalled being shelled on the way up and splattered with pieces of dead mule and blood. Echoing Major Nangle's experience of the town, just to reach Castle Hill and the route to Hangman's, Simpson had to navigate his column of porters and mules through the stinking remnants of Cassino. 'Here the going became very difficult with the rubble from shattered buildings and bomb craters to contend with. As I skirted one stricken NZ tank, its gun at a drunken angle, I stepped off the edge of a huge crater, pitching forward to end wedged in the twisted metal of a bedstead. Struggling to free myself, as my men ringed the rim of the crater looking for me, I clawed my way up and we passed on until I was able to locate the tape marking a route up to the castle.'

At the castle, Simpson's porters refused to move any further; 'there was nothing for it but to offload everything and, draping ourselves with as many bandoliers as we could carry, together with other supplies, we set off. As we neared Hangman's Hill the Gurkhas guided us through their positions with little hisses of welcome.' Meanwhile the 1/4th Essex in the castle remained vulnerable. The position was completely over-looked by German snipers and machine-gunners on Monastery Hill. Tom Simpson remembered them 'pouring multi-coloured tracer down into the courtyard, the red, green and orange bullets bouncing off the walls and ground alike'. Even the gateway was under hostile observation, so any movement could only be made at night, and on the evening of 18 March, some Essex were killed by friendly tank fire, misdirected from the town. Some men were buried; the bodies of others were thrown down the cliff face. To expand his grip on Hangman's, in order to use it as a springboard to seize the abbey, on the fourth night of the battle, 18/19 March, General Galloway sent his Rajputanas up to relieve the Essex in the stone-walled fortress, who in turn were to move up to join the 1/9th Gurkhas at Hangman's.

The Fallschirmjäger's commander, General Heidrich, was by now aware of the threat to the abbey from the troops ensconced at Hangman's Hill. He had also worked out that the Gurkhas were completely reliant for supplies, reinforcements and casualty evacuation on the logistics chain that ran through the castle. Heidrich reasoned correctly that to recapture the castle would undermine the whole Allied assault, for from there fire could also be brought to bear on the town. At about 5.30 a.m. on Sunday 19 March, just as the Rajputanas had taken over at the castle and first hairpin and two Essex companies were moving up towards Hangman's, a significant Fallschirmjäger counterattack broke and streamed down the hillside. Initially the oncoming soldiers were thought to be an Indian carrying party until the shape of their helmets was noticed. The paratroops simply steamed through two platoons of Essex and Rajputanas in the open, surrounding a mixed body from the two battalions in the castle keep, numbering about 150. Inside were two Essex majors, Frank Ketteley, of A Company, and Dennis Beckett, commanding C (the other two companies were by now climbing up to Hangman's Hill), some sappers, a gunner OP party and six Fallschirmjäger prisoners, including a sergeant major. Intense machine-gun fire swept the castle for about ten minutes. 'I have never known anything like it. It came from every angle,' Major Beckett wrote later.

With supporting fire from above, the troops of 1st Battalion/4th Fallschirmjäger Regiment threw themselves at the castle walls several times but could not break in, each wave being preceded by ferocious machine-gun fire and grenades, and repelled in the same manner. Beckett, then twenty-six and commanding C Company of the 1/4th Essex remembered that: 'The first attack very nearly succeeded. One or two tried to penetrate the courtyard and many were stopped only a few yards from the walls. We broke him up with Mills grenades, Tommy guns and Brens. The lull did not last very long. The enemy had taken advantage of his first push to occupy very favourable ground and this time began with a shower of stick grenades . . . Defensive fire was therefore laid on very close in, and as the [third] attack started a "blunderbuss" of artillery, mortars, medium machine guns and small arms was brought to bear.'

These skirmishes took on a medieval twist as Bren gunners fired at their opponents through arrow slits, paratroopers attempted to climb the walls, and at 9.20 a.m., part of the north-west wall was destroyed by a demolition charge, burying twenty-two of the defenders. However, all the Fallschirmjäger trying to enter via the breach were cut down in a hail of hand grenades, and Bren, Sten and Thompson sub-machine-gun fire, though Major Ketteley was wounded in the head; 'we talked a bit and then he died', recalled Beckett. Support Company of 1/4th Essex were stationed on the Fallschirmjäger's left, atop Point 175, and directed mortars and enfilading Vickers machine-gun fire, while friendly tank from the town was used to prevent the Fallschirmjäger from completely encircling the castle.

After three attempts, the violent assaults ebbed, by which time those in the castle had fired over 8,000 rounds and 1,500 mortar bombs, but every Essex officer had been killed or wounded (Beckett was hit three times). The Germans had lost almost 200 out of 250 attackers. However, the attitude of the six Fallschirmjäger prisoners altered remarkably in these strange circumstances. All except the sergeant major volunteered as stretcher-bearers, two of whom were killed while bringing in casualties. Another threw Major Beckett out of the line of fire of a sniper he had noticed, saving the former's life from the attentions of a colleague. Perhaps evidencing a form of shellshock, or it might have been bonhomie, the German sergeant major 'disdaining cover, walked in the open with the air of a supervisor of events. When the [last] attack was beaten off he congratulated Major Beckett on a soldierly performance and presented the Essex officer with his fur-lined paratrooper gauntlets as a trophy of the occasion.'

That afternoon, at about 3.30 p.m. a truce was arranged for both sides to evacuate their casualties. Several traces were arranged during the fighting in the town and on the hillside, in daylight hours. Such respites took time to organise because aircraft, artillery, snipers and machine gunners all had to be warned to hold their fire. These temporary interruptions to combat were much welcomed, not only as a means to recover and swap casualties (sometimes stretchers were loaned for the purpose) but in the unforgiving terrain medicines, food, water and cigarettes were also exchanged.

Although the German attack had failed, it had managed to isolate the 1/9th Gurkhas and seventy Essex (of whom thirty were wounded) up on Hangman's Hill. After the battle, Philip Brutton of 3/Wesh Guards remembered 'the smell of dead bodies was particularly bad both in the castle and on the way up . . . we counted seventy-four bodies of different regiments and nationalities, all unburied'.

Along the Cavendish Road, a surprise New Zealand tank attack was under way in tandem, against the far side of the monastery. Galloway realised that now was the moment to spring out from Hangman's Hill and seize their objective. While the Fallschirmjäger were licking their wounds, he ordered the 2/7th Gurkhas of his 11th Indian Brigade off Snakeshead Ridge, down into Cassino and up to the castle, in order to reinforce the group at Hangman's Hill. Among them was twenty-year-old Lieutenant Eric David Smith, a regular officer, born in Scotland, commissioned in 1942 and nicknamed 'Birdie' on account of his beaky nose.

Smith reached the castle shortly after the assaults. From the outside its jagged walls looked like 'a gigantic decayed tooth, with the top whittled away by shell and mortar', while inside was a scene of 'maximum activity, chaos, confusion, of men who defended the walls with desperate courage, and of men huddled behind piles of rubble, some wounded, many worn out and several who had given up completely'. He encountered the 'commander of the beleaguered castle was a young major [Beckett], with his arm in a sling, unshaven, exhausted but radiating a calmness and courage that was inspiring those men who were still willing to fight and defend the position. Behind his quiet manner was a fierce determination, it was this strength of purpose that saved us.'

Smith was eventually ordered back down the hill to liaise with the rest of his battalion. He recalled the mind-numbing tiredness of his men: 'Officers, British and Gurkha, shouted at, scolded, cajoled and assisted men as they collapsed. At times we had no alternative but to strike soldiers who just gave up; all interest lost in everything, including any desire to live. By dint of all the measures we could think of most of the battalion reached their transport.'

On the way down, Smith met a huge Sikh sheltering behind rocks who pointed out that he could either take a shortcut, which was subject to sniper fire, or the treacherous path he had used earlier in his ascent. 'One way you get shot, Sahib, the other you slip to your death. But,' he grinned without humour, 'if you go that way [pointing to the short cut] you are on your own, we won't move out to help you, even if you are hit.'

'Why?' Birdie asked.

'Why? Why? The Sahib asks why? Because we've already lost men doing crazy things for British Sahibs. Now do them yourself.'

Smith recited a prayer and, testing his private courage, twice ran crazily downhill, on both occasions a sniper flicking at his clothing or webbing. 'Breathless, in tears and humbled to find that fear had caused my bowls to move, I lay as dead until a glance at my watch spurred me on.' He then hurried on to brief his NCOs before darkness, 'trying to ignore my shaking hands and the tell-tale wet patch down my trouser legs'. Smith later chronicled the breakdown of his battalion's CO, and sacking of a company commander before the end of the third battle.

Heidrich threw further attacks against the castle, but these were easily broken up by pre-registered artillery and mortar fire, yielding more prisoners. Also trying to reach Hangman's was Lance Corporal A. J. Smith of the Essex, who remembered making his way through the archway of the castle that night and finding 'a sangar of dead bodies'. Shortly afterwards a mortar bomb landed in front of him. 'After the initial stunning, I found I had fourteen different holes in me, luckily none very large, and four other chaps were hit also.' In fact, the moment to seize the monastery had already passed and Smith's 2/7th Gurkhas were recalled to counter the threat of German infiltration up on Snakeshead. Freyberg also shared Fallschirmjäger General Richard Heidrich's appreciation of the castle as the Allied 'centre of gravity' and that same night, 19/20 March, moved up a fresh battalion, 6/Royal West Kents to secure it. They came from his reserve 78th British Division, instantly recognisable by the impressive battleaxe shoulder badges. This move, however, was defensive and an acknowledgement that the initiative had passed over to the Germans.

With the weather deteriorating again into 'a blizzard of unexampled severity', on 23 March, Freyberg told Galloway to withdraw his men from their isolated outposts across Monastery Hill, yielding the mountainside to Heidrich's men. The third battle for Cassino spluttered to a muddy, snowy and exhausted halt. The recall signals for the withdrawal of the 4th Indian Division were sent by carrier pigeon, thereby ending with three trained birds what had begun with hundreds of four-engined bombers.

8

Man versus Nature

ANOTHER DIVISION, transferred to Cassino to relieve US II Corps in January 1944, came from shores more distant even than those of the 4th Indian Division. They wore no badge as such, just a small, woven shoulder title that proudly bore the words: New Zealand. When the Kiwis first arrived in Fifth Army's sector they were welcomed, as is traditional, by its commander Mark Clark with a special Order of the Day: 'Dear General Freyberg, It is with a great deal of pleasure and pride that I welcome you and the officers and other ranks of the New Zealand Corps into the Fifth Army. I assure you without reservation that I have the utmost confidence in your leadership and in the battle-trained troops of the 2nd New Zealand and 4th Indian Divisions, both of which have established such enviable records in the hard fighting in the desert, in North Africa, and here in Italy. I look forward with great anticipation to your forthcoming operations with the firm belief that they will affect in a large manner the outcome of our present campaign for the capture of Rome.'

The trouble was that Clark didn't mean a word of this. He felt awkward, intimidated even, alongside the vastly more experienced and older man, Freyberg. When Alex had originally proposed moving General Freyberg's men from the west of Italy to the Cassino front, Clark had retorted:

'Hell, I don't want any troops from the Eighth Army.' Later, after the war, Mark Clark elaborated on his comments, saying that Bernard Freyberg scared him 'because he was a prima donna'; he 'had to be handled with kid gloves . . . He was a great big fellow and had won the Victoria Cross in World War One.'

Moustachioed, stockily built, and at over six feet tall, 'Tiny' Freyberg was an imposing figure who evoked both adoration and envy. He was certainly one of the most outstanding soldiers, of any nation, of the twentieth century and quickly became a legend in his own lifetime. But for many years, in Britain and New Zealand, wrote a subordinate, 'it was a sort of heresy to be critical of Freyberg, either as leader or as a tactician'. An Englishman by birth (he was born in Richmond, Surrey) Bernard Freyberg's family moved to Wellington, New Zealand, when he was two. A distinguished swimmer, yachtsman and rugby player, in 1913 he left the Antipodean islands to fight in the Mexican civil war under the revolutionary leader Pancho Villa. On the outbreak of war in Europe, using money he had won prize-fighting, Freyberg travelled to England where he was interviewed personally by Winston Churchill (then assessing officer candidates as First Lord of the Admiralty) and commissioned, fighting almost immediately at Antwerp in the Hood Battalion of the newly raised 63rd (Royal Naval) Division.

Serving with them at Gallipoli in early 1915, Freyberg used his athletic prowess to swim ashore, light flares to distract the Turkish defenders, and return, for which he was awarded the first of an eventual four DSOs. In November 1916, as a temporary lieutenant colonel, and though wounded four times in twenty-four hours, he led a successful battalion attack at Beaucourt-sur-Ancre on the Somme, which brought him his VC. By April 1917, at the age of twenty-eight, Freyberg, an acting captain, had been promoted to brigadier general, subsequently winning a CMG, two further DSOs, a *Croix de Guerre*, and six Mentions in Despatches, so ending the war as one of the youngest, most decorated and able – though much wounded – British general officers. The First World War had cost the lives of two Freyberg brothers, Oscar at Gallipoli in 1915 and Paul on the Western Front in 1917. Bernard, the youngest, and Cyril, an RFC pilot, survived, and this personal tragedy of family loss became a metaphor for Freyberg of the wider sacrifice of New Zealand's young men; his future military thinking would be influenced by the need to preserve the next generation of young Kiwi males from excessive casualties. One of his staff officers would recall at Cassino, 'the general pointed out to me the . . . appearance of the ground on both sides of the Rapido River – shell holes filled with water – and said: "Reminds you of Passchendaele, doesn't it? But we'll have no more Passchendaeles."'

By 1918, Freyberg had been wounded in action nine times – though Winston Churchill, a personal friend, 'recorded that one day in the 1920s, when he was staying at a country house with him, he asked him to show his wounds. He stripped himself, and Churchill counted twenty-seven separate scars and gashes. To these he was to add, in the Second World War, another three.' Freyberg failed by a whisker to enter Parliament in 1922; a heart murmur forced him to retire from the army as a major general, aged forty-eight in 1937, but such was his fame he was offered command of the 2nd NZ Division by the New Zealand Government two years later, on the outbreak of war. The division would see two years of active warfare before Italy. They went to Greece in March 1941 and Freyberg was chosen to command the Crete garrison ('Creforce') of 42,000 – essentially a coalition corps command of Britons, Greeks, Australians and Kiwis, against an expected dual air and seaborne invasion of the island. He was also admitted to the secret of Ultra strategic intelligence derived from Bletchley Park intercepts. Although the Wehrmacht prevailed at Crete, it was at the expense of around 5,000 casualties and nearly 400 transport aircraft, which broke the back of the German airborne corps, and Freyberg managed to evacuate more than half his force by sea.

As overall commander of the Allied forces on Crete, the defeat resulted in criticism of Freyberg's handling of the campaign by several subordinate brigadiers. He soon restored his reputation and by early 1942 had been knighted and promoted to lieutenant general, taking his New Zealanders (two of whom had been awarded Victoria Crosses on Crete) to North Africa. Injured again in June 1942, the bizarre romantic in Churchill would see an old-world chivalric nobility in Freyberg's battle wounds and his desire to be at the vanguard of the action, describing him as 'the salamander of the British Empire' – after the lizard which could allegedly live in fire and survive. Churchill telegraphed his general on 3 July 1942:

'Deeply moved to hear of your new wound and new glory. Trust that your injury is not serious and that you will soon be back commanding your splendid division. All good wishes to you and them.' At El Alamein in October–November 1942, Freyberg's division played a key role in Montgomery's breakthrough, and during the subsequent pursuit of Rommel westwards across the desert to Tunisia, his New Zealanders managed a series of well-executed left hooks, outflanking successive enemy positions; in April–May 1943, Freyberg was briefly elevated to lead XIII Corps, a very powerful formation which included an armoured brigade, extra artillery and a Free French formation. Monty referred to him as 'easily his best divisional commander', but Freyberg and his New Zealanders also featured highly in the Germans' esteem: a note penned by Rommel's chief of staff, Fritz Bayerlein, read: 'Our men had once again fought with extraordinary courage. Unfortunately, the New Zealanders under Freyberg had escaped. This division, with which we had become acquainted back in 1941–42, was among the elite of the British Army and I should have been much happier if it had been safely tucked away in our prison camp instead of still facing us.'

Ongoing losses in the division (Alamein alone had cost around 3,000 casualties) and problems of reinforcement caused the New Zealand Prime Minister, Fraser, to veto their participation in the Sicilian campaign, but Freyberg was able to lead his division ashore at Taranto in October 1943. They by now had refitted to become a unique formation in Italy, 20,000-strong with 2,800 vehicles, for one of its three infantry brigades had been re-equipped with armour, giving it the ability to fight not only a break-in battle, but execute a pursuit in the event of a break-out. The armoured brigade was formed by rerôling the 18th, 19th and 20th infantry battalions as tank regiments, and the resultant experience of armour crews intimately understanding the needs of their fellow infanteers would contribute greatly to the success of this most innovative of concepts. Since the division's creation in 1939, it had also contained the unique 28th (Maori) Battalion in addition to the nine infantry battalions and other support units that formed the three brigades of his division. Nevertheless the autumn of 1943 still cost the Kiwis another 400 killed and 800 wounded before they arrived at Cassino. An intelligence document of Senger's XIV Panzer Corps recognised the New Zealanders as a formidable fighting unit: 'The NZ soldier is physically fit and strong. He is well trained and formidable in close-range fighting and steadier than the Englishman. He does not shrink from hand-to-hand fighting. In many cases strong-points had to be wiped out to the last man as they refused to surrender.'

Rumours were rife among the New Zealanders about their new destination. There was talk they were about to move 'to a rest area – back to Egypt – to England for the Second Front – to Yugoslavia – southern France – garrison duty in North Africa – to the Pacific – going home'. Most troops believed they were returning to southern Italy, back to Taranto maybe, and only became aware of their destination when they saw the distant glow of Mount Vesuvius in the night sky.

Charles Dickens, after visiting Cassino abbey in 1845, also travelled to see the huge volcano, which dominates the south-east approaches to Naples and was responsible for smothering Herculaneum and Pompeii in AD 79. Dickens wrote of watching it, 'bright and snowy in the peaceful distance', Vesuvius 'disappears from the prospect, and we watch for it again, on our return, with the same thrill of interest: as the doom and destiny of all this beautiful country, biding its terrible time'. Miles Hildyard, a captain with the Sherwood Rangers Yeomanry at Cassino, was transfixed, as most soldiers were, by Vesuvius: 'the whole thing is vastly hellish . . . From the country, the volcano seems to puff smoke all the time, but in fact it throws up about every half-minute red hot lumps most of which fall back again inside the cone.'

It took the New Zealand Division a week to arrive in the Cassino theatre, traipsing west across Italy from the Adriatic sector. This mass movement of thousands of troops and vehicles was accomplished in great secrecy; as part of the deception to conceal the departure of 4th NZ Armoured Brigade, 'a Royal Armoured Corps camouflage unit placed dummy tanks in position . . . and a patrol of Spitfires kept the sky clear of enemy while the tanks withdrew'.

The division approached Cassino up the Via Casilina (Route 6), a 'busy highway running through a rain-sodden and dejected landscape, past the litter of battle and grey stone buildings wasted by war and splashed with mud. It was under the tight control of American military police, models of brisk, or even brusque, efficiency, and the strange driver felt at first like a bucolic drayman plunged into the traffic stream of a metropolis.' As they arrived, in incessant rain, they found that clay had become mud, bomb and shell craters subsided into lakes, and roads transformed into wheel-rutted quagmires. Private Feist, a driver with the Royal New Zealand Army Service Corps (RNZASC), wrote of the outgoing troops: 'the Yanks have about everything imaginable in equip-ment . . . they believe in waging war in comfort, and are generous with their goods and facilities. Hot showers, "cawfee", "seegars" and "candy" – to say nothing of Lucky Strike cigarettes – are freely offered to our drivers when they call, as many do, especially around meal times.'

Fallschirmjäger Sergeant Helmut Gille arrived at Cassino with the rest of his paratroop division as reinforcements shortly after the New Zealanders, and was posted up onto the hillside. Once the 15 February bombing raid on the abbey stopped, Gille remembered how he and his men entered the abbey grounds and set up sniper positions among the rubble, able to watch every move the Kiwis made. North Islander Stuart Hayton of Taranaki was one of those Helmut Gille watched. Hayton served initially with 21st Battalion, arriving in Italy with the eleventh reinforcement draft for the New Zealand Division, before being commis-sioned as an intelligence officer. At Cassino he recalled: 'It was winter time and bad news because it was high up, cold and there was snow. I remember we were very much under observation from Monte Cairo which is right alongside Monte Cassino but a much higher mountain. When they bombed the monastery we had a prime view from the eastern side. We looked across and watched it dissolving in all the bombing.' After a few bombs had been dropped 'you couldn't see anything but clouds of smoke and dust. At the time it looked as if they were using it as a defensive position, because a lot of fire was coming from the direc-tion of the monastery . . . They had a lot of [weapon] pits on the front. It was there and it had to be neutralised.'

Jim Wright also volunteered for the RNZASC, when he turned nine-teen. At Cassino he drove ammunition, food and petrol up to the front, observing: 'after the Yanks bombed the abbey, it just gave Jerry a crater to shoot from. Their snipers were deadly. God, that was frightening.' The limit for overseas service was twenty-one, so, like many others, Wright lied about his age and was posted to Italy as a driver. He remembers his lonely night-time ammunition runs, driving slowly along roads carved through rubble. He would often pass a wrecked statue of the Madonna, which spooked him, as her eyes seemed to follow his truck: 'we'd peer out into the darkness; there were craters and blown-up buildings everywhere. No lights. Total darkness. If it was a full moon, we wouldn't go. When we got near the front line, we would just unload our ammunition. No one would talk.'

The men receiving the supplies in the New Zealand artillery were sited with those of the rest of the corps, grouped in massed formations behind the Rapido, their guns emplaced 'in a muddy river flat' facing north-westwards across the river towards Monte Cairo. The abbey 'seemed at a distance of four miles or so from the gun areas to be so close that they could reach out and touch it'. It was hard not to think of it, declared the official history, as one 'gigantic and evil barracks with Germans at every window. Putting guns in below it was like undressing in Piccadilly Circus or Times Square – ludicrously open to a public and hostile gaze.' Like the Western Front, the landscape had been pulverised: 'leafless and mangled trees were everywhere, farmhouses lay in ruins, shell holes (some of them of monstrous size) scarred the land like an ugly rash, filled with water and edged with mud, and as the incessant gun fire grew louder there were many refugees to be seen'.

Each artillery battery had its own observers – usually sited on Monte Trocchio – such as Captain John Williams of 99th Light Anti-Aircraft Regiment, Royal Artillery. Captain Williams's British unit had been an infantry battalion until 1941 when it was converted to an anti-aircraft role. Once the Luftwaffe air threat receded, William's outfit was rerôled again for Italy, this time with 4.2-inch heavy mortars capable of throwing high explosive or concealing smoke more than two miles towards the distant German lines, in support of Allied infantry or armour attacks. 'Continuous German shelling and mortaring, to which I was subjected, had completely devastated the whole area,' Williams remembered, as he retraced his old route up Mount Trocchio, along a twisting, stony, rutted path, through olive groves, to a tiny plateau of scrub and grassland where his unprotected observation post had been sited. 'This was the trail I used in the dark then; I followed white tape through a minefield, lit continuously by the thousands of gun flashes as the guns opened up on our front.' One method of countering German artillery was to spot the muzzle flashes of their guns – flash-spotting – via optical instruments located in observation posts on Monte Trocchio, which were under fire for much of the time. Several units manned their exposed posts on Trocchio continuously for fifty-two days, clocking up an average of seven locations spotted per day. When German guns used flashless powder or were in positions with good cover, then audio sound-ranging equipment employing sets of microphones was used.

South Islander Russell Kidd served as a signaller with 6th Field Regiment, Royal New Zealand Artillery. His job was to lay communication line out to his regiment's 25-pounder field guns. He had already spent two years fighting in North Africa, including Alamein, where he lost a brother. Kidd's field regiment was one of three (4th, 5th and 6th) in the New Zealand Division, each of which contained three batteries of eight 25-pounder guns. Once targets had been identified by forward observers or the infantry, Kidd's colleagues would receive orders to fire different kinds of shoots via codewords: those coded 'Mike' were for all the regiment's twenty-four guns to fire; 'Uncle' was for the division's entire seventy-two guns; 'Victor' were more important, for the massed New Zealand Corps artillery, and 'Whiskey' required all the thousand-plus guns in the Fifth Army. The New Zealand gunners were also given different kinds of fire missions: a 'Murder' target plus grid reference was a concentration of all guns on a pinpointed location. A signal coded 'Rumpus' was a concentration of fire into a rectangular-shaped zone: the whole zone could be moved and searched for enemy; while a 'Stonk' was a linear target of about 600 metres, identified by its centre point.

Despite his calling as an Anglican priest, Pat Gourdie, a thirty-one-year-old padre with the Kiwi 18th Armoured Regiment, summed up the view of many in the NZ Division: Monte Cassino abbey 'was like a bird of ill omen brooding over us . . . I'm bloody glad it was blown to bits.' Gourdie, later awarded a DSO, was one of about fifty padres attached to the division, and was keen to stress that he did not want to see the sacred building bombed, but that it was unavoidable once the Germans decided to make it the bastion of their Winter Line. Though designated a non-combatant, Padre Gourdie, a committed pacifist, nevertheless at the front one day 'held a revolver over the top, and pulled the trigger – just so I could say that I had fired a shot whilst away'. Another New Zealand 6th Field Regiment veteran, Bryan O'Connor, on a return visit to Cassino looked up at the rebuilt Benedictine abbey on the hilltop and echoed Padre Gourdie's thoughts about the structure: 'Bugger that thing,' he said.

From 3 February, when Freyberg was elevated to corps command in charge of the British, Kiwi and Indian Divisions, it was vital at this crucial stage in the struggle for Cassino that the New Zealanders be left in a safe pair of hands. Although a handover in mid-battle is never desirable, Freyberg could feel confident in the division's new commander: Brigadier (acting Major General) Howard Kippenberger. A South Islander, 'Kip' was an extremely cool commander under fire who had seen action in the First World War, being seriously wounded in 1916 on the Somme. He too had served in Greece, and temporarily commanded a brigade on Crete, which brought him a DSO. In North Africa, he earned a second DSO leading his brigade, and the division during Freyberg's absence. Kippenberger had natural command ability and had spent much of the inter-war years reading about military history and strategy, so prepared himself – with no staff college education – for higher command. Cast in Freyberg's mould, and New Zealand-born, in February 1944, Kippenberger was the most obvious successor to lead his fellow countrymen at Cassino. However, Freyberg was in the unenviable situation of being quite new to corps command himself, with an inadequate staff, and commanding two brigadiers (Dimolene and Kippenberger), who were themselves arguably still finding their feet as acting divisional commanders.

After the aerial bombing of the monastery on 15 February, it was intended that Kippenberger's New Zealanders would strike at Cassino town at the same moment the 4th Indian Division attacked the monastery and Point 593. But the delays suffered by the Sussex and Gurkha battalions forced the Kiwis to delay their attack by two days. As the scattered battalions of the Indian Division stumbled across the stony ravines to attack the heights around the abbey on the night of 17/18 February, the 5th New Zealand Brigade – comprising the 21st (Auckland), 23rd (Canterbury-Otago) and the 28th (Maori) Battalions – attempted to enter

Cassino town. Prior reconnaissance had revealed the strength of the German defences. Everywhere was either mined, strewn with obstacles covered by fire, or waterlogged. Shell holes were a perennial hazard, with tanks and infantry unable to get through and the deep craters and holes quickly filling with water when it rained. The only possible approach appeared to be via the railway line that entered Cassino from the south-east, an embankment just wide enough to take tanks. The Germans had already made twelve separate demolitions along the embankment, and these first had to be bridged. Four had been repaired by the time the Maori Battalion picked their way along the embankment overnight.

By dawn on 18 February, two companies of Maoris reached and secured Cassino's railway station and some locomotive sheds which curved around with the railway track (called the 'Round House' positions), but were attacked throughout the day by German infantry and tanks – including two captured Shermans. One of the German defenders, *Oberfeldwebel* Hoffmann, remembers approaching the engine shed, creeping up on the Maoris with pioneers from 71st Infantry Division, when 'suddenly all hell broke loose around us with dozens of hand grenades landing at our feet. We immediately took cover and fired back. During this exchange many of my engineers went down. I suffered a few shrapnel pieces in the lower leg, which I hardly noticed in the turmoil. Although getting stuck, the attack by the engineer platoon stopped the momentum of the Maoris and prevented them from fully capitalising on their success.'

As German tanks and infantry who knew the ground scuttled through the ruins, the two Maori companies withdrew in the mid-afternoon of 18 February. As their own armour and anti-tank guns could not get forward, they had no means of overcoming the panzers: of the 200 who had started, 130 were either dead or injured. With the 4th Indian Division unable to make headway on the heights and the New Zealanders fixed in the town, Freyberg, watchful of casualties, called off further attacks. As the Kiwis withdrew, Tenth Army's Vietinghoff phoned Kesselring's underground headquarters at Monte Soratte, twenty miles north of Rome with the news:

> Vietinghoff : 'We have succeeded after hard fighting in retaking Cassino station.'
> Kesselring: 'Heartiest congratulations.'

Vietinghoff: 'I didn't think we would do it.'

Kesselring: 'Neither did I.'

Vietinghoff: 'North of Cassino also very heavy attacks have been beaten
off. 400 dead have been counted on 1st Fallschirmjäger Regiment's front
. . . Our losses are pretty heavy too.'

Kesselring: 'Convey my heartiest congratulations to 211st Regiment,
and 1st Fallschirmjäger Regiment not quite so strongly . . . I am very
pleased that the New Zealanders have had a smack in the nose. You
must recommend the local commander for the Knight's Cross.'

For Operation Dickens – third Cassino – Freyberg had envisaged a brisk
resumption of the offensive, to be preceded by another massive air raid,
this time on the town. The 6th New Zealand Brigade (24th, 25th and
26th Battalions), who had relieved the Americans on the northern
outskirts of the town on 22 February, were to withdraw half a mile while
a massive bombing raid hit the town, then attack down the road from
Caira as soon as the bombers had departed, with 25th Battalion leading
and 19th Armoured Regiment in support. At the same time, as we have
seen, 4th Indian Division would attack on their right, hoping to seize
the hairpin bends of the zigzag road leading to their ultimate objective
– the abbey itself.

In devising Dickens, Freyberg was doubtless swayed by personal
history. Reaching back to the 1916 days of his VC on the Somme at
Beaucourt, or Passchendaele in 1917, he had seen how huge artillery
barrages obliterated enemy positions – the 1944 equivalent was aerial
bombing. There may also have been an element of score-settling, for
Freyberg would also have known, from captured German prisoners and
from Ultra decrypts, that the new defenders of Cassino town were Richard
Heidrich's 1st Fallschirmjäger Division. Heidrich, his three regimental
commanders – Oberst Karl-Lothar Schulz, of 1st Fallschirmjäger
Regiment occupying the town; Ludwig Heilmann of the 3rd Regiment
around the monastery; and Erich Walther, leading the 4th Regiment in
the hills beyond – his artillery brigade commander, Oberstleutnant Bruno
Schram and many other senior members of the division were veterans
of the 1941 campaign on Crete, which Freyberg and his forces had so
famously defended at a cost to the Kiwis alone of 300 dead and 1,800

captured. It is impossible to believe there was not an element of a 'return match' in Freyberg's mind. Freyberg was also under personal strain for on 14 February news had come that Freyberg's son Paul, an officer in the Grenadier Guards, had been captured at Anzio. (He would later escape with friendly partisans helping him into the neutral sanctuary of Vatican City, from where he was freed when Rome was liberated in June.)

For weeks the Allies waited for a change in weather that suited the air force. During this time the NZ Division's troops remained in a constant state of readiness to launch Operation Dickens, enduring atrocious conditions and hard-to-justify casualties from exposure, shells and bullets caused by the daily diet of artillery exchanges, raiding parties and patrolling. In the three weeks until the third battle began, the three battalions of 6th NZ Brigade lost 263 men, and the Indian Division about the same. Ironically, this was reminiscent of Passchendaele, the 1917 battle Freyberg was desperate not to repeat.

The Kiwi armoured units had been obliged, because of the waterlogged approaches to Cassino town, to sit out the second battle, and found the period of prolonged inactivity and weather particularly challenging. A 20th Armoured Regiment officer recalled 'the bitter cold and the enormous fire we had going all night. The men were even colder; and some of them had their boots stolen. There were not enough houses to go round and many of the men were quartered in bivvy tents and lorries, where living conditions were cheerless. At night the wind flapped and tore at the canvas and draughts found entrance to even the most carefully made bed. Some of the men made ingenious charcoal stoves from ammunition boxes and shell cases.'

In a neighbouring British unit of 78th Division, Ray Dighton of 1/ East Surreys (in 11th Brigade) found himself manning a waterlogged trench overlooking the Rapido River most nights with his mate, Fred. Boots and clothing were in short supply and Ray's recollections reveal how brutalised to war the division had become by March 1944: 'Fred one night slipped down to the river and took the boots off a dead German. He wore these every time we had to stay in the trench. I thought I would like a pair too. With Fred holding [another dead] . . . body down with his foot, I tugged the first boot off, but when I came to the second, I pulled the whole leg off at the thigh. Fred took the jacket off the

German and wrapped it around the thigh and held it tightly while I successfully wrenched the boot off the dead soldier's foot.' Padre Pat Gourdie remembered the 'funny, cheesy, sour vinegary smell' he associated with the German dead. Others recalled on quiet nights the sound of rats tearing at the corpses. While waiting for 'Bradman', the 5/Northamptons, of the same brigade as Ray Dighton and his Surreymen, found that life manning the 'semi-liquid quagmires' of outposts in the Rapido valley, or sangars up on the frozen heights was very grim indeed: 'Between the lines lay innumerable bodies – those of British, Indian, American and German soldiers who had fallen in the close fighting of the past few months. They lay in the open as it was impossible to remove them. At night time some of them were covered up with stones after putting a blanket, lime and creosote on them to hasten decomposition. Graves were quite out of the question.'

Meanwhile, in preparation for 'Bradman batting', transport units ferried troops, fuel, rations and vast quantities of artillery ammunition to camouflaged dumps just behind the front. A single platoon of the 4th New Zealand Reserve Mechanical Transport Company recorded that they shifted '113,000 25-pounder shells (enough to give each gun in the division about 1,570 rounds), 5,000 smoke generators (gadgets about the size of thermos flasks which, when lit, poured out columns of smoke), and over a thousand [propaganda] leaflet shells'.

The enormously capable Howard Kippenberger had done much to 'bed in' his division and Cassino and keep their morale high, while waiting for 'Bradman to bat'. On 2 March, his military career came to a painful halt, as the last page of his diary observed: 'Corps conference at 1400 hours. Went with [Captain] Frank Massey up Monte Trocchio afterwards and, coming down, stepped on a mine and had one foot blown off, the other mangled and thumb ripped up. Frank slightly hurt.' Kip had stepped on a *Schü*-mine, on a supposedly clear path. His other foot would be amputated by the end of the day.

In Kippenberger another vital cog of Freyberg's trusted command team had been removed. Kip was swiftly replaced by Brigadier Graham 'Ike' Parkinson, formerly commanding 6th NZ Brigade: but as one Kiwi soldier reacted: 'there goes our best man. He is irreplaceable.' With Tuker, Dimoline and Kippenberger gone by March 1944, there was no officer left in Freyberg's command with the seniority and experience to challenge him.

Weather conditions had eased sufficiently on the ides of March – Roman festive day of the god of war, Mars – for 'Bradman to bat', the codename for the air attack. The second big Allied air offensive on Cassino this time aimed at destroying the town and any Germans who happened to be in the vicinity. Major Rudolf Böhmler, commanding 1st Battalion of Heilmann's 3rd Fallschirmjäger Regiment in the town, described how 'the leading bombers opened their bomb-hatches punctually at 8.30 a.m.', and came in an endless stream. 'The very first wave enveloped Cassino in a pall of dark grey dust, hiding from view the horror below, where men, houses and machines were being blown to pieces. In this hell, it seemed as though all will to resist must be quenched . . . and all life be brought to an end. As wave succeeded deadly wave, the inferno seemed endless.'

War correspondent Christopher Buckley watched the raid: 'They were attacking with a far greater intensity than on the [previous] occasion . . . Sometimes they flew in formations of eighteen, sometimes of thirty-six. Sometimes it was the heavies, Fortresses and Liberators; sometimes the mediums, Bostons and Mitchells.' Further down the Garigliano, Major Hardy Parkhurst of the 2/Northumberland Fusiliers climbed a hill for the view and noted the strange juxtaposition of images: 'Spring flowers are coming up everywhere. The clusters of violets are especially beautiful and so are the anemones . . . Waves of bombers were going over continuously and the whole Cassino area was a mass of drifting smoke.' In all, some 455 bombers – B-24 Liberators, B-17 Flying Fortresses, B-26 Marauders and B-25 Mitchells – dropped 992 tons of bombs on Cassino, while another 260 were prevented by cloud cover from making their attack. Some 280 P-38 Lightnings and RAF Spitfires lurked above, keeping guard.

Freyberg's corps headquarters was at Cervaro, in the hills directly opposite and three miles east of Cassino. It was from where he watched the bombing with generals Alexander, Devers, Clark, Eaker of the MAAF and Major General John K. Cannon of the Mediterranean Allied Tactical Air Force (MATAF). Unknown to Freyberg, Eaker was privately dubious about this second raid, writing to the US Chief of Air Staff that 'little useful purpose is served by our blasting the opposition unless the Army does follow through. I am anxious that you do not set your heart on a great victory as a result of this operation. Personally, I do not feel it will throw the German out of his present position completely or entirely, or compel him to abandon the defensive role, if he decides to hold to the last man.' With six senior generals observing, 'the picnic atmosphere was both inappropriate and unavoidable', wrote the New Zealand official historian. 'None who saw it will forget the terrible one-sidedness of the spectacle: there was an insolent meting out of punishment as the great bombers, unwavering and impeccable, opened their racks upon the suffering earth. The sky had been swept clear of enemy fighters and the bombers were unchallenged except by a nest of anti-aircraft guns south of the Liri, which fired ineffectually as the attackers wheeled away from the target; and even this fire was silenced half-way through the morning.' Freyberg recorded, 'flashes of flame from bursting bombs leaped from the buildings and from the slopes above the town, explosions reverberated through the hills and shook the ground under our feet'. Elsewhere, Oliver Leese watched in company with Sydney Kirkman of British XIII Corps, Charles Keightley of 78th Division and Major General Evered Poole of the newly arrived 6th South African Armoured Division.

North of Cassino, a signaller from 25th New Zealand Battalion, 'felt the shockwave, which blew me over backwards about ten yards'. The history of the 19th NZ Armoured Regiment recorded that 'it was an awesome exhibition of Allied air might, but the watching troops, elated at first, were soon uncomfortably aware that the term "safety bomb line" meant little to many of the bombardiers up above. Some of their missiles found marks as much as five miles within our own area, and there were many unexpected casualties. Much bitterness naturally resulted. It was with justifiable relief that the troops waiting to go into the attack watched the last group of planes disappear shortly before midday.'

Directly underneath the raid, at Cassino town, were the Fallschirmjäger. Major Böhmler wrote of bombs which 'tore gaping craters in gardens, fields, and meadows; whole streets collapsed suddenly into a mountain of rubble; trees flew through the air, as though hurled by some giant hand'. Also on the receiving end was Leutnant Schuster of 7th

Company/2nd Battalion, who survived to recount: 'direct hits – here, here and here; a hand sticking out of the debris told me what had happened. When I got back, the men read in my eyes what I had seen. The same, unspoken thought was in all our minds – when would it be our turn? The crash of bursting bombs increased in intensity. We clung to each other, instinctively keeping our mouths open. It went on and on. Time no longer existed, everything was unreal . . . Rubble and dust came pouring down into our hole. Breathing became a desperate and urgent business . . . Crouching in silence, we waited for the pitiless hail to end.'

'No tree escaped damage, no piece of ground remained green,' wrote Senger. 'On my lonely walk the only accompaniment was the jarring explosion of shells, the whistling of splinters, the smell of freshly thrown-up earth and the well-known mixture of smells from glowing iron and burnt powder.' As a corps commander walking through shellfire to join his divisional commander, Heidrich, at the front-line headquarters of the 3rd Fallschirmjäger Regiment, Senger was also practising the German doctrine of commanding as far forward as possible: senior leaders should move towards their subordinates for combat reports, not the other way around. In contrast, Senger noted that the command elements of 5th New Zealand Brigade were rarely seen entering Cassino or their battalion HQs in the first two days.

As the bombers ceased at midday on the 15th, nearly a thousand guns from the assembled Allied batteries – American, British, Indian, Free French, and New Zealander – opened up; even three giant eight-inch railway guns of the 1st Italian Armoured Artillery Regiment, which had escaped German capture in September 1943, added to the firepower. The Kiwi gunners were unprepared for the volume of fire that erupted from their own lines. 'From midday onwards, the ground all round them seemed to be flashing fire and puffing up clouds of smoke as though it had suddenly turned into a vast and highly active volcanic region.' Monte Cassino was 'flashing and puffing in quite a different way until it was smothered with smoke and dust and the town became a blur that was jagged with fragments flung into the air'.

That evening, ten miles down the Garigliano towards the sea, Captain David Cole, signals officer of the 2/Royal Inniskilling Fusiliers, remembered that 'the endlessly flickering light of the American guns at Cassino' gave a 'festive look to the distant mountains'. Meanwhile, during the afternoon, P-47 Thunderbolts, A-36 Invaders, A-20 Havocs and P-40 Kittyhawks operating as fighter-bombers attacked targets in the town. To the intense embarrassment of Eaker and Cannon, a few of their aircraft managed to hit Eighth Army headquarters with five bombs, and a French field hospital, both a considerable distance away, killing seventy-five Allied troops, forty civilians and wounding 250. Neither general would have been impressed, either, to read that after-action analysis concluded only half of the 1,000lb bombs were dropped within a mile of the aiming point, while a mere eight per cent were within half a mile.

Examination of Freyberg's orders for Operation Dickens reveals that the main bombing was to be followed by tactical air support working in conjunction with ground forces, if operations at Anzio permitted. The latter was what was really required throughout, but the whole NZ Corps ground assault plan was fatally flawed because it would be timed to suit the air force: infantry and armour would attack when the bombers had departed, whenever that was. Yet, Allied doctrine *already* established in North Africa had determined that air forces should work to the army's timetable. However, the idea of tactical air managing to achieve anything after the bombers had completed their mission was stretching credulity – fighter-bombers were likely to encounter a target completely unrecognisable compared with their neat, pre-mission aerial photographs. Furthermore, response times for close air support were up to two hours, when any moving targets such as armour or self-propelled artillery were likely to have fled.

Shortly after the bombing of Cassino, the Allies applied a more intelligent use of air power. On 19 March, Cannon, commanding MATAF, issued orders for Operation Strangle, designed to interdict German road, rail and sea communications, and eventually force a withdrawal from the Cassino and other Gustav Line defences. The operation would last until 11 May, when the fourth battle, Operation Diadem, began. The aim of Strangle was to immobilise the Italian rail system, where stations, marshalling yards and repair depots became the primary targets of Cannon's medium bombers, while bridges, tunnels, moving trains, viaducts and rail lines were to be attacked by fighter-bombers, operating from Corsica, which could also pounce on roads and vehicles. As well as the 1,700 aircraft in Cannon's MATAF, up to 2,000 bombers from the MAAF attacked rail, road and coastal targets – generally chosen north of Rome as far as Pisa, Florence and Rimini, to suggest this was an independent air offensive, and not a precursor to another Allied assault.

There is no evidence the Germans were fooled. They soon realised the Allied air offensive was aimed at preventing rolling stock from running to the Cassino or Anzio fronts, and though their estimated flow of supplies slowed from 80,000 tons per day to sometimes only 4,000 tons, the Germans proved masters of improvisation. General de Flieger Rudolf Wenninger, appointed by Kesselring with 'special responsibility for the maintenance of rail communications in Italy', simply arranged for everything needed to be ferried south of Florence by truck and at night – or by day when the weather was poor. Operation Strangle did, however, manage to impede German movement by day; it resulted in over 10,000 motor vehicles being destroyed, prompted a huge increase in fuel consumption and diverted resources to repairing the infrastructure and would have important consequences for German tactical troop movements when the fourth battle for Cassino began.

Nearly two millennia had passed since the AD 79 eruption of Mount Vesuvius; now the volcano chose again to spew lava. Between 17 and 23 March 1944, troops of both sides watched as it glowed red, and then belched smoke and ash. American Leander K. Powers, one of thousands of Allied servicemen on leave or in hospital throughout Naples, noted in his diary for Friday 17 March: 'huge red streams of lava flowing down the sides' of Mount Vesuvius; 'it was a sight to behold. Never had we seen such at night – usually a faint red glow at the most. As we watched the streams, like giant fingers flowing down the sides, we could see a glow in the sky. All during the night and Sunday there were quakes of the earth with tremendous roars – similar to thunder . . . The windows rattled, and the entire building vibrated.'

By Sunday night, 'streams of fire were shooting thousands of feet into the air, and the countryside was lit up for miles around. Oft times the entire top of the mountain looked as if it were a blazing inferno.' On the 19th, Powers learned that a stream of lava was flowing down the side towards Naples, so rode over to see it, 'a huge mass of fiery coals some twenty feet high, and 200 yards wide, destroying everything in its path. There were many people evacuating their homes, which we saw destroyed as the lava pressed on. At night, the sky and countryside was bright for miles around. Flames were shooting into the sky for thousands of feet.'

Gunner Spike Milligan was resting in a tented camp at Torre Del Greco, 'a dust and rags village astride the Salerno-Naples road on the south side of Vesuvius'. The volcano 'had started to belch smoke at an alarming rate, and at night tipples of lava were spilling over the cone'. Massive Allied resources were being diverted into reassuring and rescuing the inhabitants in nearby towns and villages. Spike was ordered to warn the locals to leave: 'It was evening when I set out in the jeep. Due to the smoke, it was dark before sunset. A strange unearthly light settled on the land, reminding me of those Turner chiaroscuro paintings . . . the mountain [was] rumbling and the cone glowing scarlet like the throat of a mythical dragon.' Driving back by the light of Vesuvius, 'the lava was now flowing down the sides towards the sea, the rumbling was very loud. The camp was all awake and in a state of tension. Men stood outside their tents staring at the phenomenon, their faces going on and off in the volcano's fluctuating light.'

In the midst of a hellish Cassino campaign, the Allies found themselves involved in a major emergency and disaster-relief operation. The cost was high in machinery, if not personnel: the 340th Bombardment Group (in which Lieutenant Joseph Heller was serving) were based on Pompeii airfield at the time and lost nearly all of their eighty-eight bombers, which were covered with hot ash that clogged engines, melted rubber and burned through airframes, Plexiglas and control wires. The lava flow reached and destroyed most of San Sebastiano, which Sergeant Norman Lewis observed: 'the lava was pushing its way very quietly down the main street, and about fifty yards from the edge of this great, slowly shifting slagheap, a crowd of several hundred people, mostly in black, knelt in prayer. Holy banners and church images were held aloft, and acolytes swung censers and sprinkled holy water in the direction of the cinders.'

Though Neapolitans had lived with the menace for ever, in 1944 the spectacle was a once-in-a-lifetime sight that featured in the letters home of all servicemen in the vicinity. While Vesuvius erupted, the vital work of unloading cargo in the port of Naples continued, in order to meet the huge demands of the Cassino and Anzio fronts. Churchill wrote of the event: 'On 24 March, a report to the Naval Commander-in-Chief stated, "The Naples group of ports is now discharging at the rate of 12 million tons a year, while Vesuvius is estimated to be doing 30 million a day. We can but admire this gesture of the Gods."'

9

Kiwis at Cassino

Back at Cassino, the Allied air forces had tried to compete with the forces of Vesuvius in their mission to bomb the Germans out of the town. Once the raid of 15 March had subsided, the 25th New Zealand Battalion began to pick their way into the ruins, using the route running south from Caira village as their axis, which they named 'Caruso Road', while the 26th Battalion used another to the north-east, 'Pasquale Road', and made for the station. When the NZ battalions had withdrawn temporarily to avoid the bombing that morning, German troops reoccupied some of their old positions, including the stone-built gaol and a nunnery on the northern edge of town, and dug their way into the rubble to await the inevitable ground assault.

The Kiwi attackers moved cautiously, aiming for the castle and the Excelsior Hotel (dubbed the easier to say Continental Hotel by troops), but found the streets utterly choked with rubble, an effective barrier to their armoured support. Tank crews had the novel experience of being obliged to exit their vehicles and clear paths with pick and shovel. The greatest gain was the capture of the castle on Rocca Janula by the 25th Battalion at around 5 p.m., and being able later to hand it over to 1/4th Essex of the Indian Division. Allied photographers snapped the small numbers of Fallschirmjäger who had been captured and ushered to the rear, up the Caruso Road. After the aerial bombing, Clark's HQ had arranged for psychiatrists to be on hand to examine the effects of bombing on their prisoners. One observer noted merely that, 'the para-troops, mostly boys in their teens or early twenties, seemed to know what was expected of them. When they were asked about the bombing they forced a smile, shrugged their shoulders and said that it was nothing. Their attitude was that of a schoolboy who, emerging from the head-master's study rubbing his behind, defiantly informs his friends: "It didn't hurt." Of the first 300 prisoners to come in, only one was found in a nervous condition directly attributable to the bombing.'

The evening brought a resumption of torrential rain, which filled craters and cellars, drowning those who had survived the bombing but been trapped by debris, and hampering the movements of the living. That first night was, by all accounts, miserable – neither side had hot food, were wet through, cold and hungry and the attackers' wireless sets were quickly soaked and useless. Fred Majdalany, who took part in the later stages of the battle as a company commander with 2/Lancashire Fusiliers (of 78th Battleaxe Division), winning an MC, described how the 26th NZ Battalion headed towards the station, 'having taken three hours to cover the last 650 yards in pitch blackness, each soaked man of them clinging miserably to the bayonet scabbard of the man in front'.

The already depleted Fallschirmjäger in the town had lost perhaps half their number again in the bombing; survival was very much a lottery – due to luck, not necessarily professional skill. Some lived because they sheltered in strong cellars; others had withdrawn into caves in the cliff face underneath Castle Hill and Monte Cassino abbey. As the 24th NZ Battalion was also fed into the rubble, they found they were up against quite small bands of survivors, company and platoon groups, who fought back. The training of the Fallschirmjäger played to the defenders' advan-tage. Almost any other kind of unit would have crumbled, but because paratroopers were expected to land in disorganised small groups, operate leaderless and independently if necessary, and were armed with large numbers of automatic weapons and stick grenades, the very circumstances of Cassino after the bombing raid triggered their robust training. Not only did bands of Fallschirmjäger survive, but were sufficiently unified to feed their casualties out of town, and reinforcements in.

Others occupied vacant structures, while some of the 14th Panzerjäger (anti-tank) Company even disassembled their weapons and carried them to one of the main bastions of resistance, the Hôtel des Roses (never actually an hotel, though at one time owned by Baron de Rosa, hence the name). This was a large, stone building situated on the corner where the road to the abbey left the Via Casilina and began to climb. Company commander Oberleutnant Joseph 'Jupp' Klein of 1st Fallschirm-Pioneer Battalion recalled 'we chose the upper floors as our troop headquarters while the cellar became the troop shelter'. His assignment was to dig tunnels from the Hôtel des Roses under the road behind that ascended to the monastery to machine-gun nests that overlooked the Rapido. 'Because the dams of the Rapido River had been opened before our deployment, the whole area was swampy and impassable for enemy tanks.' From his vantage point, Klein 'didn't envy our foes down there as they were lying in the wet and all they seemed to have for cover from the frequent rain was a piece of tarpaulin covering their shelters. They had one real advantage, however, which was the fact that any artillery shells fired at them would simply be absorbed into the swampy ground and hence could not harm them.'

Five hundred yards north was the other lynchpin of the defences, the 'Continental' Hotel, which looked due east, straight down the Via Casilina towards Monte Trocchio. It housed the battalion HQ and a company of the Fallschirmjäger Regiment, under Hauptmann Ferdinand Foltin, and a platoon of pioneers. Unknown to the Allies, behind the hotel were natural caves leading into the cliff faces, where a garrison of over a hundred men sheltered from the bombs. Feldwebel Georg Schmitz commanded a platoon of pioneers based in the Continental, and sat out the bombing in the cave behind it. He recalled that one assault gun which had survived, rodent-like, would scurry in and out of its lair in the basement of the Continental.

Earlier that day, immediately following the bombing, Ira C. Eaker (despite his private scepticism) announced to the media: 'Today we have fumigated Cassino and I am most hopeful when the smoke of today's battle clears we will find more worthy occupants installed with little loss of our men . . . Let the Germans well ponder that what we have done on the ides of March to their fortress of Cassino, we shall do to every fortress where he elects to make a stand.' By the same evening, he would be obliged to eat his words.

On the second day, 16 March, the 19th NZ Armoured Regiment pushed further into town, but needed the help of bridge-laying tanks to cross craters and culverts. Several Shermans threw tracks or became bogged in the morass of liquid mud congealing in craters; others were hit by anti-tank weapons and mines, but even if immobile were able to offer support to the infantry. Snipers were everywhere and especially lethal to infantry commanders and armour crews. However, as fast as a sector was cleared, the Fallschirmjäger would reappear: with weeks of local knowledge behind them, the defenders had a great advantage over the Kiwis.

In darkness they were able to infiltrate back from their own lines, reinforce old strongpoints and establish several new ones. The experience of one of 25th NZ Battalion's platoons was not untypical. No. 7 Platoon, which was just twelve strong at this stage, 'shared a house with the enemy for three days and for thirty-six hours lived on iron rations and cigarettes'. They could hear the Germans moving about on the roof and next door, but could do nothing 'as all exits were covered by a German strongpoint across the street in front and grenade-dropping snipers on the roof'. It was not long after that 'that the reason for a mysterious tapping in one wall, of the night before, was felt . . . over half the ceiling and back wall were blown into the room . . . a demolition charge had been placed high up on the back wall. Fortunately, the platoon organised quickly, and the hole in the roof, the front of the house and the flooded alleyway were quickly covered. Attempts to rush the house were discouraged by lobbing grenades through the hole in the roof, and down into the alleyway.'

Pulverised brick and plaster from wrecked buildings, mixed with rain, was churned by tracked vehicles into a mud that possessed the consistency of glue, which oozed everywhere, forming hidden hazards for humans and armour alike, then set solid, creating impossible repair challenges for the engineers. Some German panzers and self-propelled guns had survived, having reversed into handy basements before the bombing, and their crews now cleared fields of fire or created rat-runs down which they could scoot from cover to cover. One panzer, completely entombed in a collapsed house, was used as a German artillery observation post and a subterranean passage made, enabling its crew to man the position. On 17 March, an attack on the railway station developed with New Zealand infantry and armour advancing from the town, the opposite direction to the previous Maori attack a month before. 'We found that the streets just did not exist,' wrote one tank troop commander; 'there was nothing but rubble everywhere and all our previous recces and plans went overboard. I couldn't find any semblance of the roads . . . so we nosed the tanks through a few gaps.' From there, 'I had no alternative but to get out of the tank and crawl forward among the rubble to find a track . . . Machine-gun fire was rattling like hailstones on the tank as we made our way to the station, firing on the move with the 75mm at any building that looked suspicious.'

The attrition in Cassino would eventually cost the 19th NZ Armoured Regiment two-thirds (forty) of its tanks, and over sixty crewmen killed or wounded. However, by the evening of 17 March, 26th NZ Battalion held the station area, the Round House and a small dominating mound referred to in official histories as 'the Hummocks' or 'the Pimples' (though veterans knew it as 'the Tits'). The station garrison was resupplied at night by jeep. Above them, the Essex in the castle and Gurkhas clinging on to Hangman's Hill were able to subdue some German fire and distract more from decimating the New Zealanders busy in the town.

By the close of the third day, roughly two-thirds of Cassino town was in Allied hands, but the well-built solid bastions of the Hôtel des Roses, the Continental and the abbey itself resolutely defied capture. To the south of the town, downhill from the old colosseum, lay an old abandoned seminary, known in 1944 as the Baron's Place from its imposing appearance, which also remained in German hands, enabling their reinforcement and resupply of the town, and – with the remaining German strongpoints – blocking all access to Route 6, the Via Casilina. The Hôtel des Roses in particular seemed to resist all kinds of fire from 25-pounders and the medium 5.5-inch artillery. This so infuriated the New Zealand CRA, Brigadier Steve Weir, that later he went up to a vantage point near the Corps HQ at Cervaro with the commanding officer of the US 936th Field Artillery Battalion and personally conducted a shoot with a 240mm gun on the hotel, finally doing a good deal of damage to it.

On 18 March, *The Times* picked up on the exhaustive nature of this slogging match in the ruins, informing its readers with a mixture of over-optimism and respect for the enemy: 'The battle for Cassino pursues its grim course across the ruins and rubble of the town. Forces of the Fifth Army have gained all but the south-west part of Cassino, and the Germans are making a determined effort to retain what hold they still have in that part of town. New Zealand troops formed the spearhead of the assault on Cassino, and, with Indian troops, have also taken hill positions overlooking the town. Remnants of buildings and masses of debris have been transformed by the enemy into strongpoints, each one of which has become a sniper's post.'

During the afternoon of the fourth day, while the 24th NZ Battalion were busy in the centre near the Hôtel des Roses, the 25th NZ Battalion were north of Route 6, and the 28th Maori Battalion was committed to try and clear the south-west corner of the town, adjacent to the 26th NZ Battalion around the station, Round House and Hummocks. A company of sixty-two Fallschirmjäger tried to wrest the Round House complex off the Kiwi occupants but were driven off, losing two-thirds of their number in the attack.

So far the battle in Cassino had absorbed four Kiwi battalions of infantry and one of armour, while behind the lines there was grim attrition of another kind. Against the backdrop of awful weather, cold, continuous noise, dust, smoke, shelling, lack of sleep and the stream of casualties, other matters could tip a soldier over the edge. When one of RNZASC driver Jim Wright's acquaintances got bad news from home, that his girlfriend had gone off with an American, 'he pulled out a pistol and put the barrel under his chin and killed himself. We wrapped him in a grey army blanket . . . And then we waited for the chaplain to come around. Once he got there, we carried my mate and dropped him down a hole. I remember the sound he made hitting the bottom. After the war, every time I dropped a dead ewe down the offal pit, the sound reminded me of that night.'

In England, the Eton- and Oxford-educated influential backbench MP Harold Nicolson was relaxing in his beautiful country house, Sissinghurst Castle, in Kent. Married to the author and poet Vita Sackville-West, they had created some of the most stunning gardens anywhere in England; yet he was profoundly ill at ease, and wrote in his diary for Monday 19 March that he had been to his constituency for a meeting, 'where they are annoyed with me for having said that Monte Cassino was more important than Nigel's [his son] life or mine'. Nicolson had earlier in the month debated the issue of whether to sacrifice lives in order to spare works of art, taking the extreme, and passionate, view that the latter were irreplaceable, 'whereas no lives are irreplaceable'. He had gone on to argue hypothetically that he would rather his son, who was serving with the Grenadier Guards in Italy, were killed at Cassino, than the monastery be destroyed, though he did not then know that his son *was* at Cassino. The debate illustrated the degree to which the fighting at Cassino and destruction of the monastery had ignited the passions of the whole nation – for and against.

The day was also to witness the most inspired and bold attack of any in the four Cassino battles, when an armoured column attacked the monastery area itself, arriving from a hitherto unexpected quarter. The Cavendish Road, the five-mile former mule track leading out of Caira village, emerged between Snakeshead and Phantom ridges into a bowl-shaped plateau christened 'Madras Circus' in honour of the 11th and 12th Indian Field Park Engineer Companies who had worked on the project. Beyond, lay paths to the German-held Albaneta Farm complex and the monastery. Albaneta was a lynchpin of the German defences, and its loss would finish the Germans in the monastery, for a ravine led south from the stone farmhouse down to the Via Casilina up and down which all reinforcements, logistics and casualties were moved, as one local Fallschirmjäger commander recalled: 'from the point on the Via Casilina [Route 6] where they took over from the lorries, the pack-animal personnel, night after night, carried supplies up the hillsides. Their only way lay through the dreaded "Dead Man's Gully", which was under constant and concentrated fire, was strewn with the corpses of man and beast and filled with the odours of decay.' It took two hours to reach Albaneta and an hour and a half to reach the monastery. 'The narrow mountain path was littered with boulders, rocks and frequently came tumbling down . . . If the column were caught by enemy fire, the men, of course, took what cover they could, but the animals often broke loose and went hurtling down the precipitous hill-sides; or some animal would be hit, and then the man had to take over its heavy load by himself.'

The plan was originally to use the Cavendish Road to launch an attack at the back of the monastery on the morning after the aerial bombardment, but all dates had now changed. The fresh and ill-thought-out plan seems to have emanated from an overworked New Zealand Corps HQ. A total of forty-seven tracked armoured vehicles from three different national forces (New Zealand, America and India – a command nightmare) were assembled and placed under the command of Lieutenant Colonel John Adye, the Indian Division's acting commander Royal Artillery (a curious choice, for he had no experience of leading armour). When the New Zealand squadron commander requested infantry support for the mission he was told the Indian brigades had lost so many casualties that no riflemen would be accompanying them.

Although widened to take armour, with towering cliffs on one side and a sheer drop on the other, the thirty-ton M-4 Shermans and fifteen-ton M-5 Stuarts ('Honeys') might have wished for a wider thoroughfare up the Cavendish Road. The vehicles made their way part of the way up the track, and then waited under camouflage nets for the off. While Sandy Galloway of 4th Indian Division was trying to organise a Gurkha attack on the monastery from Hangman's Hill and the Essex were under attack in their castle, the armour was let loose. The vehicles began labouring uphill at 6 a.m. in a heavy morning mist, the track rising 800 feet in a mile and a half, with two sharp bends and an average gradient of one in four. By 7.30 a.m. they reached Madras Circus.

While some of the American armour peeled off to deal with German positions on Phantom Ridge, Colonel Adye's tank, among others, shed a track on the stony terrain, and S-mines went 'off like crackers under the tracks'. Nevertheless, the New Zealand Shermans lumbered on to attack the monastery, although confined to the single track, with their commanders vulnerable to Fallschirmjäger snipers. For one tank commander, Corporal Dick Jones, 'it was getting very uncomfortable with the head out, I tried commanding with the turret closed, using the periscope, but between fumes from the guns and the rough going found it impossible'.

The tanks advanced, leapfrogging each other in 300-yard bounds, each tank giving covering fire in turn. Just as Buck Renall, Corporal Jones's troop leader, gave the word to move, 'a German crawled out of the scrub waving a white flag. I think that if we had had infantry we could have captured many prisoners as they were starting to appear everywhere. As we leapfrogged our way forward it became obvious that we had caught Jerry napping. Buck wiped out a machine-gun nest, the Germans bravely firing away at us until the end.'

Dick Jones's tank reached and attacked the Germans at Albaneta Farm, while Buck Renall was sent on, down the track which rounded the southern shoulder of Point 593, with the Liri valley in full view to their right. 'Two tanks were to cover Albaneta House as we were certain some Jerries must be there – we had seen four pop up from behind a wall some time earlier,' explained Major P. A. Barton, the NZ squadron leader. 'It was not possible to get around the rear of the house as it was perched on the edge of a gully and the going was too tough . . . Renall disappeared around the corner and we waited anxiously to hear from him. All went well for a while and then silence. I cannot remember now that we ever heard any more over the air from Buck Renall.'

Trooper Frank Bruce, in Renall's tank, remembered reaching the crest of the slope and 'could see the back of the monastery. There was a gap of about twenty yards and we could see Germans running across and down a steep hill.' The Sherman was less than half a mile away from the abbey – tantalisingly close. Just when the odds were tipping in the Allies' favour, fate intervened. The audacious Renall, commanding from out of his cupola, was killed by a headshot from a Fallschirmjäger sniper. At the same time other defenders had woken up and used *Panzerschreck* bazookas to damage the tank, forcing it to withdraw all the way to Madras Circus.

Faced with this setback on a narrow mountain track, Colonel Adye and Major Barton radioed back for orders and were eventually told to resume the attack, which they did after rescuing several trapped tank crewmen. This time, it was US tanks that led the assault towards Albaneta and the monastery. On the receiving end, in the HQ of 2/Battalion, 4th Fallschirmjäger Regiment, a large cavern in the cliff face, a report arrived of enemy tanks, which battalion commander Rudolf Böhmler explained, 'was regarded as a feeble joke. No one thought it possible for enemy armour to have penetrated into the steep, rugged, mountain country.' But Oberleutnant Eckel commanding the anti-tank company was sent to investigate, and 'from the shelter of a rock they suddenly caught sight of a number of enemy tanks, rattling along a narrow mountain path'.

Several of the tanks were 'circling round the fortress-like Albaneta, firing wildly in all directions', and Eckel despatched one, but three followed the route taken earlier by Renall's New Zealand troop and drove towards the monastery. Beyond the headquarters cave the track funnelled in to a narrow defile with a wall of rock leading to Point 593 on one side and a sharp drop on the other: a bottleneck, perfect for an ambush. At point-blank range, Eckel immobilised the leading American Stuart, dubbed 'Dead Eye Dick', commanded by Lieutenant John A. Crews, with a single shot from a *Panzerschreck*. Finding some Teller (anti-tank) mines, Eckel hastened ahead of the remaining armoured vehicles to lay them across the track.

A second Stuart, 'Devil's Playmate', commanded by Sergeant Lawrence R. Custer, manoeuvred around Lieutenant Crews's disabled tank and hit these mines further on. From interpreting photographic evidence, Custer seemed to have advanced almost as far as Renall earlier in the day, before this second armoured attack also faltered. Thereafter, the assault petered out, as the attackers tried to rescue crewmen from the damaged tanks, and other US Shermans and Stuarts were disabled or bogged, so that by the time the remaining vehicles withdrew to Madras Circus at about 5.30 p.m., nineteen of the forty-four tanks that started had been disabled in some way, with twenty-nine Allied crewmen killed, wounded or captured.

'Panic now gripped the crews of the surviving tanks,' wrote Rudolf Böhmler. 'Turrets were torn open, the crews poured out and sought safety in headlong flight. But they did not get very far. From all sides a murderous fire was opened on them; some fell at once, others tried to put up a fight, but they quickly realised the hopelessness of their position and surrendered.' Although Böhmler's account doesn't in any way accord with the Allied post-action reports, in essence, using the best weapon of all – surprise – the Allies had come to within an inch of unhingeing the German defences and taking the abbey. That they failed was down to a lack of infantry support, which had been requested. Air support had not been requested, and was vital: the whole business had been rushed and was poorly planned. There is no doubt that a couple of companies of infantry plus a troop of engineers working with the Shermans and Stuarts would have swept through the positions and into the monastery before the Germans could have reacted, but Allied armour on its own would never have survived, even if it reached the abbey complex. A brilliant opportunity had been squandered.

The tank attack along the Cavendish Road, Freyberg's last major attempt to seize the initiative, cost the 20th NZ Armoured Regiment eleven casualties and sixteen tanks disabled. The month as a whole was far deadlier with fifty-four killed, wounded or captured, while most of the unit's vehicles at some stage were disabled by enemy fire, throwing tracks, getting bogged down or tipping into ditches. Scenting a good news story for the German propaganda machine, a German cine cameraman happened to be on Point 593 that day and recorded footage of the tank attack on Albaneta, which was shown in the weekly newsreel *Die Deutsche Wochenschau*, the camera lingering on crippled Allied tanks amid the abbey's ruins.

After nearly a week in Cassino town, the main aim of the attack – to gain control of the Route 6, the Via Casilina, and thus storm the Liri valley – had not been achieved. The third battle had, in fact, dissolved into a muddle of six New Zealand battalions, plus armour, trying to overcome the remaining German centres of resistance based in several big stone buildings that had somehow survived the bombing and shelling. In their reports, most Allied newspapers reached out for the language they had used a year earlier to describe the Stalingrad campaign, perhaps hoping that Cassino, too, would prove the graveyard of another German army. On 20 March, *The Times* told its readers: 'By last evening the New Zealanders, fighting their way through the rubble of demolished houses, had quenched German resistance in the town except for two strongpoints.' Their 'progress across the wreck of the town has not been easy. The Germans had prepared deep shelters in the hillside caves, whence they emerged after the bombardment and resisted stubbornly. The movement of our supporting tanks was made difficult by the immense mounds of rubble caused by our bombing.'

Freyberg, to further protect his forces, now ordered a permanent smoke screen over Cassino by day, which all found detrimental. New Zealand infantry complained the smoke stung their eyes and throats, while the Germans at times needed respirators, and the Allied field artillery batteries, firing up to 10,000 rounds per day, soon found they were dealing with worn barrels and blistered hands. Sometimes, wind blew the smoke backwards, filling gun positions with the stuff and suffocating gunners, who were obliged to don gasmasks, and several were medically evacuated to be treated for the after-effects of their own smoke.

After a conference with his divisional commanders that same day, Freyberg agreed to refresh the attack by inserting the 21st NZ Battalion shortly after midnight to attack the Continental Hotel area, but on 21 March a whole platoon of its D Company were spotted by German troops in the hotel, surrounded and taken prisoner. A German cameraman was on hand to film the mass capture. In the images, the Kiwi prisoners appear understandably very nervous: they had just been searched and several were found to be carrying Fallschirmjäger jump badges, taken from dead or captured paratroops.

The Nazi Party's newspaper *Völkischer Beobachter* reviewed the Wehrmacht's success '*in dem Krater Bereichen Cassino*' ('In the Crater Fields of Cassino') with words of uncharacteristic veracity: 'Last Wednesday morning, in beautiful sunshine following a relatively quite night punctuated by the usual raids, hundreds of four-engined bombers, pursuit bombers and escorts hurled themselves upon the Cassino area in deeply echeloned waves for almost three hours . . . An Indian division attacked from the north of the town and a New Zealand division made another frontal assault against the bulwark which till then had put up such a glorious and extraordinarily powerful defence . . . even now, in spite of the heaviest air and ground bombardment of our positions so far, the enemy had deluded himself . . . Bitter resistance, above all by the paratroops who again defied death in their defence of this position on the southern front, meant that the first day brought the adversary only minimal territorial gains in a totally ruined town, and, as in all his attacks, he again had to suffer the severest losses.'

Freyberg still felt he could take the town. When, at an army commander's conference, Mark Clark suggested: 'I think you and the Boche are very groggy,' Freyberg stubbornly insisted that his corps could carry on. Despite having a reputation for a 'band of brothers' style of command, for welcoming and incorporating advice in formulating his plans, on 21 March he was deaf to pleas from his superior to cease. Similarly, before the bombing of 15 February, Freyberg had refused to meet what he called 'a soviet' of divisional commanders, Dimoline and Kippenberger, who had come to press their pleas for an alternative to his plan.

Eventually, Freyberg was forced to conclude that to continue attacking with fresh troops (Keightley's 78th Battleaxe Division) might be reinforcing failure, and – more importantly – he ran the risk of committing his reserve, kept back in case a swift pursuit was necessary up the Liri valley. Managing to punch through the Gustav Line, then being unable to exploit the opportunity due to a lack of reserves, led to the 78th not being committed, except in holding the castle. This meant that any further action in the town would have to be undertaken by the New Zealanders themselves.

On 22 March, elements of three Kiwi battalions, 21st, 23rd and 25th, tried to subdue the German defenders around the Hôtel des Roses; their failure to do so signalled that Freyberg's corps had run out of ideas and exhausted its fighting strength, something that Freyberg could no longer deny when on 23 March he met his divisional commanders, Galloway of the 4th Indian, Parkinson of the New Zealand and Keightley of the 78th. He immediately called Clark, who agreed, and General Alexander himself arrived at Cervaro that afternoon to discuss dispositions, no doubt relieved that this phase at Cassino had ceased. The New Zealand Corps had only ever been a temporary device with which to resume the offensive after the first battle of Cassino. On 26 March, Freyberg's corps was dissolved and the Allies went over to the defensive.

On the same day, Lieutenant Richard Gade of the British Army Film and Photo Unit (AFPU) accompanied the 25th NZ Battalion (who would lose six officers and 217 men, out of an establishment of thirty-five officers and 741 other ranks) into Cassino on the evening of 25–26 March, skirting 'the deepest craters I have ever seen. They were like wells. Way down in the bottom of each was water which reflected the dim skylight . . . In the gloom you couldn't tell whether you were stepping down messed-up streets or over house tops. It was all the same . . . Puffing, grunting men were unhitching their webbing in the dark.' Gade found their New Zealand accents strange and new. 'Flat-toned, drawn-out vowels. And you could rarely tell from tone of voice who was an officer and who was an OR [other rank]. They seem to all talk the same way. Much of their conversation concerned people called Pommies. After a few minutes I got it – the Pommies are English.'

On the same day that Freyberg originally issued orders for Operation Dickens, 22 February, Alexander's chief of staff, John Harding, had submitted his own appreciation of the problem, which would become the plan for fourth Cassino, Operation Diadem. Freyberg could simply have waited until Diadem but instead he had chosen carry on chipping away at Cassino. The reasons Freyberg persisted with the third attack were varied. He realised he needed to keep the initiative and carry on whittling down his opponents, and indeed Clark stated he required action that would take the pressure off Anzio, although the situation there had eased. Freyberg may have felt the Germans were about to collapse, and another attack would succeed; he may also have assumed the weather was changing (hence his surprise when Dickens was continually postponed). Wilson, Alexander, Clark and Freyberg also shared a sense of frustration that those assets the Allies possessed in abundance – aircraft, artillery and armour – were of limited use at Cassino, and to date had been minimally employed; Freyberg was perhaps reaching out to use these weapons because he *had* them, not because they were the most appropriate.

The need to keep casualty numbers down by resorting to any technological method was also at play in the background, both from his own experience and the insistence of New Zealand's Prime Minister (between November 1941 and May 1943 combat in North Africa had already cost the New Zealanders over 11,000). Freyberg's deputy, Howard Kippenberger, who knew him very well, however felt privately 'the only sort of battle in which General Freyberg was any good was the . . . set-piece battle, of which he was a master', a criticism that was often labelled at Montgomery. What 'Kip' meant was that a fluid battle with many circumstances beyond his control was too much of a challenge, but one set within geographical confines, between known opposing forces, to a predetermined timetable, was easier to control – and win – and Freyberg may thus have felt that a third 'set-piece' chip at Cassino was too much to resist.

'There was something almost obsessive about Freyberg's behaviour from the moment he came before Cassino,' wrote the historian Richard Holmes. 'I do not think it a coincidence that from the first he was like a moth to the flame of the positions held by the German paras, the very men who had bundled him humiliatingly out of Crete in May 1941.' There may have been an element of hubris – a desire to be acknowledged as the victor of Cassino, where so many other Allies had failed. Freyberg held out for a breakthrough: from mid-February he had received reinforcements in the form of 78th Division, several extra batteries of artillery and Combat Command B of the US First Armoured Division; with nearly twenty infantry battalions, almost a thousand guns and 300 tanks, he had on hand two armoured brigades with which to race up the Liri valley when the breakthrough came.

Freyberg was clearly aware of (but deaf to) the potentially counter-productive effect of strategic bombing of Cassino town, indeed Colonel Stephen B. Mack of US XII Air Support Command warned him that the streets would be choked with rubble, closing access to tanks 'for at least two days', and huge bomb craters that would challenge infantry.

There were also higher level issues. The real reason why Alexander, Clark and Freyberg felt obliged to continue battering away at Cassino was political pressure emanating from Churchill himself, whose baby the whole Italian campaign was (Roosevelt and Marshall by now having their eyes fixed firmly on Normandy). First, the Churchill-sponsored landing at Anzio in January had made no headway; now Cassino was proving just as obdurate to the amateur tactician. 'I wish you would explain to me,' wrote Churchill to Alexander, his favourite general, in an uncharacteristically terse secret telegram of 20 March, 'why this passage by Cassino, Monastery Hill, etc., all on a front of two or three miles, is the only place which you must keep butting at. About five or six divisions have been worn out going into these jaws. Of course, I do not know the ground or the battle conditions, but, looking at it from afar, it is puzzling why, if the enemy can be held and dominated at this point, no attacks can be made on the flanks. It seems very hard to understand why this most strongly defended point is the only passage forward, or why, when it is saturated [in a military sense], ground cannot be gained on one side or the other. I have the greatest confidence in you and will back you up through thick and thin, but do try to explain to me why no flanking movements can be made.'

The diary of his CIGS, Brooke, for 20 March, is revealing on the background to this missive: 'One of the worst of Cabinet meetings with Winston in one of his worst moods! Nothing that the army does can be right and he did nothing but belittle its efforts in the eyes of the whole Cabinet. I cannot stick any more meetings like it!' Alex, unaware of Churchill's mood, and with enough on his plate without Winston's demands, replied the same day in a polite, fluent telegram that was probably drafted by John Harding. In it, Alexander spelled out Harding's vision for Operation Diadem, concluding: 'I am meeting Freyberg and the army commanders tomorrow to discuss the situation . . . The Eighth Army's plan for entering the Liri valley in force will be undertaken when regrouping is completed. The plan must envisage an attack on a wider front and with greater forces than Freyberg has been able to have for this operation. A little later, when the snow goes off mountains, the rivers drop, and the ground hardens, movement will be possible over terrain which at present is impassable.'

Churchill was sufficiently mollified to cable back on 21 March: 'Thank you very much for your full explanation. I hope you will not have to "call it off" when you have gone so far. Surely the enemy is very hard-pressed too. Every good wish. The war weighs very heavy on us all just now.' The pressure was off – for the moment.

10

Poland the Brave

IT WAS CLEAR to Alexander and Wilson that each of the previous three attacks at Cassino had failed because of the scale of operations attempted: far too few divisions had been employed, with too few resources, on too narrow a front. As early as 5 March, *before* the third battle, Alexander had discussed regrouping and relocating his forces with his two army commanders, Clark and Leese. In April, General John Harding confirmed these groupings and devised Diadem, to correct the flaws of the earlier schemes.

Harding concluded the Allies needed to virtually abandon ongoing operations on the Adriatic coast and concentrate *all* combat power in the west. This would enable simultaneous, corps-sized attacks on Cassino where previously there had been divisional assaults, and elevate the fourth battle from a series of tactical operations to a fluid, interconnected operational-level plan. Harding with Diadem saw an opportunity to not merely gain ground but degrade German formations to such an extent that they would need to be replaced from another theatre – in other words, that the breaking of the Gustav Line would not be an end in itself, but a means – with the troops at Anzio – to destroying the German presence in Italy.

Diadem was inspired, pure *Blitzkrieg*, and would be the largest set piece Allied assault to date. It has been overlooked in history because of the Normandy battles which stole the headlines and commenced a mere twenty-five days later. Under conditions of maximum surprise, it was planned that massed artillery fire and aerial support would create breaches in the Gustav Line, in conjunction with engineers and infantry; and through this breach Allied armour and motorised units would pour, outflank and then pursue the enemy.

The ultimate prize at Cassino, capturing the abbey, would fall to a national army which had had the toughest journey getting there, and a people that owed the Allies very little. By 1944, most Poles had already endured more hardship before seeing shots fired in anger than most average combat soldiers would see in their careers.

In September 1939, Germany and Russia partitioned Poland almost equally between themselves and started to repress Poles immediately. (Much later in his career the Polish corps commander at Cassino, General Anders, would joke with George S. Patton that 'if his corps got caught between a German and Russian army, he would have difficulty in deciding which they wanted to fight the most'.) German excesses in Poland were bloody and overt, while in the Soviet zone the NKVD moved in to eliminate the Polish military and cultural elite: as many as 1.7 million were rounded up and sent to Siberian gulags. The Polish community in exile soon realised that many of its top leaders were missing: over 20,000 were later found executed with a pistol shot to the back of the head in mass graves uncovered in the Katyń Forest, near Smolensk.

After the defeat of their own country in 1939, Poland's servicemen were ordered to carry on the fight elsewhere and saw action in the French campaign of 1940. After Dunkirk, some 35,000 Polish airmen, soldiers and sailors arrived in Britain, making up the largest non-Commonwealth military force in the country. Polish troops evacuated to Britain in 1940 formed I Polish Corps, based in Scotland, which eventually sent the 1st Polish Armoured Division to Normandy in 1944 and deployed the 1st Polish Parachute Brigade over Arnhem in September the same year.

With the German invasion of Russia on 22 June 1941, Stalin needed his Polish prisoners to form fighting units under Russian command to repel the Nazi invaders. In British eyes, Poland's fighting reputation remained high, so one of Churchill's stipulations in return for aid to the Soviet Union was the release of the remaining Poles from the Siberian gulags to which they had been banished; no one knew how many were still left alive of the original 1.7 million deportees, who could form an independent force.

The man chosen to lead this force was the charismatic and determined Lieutenant General Władysław Anders, born in 1892 to a Baltic-German father in what is now and had previously been Poland, but was then Western Russia. As a young officer, he served in a Tsarist cavalry regiment during the First World War. September 1939 found him commanding the horsed *Mazowiecka* Cavalry Brigade, which engaged German mounted units with some success, before being wounded at least eight times and captured by the Soviets. Subsequently he was jailed and tortured for having 'betrayed the international proletariat by fighting the Bolsheviks in 1918–1920'. In March 1940, he was transferred to the headquarters of the NKVD in Moscow, the Lubyanka prison, where he faced a year of interrogation, fear and poor health, but escaped execution.

Six weeks after Barbarossa, on 4 August 1941, Anders was surprised to be hauled out of prison and told that the head of the Polish government in exile, General Władysław Sikorski, had signed an agreement in London on 20 July enabling the formation, training and equipping of a two-division Polish corps within the Soviet Union, which he was to lead. Following the signing of a further agreement in Moscow on 14 August detailing force numbers, news spread through the gulags of the Poles' 'freedom' to join this army, under what the Soviets termed an 'amnesty'. With the deadly Siberian winter approaching, and afraid that orders for their release would be revoked, swarms of Poles began dragging themselves from camps scattered throughout the Soviet Union – frequently walking in sub-zero conditions – to the nominated concentration area of Buzuluk where they lived under canvas with inadequate rations, clothing and equipment. Yet, Soviet cynicism towards the Poles persisted and only intense lobbying in December 1941 resulted in higher agreed force levels and a move to the less harsh climes of Kazakhstan.

Churchill had already backed the Poles by sending them military clothing. Sixteen-year-old Franek Rymaszewski remembered the 'still freezing temperatures at night in the south of Russia, and mud and slush in daytime. We slept in Soviet-made summer tents on the ground without any heating, 18–20 soldiers to a tent . . . But instead of rags and lice I now wore new, warm British battledress and real leather boots – heavenly comfort!' General Sikorski in London was determined that Poles under Russian command would liberate their homeland and thus could influence the future of their state, with 'boots on the ground'. Yet Anders knew his followers – over 70,000 men and as many dependants again – were undernourished and weakening through typhus, malaria, dysentery and jaundice, and would only survive if they left the Soviet Union altogether, perhaps moving to more benign British control in the Middle East. He argued that from there they could participate in an Allied drive through the Balkans and into southern Poland.

Colonel Klemens Rudnicki, who had led the 9th Lancers in September 1939, remembered of this time: 'In the spring, diseases again began to decimate our division; first typhus, then typhoid fever, brought to us by new recruits and civilians . . . The doctors were almost helpless; there were no medicines. For a long time ten to twenty people died each day.' Anders won his argument only after Stalin decided to reduce the already meagre rations to the Polish contingent in March 1942, permitting 'non-essential personnel' to depart for Jumbo Wilson's British Ninth Army, based in Iran. It was certainly the case that many – if not most – Poles owed their lives directly to Anders's overbearing personality in getting them out of Russia; this remained the case as his uniformed force moved to and fought at Cassino. As his deputy commander in Italy, Lieutenant General Bohusz-Szyszko later noted: 'I must say that every Polish eye was fixed on our corps commander, General Anders. Always calm and confident of victory, he was a source of inspiration to all of us. His superb assurance sustained us in adversity . . . And this faith spread to the humblest private.'

During April and August 1942, over 45,000 Polish soldiers, plus 25,000 families, were moved across the Caspian Sea to Pahlevi on the Persian coast (Iran); others, escapees from collective farms and gulags, managed to make their own way overland. Tragically, 2,806 refugees died within a few months of arriving and were buried in cemeteries throughout Iran. After this exodus, the Soviet door slammed shut, for Stalin then decreed those Poles remaining would be Soviet citizens. No one counted the total of these 'non-essential' Polish refugees who arrived in Persia, but it is thought to be between

114,000 and 300,000. Over 13,000 of the arrivals were children, some of them orphans whose parents had died on the way – starving mothers had pushed their children onto passing trains in the hope of saving them. The majority of fit survivors, including children as young as fourteen, volunteered for Anders's force; others began life in refugee camps, eventually to move on and found the Polish diaspora in the United States, Britain, Canada, Australia, South Africa, New Zealand and elsewhere.

At this stage Anders realised he was lacking experienced officers and NCOs, of whom around 15,000 were known to have disappeared in Soviet captivity. With the discovery of the Katyñ graves, Moscow broke off diplomatic relations with the London Poles in April 1943 following Sikorski's request that the International Red Cross investigate the massacre, but Anders and his Poles were by now safe outside the USSR. His boss, General Sikorski, however, died in July 1943 when his RAF transport plane, on a return flight from inspecting Anders's Polish Corps, crashed after leaving Gibraltar, in circumstances that have never been properly explained. Anders reluctantly replaced Sikorski as the Polish figurehead, carrying on his shoulders the hopes of a nation scattered around the world, expecting to return home.

By June 1943, most of the surviving Polish non-combatants had been moved to India, while Anders's force – now named II Polish Corps – had been joined by Colonel Stanisław Kopański's 5,000-strong Independent Carpathian Rifle Brigade (formed in 1940 from Poles who had escaped from their homeland via Romania and Syria to Palestine) which had fought at Tobruk; it was enlarged to 13,200 and renamed the 3rd Carpathian Rifle Division. The division's badge was a green fir tree on a bisected red and white background, Poland's national colours – the fir was to remind its wearers of the forest-covered Carpathian Mountains back home. There were also some 1,200 volunteers of the Polish Women's Auxiliary Service (ambulance and truck drivers, couriers and mechanics, who wore the distinctive Australian slouch hat) and 3,000 underage men and women who formed the Labour Auxiliary Service. They also brought with them their mascot, an orphaned Iranian bear cub named Wojtek (Slavic-Polish for 'happy soldier') which, close to death, had been adopted by soldiers as they drove from Persia via British-occupied Iraq to Palestine in April 1942. Officially enrolled in the Polish Corps, and possessing the correct paperwork, as Private Wojtek he would eventually accompany his unit to Italy.

In August 1943, at the US-British-Canadian Quebec conference, code-named Quadrant, Churchill got agreement to send II Polish Corps to Italy. In Palestine, they were all reissued with British battledress sporting Polish rank and insignia, weapons and equipment – including 660 artillery pieces, 600 mortars and Vickers machine guns, 170 tanks, 180 armoured cars, 5,300 trucks – 12,500 vehicles in all. Meanwhile some kindly Polish commanders looked the other way as nearly 3,000 Polish Jews disappeared from Anders's units, and recorded their disgust at having to help British military police search *kibbutzim* for them as the rest of the corps moved finally to Egypt. Several convoys of Polish destroyers and merchantmen shepherded the corps from Egypt to southern Italy, where they spent the first months in Italy in Eighth Army's sector, holding the line and patrolling along the River Sangro. On 29 December 1943, the Independent Commando Company was the first Polish unit to be bloodied in a raid on German positions along the River Garigliano. On 13 March, the 5th Kresowa Infantry Division relieved 2nd Moroccan Division at Castel San Vincenzo.

Nine days later, on 24 March, Oliver Leese visited Anders at his HQ in Vinchiaturo (east of Monte Lungo) and formally requested him with his chief of staff, Colonel Casimir Wisniowski, and interpreter Prince Eugene Lubomirski, to take part in the forthcoming fourth battle of Monte Cassino. Despite the presence of Lubomirski, Leese felt the gravity of the moment and made the request in a mutual language – schoolboy French. Afterwards Anders wrote: 'It was a great moment for me. The difficulty of the task assigned to the Corps was obvious . . . I realised the cost in lives must be heavy, but I realised too the importance of the capture of Monte Cassino to . . . Poland, for it would answer once and for all the Soviet lie that the Poles did not want to fight the Germans. Victory would give new courage to the resistance movement in Poland and would cover Polish arms with glory. After a short moment's reflection I answered that I would undertake the task.'

Harold Macmillan, Resident Minister in North Africa, visited Anders for lunch in April 1944 and thought him 'very attractive – a keen soldier and a powerful political controversialist. Fortunately, for the time being the former interest is uppermost in his mind. But naturally memories of Poland, fear for his fate, and equal hatred of Russians and Germans are never far removed from his thoughts.' Though Anders accepted his corps' mission with alacrity, it was not a decision taken lightly. He was acutely aware that, with three failed attacks, he ran the risk of losing his irreplaceable unit. On one hand, he knew Germany and Russia would welcome a Polish defeat, but on the other, success at Cassino would raise the morale of his own force, and of Poles worldwide. Whether he liked it or not, Anders realised he was not only the commander of a fighting formation within Britain's Eighth Army, but he was also a national leader, morally responsible for the thousands of civilians who had, Moses-like, followed him out of the Soviet Union: he was the man they trusted to take them home. Anders was, to a certain extent, already prepared for this moment, having been warned by Oliver Leese in February (the day after the monastery was levelled) that if the next attack by Freyberg's New Zealand Corps failed, he proposed using Anders's Poles in their place.

Final orders for Diadem were issued on 5 May by Alex's headquarters, the Allied Armies in Italy. Fifth Army's front was shortened, its right boundary drawn in westwards from the Liri valley, and Eighth Army's operating zone extended to include Cassino town and the Liri valley. This now meant that Oliver Leese could transfer much of his army's combat power to his left wing to help assault the Cassino area. Diadem envisaged four army corps attacking the Cassino front simultaneously: US II Corps and Juin's French Expeditionary Corps of Fifth Army; and British XIII Corps (comprising 4th, 78th, 8th Indian and 6th Armoured Divisions, plus 1st Canadian Armoured Brigade) and Anders's Polish II Corps. On the eve of Diadem, the Polish Corps numbered 53,508 men and 1,290 women. During the coming months, in an effort to replace substantial casualties, some 35,500 captured Poles who had been conscripted into the Wehrmacht were also offered places in the corps, after first being screened and then sent for training to the Polish 7th Reserve Division back in Palestine.

Alexander, Clark and Leese had managed to assemble in combat power the equivalent of seventeen divisions, over 300,000 troops, in the eighteen miles between Cassino and the sea. Here the Allies hoped to imitate the *Blitzkrieg*-type war at operational level, borrowing from the best German principles of attack. Opposite the Liri valley, with British XIII Corps and the Canadians behind, the Allies would create a *Schwerpunkt*; the centre of gravity or point of maximum effort, where the decisive action would be achieved. A corps either side would enable the break-in and then would guard the flanks – the French to the left, the Poles to the right. They were practising what Panzer commander Heinz Guderian often preached, '*klotzen nicht kleckern*' – 'strike concentrated, not dispersed'. A glance at the Allied order of battle confirms that most of the Allied armour lay with the *Schwerpunkt* waiting to break into the Liri valley.

Part of Diadem's genius lay in the fact that it did not rely on the obvious movement corridor of the Liri valley for its success; for this Harding had to thank the Frenchman, Juin. General Alphonse Juin had a personal aversion to attritional, frontal attacks of the kind he had experienced in the First World War and had witnessed more recently at Cassino. He drew Harding's attention to the possibility of using the Aurunci mountain range to the left of the Liri valley as a movement corridor for the experienced mountain warriors of his corps. This would be the last place the Germans would expect an attack: the Aurunci were considered impassable and German eyes were on the Liri valley, Cassino and Anzio.

While the Allies possessed an overwhelming material abundance of men and resources, this size could in itself become a hindrance, leading to slow, clumsy decisions, and even slower manoeuvres. Speed would be of the essence, for a swift advance could paralyse the enemy's ability to react. Moving faster than their opponents, Allied mobile forces aimed to act before the Germans could formulate a response. Alexander hoped that every German reaction would require time to gather intelligence, make a decision, issue orders, and act. Similarly, if there was pressure all along the German fronts at Cassino and Anzio, Alexander and Harding hoped the simultaneous nature of the rapid decisions forced on Kesselring might allow the Allies to perform this cycle quicker than the Germans, and permit Diadem to achieve spectacular results.

However, arrayed opposite the Allies was Vietinghoff's Tenth Army, with the majority of the front about to be attacked in the capable hands of General Frido von Senger and his XIV Panzer Corps, all well versed in *Schwerpunkts*, *Blitzkriegs*, and everything else the Allies were belatedly attempting to imitate. Their inter-corps boundary had been shifted to the line of the River Liri, in the middle of the valley, so that Senger's XIV Corps had responsibility for the south and General der Gebirgstruppen Valentin Feuerstein's LI Mountain Corps took over the northern sector, including the heights of Monte Cassino. Feuerstein's front was defended by the 1st Fallschirmjäger Division between the town of Cassino and Point 593. Further to the north, the sector up to Monte Caira was held by the 5th German Mountain Division; beyond them lay some of the long-suffering 44th Hoch und Deutschmeister Division. In the valley was a medley of units: the 115th PanzerGrenadier Regiment, two battalions of 305th Division and the Parachute Machine-gun Battalion of 1st Fallschirmjäger, known as *Kampfgruppe Bode*, after its commander. Whereas Diadem incorporated masses of fresh Allied troops, all these German formations, if used to the terrain, were stale, battered and severely under strength.

Opposite Juin's French Corps in the Aurunci Mountains were the 71st Infantry Division, with three battalions from 44th Division under command, while the 94th Infantry Division were also in the hills, but overlooking the coastal sector, opposite Keyes's US II Corps. Most of 90th PanzerGrenadier Division was on call as Tenth Army reserve, while the remainder of 15th PanzerGrenadier Division was split up into battalion-sized reserve battlegroups, something to which Senger took great exception. The act had been made in Senger's absence, and after the battle, he would always argue that keeping 15th PanzerGrenadiers intact as a powerful reserve force would have made more sense than frittering away the formation in little battlegroups. Their firepower, by now eroded, still included around 230 artillery pieces, with forty six-barrelled *Nebelwerfers*. One of the most feared weapons, *Nebelwerfers* could be towed from site to site, using 'shoot-and-scoot' tactics, and send a concentration of fire very accurately over the mountains for around four miles. Its rockets were delivered in 'stonks' of six, their arrival being heralded by a high-pitched scream emitted from the warheads – hence its nickname of 'Moaning Minnie' – with terrifying effect: 'The moan grew loader. We ducked into trenches. I had time to notice the exact growth of my fear. It began in the calves, welled up through the loins and stomach, and finally struck home in the throat. As the moan changed to a deafening roar, I think I screamed. A series of explosions shook the ground.' Most of the German machine-gun nests had also survived the successive bombardments intact, and laced the battlefield with deadly overlapping and interlocking arcs of fire.

General Anders's task amidst this massive array of fighting power was to attack and capture the area of the Monastery Hill from the north and north-east and to dominate Route 6, until a link up could be made with British XIII Corps to the west. The Polish effort was always conceived of in wider terms than the capture of the monastery; the ultimate objective was to reach the Hitler Line (in the Liri valley) and outflank it to the north-east. In order to better understand the ground, on 7 April Anders made an extensive low-level reconnaissance over the battleground in a spotter aircraft.

Whereas the previous American and Indian Division attacks had followed the single axis of Snakeshead Ridge, Anders saw that terrain would allow two narrow divisional axes for his corps, both starting up the narrow track from Caira village – Cavendish Road. Romuald E. Lipinski, in the mortar platoon of the 12th Podolski Lancers, remembered his nerve-wracking march up into the hills: 'We were told that any talk while marching was forbidden because the enemy could hear and that would bring artillery fire on us.' It was impossible to walk outside the footpath due to landmines scattered everywhere. 'We were walking in complete silence, it is hard to estimate how long did we walk, but finally we reached the positions of our predecessors. I think they were British. We did not have to change anything as far as our equipment is concerned: they had their mortars in place with various targets marked. One of them was the monastery.'

The 3rd Carpathian Division were to move along Snakeshead Ridge and destroy the German defences at Albaneta Farm and on Point 593, overlooking the monastery, and held by 1st Battalion/3rd Fallschirmjäger Regiment. Simultaneously, the 5th Kresowa Division would clear the lower slopes of Monte Cairo, via Phantom Ridge to seize the Colle Sant'Angelo (occupied by Hauptmann Kurt Veth's 2nd Battalion/3rd Fallschirmjäger Regiment). All this high ground overlooked the monastery. Ironically, Anders discovered that while shelling and aerial bombing had destroyed most of the monastery complex, the only part left relatively intact was the thick north-western walls, containing rows of tiny, loophole-like windows – exactly the face he was now obliged to assault. In fact, as they soon discovered, the monastery was not the key to the defensive positions, but Point 593, which dominated both Route 6 and the religious settlement.

This peak had, in fact, also been used in earlier centuries for defence, and contained the remains of a small, star-shaped fort.

German defensive sites opposite the Poles appeared to form two rings running along high ground above the monastery, like a figure of eight, with Point 593 at the centre. The rim of one ring comprised the high ground of Point 593, Phantom Ridge, Colle Sant'Angelo, and the Albaneta Farm complex. The other covered Monastery Hill itself and the ground where much of the Polish cemetery now lies. All the German strongpoints around both rings were like seats in the top row of an amphitheatre, from which every scrap of ground could be seen, with no possibility for an attacker to approach unobserved – after months of fighting there was not a scrap of vegetation or tree cover, just bare rock and scree. Most of the stones were loose, which meant that creeping about even at night had its disadvantages. The Poles were actually issued with rubber-soled shoes for night operations. The obvious approaches to most positions were further protected by endless coils of barbed wire and scattered mines, requiring concentrated mortar or artillery fire to eliminate.

The Germans, however, could resupply at night, and had enlarged several natural caves for additional shelter, some completely protected on reverse slopes. Each German position sited along these rings of high ground had all-round defence, and could cover the front or rear of any other position. This meant that the capture of any one position could not defeat either ring; only by capturing at least half of a defensive ring by simultaneous assault could any progress be made. Unless the dominating height of Point 593 fell, it was unlikely that any other positions could be taken and held. Another headache for the Poles was the lack of cover implied only a limited number of forming-up places from which to launch attacks, meaning that simultaneous assaults on several positions were impossible. The other dominating site in German hands was the Massa Albaneta. The complex is now an ivy-clad ruin, but as the remaining masonry and walls hint, it was once a substantial fortified stone monastery, built as an adjunct to the main abbey in the early eleventh century. Its thick stone walls, outbuildings and cellars were variously used as a medical facility, regimental headquarters and supply depot, and were an obvious focal point for the German defenders.

The plentiful supply of loose stone blocks lying around were refashioned by the Germans into pillboxes and bunkers. Consequently it was also an attractive and obvious target for Allied fighter-bombers and artillery. The defenders were well aware of this so stationed much of their local combat power in the surrounding gullies and caves, which were more difficult to locate or subdue. Both sides found the medical and logistics needs of the troops up in the hills were magnified in the May battles due to the heat, and supplying water in particular proved problematical. Wrote a Pole of his rations: 'We are all half-starved, for the food is really bad. We have biscuits, beef and bacon, but these rations are of such inferior quality that very few of us can swallow them . . . I can remember a mule running away with a load of full [water] cans. One of our men ignores the shooting and goes after the animal with a rifle. In the end he is forced to kill the animal rather than lose the precious water . . . Such are the conditions in which we live . . . Tired, hungry, thirsty and surrounded by rotting corpses.'

Meanwhile Wojtek the bear had, to the amusement of all, become accustomed to riding in the front seat of his unit's jeeps. The noises of battle, shelling and gunfire seemed not to affect him. Legend has it that the animal was handed a heavy ammunition box, which he then loaded effortlessly onto a vehicle, and thereafter became a fully integrated member of the loading team, shouldering boxes alongside his mates for the rest of the Cassino campaign. A Polish soldier-artist produced a picture of Wojtek carrying a large artillery shell in his arms, which immediately became the badge of the 22nd Transport Company, worn proudly on their uniform sleeves and painted onto the unit's vehicles.

Crucial to Diadem's success was the requirement for a sophisticated deception plan; this was codenamed Operation Nunton. The first aspect of Nunton was to suggest that the Allies might try a further left hook along the coast north of Rome; the concealment of the arrival of the Canadian and Polish corps, and disguise of the move of the French from the areas of Monte Cairo and Monte Castellone to the Garigliano River, opposite the Aurunci Mountains. But the second was the strict control of daytime movement, suppression of noise and continuance of normal routines to reinforce the impression that a major attack was not imminent – indeed, Ultra intercepts confirmed the Germans' false sense of security.

Between 23 and 28 April, the Poles, and all of Alexander's other troops, assembled in conditions of great secrecy, which meant no patrolling – the risk of capture was too great. The Polish Corps took over positions in the hills occupied by British 78th Battleaxe Division, who had been holding Snakeshead Ridge and the tracks from Caira ever since taking over from 4th Indian Division at the end of the third battle in March. One British officer noticed the Poles 'could never wholly conceal their slight impatience with our attitudes. They hated the Germans, and their military outlook was dominated by their hate. Their one idea was to find out where the nearest Germans were and go after them. It was praiseworthy, but often impractical.'

To support II Corps, Polish artillery had to be sited as far forward as possible, which meant putting the guns into the flat Rapido valley, unfortunately under enemy observation from Monte Cairo and Monastery Hill. Thus the artillery, too, could only be moved at night, and had to be extremely well camouflaged and remain silent until the actual attack started. They, and the rest of Alexander's 1,600 guns, would be screened continuously by smoke for the whole period of the attack, to prevent accurate counter-battery fire. Romuald Lipinski recalls emptying his pockets of all personal possessions in an olive grove prior to the attack. 'We were told to deliver to the headquarters all papers that could identify us by name or by the regiment. All personal papers, letters to our families, documents, etc., had to be collected and left with the regimental office. The only thing that we were allowed to retain were the dog tags, and the equipment that consisted of one blanket, mess kit, and of course, our side arms, in my case my rifle, and ammo.'

In contrast to the earlier three assaults, all Alexander's attacking corps were extremely well resourced (beforehand the Poles dumped over half a million rounds of artillery ammunition for the 294 guns supporting them, and 40,000 rounds of mortar ammunition). This required a huge logistics effort, for the closer to the German lines that combat stores and men were brought, the quieter the operation had to be. The treacly mud of the Rapido plain prevented even four-wheel-drive trucks from getting close to the guns, which meant long columns of men and mules silently picking their way over a torn landscape at night, without lights, portering loads forward, just as an earlier generation had done in the First World War.

Waiting for the 'off', Lipinski and his mates of the 12th Lancers observed that there was always a shortage of food and water: 'everything had to be brought by mules or in the final stage by men. Sometimes the mules were scattered around on the way up by German fire, got blown up on the mines, and only a fraction of the supplies arrived.' As he made his way towards the Polish assembly positions, Lipinski saw all around 'a living testimony of what war is all about. There was not one tree that did have its branches green with leaves. There were only naked limbs, stumps, sticking out here and there. Grass has disappeared also. Bare rocks, covered with dust, unfriendly, were everywhere. Also, there was a testimony of what was there in the past – dead bodies. Some were half decomposed, some half covered with dust or whatever dirt could be scraped from the surface, in most cases, they were covered with lime. These were the reminders of the ferocious fighting that was going there for four months, since January . . . The entire history of the battle could be read from these corpses.'

The first few days of May 1944 were bright and sunny, and waiting troops happily exchanged the mud of winter for the dust of summer. Dawn on 11 May was overcast and some rain fell, but at exactly 11 p.m. that evening the peace was shattered by 1,600 Allied guns beginning a detailed shoot, to systematically destroy all known German gun and mortar positions over the next forty minutes, before switching to suppress the infantry's first objectives. The Allies achieved complete surprise, so much so that many senior Germans were absent. General von Senger wrote that he and Vietinghoff 'had been superfluously ordered to meet Hitler to receive our decorations, after which we had gone on leave', while Army Group C's Chief of Staff, General Westphal, and XIV Panzer Corps' Chief of Staff were also away. The departure of so many key players undoubtedly slowed down the Wehrmacht's response to Diadem in the opening days, allowing the Allies to rapidly overtake the Germans in the speed of their decision-making. Polish Cadet Officer Skaznik remembered of the impressive bombardment: 'tracers like illuminated flying beetles streaked across a multi-coloured sky that reminded me of the aurora borealis'.

Aware of the importance of his task, General Anders deployed three Polish combat photographers to accompany his troops, while Alexander and Leese both issued 'orders of the day' (an old technique of Monty's, to inspire the Allied armies into battle) on the eve of battle. Anders distributed his own moving and patriotic exhortation: 'We go forward with the sacred slogan in our hearts: God, Honour, Country.'

11

Winning Cassino

T HE INFANTRY OF the two Polish divisions began to cross their start
lines shortly after 1 a.m. on 12 May. The Poles were unlucky, for
the Germans had chosen the same night to relieve many of their troops,
so there were double the number of Fallschirmjäger as usual, and the
extra firepower soon pinned down the assaulting battalions of the 5th
Wilno Brigade, who were preceded by engineers, mine-clearing and
route-marking from their forming-up areas towards Phantom Ridge.
The forward battalions of the Kresowa Division suffered one in five
casualties and were halted by murderous fire which made further movement impossible.

The area was soon overwhelmed with casualties under the increasing
weight of enemy fire, and counterattacks. As the slopes of Phantom
Ridge had been pre-registered by German mortars and artillery, the
Poles found themselves in the middle of a rectangle of defensive fire on
rocky ground which offered no suitable shelter. This hideous situation
continued until one in the afternoon, twelve hours after they had left
their start lines, when the divisional commander ordered the remnants
to withdraw.

The infantry of the 1st Carpathian Brigade left their forming-up area
at the same time to attack Snakeshead Ridge, Point 593 and then Albaneta

Farm, supported by a troop of tanks, which could use the track that originated in Caira and ran in the lee of Snakeshead. To preserve surprise, the soldiers exchanged boots for canvas shoes and, each carrying extra bandoliers of ammunition, crept towards their line of departure at a building overlooking the abbey, known to the Poles as the *Domek Doktora* (Doctor's House). Lieutenant Edward Rynkiewicz described the location, which also possessed two fresh water springs, as 'a heap of debris'. Dozens of bodies were scattered everywhere, including a soldier of 4th Indian Division, killed in March; the others 'belonged to various nations, as we could see from the remains of their uniforms. The place was alive with rats, big bloated creatures which scurried about with impunity while we slept. The sickly sweet smell of decaying flesh was nauseating and we could do nothing to rid ourselves of it.'

Their advance soon rushed Point 593, but eventually found the withering fire from Albaneta too much on the exposed, rocky peak. Alerted from the earlier use of tanks back in February, much of the track leading to Albaneta had been mined by the Germans, and the Polish mine-clearing sappers working ahead of the armour lost eighteen out of twenty, several tanks being lost. Covered by artillery and Nebelwerfer fire, the Germans launched seven unsuccessful counterattacks before midday, but Polish casualties were so high that only one officer and seven men remained unwounded on the southern slopes of Point 593. A final counterattack by the last German reserves (just fourteen men available out of the entire 3rd Fallschirmjäger Regiment) forced the Poles to withdraw at about 7 p.m. However, some, like Edward Rynkiewicz, who had found shelter in the enlarged caves just below Point 593 were eventually taken prisoner.

It would be misleading to picture large groups of men advancing in formation across the slopes during this assault; due to the exposed nature of the ground, it was rather more a haphazard affair. As one Polish eyewitness remembered: 'a group of five to ten Germans, armed with hand grenades and machine guns, would suddenly leap out of the ground and capture one of our positions. Then, just as quickly, a handful of Poles would spring up from nowhere and drive off the Germans in the same manner.' Another Pole wrote: 'Soldiers, even when wounded, are reluctant to retreat. We stayed where we were and sought the best cover we could find or contrive. We could not dig in, for the ground was too hard, so we filled sandbags with rocks and made small shelters.'

However, the cost to the defending 1st Fallschirmjäger Regiment of Heidrich's 'Green Devils' was even higher, for they could not replace their losses. One complete battalion was virtually annihilated by Polish artillery, and the strength of some companies was whittled down to twenty men – and the Poles now knew most of their positions. Hauptmann Kurt Veth of 2nd Battalion/3rd Fallschirmjäger Regiment noted of his own casualties: 'Impossible to get wounded away . . . Great number of dead on the slopes – stench – no water – no sleep for three nights – amputations being carried out at battle headquarters.' Veth also recorded how his men were obliged to wear gas masks because the stench from the dead was intolerable in the hot May sun.

Meanwhile, Sidney Kirkman's British XIII Corps' (4th British and 8th Indian Divisions) attack down the Liri valley had begun more or less according to plan, with the leading elements managing to establish a small bridgehead on the western bank of the River Gari. Artillery and mortar fire was lighter than expected because most of the local German defensive fire was concentrated against the Polish Corps on the high ground. As the Poles were withdrawing, XIII Corps had managed to advance nearly a mile beyond the river, but the Bailey bridges were proving a problem, with vehicles and equipment queuing to get across.

During the afternoon of the first day, Oliver Leese arrived at General Anders's HQ and realised that the attacks by the Poles and Kirkman's XIII Corps were not well enough coordinated. This had allowed the Germans to shift their fire and reserves along interior lines, hammering first one Allied corps, then the other, and stalling the advance indefinitely; what was needed was for both corps to attack again, with much closer liaison, maintaining pressure on the defenders, and preventing them from disengaging any reserves committed. Anders was fighting a tactical battle, but Oliver Leese's concern was at the operational level, manoeuvring two army corps, side by side. They agreed to postpone further attacks in the heights until XIII Corps had advanced further down the Liri valley, in particular so that British guns could better support the Poles with shoots directed at German reverse slope positions. Anders's next attack was to be coordinated with the deployment of the reserve

British 78th Infantry Division across their first objective phase line, codenamed 'Pytchley'.

In the heights, the first attack had cost the Poles 4,000 casualties for no gain, and rather than erode the Polish battalions further – the whole corps had dwindling resources of manpower – Anders had his men dig in and consolidate the positions they had, which meant using the night to patrol, or pile up and reinforce their stone sangars. One of those patrolling was Wladek Rubnikowicz, who had been a cadet in the Polish Army in 1939, spent thirteen long months in Bialystok prison and another year in a gulag before joining the great migration through Iran, Iraq and Palestine. There he was recruited into the 12th Podolski Lancers, the reconnaissance regiment of the Carpathian Division. By rights he should have been in an armoured car, but in the fight for the hills around Monte Cassino, Polish pride dictated that everyone take their place in the infantry battle. Wladek remembered the lull after the first Polish attack. 'We were in a lovely meadow below Snakeshead Ridge. You couldn't move by day . . . [or] you would be shot.' He was just behind three men when a shell came over and exploded right of top of them. 'Two of the men disappeared into thin air. There was nothing left. But on a bush nearby I saw the ammunition belt and the stomach of the third. That was all that was left.' The patrols brought in prisoners, and from them it was realised that some of the 1st Fallschirmjäger Regiment had been withdrawn from the hill to reinforce positions in the valley, against the British 4th Division.

A Polish platoon commander remembered: 'We lived in a shifting murk of drifting smoke, heavy with the pestilential reek of death. The very ground we clung to was trembling under the artillery barrage. Yet at night-time, when the guns stopped firing, we could occasionally hear nightingales singing.'

While Polish artillery continued to bombard key German positions, two squadrons of Sherman tanks from the 4th Armoured Regiment, nicknamed 'The Skorpions', attempted to grind forward in small sorties, working with Polish engineers, who slowly cleared a path through the minefield, while fighter-bombers attacked German guns around Albaneta. Taking crossfire, the sappers ingeniously worked from underneath the tanks, as the 5th Division's engineer commander recorded: 'I watched one of the engineers crawl out from beneath the tank and remove the cap from a Teller [anti-tank] mine. As soon as he had done the job, he darted back to the protection of the tank and lay there until the Germans had stopped firing. Then a second sapper wriggled forward to deal with another mine in exactly the same way. After each sapper had disposed of three or four mines, the first tank pulled back and the sappers on the reserve tank took over. We continued with this system for three hours in broad daylight, clearing approximately a hundred mines.'

In many ways, sustaining the Poles in the mountains was as much of a challenge as contesting the peaks with the Germans. By now five Cypriot mule companies were attached to the Polish Corps – having no spare labour of their own – which toiled up and down the narrow Cavendish Road leading from Caira into the hills behind Monte Cassino. En route, Stanislaw Bierkieta, a platoon commander in the 15th Pozañski Lancers (the reconnaissance regiment of the Kresowa Division), recalled a sudden shout from a military policeman to 'take cover': 'I jumped behind a dead mule and found myself lying next to a very dark-skinned chap, who I assumed was a Cypriot. Once the MP declared it was safe to move on, I stood up and then noticed my neighbour remained on the ground. "You can get up now," I told him. He didn't respond. I then realised I had been taking cover next to the blackening corpse of a man killed some time beforehand.'

Over 13 and 14 May a new main effort was devised for 5th Kresowa Division to gain control of the northern defensive ring, Colle Sant'Angelo and Point 575, and link up with the right flank of British XIII Corps. This would isolate any remaining Germans around Monte Cassino. Anders knew that the defenders had only two weakened battalions and a reserve battalion left, while Allied successes down in the Liri valley were bound to draw away even more of Heidrich's already badly eroded Fallschirmjäger Division, and indeed 1st Parachute Regiment had been withdrawn and sent to reinforce the defence against British 4th Division, where the threat was considered greater.

Orders were issued on 14 May for a fresh attack by both divisions beginning at 6 a.m. on 17 May, with an hour's softening up by the massed guns of the Polish Corps. H-Hour was set for 7 a.m., coinciding with

XIII Corps' renewed attack down in the valley. The assault was preceded by a successful overnight raid by the 6 Lwowska Brigade on Phantom Ridge which captured its northern slopes; using the newly won positions as a springboard, a battalion quickly stormed Colle Sant'Angelo, advancing just behind an artillery screen and by 7.30 a.m. were in control of all but its western slopes, where a series of machine-gun nests continued to give trouble. Major General Sulik's Kresowa Division subsequently fought all day for the hill, but in the face of their own losses, counterattacks and German artillery fire, could not quite manage to clear the area. Running out of ammunition on the slopes of Colle Sant'Angelo, and in the face of yet another counterattack, one forward company began hurling stones at the Germans while singing the Polish national anthem to keep up their spirits.

Meanwhile Duch's 3rd Carpathian Division spent the day working their way towards Albaneta Farm and Point 593, with infantry, tanks and engineers working closely together. The advance was painfully slow, with the Poles caught in crossfire from Colle Sant'Angelo, Point 593 and Albaneta Farm; but by the evening of 17 May they were within 150 yards of the farm. Point 593 changed hands several times during the day, as both sides were aware of its importance; the 2nd Carpathian Battalion initially managed to take the crag, but with casualties mounting, their effort started to falter. Oberst Ludwig Heilman's 3rd Fallschirmjäger Regiment counterattacked and won it back with covering machine-gun fire from the rest of the defensive rings; at 2.30 p.m. Lieutenant Colonel Karol Fanslau, a Polish battalion commander, was killed leading an assault on the heights, which was halted only fifty yards from the summit. Results during the day had been achieved mainly by hand-to-hand fighting, while over 200 sorties had been flown overhead to bomb mortar and gun positions. The Poles were utterly exhausted and as the fighting died down, dug in to defend their gains. After a hard day's fighting they had come close to breaking the enemy's northern defensive ring. That night, patrols could hear the noise of movement, which indicated that some of the Fallschirmjäger were thinning out, but there was nothing the tired troops could do to prevent some of their opponents from, wraith-like, slipping away. Meanwhile, any idea of pushing on towards the monastery during 17 May was cancelled because of the remaining threat from German reserves around Albaneta. Yet the four-month battle for Monte Cassino monastery had in fact already culminated – and was about to end in a way that would surprise the Allies.

The next morning at dawn the Poles tried again and managed to finally seize Point 593 by 7 a.m., then went on to capture the lower slopes by mid-morning. Earlier, the Poles had intercepted radio traffic indicating the Germans had ordered a retreat from the monastery. Heidrich, 1st Fallschirmjäger Division's commander, had refused to comply with an order from LI Mountain Corps to redeploy his men to the valley, so Kesselring personally intervened, and this extra wireless traffic alerted the Poles, many of whom were fluent German speakers. At first light, scouts from the Kresowa Division were surprised to find Albaneta Farm abandoned. Likewise, the Carpathian Division's 12th Poldolski Lancers were sent forward to see whether the monastery was still defended; given the paucity of intelligence about the German withdrawal and the determination shown by the Green Devils so far, the reconnaissance must have seemed like a suicide mission.

Robert Frettlöhr was among the Fallschirmjager in the monastery as the Lancers approached. He had been to report inside the abbey, and waited for a pause in the shelling: 'We went and ran like mad to get round the corner of the monastery wall at the bottom . . . what I remember is a big flash.' A grenade had exploded somewhere in the vicinity. 'When I woke up my left leg was like a big balloon, but I knew the monastery was only a couple of yards on the left and I knew the way to get in. I crawled along to the first aid post which was down in St Benedict's Crypt, and they bandaged my leg and said, "There is no way you can walk."' At that moment Frettlöhr realised he would most likely be captured, or worse. Unable to move, he simply waited, expecting to be killed by his captors. 'Then the morning came, we heard shouts of "The Tommies are coming!" A Polish platoon came into the monastery in the morning and asked us: "Are there any mines?" and I said, "No, this is the first aid post." So they came in and we talked to them . . . We had been in that battle for months on end. We were filthy, lousy, full of lice, unshaven; we must have looked a hell of a sight.'

The Polish cavalrymen entering the monastery's remains discovered only wounded Fallschirmjäger, corpses and rubble. Thereupon the Lancers hoisted a home-made regimental pennant pinned to a branch, signifying the battle was over, shortly followed by Polish national colours (and later still a British flag). At 10.15 a.m. Master Bugler Emil Czech stood on the ruined walls and played the *Krakow Heynal* trumpet call. General Władysław Anders knew, as the famous notes echoed around the hills, that this would be a much-witnessed, much-recorded symbol that Poland had struck back. By 4 p.m. a Polish platoon had made contact with units of the British 78th Division advancing along Route 6.

Allied war correspondents, wearing uniform, and treated as officers, were not far behind, sensing a good story. The abbey's capture was hot news across the English-speaking world, exactly as General Anders had hoped. The *Daily Telegraph*'s Graham Beamish recorded on 17 May, 1944: 'The Poles have been battling up the slopes of the Albaneta massif . . . I was with the Carpathians, those magnificent fighters who made history at Gazala and Tobruk. They were the spearhead of the attack . . . Polish infantry attacked on the rugged mountain feature 1,000 yards from their starting line. After a sharp, fierce clash, they captured their first objective in two hours. There were desperate hand-to-hand clashes . . . The Poles have achieved almost impossible feats.'

The fight for Colle Sant'Angelo, meanwhile, continued into 18 May unabated, with 5th Kresowa Division having to form improvised reserves from the divisional anti-tank and anti-aircraft regiments, spare drivers, military policemen, and others who could hold a rifle, which were put under the command of Colonel Rudnicki. The Germans managed to recapture part of Colle Sant'Angelo, and were not finally subdued until just after six in the evening, but fighting had already spread to the last major German position, Point 575, assaulted the previous day without success, and which overlooked Route 6. There the Fallschirmjäger resisted stubbornly, amidst the crevices and fissures of the hillside, for the Germans had understood that the Poles did not take prisoners: they fought on to the very end and few surrendered; the area was not clear until well into the night of 18/19 May.

While the monastery may have been relatively empty when the Poles arrived, most of the other peaks were not, and it is hard to agree with some accounts claiming the Polish Corps succeeded only because the Germans had already withdrawn. The exceptionally hard fighting had almost wiped out 1st Fallschirmjäger Division, so as to make its continued tenure of Monte Cassino impossible. Almost immediately swarms of visiting soldiery descended on the ruins, perhaps out of curiosity or possibly in revenge for the object that had cost them so much suffering. The monks later recorded: 'The human hyenas had fallen upon it, ransacking the ruins and pillaging everything they could lay their hands on.'

On his way to explore the abbey immediately after the battle, British sapper Major Tony Daniell recorded meeting a Carpathian Pole on the morning of 18 May. 'He had two roses in his cap and some parchment books in his hand which he had found in the wreckage. As he passed me he said, "We have not met the Germans since Tobruk but we have not forgotten those days."' The struggle for Monte Cassino left a lasting impression on the Poles who fought for it; one young officer in the 6th Carpathian Battalion later recalled the inspiring example of Company Sergeant Major Franciszek Sochacki who was, 'a regular NCO, then in his fifties. He was a real soldier. Although badly wounded by machine-gun fire he refused to retire without reporting to his commanding officer. We urged him to pull back as far as possible, but his reply was, "No, I can't leave the company without telling the commanding officer." Shortly afterwards a burst from an enemy machine gun finished him off. Before he died he drew himself erect and gasped out, "Sir, I'm killed!"'

Anders himself was soon on Monastery Hill, 'the battlefield presented a dreary sight. Corpses of Polish and German soldiers, sometimes entangled in a deathly embrace, lay everywhere, and the air was full of the stench of rotting bodies. There were overturned tanks with broken caterpillars,' he noted. 'Crater after crater pitted the sides of the hills, and scattered over them were fragments of uniforms and tin helmets, Tommy guns, Spandaus, Schmeissers and hand grenades.' He observed that of the monastery itself there remained only an enormous heap of ruins and rubble. 'A cracked church bell lay on the ground next to an unexploded shell of the heaviest calibre, and on shattered walls and ceilings fragments of paintings and frescoes could be seen. Priceless works of art, sculpture, pictures and books lay in the dust and broken plaster.'

Even though they had endured nameless horrors on their way to Italy, it was the devastation that most Poles remembered. As with soldiers on the Western Front of the First World War, the first signs of life returning to the battlefields were poppies. The cost to the Polish Corps of seizing the hills overlooking Cassino was high, not least among the commanders. Two out of three brigade commanders and four out of nine battalion COs were killed or wounded; in total 281 officers and 3,503 other ranks became casualties. Wladek Rubnikowicz reflected: 'Of course we were thrilled to have taken Monte Cassino. When we captured it we all felt as though we had shown everyone what we were capable of.' Ever since the bombing of 15 February the fight for the abbey had been headline news around the world – one reason why the fighting was so prolonged for what had become a symbol of military prowess for both sides.

As the *Daily Herald*'s correspondent, Arthur Helliwell, reported on 19 May 1944: 'The bodies of the heroes – brave soldiers of Poland – line the narrow, tortuous goat track by which I climbed to all that remains of the historic monastery of Saint Benedict today. They lie in the rigid, ungainly attitudes of violent death, over the slopes up which they fought so gallantly. It took us two and a half hours to climb the 1,700 feet to the monastery, following a white tape that snaked among the rocks to indicate a path free of mines . . . It was a gruelling nightmarish journey, even in broad daylight. What it must have meant to fight over such country. Indeed, it seems incredible that the Poles, under such conditions, were ever able to force the Germans back.'

The Polish Corps would incur more casualties during their advance up the Liri valley, when they attacked Piedimonte over 20–25 May and fought on in Italy to the war's end, almost exactly a year later. They buried about 900 Germans found in the monastery area, and during preparations for the fiftieth anniversary commemorations two more skeletal Germans were discovered, still clutching their rifles, in the brush just below Point 593.

It was between the monastery and Point 593, the two hardest-fought objectives, where the Poles buried their dead: twin Polish eagles flank the entrance way to the cemetery, officially completed on 1 September 1945: the sixth anniversary of Poland's invasion in 1939. Here 1,054 soldiers lie in individual plots, spread out across the steep terraces. After the fighting had ended soldiers continued to die, as the deputy corps commander witnessed, 'one of our men picked up a revolver that was lying in the grass. The poor fellow was killed instantly by the frightening blast that followed his imprudence.' At their head, the dead warriors were joined in 1970 by General Władysław Anders, whose dying wish after a long exile in London was to be buried with his men at Cassino.

The citation awarding a CB (Companion of the Order of the Bath) to General Anders immediately after Diadem makes it quite clear that the honour was also recognition of the Polish Corps' collective courage. But General Alexander's words, spoken at Cassino on 25 May 1944, when Anders received his decoration, were also a carefully crafted attempt by the Allies to keep the Poles in the battle, for they were all broadly aware from the Tehran Conference the previous year that the Western powers intended to leave Poland in the Soviet sphere of influence at the war's end.

At Tehran, Stalin had pressed for a revision of Poland's eastern border with the Soviet Union to match the line set by British Foreign Secretary Lord Curzon in 1920 and expressed his opposition to the Polish government-in-exile in London, who he claimed fatuously, 'were closely connected with the Germans and their agents in Poland were killing partisans'. According to newly released papers of secret talks held at the Soviet embassy in Tehran on 1 December 1943, Churchill himself seems to have initiated acceptance of a post-war Soviet-dominated Eastern Europe. He stated that if the Polish government-in-exile refused to accept the deliberations of the Allies 'then Great Britain would be through with them and certainly would not oppose the Soviet government under any condition at the peace table. The British government wished to see a Poland strong and friendly to Russia.'

Aware of Allied policy towards Poland, there is no doubt that Alex, who greatly admired the Polish Corps, would have found parts of Anders's citation speech difficult. 'It was a day of great glory for Poland when you took this stronghold the Germans themselves considered to be impregnable,' he told the Polish leader. 'It is not merely a brilliant beginning: it is a signpost showing the way to the future . . . I pay my tribute to you.'

12

Trouble in the Liri

T HE POLISH FLAG fluttered in the slight breeze. Around it lay the saw-toothed remains of the monastery, where dust and flies settled on the dead in the stillness. Men began to round up prisoners, tend to the wounded, bury the dead and search for their friends. Other Polish units pushed on. After a hard week of fighting Anders's Corps had achieved the seemingly impossible, but their job was not yet over. The aim of their attack had been to snuff out the defenders of the high ground, to enable their comrades of the Eighth Army to advance down the Liri valley below.

In contrast to the unforgiving winter, a benevolent May sun now glinted down on the scene, picking out the serpentine River Liri meandering its way towards the Rapido (at this juncture named the Gari). Where the two silvery coils of water met, the wider river acquired a new title, the Garigliano, fusing the names of its constituent waters, and ebbed into the sea, twenty miles away.

The valley below the monastery, taking its name from the river flowing down it, was for the Allies the main movement corridor stretching towards Rome, and down it ran a disused railway line and the Via Casilina – Route 6, which led directly to the Eternal City. Although to an observer up at the monastery it seemed flat, the reality at ground level was different:

a maze of small hillocks, often surmounted by stone-built villages, confusing tracks that led to every compass point, smudges of woodland, and small rivers, which ran across the valley at right angles to the axis of advance.

This was Eighth Army's battlefield, and since the Poles first began their attack on 11 May, Allied troops had also been battering away, trying to access the Liri valley. To get there required assault river crossings and penetration of the Gustav Line which had held up all previous attacks. However, this alone would not be enough; they also needed to swamp a secondary defensive position, the Senger (formerly named the Hitler) Line, nine miles further up the valley, to which Vietinghoff's defending Tenth Army would withdraw. Meanwhile, Juin's French Expeditionary Corps and beyond them, Keyes's US II Corps would be advancing through the Aurunci mountain range, to their left. It all required careful coordinating, deft timing – and an enemy who would dance to the Allies' tune. In their favour, the architects of Operation Diadem, Alexander and Harding, hoped that the better weather, improved ground conditions, massive logistics and far greater numbers, would help finally overwhelm their opponents.

A large, extrovert, old Etonian, and Coldstream Guardsman, usually genial but 'prone to sudden explosion', Sir Oliver William Hargreaves Leese had 'virtually inherited Eighth Army' from his old chief Montgomery at the end of December 1943, as well as a baronetcy from his father in 1937. Monty, though, was an incredibly difficult act to follow, and some thought Leese a shadow of his former boss. Nevertheless, he had an agile brain, tremendous energy, and a powerful personality.

In his forty-ninth year, Leese's task was to oversee his Eighth Army's activities with two army corps ranged opposite the Liri valley, Cassino town and on the heights around the abbey. To his left, Mark Clark's Fifth Army would attack simultaneously, also with two corps. As the Poles began their assault on the monastery heights, Sidney Kirkman's British XIII Corps were to attack over the Rapido. Where the US 36th Texans had tried and failed to cross the river in their assault of 20–21 January, at the cost of almost 3,000 casualties, Kirkman was now to throw at the same problem two divisions, operating side by side: Major General Dudley Russell's 8th Indian Infantry Division to the left and on the right, Dudley Ward's 4th British Division moving along the foot of Monte Cassino, and the southern edge of Cassino town. At the moment of attack, Royal Engineers would bridge the Rapido and, under cover of the preliminary bombardment, erect seven bridges along a ten-mile stretch codenamed Amazon, Blackwater and Congo (in 4th British Division's sector), and Cardiff, London, Oxford and Plymouth (in 8th Indian Division's area).

Across the divide, behind the Gustav Line, were the remnants of German formations that had resisted attacks, in some cases since January. Rather than a continuous line of defenders, terrain and manpower shortages dictated that Vietinghoff, Senger and Feurstein, the other corps commander, positioned their dwindling manpower where they could dominate patches of ground, creating an interlocking web of fire overseeing natural obstacles. The centuries-old stone villages and small rivers assisted this battleplan, with the addition of minefields, artillery and a few panzers which could scuttle two and fro in the dense spring foliage. Along the Gustav Line were many small battlegroups, all-arms groupings of twenty to a hundred men, like that of Leutnant Joseph 'Jupp' Klein, veteran of nearly 200 parachute jumps, commanding a company of Fallschirmjäger engineers. In 1944, the twenty-three-year-old was already a battle-hardened veteran of the fighting on the Eastern Front, where he had been wounded, and Sicily. In the same company was his friend and fellow officer Leutnant Hermann Volk, two years his senior, who had joined the Fallschirmjäger back in 1940 and jumped into Crete in May 1941 as an NCO paratrooper. Their company was one of four in the 1st Parachute Engineer Battalion commanded by Major Ernst Frömming. On his first operational jump, into Crete, Frömming's chute had malfunctioned and opened in the plane. Refusing an order to return and fly in later, he jumped with his chute open anyway, and survived. In Sicily his engineer battalion was already credited with destroying 146 bridges, slowing down their opponents, and laying more than 5,000 mines. At full strength, Frömming's engineer battalion numbered about 600 men; only seventy-two, including Klein and Volk and Frömming would escape from the Liri valley.

The defenders were so unaware of the impending assault that Lieutenant Colonel Henry Cubitt-Smith of the 1/12th Frontier Force

Rifles (in Russell's attacking 8th Indian Division) recalled 'creeping down to the river with my intelligence officer and a signaller to the water's edge, where we heard a gramophone being played in the strongpoint we were to capture'. Alive to the need for personal reconnaissance, Cubitt-Smith had earlier persuaded the supporting tank unit, 11th Ontario Armoured Regiment, to give him a flight over the monastery, which he could see a few miles distant, in their Auster spotter plane. Yet to be captured by the Poles, he was 'amazed at the immense thickness of the ruined walls', he recalled, and realised why his colleagues of 4th Indian Division had failed in their earlier endeavours to take the huge religious complex.

Every participant recalled the Allies' spectacular opening barrage, at 11 p.m. on 11 May, which would launch Anders's Poles at the monastery and Kirkman's XIII Corps across the river below. It was partly the spectacular noise at the end of a quiet evening, but also the flickering light from so many gun barrels, momentarily turning night into day, which remained seared in everyone's memory. 'The element of fantasy was always present in Italy,' wrote the historian of the 17/21st Lancers: 'at Cassino it was fireflies, and the nightingales which sang continuously every night, even through the heaviest artillery.' While the guns were breathing their fire, the 1/Royal Fusiliers, 1/12th Frontier Force Rifles and 1/5th Gurkhas of Brigadier Charles Boucher's 17th Indian Brigade started to cross by assault boats (like the Texans), opposite Sant'Angelo in Theodice. At this stage nature intervened, 'suddenly the countryside became engulfed in a mist thicker than a London pea-soup smog. Visibility was reduced to one yard. Holding hands and bayonets the men edged their way forward, falling into huge shell holes and craters.' Both the attacking Indian brigades had difficulty securing the far banks of the Rapido due to the tenacity of the defenders in their sector, grenadiers from 576 Regiment of General Hauck's 305th Infantry Division. This formation, whose troops were strung all along the Gustav Line, between the valley and the coast, was another unit reconstituted from a division destroyed at Stalingrad, and had already fought hard and well against the French, north of Cassino during December and January.

Cubitt-Smith's troops of the Frontier Force Rifles attacked 'two-up', with D Company (Dogras) and C Company (Pathans) to the left, and

A Company (Sikhs) to the right, with B (Punjabi Mussulmans) in reserve. Although badly cut up by fire, and losing two company commanders, the Frontier Force were across the thirty-foot-wide river in a couple of hours, necessitating the bridges to be assembled quickly to get tanks over to support the infantry. In the mist, Cubitt-Smith remembered hearing his Pathans 'shouting lustily to demonstrate their presence', and shortly afterwards interrogation of their first German prisoners showed that the 'unexpected battlecries in the fog had a demoralising effect on the defenders'.

Downriver, the 1/Argyll & Sutherland Highlanders, 3/8th Punjabis and 6/13th Frontier Force Rifles of the 19th Indian Brigade experienced similar challenges, with assault boats being holed by machine-gun fire or swept downstream. However, their engineers had studied the Texans' failed attack of January and made plans: rope and wire had been stretched across the water previously, enabling boats to be pulled to and fro. On the night of 11/12 May, under cover of a barrage and darkness, Oxford and Plymouth bridges were constructed, the latter being – uniquely – launched over the river on the back of two turretless Shermans, across which tanks of the Ontario and Calgary regiments of the Canadian 1st Armoured Brigade thundered to the rescue – the first Canadians to see action in the Cassino battles. During this fighting, Sepoy Kamal Ram of the 3/8th Punjab Regiment was awarded the Victoria Cross for destroying four machine-gun posts in the first few hours. London and Cardiff bridges were eventually completed on 14 May.

Dudley Ward's British Division also sent battalions over by boat: 2/King's Liverpool, 2/Somerset Light Infantry and 2/4 Hampshires of 28 Brigade on the left; and 1/6th East Surreys, 2/Beds and Herts, 2/Duke of Cornwall's Light Infantry of 10 Brigade on the right. Likewise, these needed to be helped and reinforced by tanks. Although three field companies of engineers were assigned to the task, not one of the 4th Division's bridges was completed by nightfall on the first day because of the sheer force of German opposition. By the second night, 12/13 May, all the division's three engineer companies had been assigned to the construction of the northernmost crossing point, Amazon – a Class 40 (that is, capable of taking a 40-ton vehicle), 70-foot Bailey bridge. Throughout, sappers were harried by sniper and machine-gun fire, and silhouetted by the Germans firing rounds beyond the engineers, illuminating them for accurate shelling and mortaring. The action was immortalised in a vivid and detailed painting by the famous British artist Terence Cuneo. Some 'friendly' counter-battery fire fell uncomfortably close until hurried calls to 'pitch them up' silenced the German guns for a while. Meanwhile, fellow Royal Engineers began mine-clearing operations on the far bank, the need for which was made clear when the officer in charge of the recce party lost a foot to a *Schü*-mine.

Behind schedule, at 3 a.m., the assembled Amazon was pushed out on rollers towards the far bank of the Rapido. Major Tony Daniell of 59 Field Company recalled that for some time 'one particular Spandau on the left had been causing almost continuous interference and quite a few casualties. So Sergeant Arthur Parry of 59 Field Company decided to go across on the launching nose and deal with this man. He lay full length on the leading transom until it grounded, and at once ran a few yards along the [far] bank, throwing himself on the ground to take cover. When the Spandau opened fire, he got the direction and made a dash towards the spot, firing two magazines of his Tommy gun. The Spandau did not fire again.'

Parry later set off to deal with another Spandau machine gun – referred to by soldiers as 'the Devil's paint brush' – and en route rescued the recce officer who had stepped on the *Schü*-mine. He silenced this second machine gun and earned himself a Military Medal for his night's endeavours, though, as is often the nature of matters with brave men, Parry would be killed in combat a month later. At four in the morning Amazon bridge was almost complete. Still under fire, every available sapper, and a small bulldozer, started to push it into position. With only twenty feet left to go the bulldozer seized up, its radiator and sump punctured by shrapnel. A desperate Royal Engineers officer tried to rouse the crew of a tank waiting to cross but found 'all the hatches were closed and there was absolutely no sign of life within'. Since nightfall, a tank squadron had arrived in the vicinity, waiting for the moment to cross. 'I redoubled my shouts and beat on the armour with my fists until my knuckles bled, but could raise absolutely no response. It was like a nightmare. I felt as useless as an ant on the hide of an elephant. In desperation I was reduced to the inanity of kicking the tank with my toecaps.' The crew inside were all asleep, 'separated from me by two inches of steel. Finally I climbed up onto one of the sprocket wheels, took out my revolver, and with the butt, beat a furious 1-2-3, 1-2-3, on the armour plate of the turret.' Eventually, the driver's visor opened 'and I was aware of a dim light coming up from the interior and a sleepy eye regarded me. I explained our predicament, asked for his help and without a moment's hesitation the driver agreed.'

The Sherman was impressed first into pulling the bulldozer out of the way, then pushing the bridge into its final position. Within an hour Amazon was open for business – but at a cost of 83 out of the 200 Royal Engineers. The men and machines of C Squadron, 17/21st Lancers started to pour cross. Only afterwards, on 14 May, could 4th Division's engineers turn their attention to building Blackwater and Congo bridges.

Amazon proved key to the momentum of the 4th Division's attack, though few Germans ever witnessed the assault; in daylight hours all the crossing sites were curtained with smoke, meaning that German artillery on the Cassino heights could aim in the general direction of the bridges, but could not correct their fall of shot to destroy their targets. Air superiority also hampered the activities of German guns, and movement of their reinforcements. Allied close air support to XIII Corps in the valley or Anders's Poles on the heights was challenging due to the proximity of their opponents, and in these early days, calls for aerial assistance were frequently refused for fear of 'friendly fire' casualties. Once beyond the bridges, the Allies benefited, as Alexander had hoped, from much drier ground, meaning that they could deploy tanks where none could have manoeuvred in the earlier months.

Back in the 8th Indian Division's sector, the settlement of Sant'Angelo in Theodice, which overlooked the Rapido, had defied capture since US 36th Division's attempts in January. The ruined village, adapted by the Germans into a bristling fortress, was now an unrecognisable heap of debris. The defenders had held out amidst the rubble until mid-afternoon of 13 May, when the village fell to 1/5th Gurkhas, at a cost of 129 Nepalese infantrymen, battling to free a village they couldn't pronounce, so far from their homeland. Many of Cassino's surrounding settlements were little more than ruins. 'It is not possible that once these places stood up foursquare and people lived in them,' wrote Martha Gellhorn. 'No cyclone could have done as thorough a job as high explosive has. After a while you do not even notice the sliced houses, the landslides of rubble, the torn roofs.' An American ambulance driver saw the devastation: 'buildings were as skeletons, half standing in crumbled heaps, iron and steel twisted and torn. All horrible and black. It is like looking into the eyes of a lunatic and being able to see into his brain. It is an awe-inspiring sight at first but in reality horrifying.'

The hillsides, and pre-war buildings constructed of local stone, remain scarred with high-velocity fracture patterns today caused by impacting shells, from which quite small fragments could prove fatal. Conveying casualties over this prehistoric landscape was challenging in the extreme and a constant drain on manpower. The wounded also inevitably included those Italian civilians who had been unable to escape before being caught in the combat zone; those who had stayed indoors and retreated underground hoping for the best. Buildings were often uninhabitable above ground and cellars were highly prized – just as many diarists recorded on the Western Front in the First World War. The (relatively luxurious) living quarters of medics at one first-aid station were 'a very cold room in another cellar. Half the dirt floor had been covered with old doors to keep the damp from the mattresses they slept on. There was a table with a marble top, an iron stove that barely worked, two kerosene lamps, four uncertain chairs, an upright piano with planks for legs, a radio, some mice, a pervading odour of damp and good thick walls.' This closely observed passage could have come from Siegfried Sassoon or Robert Graves in 1917, but was Italy in 1944. John Myers, a Royal Artilleryman with British X Corps, remembered that the hard surfaces in farmyards were a favourite choice for his gun positions, 'until we found that houses were an easy target to spot on the map . . . When positioned near a farmhouse we would use the outhouses for shelter from the cold and rain. We sometimes slept there with the animals. They were as good as central heating.'

On 13 May, as Sant'Angelo fell, just beyond in a hamlet called Vertechi Captain Richard Wakeford of the 2/4th Hampshires rallied his badly chewed-up company, while his supporting armour of the 19th NZ Armoured Regiment was held up by a tributary of the Rapido named the Pioppeto. The stream had unfortunately not been identified as a major obstacle and other armoured units, including the 16/5th Lancers, would be bogged down here, requiring further bridging operations. When subsequently attacking a hill the following day, Wakeford's company again came under heavy fire, and although wounded in the face and both arms, he pressed on with the attack. Armed with a revolver, he went forward, killed a number of Fallschirmjäger and took twenty prisoners. For his leadership, the much-wounded Wakeford was awarded a Victoria Cross.

With the Rapido River line crossed and his two forward divisions beginning to eat into the edge of the Liri valley, Eighth Army commander Oliver Leese found he had a fluid battle developing and needed to retain flexibility. Originally it was assumed that the passage up the all-important Liri would only be possible if the French on the left and Poles on the Monte Cassino massif to the right could conquer the mountains either side. Juin's Frenchmen were, however, breaking through the Gustav Line in the Aurunci Mountains far more quickly and deeply than expected. So, in order to take advantage of the unexpected progress by the French and help the Poles, who were still struggling with the abbey's defenders on his right, Leese decided to deploy his next wave of attackers forward, the 78th Battleaxe Division, much earlier than originally planned. Although ordered to move forward on 13 May, such was the traffic chaos on the narrow Bailey bridges and small dirt tracks that the division only entered the Rapido bridgehead on 14–15 May.

Their divisional commander, Charles Keightley, needed to control his move forward, and keep parallel with the divisions on his left, and so resorted to the common military solution of 'phase lines' by which his men could move forward in tactical bounds of short distance. A bit like leapfrogging, this allowed tight control of units in confusing terrain. The completion of each phase would be signalled by a codeword. Nodding to his own cavalry background, Keightley named his phase lines after four famous English hunts, Grafton, Pytchley, Fernie and Bedale, terminology appreciated by some of the debonair horsemen of his supporting tanks, the blue-blooded 26th Armoured Brigade, commanded by Brigadier Neville Mitchell. Also travelling with the armour was 12/Royal Horse Artillery, otherwise known as the Honourable Artillery Company (mostly well-connected reservists who worked in the City of London), equipped with self-propelled Priests, 105mm howitzers. Each armoured regiment was supported by a battery of eight guns – C Battery accompanied 16/5th Lancers, D escorted 2/Lothians, while F kept company with the 17/21st Lancers.

Battery commanders and their observation post (OP) officers travelled in converted Shermans with the tank regiments to call down fire as needed. C Battery of the Honourable Artillery Company crossed over Amazon bridge with the 16/5th Lancers on 13 May to find that fog, 'thickened no doubt by the smoke screen which still hung around the bridgehead, had reduced visibility to ten yards. Moving blindly through close country such as this, a tank might at any moment become the victim of a bold ambush. Thus Captain Massey's tank was knocked out by a German who, emerging suddenly from cover, placed a couple of sticky bombs on the turret.' Allied armour generally had an awful time in the unforgiving terrain of the Liri: the 17/21st Lancers' historian recorded their casualties for the first six days as fifty-seven officers and men killed or wounded, brought about by several challenges: 'First, the thick, difficult ground, intersected by marshes, rivers, dykes, where physical obstacles hindered the advance as much as enemy fire. Secondly, the mountain observation posts, from which enemy artillery and mortar fire was directed on to the battlefield . . . This is real war, and makes Africa seem a picnic.'

On his first day of action at Cassino, above the Rapido, another Honourable Artillery Company gunner probed his way 'slowly over the ruins of Sant'Angelo . . . one great mass of rubble and the tank lurched and ground its way through the bricks and stones while I wondered if we would shed a track'. Further down the road to Cassino and the monastery, 'dead mules and men scattered the road which was lined with dugouts; bits of clothing and equipment were thrown all over the place. On a clump of barbed wire hung the mangled remains of a German, and above all there was the sickening stench of the dead, putrefying and swelling in the scorching heat of the sun.'

At 9 a.m. on 15 May, units of Charles Boucher's 17th Indian Brigade came under strong German counterattack, where Cubitt-Smith proudly recalled one of his Sikh officers 'telling his men they could not withdraw, must not surrender, and should die to a man. Fortunately this did not become necessary,' and the attack petered out with seventy prisoners

Montecassino - Lato nord e nord Ovest della Badia

Pre-war view of the abbey from the north-west. Taken from what became known as Snakeshead Ridge, after the destruction of 15 February 1944, this was the only portion of the religious complex to remain relatively intact but, for reasons of terrain, was where all infantry attacks had to be launched.

On 15 March 1944, Freyberg launched Operation Dickens, preceded by a massive air raid, after which every Allied gun pounded the town, 'from midday onwards Cassino was flashing and puffing until it was smothered in smoke and dust and the town became a blur with jagged fragments flung into the air'. Photo taken from Freyberg's HQ, three miles distant.

The thousand-yard stare of an exhausted soldier in his foxhole who has been under prolonged fire. The unrelenting conditions at Cassino provoked a huge number of psychiatric cases, as high as ten per cent of all casualties in the Allied armies, but unrecorded by the Germans.

Monday 19 March 1944 saw the boldest assault of the four battles, a tank attack up the Cavendish Road. Looking like this, the five-mile former mule track that snaked steeply through the hills behind the abbey had been widened by Indian Army sappers to take armour, but remained a precarious drive. Hurried planning and a lack of infantry support caused the venture to fail, and a brilliant opportunity to capture the monastery was squandered.

The propaganda war at Cassino was vicious with millions of leaflets fired by shell or dropped from aircraft, by both sides. The Germans targeted the Allied coalition partners, trying to create rifts amongst the different nations. This leaflet tried to persuade the Poles that they would suffer the same fate as Indian and French North African troops who had already attacked the monastery.

After breaking through the Gustav Line, 1 Canadian Corps led by General 'Tommy' Burns, was unleashed to advance up the Liri valley and overwhelm the Hitler Line. It encountered a series of well-defended villages that had to be cleared, house by house.

Both sides found at Cassino that three quarters of all casualties were inflicted by indirect (artillery and mortar) fire. These Germans, caught in the open without trenches or bunkers to shelter in, were highly vulnerable.

General Alphonse Juin's French Expeditionary Corps, which eventually totalled 112,000 men in five divisions, played a key role in the first and fourth battles. The American-supplied tank and mule illustrates their bizarre mix of ancient and modern methods of war.

Goumiers. The very name struck terror amongst German troops. Part of Juin's corps, this force of 13,000 recruited in Morocco were skilled mountain troops, and split open the Gustav Line in the fourth battle. 'These are the boys who are expert at knife work,' remembered one soldier; Clark admired them, but one in four were killed or wounded.

The message on this propaganda leaflet may have summed up the war for Allied troops. The weather was anything but sunny for much of the attritional Cassino campaign, and even Mark Clark felt that 'behind every hill there's another river, and behind every river, there's another hill'. However, conditions were just as bad for the Germans. The leaflet is singed top and bottom, indicating it was fired by an artillery shell.

US troops make their way up into the hills. In the fourth battle it was the rapid progress of the 85th and 88th divisions of Geoffrey Keyes' II US Corps through the Aurunci mountains that led to the link-up with the Anzio force on 25 May. One surgeon had to send back a medical colleague whose became unwell. 'He has been a fine and brave companion and excellent medical officer, but a man over thirty-five is already too old for rugged mountain warfare'.

Throughout the four battles, all Allied troops came to rely heavily on mules for logistics, and employed nearly 15,000, often led by volunteer Italian and Cypriot troops. They could operate where vehicles could not; one journalist reported rounding a curve and seeing 'two trucks which had plunged down a ravine and were hanging on the mountainside'.

Determined German soldiers were difficult to dislodge from the many solid stone houses of the Liri valley. Leutnant 'Jupp' Klein with a band of thirty-eight *Fallschirmjäger* defended a farm like this for several days, holding up a British battalion and destroying thirteen tanks.

Although the Allies commanded the skies by day, German aircraft bombed Fifth and Eighth Army troops most nights, necessitating this British 40mm anti-aircraft gun position. A Canadian soldier remembered 'No matter where the Luftwaffe dropped their bombs they would do some damage. The high concentration of troops, trucks, tanks, guns in the area guaranteed success.'

Despite Allied pressure in the Liri valley, Senger's XIV Panzer Corps managed a fighting withdrawal, saving much of their manpower and equipment, like this 88mm gun, being whisked through a ruined town. German officers kept an iron grip on their men, one insisting 'the word "impossible" does not exist in the soldier's dictionary.'

Both sides treated each others' casualties fairly, recognising they were all at war with nature. 'Their stretcher bearers appeared like magic amongst our own parties, instructed by no one but equally devoted. A German doctor snapped out orders impartially to both sides in both languages', remembered one officer. Italian civilians were frequently caught up in the fighting, too.

On 19 March 1944, the Allies initiated Operation Strangle, hoping to interdict all movements of troops and logistics to the Cassino and Anzio fronts by aerial bombing. It failed because the Germans proved masters of improvisation and repair; here a damaged train has been shunted off the track and (foreground) bridge replaced.

The *Pantherturm* was a revolving turret from a Panther tank fixed to an underground concrete bunker. Nineteen-year-old Herbert Fries used one of these to immobilise seventeen Allied tanks in three days. This one has been blown off its mounting by an Allied shell.

The build-up of Allied vehicles in Naples. Materiel superiority contributed to the huge traffic jam of six divisions competing for road space in the narrow Liri valley in late May. One soldier wrote of 'an endless column, nose to tail, either waiting with engines running in the overpowering heat and dust or tearing through narrow lanes trying to catch the vehicle in front.'

Jubilant Romans welcome the Allies. Kisses were exchanged for cigarettes and troops showered with fresh flowers and baskets of cherries; 'this is the first place where I have seen folk decently dressed or any pretty girls', noted a South African. The Colosseum and other ancient buildings had witnessed the passage of conquerors and liberators through time, remembered Charles Dickens, 'despoiled by Popes and fighting Princes'.

taken and thirteen anti-tank guns destroyed. Through the rest of the day, Dudley Russell's 8th Indian Division, supported by 1st Canadian Armoured Brigade (the Ontario, Three Rivers and Calgary regiments) ground forward through difficult countryside – full of small, rolling hummocks, woods, dried-up water courses, with towns and villages perched on heights overlooking the attackers' line of advance – each travertine stone-built farmhouse concealing a German position. This land had been beyond the reach of each side's artillery in the earlier battles and was untouched, verdant terrain, much splashed with the pink of cherry and other trees. Dudley Ward's 4th Division had also adopted their own phase lines – geographically different to the 78th's – and named rather less prosaically Brown, Blue, Red and Green. Keeping up, on their right, Keightley's Battleaxe Division and 26th Armoured Brigade negotiated similar terrain.

Harrow-educated John Coldwell-Horsfall would write three erudite volumes of his Second World War experiences when he joined as the second-in-command of 2/London Irish Rifles in the Battleaxe Division. His description of the terrain speaks for the many units – British, Indian, Polish, Canadian, South African – that would fight through this valley. Then aged twenty-nine, he remembered the Liri countryside like this: 'Reliance on air photos had its shortcomings, and with their deceptive tendency to indicate all ground as flat it is hardly surprising that the landscape was quite different to what we had deduced from them. There was no substitute for map reading. The countryside was quite closed in, with forward visibility usually only a few hundred yards at best, and often nothing at all owing to trees. The terrain in fact was a vast arboretum, solid with fruit trees and other shrubs set in a maze of small hillocks and dips with boggy bottoms to them. The cover in this respect was quite good, but in fact it was ideal defensive country for the enemy – though the drifting smoke and the mist patches soon made aimed fire impossible to both sides.'

Horsfall had already seen action in Palestine before joining the BEF in France and Belgium, where he was awarded his first MC for gallantry and leadership, having led 70 of the 112 men in his company safely out of Dunkirk. 'Under fire,' one of his platoon commanders recalled, 'Horsfall would walk about as unconcerned as if on a stroll in the park.'

A force multiplier all by himself, and a tall man of distinguished countenance, he could – and did – inspire a battalion with his habit of always
wearing a peaked officers' cap, even in the battle zone, only resorting
to a steel helmet when actually leading an attack.

Forward left on Keightley's divisional front, Lieutenant Colonel 'Bala'
Bredin's 6/Royal Inniskilling Fusiliers (the 'Skins') reached the Pignataro-
Cassino road (Line Grafton) at midday, parallel with the spearhead battalion
of 11 Brigade on their right, the 5/Northamptons. Another pair of battalions
– 2/London Irish Rifles to the left, 2/Lancashire Fusiliers to the right –
started to move through them and beyond to Line Pytchley, but at this
moment German defensive fire rained on the former, killing many in
battalion headquarters, including Horsfall's great friend and commanding
officer, Ion Goff, and John Loveday, CO of their supporting armour, the
16/5th Lancers. As Horsfall moved forward to take over 2/London Irish
(seconds-in-command were routinely left out of battle for just this eventuality), the battalions dug in, and despite support from all seventy-two
guns of the Battleaxe's artillery and a squadron of tanks, accurate German
fire preventing their attack from being renewed until the following morning.

The next day, 16 May, the 16/5th Lancers 'did not move until our
men reached the first rise several hundred yards ahead. Then the tanks
motored slowly forward to cover them on to the next lot of hummocks.'
This was the signal for German reaction. Supported also by the divisional
machine-gun battalion, 1/Kensington Regiment, it took the three battalions most of the day to subdue the Germans tucked away behind their
stone houses and concrete forts and gun emplacements of Baade's 90th
PanzerGrenadiers.

Horsfall described the scene in front of him: 'wrecked buildings scattered across the whole of the battle zone, and as a centre piece to it there
were the loose conglomeration of houses which formed the hamlet of
Sinagoga. All of them were fortified, and tracer was streaking across in
all directions like jets of fire outlined against the backdrop of the barrage.'
This was Line Pytchley, and a mini version of Stalingrad. Here the
Lancers' tanks opened up with their 75mms, 'a marvellous gun: a single
shell from it was sufficient to bring down a large part of the front wall
of a house'. In a number of instances 'the enemy were trapped in their
basements and cellars with the tanks on top of them'.

After hours of fighting, and after taking many prisoners, Sinagoga, the heart of the German defence in this sector, was secured by H Company, which had sustained heavy losses and was now only twelve men strong. Beyond the village Horsfall met his friend Major Desmond Woods with the scanty remains of his company. 'A bare dozen of them were visible – smothered in brick dust, and their eyes the only bright thing about them. They were barely distinguishable from their adversaries who had subsided amongst them, weapons tossed anywhere.'

'I'm afraid I've lost almost all my company,' Desmond told him.

'Never mind,' replied Horsfall. 'You're here, which is what I told you to do – well done!' The enemy was 'silent or ran for it . . . so we reigned in the tanks, put out our pickets, and motored slowly back to the village'.

The 2/London Irish Rifles lost over a hundred men and nine officers taking and defending the settlement, but killed or captured 220, while 'nine German tanks were also counted – pathetic smouldering wreckage, often enclosing the charred remains of the men who manned them'. For taking Sinagoga from Baade's PanzerGrenadiers, Horsfall received an immediate DSO, to add to the MC and bar he already possessed. Indicative of the ferocity and unpredictable nature of this fighting, another 78th Division soldier, Fusilier Frank Jefferson of 2/Lancashire Fusiliers, also won a Victoria Cross on 16 May for repelling panzer attacks successfully at *twenty yards*, with his PIAT anti-tank weapon on the outskirts of Sinagoga. 'There were badly injured and dying men from both sides scattered helplessly round the village,' Horsfall recalled; 'a number were burned beyond all hope – tanks crews, both Lancers and Germans, and two of the Vickers teams from the Kensingtons, shattered by direct hits. Enemy medical help arrived unsought and unasked as Rhys, our MO, and his German opposite number toiled together in the carnage. Their stretcher-bearers appeared like magic among our own parties, instructed by no one but equally devoted. Later, the German doctor saw to the carrying parties, snapping out strings of orders impartially to both sides in both languages.'

Horsfall's reputation in the division was only eclipsed by that of his fellow battalion commander, Bala Bredin of the 6/Inniskilling Fusiliers, who – likewise – already possessed two MCs and would win himself a DSO the following day when attacking Piumarola, just beyond their next objective, Line Fernie. In this battle, Bala would be wounded in both legs and evacuated out of the combat zone. They were now close, just a thousand yards, to their final objective, Line Bedale, which they reached at four in the afternoon.

Lurking between between Sinagoga and Piumarola were a band of thirty-eight Fallschirmjäger, the remnants of an engineer company commanded by Leutnant Jupp Klein. From Cassino town they had been ordered on the evening of 15 May to take up a blocking position in the Liri valley by the following morning. Jupp recalled leading his group across the Pignataro-Cassino Road (38 Brigade's Line Grafton) and moving through harassing shellfire to 'an isolated farm, within which, strengthened with wooden beams and rubble from adjacent walls, was a passable bunker. The windows had been made smaller to serve as loopholes and underneath was a shelter with steps leading down. It dominated the surrounding ground by 2.5 metres and impressed us as a small fortress.' Seeing some Allied armour halted unaware of the Germans' presence about a thousand yards distant – indeed 'some of them lay shirtless on top of their tanks and let the upper part of their bodies bake in the sun ... but we had been commanded not to fire unnecessarily' – Klein requested anti-tank weapons, and was soon joined by a group with three *Panzerschreck* bazookas 'led by a nervous corporal'. The *Panzerschreck* (literally German for 'tank terror') or *Ofenrohr* ('stovepipe'), as it was also known, was a short-range, reloadable anti-tank weapon and found to be a most effective antidote to a plague of Shermans. However, its weight (30lb, including an 88mm warhead) meant it was best fired from a prone position, and it required guts to take on a fast-advancing Allied tank at less than 150 yards, its maximum range.

Much to Klein's relief, some infantry also appeared led by a 'major who had previously been fighting partisans in Yugoslavia' but was not tactically wise, and insisted on placing an MG-42 crew in an isolated forward outpost. 'We tried to persuade him that they had no chance of pulling back and that attacking tanks would cut them down at once,' but Klein was ignored. 'We could only feel sorry for the poor gunners, for we knew they were prime candidates for death.'

Klein remembered the moment when his farmhouse was assaulted.

'They emerged in staggered fashion over the ridge, about ten metres apart. There must have been twenty-five Shermans rushing towards us. Behind them came the accompanying infantry. The MG-42 outpost fired one burst, then came a shot from an approaching Sherman and then stillness. We looked for our bazooka troops, but in the excitement of the first seconds they had disappeared.' The Shermans came gradually nearer to Klein's group, when 'the first, and immediately afterwards a second, was hit, other tanks were shot up and the remainder retreated to escape annihilation, their occupants jumped out and ran to the rear or wandered around as if blind. Many tank crews were set ablaze and were running back like burning torches. The tank deaths ceased and when the English infantry had disappeared, the artillery fire was silent.' Klein's little battlegroup left their battle headquarters and threw their arms around the *Panzerschreck* crews, who had not run away after all, but departed to find better fire positions. 'We counted thirteen destroyed Shermans in the distance and close to our small fortress.'

It is difficult to place the encounter precisely, for nearly all the old stone buildings have gone now, but Jupp appears to have been between Lines Pytchley and Fernie, while his opponents were almost certainly 38 Brigade and the 16/5th Lancers. The Fallschirmjägers' experiences here represent those of many of the isolated platoon-sized groups anchored in farmhouses and hamlets, whose war never made it into print. They were thrown together from a mix of PanzerGrenadiers, paratroopers and others in the vicinity, and pinned down a vastly superior number of Allied troops for over a week, with limited logistics (mostly what they could carry), no transport or air cover. Jupp Klein remains bitter about the fate of the MG-42 crew: 'A senseless death for these young soldiers. With some insight from their commander they could have been rescued. We were indignant over so much lack of judgement.'

Later the Allies shelled their farmhouse, which collapsed around them, trapping Jupp and his men in their shelter. Eventually, they managed to move the rubble from their door and free themselves. By then the battle had moved on and they were behind enemy lines. Shooting down an enemy patrol who spotted them, under cover of night, Jupp led the survivors of his gang through Allied lines, cleverly shouting 'Polish soldiers!' to British sentries when challenged. Making their way up the Via Casilina, Klein eventually managed to reunite his charges with their battalion. His CO, Major Ernst Frömming, greeted him with mock severity: 'I expected you much earlier, for there are 2,000 tank mines to be laid and I don't have anyone else available.'

13

Pursuit from Cassino

B Y THE EVENING of 13 May the Diadem battle had been raging for two full days and nights. Kirkman's two assault divisions (8th Indian and 4th British) had crossed the river, breached the Gustav Line defences opposite and established a bridgehead. To the left Juin's French Expeditionary Corps (in Clark's Fifth Army) were making commendable progress through the Aurunci Mountains, while on the right, Anders's Poles had hit stalemate on the heights around Cassino and were preparing to attack again. Generally, Leese was pleased enough with the progress to launch the Battleaxe Division forward, through the 4th British Division on his right, who had performed their task of breaching the German defences. Now, Oliver Leese decided to commit Tommy Burns's I Canadian Corps, in the form of Major General Chris Vokes's 1st Canadian Infantry Division, to relieve 8th Indian Division on Leese's left.

Commanding the Canadians, and blessed with the three forenames of Eedson Louis Millard, Lieutenant General E. L. M. Burns was known more familiarly as 'Tommy'. A First World War veteran with an MC, Burns was a puzzling and controversial figure; the forty-six-year old was undoubtedly cerebral, well qualified, but not well liked. As Canada was determined their countrymen should lead their own formations, Burns was promoted rapidly (some argue, too rapidly), on 30 January 1944, to command the 5th Canadian Armoured Division and on 20 March, to lead I Canadian Corps. He was viewed by fellow Canadians as lacking flexibility and, crucially, leadership. Unsympathetic, shortly after assuming corps command, his medical officers were instructed to be very strict about evacuating battle exhaustion cases, and only to do so when it was certain they could not be returned to their units; this was at a time when the medical profession had just recognised that a few days rest was often the most effective cure. Unkindly, Burns told his battalion COs that battle exhaustion was their responsibility and if it occurred in the coming battles 'it would be taken as a reflection on their ability'.

Chris Vokes, GOC of 1st Canadian Division, reflected the private view of some senior officers in the corps at the time of the Liri campaign, and after, writing, 'I had known Burns for many years. He had taught me as a cadet at the Royal Military College . . . [and was] highly regarded in Canadian military circles . . . I had always admired him for his great ability as an officer,' but Vokes felt that after taking command of the corps, 'I never felt comfortable in his presence. His manner was shy, introverted and humourless. He seemed most unfriendly and distrustful. Perhaps he resented my more extensive experience in operational command . . . For old time's sake I determined to tread warily and give him my loyal support.' This was a formation potentially at odds with Oliver Leese and itself, as events would show.

The Canadians had arrived at the Cassino over the previous few weeks, moving stealthily from Italy's eastern seaboard with the rest of Eighth Army. Among them was Private Stan Scislowski. Although of Polish parentage, Stan was born in 1923 at Windsor, Ontario. May 1943 had seen him aboard the troop ship USS *General Anderson,* bound for training in England; on 5 August 1943 he was posted with a draft to the Perth Regiment of Canada, landing in Italy in September. Stan had not welcomed his corps' switch from the Adriatic front: 'After a long, halting and twisting ride up and over razorback ridges, around hairpin turns, at times our outer wheels just a scant four feet from the road's edge and a straight drop for some 200 feet and more to oblivion,' his convoy finally arrived in early evening at the settlement of Acquafondata. 'Nestled in the cleavage of rock-strewn heights' a few miles north-east of Cassino, it was 'the saddest, most forlorn and derelict cluster of beat-up old buildings my eyes had yet fallen upon', he recalled. Here was 'a region so forbidding it was beyond comprehension that anyone could have made their home and eke out a living here ... And now, after the fighting had closed in, the desolation was complete, with rats and the odd stray dog the only inhabitants of the ruins. Its citizens had long since scattered to the four winds.' Coming from a Canadian, used to desolate places, the village must have been bleak indeed.

Others were more optimistic about the move, including Lieutenant Farley Mowat of the Hastings and Prince Edward Regiment (the 'Hasty Ps'). Born in 1921, Mowat would go on to become one of Canada's great writers; by 1936, he had already made his first trip to the Arctic and was writing articles on wild life for magazines. Tough, resourceful and outspoken by nature, he joined the army as a private when Canada entered the war, had led a platoon through the 1943 Sicilian campaign, and followed his division into Italy. With his observer's eye, the twenty-two-year-old Lieutenant Mowat recorded his battalion's trek from the Adriatic: 'The sun grew hotter. The mud on the roads caked, was pulverised and turned to the thick penetrating dust that had been so achingly familiar in Sicily. The troops wore handkerchiefs across their mouths and travelled stripped to the waist – their white bodies reddening in the welcome heat.' There were lighter moments too, created when the military bureaucracy managed to post the least appropriate individuals to do certain jobs. Before moving up to take part in Diadem, Mowat encountered a vocabulary-challenged company clerk who had misinterpreted their routine battalion orders to read 'Latrines: All troops will ensure that faces are covered with soil after each person has deprecated.'

Canadian infantry battalions and armoured regiments possessed fairly ornate titles, named in the English style after regions, clans or territory and in turn were often shortened to amusing nicknames. Thus the Governor General's Horse Guards of 5th Canadian Armoured Division were better known as the 'GeeGees' (but also from their initials, 'God's Gift to Hungry Girls', or 'Good God, How Gorgeous!'). A British tank brigade was also assigned to support 1st Canadian Infantry Division. Almost uniquely for the Italian theatre, it contained Churchill heavy tanks, including those of the North Irish Horse.

Waiting for the start, Stan Scislowski and his mates of the Perth Regiment were camped near Monte Trocchio, and eager to move, though their location had some compensations. 'We could all see the ruins of the abbey ... through the gathering haze. An American Long Tom battery [a long-barrelled, 155mm artillery piece] pulled in soon after we settled in for the night, and it didn't take us long to find them to be ideal neighbours. They were an Oklahoma outfit, and as to be expected, they had in their midst guitar players and fiddlers.'

Stan had been enjoying listening to the Oklahomans strumming their guitars, singing and playing their fiddles for about an hour 'when the unmistakable menacing throb of German aircraft engines came to our ears. This broke up the good-times gathering, with everybody hustling back to their own area.' While the Allies generally ruled the skies by day, each night the Luftwaffe returned to the battlefield to cause mayhem. No matter where German aircraft dropped their bombs they 'could be sure to do some damage. The high concentration of troops, trucks, tanks, guns and whatnot in the area practically guaranteed success.'

Although the Canadian 1st Infantry and 5th Armoured Divisions had been penned up in holding areas since before Diadem, restless under their camouflage nets, impatient to move, Leese's decision to commit Burns's Canadians at this stage was a brave (and, in retrospect an optimistic and possibly unwise) one, for he was now inserting another entire corps alongside the Battleaxe Division of Kirkman's XIII Corps on a narrow front over terrain that would challenge a division, bounded on the Canadians' left by the Liri river, and on the right by a deep gully, the Forme d'Aquino. Horrendous traffic jams would ensue with four divisions and over 20,000 vehicles competing for space along the few dirt tracks and Bailey bridges available. Farley Mowat remembered how, 'behind the forward units, road-building bulldozers ground through the dry soil sending streamers of dust high into the sky. The transport of an army moved up toward the front along narrow, sunken trails, whose ditches were filled with the bodies of men, and the debris of defeat. Spring lay on the land, but it was overlaid with the autumnal wreckage of war.' The West Nova Scotia Regiment found that 'more than once what the map showed as a road turned out to be merely a grassy cattle track through the fields'.

Ahead, the traffic jam meant the Canadians could only resume the advance from 8th Indian Division on the morning of 16 May, with Lieutenant Colonel Bill Mathers's Royal Canadian Regiment passing through the Bengal Lancers and advancing beyond Panaccioni, supported by Churchill tanks of the British 25th Tank Brigade. A Welsh Guards officer of 6 Armoured Division had his first sight of the Indians: 'They were Punjabi Mussulmen, great bearded fellows in turbans and flapping greatcoats. Curious smells came from their cooking fires.' Further back, one of the Perths remembered: 'On the far side of Pignataro, as we marched along a sunken road, we passed a column of turbaned Sikhs going in the opposite direction. I looked up on the embankment to my right and saw a newsreel crew cranking away at a tripod-mounted camera with the lens pointed straight at me.' Shortly afterwards 'we filed into a broad, rain-slicked meadow, speckled thickly with poppies'.

Throughout the day, forward battalions of Brigadier Spry's Canadian 1st Brigade 'bumped' stay-behind German detachments, slowing their progress, as had happened on each previous day to 8th Indian and 78th Divisions. Eighth Army intelligence had not anticipated much resistance, and issued a sharp rebuke to Tommy Burns for his troops to speed up. That night, while planning operations for 17 May, Chris Vokes of 1st Canadian Infantry Division received from Burns the message that 'General Leese is disappointed that no greater progress was made in the face of quite light opposition and [it] is very urgent that a determined advance should be made tomorrow.' A robust commander might have gone forward himself to assess whether Oliver Leese's distant judgement was correct, and either had a word with Vokes, or protested to Eighth Army HQ that the criticism was unfounded. Instead Burns did neither, meekly passing on Leese's view, an action which sowed the doubts of many that their corps commander was out of his depth.

Stung by the criticism, Vokes's division made much greater progress over the ensuing twenty-four hours. The Canadians and 78th Division were now both moving towards the Hitler Line, which stretched between the towns of Pontecorvo and Aquino, and described as 'a kind of insurance policy for the Gustav Line'. As soon as General Keightley of the 78th Battleaxe Division (on the Canadians' right) heard the news of the fall of Albaneta to the Poles, he authorised Lieutenant Colonel John

Mackenzie of 2/Lancashire Fusiliers to send 'a special patrol of three corporals, all holders of Military Medals, to convey the formal compliments of 78th Division to our Polish Allies'. They scaled the 'death gulley' leading from Route 6 to Albaneta that the Germans had used to resupply the monastery, and were on the heights when word spread of the Polish flag fluttering over the abbey. The link-up that Leese required between his troops in the Liri valley and Anders's Polish Corps had been achieved, but the cost all round had been high.

Two attempts were made to pierce the Hitler Line on 19 May: one was at Aquino, on the right boundary between the Canadians and 78th Division. Here, the 5/Buffs and 8/Argyll and Sutherland Highlanders of 36 Brigade with Canadian Shermans of the Ontario Regiment tried and failed to seize the airfield, losing thirteen tanks. Advancing through the morning fog, the battalions ran into a cobweb of barbed wire overlooked by interlocking machine-gun fire from pillboxes as the mist lifted, while the loss of the armour removed the means of dealing with the bunkers. Both commanding officers went down, and the attackers withdrew after 1 p.m.

The Canadian Carleton & Yorks and Van Doos (22ème) Regiments also tried a break-in, but were repelled. Looking back, the latter's CO, Jean-Victor Allard, wrote that he had 'a bad taste in my mouth about the whole affair'. After this event 'I retained serious doubts about the competence of commanders who had blindly made the decision to hurl us, without preparation, against lines supposed to be abandoned shortly anyway'. Farley Mowat wrote that when the scout platoon of his Hasty Ps sent back the report 'Have bumped the Hitler Line', 'a great deal was contained in that succinct sentence'. This forced the Canadian Corps to pause and spend the next three days devising a set-piece attack against the German positions, scheduled for 6 a.m. on 23 May and named Operation Chesterfield. This would coincide with General Lucian K. Truscott's breakout with US VI Corps from the Anzio beachhead.

Operationally, Leese realised that the Allies had effectively beaten the Hitler Line, for, as he hoped, the Poles now dominated the heights on his right, while Juin's French Corps were masters of the high ground to the left, stretching towards the sea. Along the Eighth Army's front of only about six miles, Leese had two corps in the valley: Burns's Canadians and Kirkman's XIII, plus Anders's Poles in the mountains. However, the very size of Leese's force would start to act as a brake on his ability to manoeuvre at speed within the confines of the narrow river valley. He was also a slave to Fifth Army's timetable, which envisaged a breakout from Anzio, and Eighth Army was required, in the manner of a pheasant shoot, to 'flush out' the 'game' from its roosts along the Liri and send them up to the 'guns' of VI Corps who should be ready and waiting a few days' hence.

However, en route and before Operation Chesterfield began, the Poles, advancing alongside 78th Division at the foot of the Abruzzi Mountains, had to contend with forward units of the Hitler Line near Piedimonte San Germano. Looking out across the Liri valley, commanding a *Pantherturm* was nineteen-year-old Herbert Fries. A *Pantherturm* was a cunning makeshift fortification comprising a revolving turret from a Panther tank fixed to an underground concrete bunker. The device was essentially a static tank with its turret at ground level. After a stint in the Reich Labour Service, Fries had volunteered for the parachute service in June 1943, and at the end of training in Germany and France was posted to the 2nd Company, 1st Panzerjäger ('tank destroyer') battalion of Heidrich's 1st Parachute Division, the formation which had defended Cassino for so long. Short in stature (ideal for a small tank turret), young Herbert and his three Fallschirmjäger comrades nicknamed their turret *Schlafmütze* – 'Sleepyhead'. On 21 May, as Polish Shermans rumbled into view, Fries and his mates withheld their fire until the last moment, disabling seven of them with their 75mm gun. Though trained as *panzerjäger* – anti-tank troops – this was their first combat from the *Pantherturm*. The next day, they knocked out six tanks that ventured too close, and on 24 May another four. For this Fries was promoted to Gefreiter (lance corporal) and awarded both classes of Iron Cross. Though the youngest, as the turret's commander, his direction had enabled the turret crew to destroy seventeen Allied tanks in three days, before quietly withdrawing by night. On 5 September 1944, Fries was decorated with the coveted Knight's Cross for his activities. Their achievement was considerable, for Fries and his mates were trained as paratroopers, not tank crew, yet they had become panzer 'aces' several times over.

Though he was up against some first-class defensive structures, Major

Chris Vokes knew the Germans did not have the men or the weaponry to equip all the positions. The collapse of the Gustav Line had been so swift and overwhelming that fewer of Vietinghoff's men and guns had made it back to this second line than expected. Vokes understood he was opposed by several battalions of Baade's 90th PanzerGrenadier Division, but was also aware that they were tired, and in no condition to withstand a major pitched battle – which is what he intended to give them. For Operation Chesterfield, he planned for two of his three brigades to hit the midpoint of the German line, between Pontecorvo and Aquino.

Brigadier Graeme Gibson's 2nd Canadian Brigade (the Princess Patricia's Canadian Light Infantry, the Seaforth Highlanders of Canada and Loyal Edmonton Regiment) would attack on the right, with tanks from the North Irish Horse. To their left, Brigadier Bernatchez's 3rd Brigade (22ème Regiment, Carleton & Yorks and West Nova Scotias) and the 51st Royal Tank Regiment were to strike at H-Hour, preceded by a fifteen-minute artillery barrage. Vokes kept back his third brigade and a regiment of tanks to reinforce or exploit as necessary. Officers and senior NCOs of the mostly Churchill tank-equipped North Irish Horse had been briefed the night before that they were supporting the 2nd Canadian Brigade, a squadron of tanks to each battalion, a troop to each company; they knew also that advancing behind Lieutenant Colonel Cam Ware's Patricias were another battalion, the Loyal Eddies.

The battleground between Pontecorvo and Aquino was saturated with complex German defences, built over six months, including trenches, cleverly sited steel-and-concrete anti-tank and machine-gun emplacements overlooking minefields and wire, laid tactically so as to draw tanks and infantry into killing zones. Particularly dangerous were eighteen *Pantherturm*, turrets like Herbert Fries's, which were near impossible to locate because of their low profile. German artillery and mortar fire had been pre-registered, lines of fire cut through the vegetation, while camouflaged snipers acted also as artillery and mortar observers. Augmenting these defences, some thirty panzers and self-propelled guns were also stationed in the vicinity to roam around taking on opportunity targets.

Serving as a troop commander of three Churchill tanks in A Squadron,

North Irish Horse, was twenty-one-year-old Donald Hunt. In 1941 he had travelled from his homeland of Eire over the border to Belfast, volunteering for the army on Armistice Day. He was among 40,000 Anglo-Irish who joined the British Army and remembered that going on leave from war-torn England to Eire, 'a neutral country, where the swastika hung outside the German embassy in Dublin', was a surreal affair. His squadron had arrived in Naples only the previous month, collected eighteen Shermans in addition to their 42-ton Churchills, and were moved up to Cassino by rail and tank transporter. The North Irish Horse, as all Allied tank regiments in Italy, relied on tank transporters for road moves, but on the winding mountain tracks, their progress was painfully slow. Donald recalled that at every hairpin bend 'the tanks had to dismount from the transporters, drive round the bend, mount the transporters again and carry on until the next bend'. Although his regiment were veterans of Tunisia, this would be their first action in Italy.

Before the 'off', Donald Hunt recalled he 'had that peculiar feeling in the pit of the stomach that occurs before a big event. I don't think fear entered into it, apprehension, yes, but even under fire there was so much to think about and do, there was little room or time for fear.' He thought the start of Operation Chesterfield was rather like a horse race, 'the Grand National. At 6 a.m. we all moved forward. The cunning Jerries, anticipating this, brought down concentrations of their own artillery and mortar fire between a hundred and two hundred yards behind our own barrage. This resulted in heavy casualties to our infantry.' In the trees were snipers, 'tied to the branches on a suicide mission'. Among all this was a 'heavy smoke screen, but worst of all was the dust, thick clouds of it. It was dry and hot, and the dust from the tanks and shells exploding created a situation like the proverbial London pea-souper fog in the old days. It was impossible to see anything. I think you would have been able to see more in the middle of a very dark night.' Later on, the Canadians encountered a badly wounded sniper, shot out off his branch by tank fire: 'when we got up to him he was sitting against a tree with a cigarette going. He had one leg off and he'd taken off his belt to make a tourniquet. His sniper's rifle had six notches in it.'

The start line was about 900 yards short of the German positions, and initially their route, with the Princess Patricia's Light Infantry following, took them through a copse of small but closely planted oaks. Hunt reckoned that it took about an hour and a half to traverse just five hundred yards. 'To have proper visibility from a tank it is essential to have your head out of the turret. Here it was impossible, what with shrapnel, snipers and shells bursting in the air, at which the Germans were adept. Closed down in a tank there is only a small visor of armoured glass to see through, about six inches long by three high.' Hunt's squadron was held up by a cleverly concealed minefield. Over the air came a message from 'Griff', his squadron commander Major Robin Griffith, to find a way around the minefield on the extreme right.

As Hunt's squadron emerged from the tree line, it was fixed by the minefield, where they lost two vehicles, and engaged by anti-tank guns, which took another four. They in turn destroyed three panzers and two 75mm anti-tank guns. However, the Germans managed to direct fire from their left, capturing the Canadian infantrymen in crossfire. In retrospect the Edmonton Regiment should have waited longer before walking into the same fire as the Princess Patricia's Light Infantry. The battle was swiftly descending into a shambles, with both the Patricias and the Eddies taking serious casualties, and men becoming scattered in the woods and blocked by the wire – exactly as the Germans had intended.

Hunt moved his tank off, searching for a way round the mines when: 'Suddenly the tank, weighing some 40 tons, lurched to the right, went crashing endlessly down, turning a somersault as we crashed and banged about landing upside down, another almighty crash and we seemed to turn the right way up again as this mighty animal bounced back on its tracks again. I have never before been so frightened, amazed and thrown about in the space of a few seconds in my life.' His tank had fallen into a deep gully and turned a complete somersault, landing upright. The driver sensibly had switched off the fuel when the vehicle started to slide, and the five-man crew was, amazingly, uninjured. Finding the engine still worked and the tracks were unbroken, but his wireless dead, Hunt jumped out and ran, zigzagging on foot back across the mined battlefield to report his predicament to the squadron leader before returning to his tank. Somehow his driver, Davy Graham, managed to manoeuvre the Churchill down to the gully floor and up the other side, and eventually over the top. Churchills had gained a reputation in Tunisia for their excellent climbing ability, and it is unlikely that the narrower and taller Sherman would ever have been able to extract itself. Had they not fallen into the gully, however, Hunt's tank would almost certainly have been brewed up by Baade's anti-tank gunners, along with much of his squadron.

To the left of Hunt's troop, the Seaforth Highlanders of Canada, supported by B Squadron of the North Irish Horse, were engaged in a similar skirmish with their portion of the line. At 8 a.m., they too had burst out of the tree line, guns blazing, and had been raked with fire from some very cool anti-tank gunners, when only a hundred yards from their objective. Five tanks were hit immediately, including the squadron commander's. By 1 p.m. the two North Irish Horse squadrons were combined and tried to further support the Seaforths, Patricias and Edmontons, but had lost collectively sixteen tanks by mid-afternoon – a squadron's worth. Hunt's Churchill somehow survived the whole day's combat, emerging from a quarter the defenders did not expect, but by nightfall his regiment lost almost half their strength, including their CO, twenty-five tanks and seventy-five casualties to German guns.

While 2nd Canadian Brigade and the North Irish Horse tanks had hit near-disaster on the right before Aquino, the 3rd Brigade and 51st Tanks made much better progress to their left, and had breached the main defences within seventy-five minutes. This was attributed to aggressive patrolling on 22 May, which brought in much valuable intelligence about the defence layout ahead. The picture for Major General Vokes at 1st Canadian Division HQ was of an encouraging advance on the left, but depressing stalemate on his right. He ordered a 'William' target (the codeword devised by Freyberg's New Zealand artillery adviser, requiring all Eighth Army artillery to switch fire onto a single target area) on Aquino which was approved instantly. At 1 p.m., thirty-three minutes later, 668 guns opened fire and pulverised Baade's PanzerGrenadiers with nearly a hundred tons of high explosive, and the defence gradually subsided. Aquino received 3,509 shells in a few minutes, leaving 'a small town in ruins, with the all-pervading smell of death. It seemed worse here,' wrote one Canadian, 'because the town must have been pretty.' By 4 p.m. German fire had noticeably slackened, and those defenders who could slipped away at nightfall.

The 2nd Canadian Brigade attack had cost 543 casualties, about one in seven of their number, and a price, calculated one historian, unequalled by any other Canadian brigade in a single day's fighting for the entire Italian campaign. Meanwhile on the extreme left, the 48th Highlanders, with support from the divisional reconnaissance unit, the Princess Louise Dragoon Guards (who found a path through the minefield), and eventually the Hasty Ps, battled their way into Pontecorvo, while the West Nova Scotias and 22ème Regiment advanced a mile beyond. Despite Leese's earlier criticism of him, Vokes had broken through in a single day, and later looked back on 23 May as 'the best battle I ever fought, or organised, even though we suffered so heavily'.

The cost in British tanks was high, too: the North Irish Horse, 51st and 142nd Royal Tank Regiments collectively lost forty-four tanks destroyed, and at least as many again disabled and subsequently repaired at night – over a third of Brigadier James Tetley's British 25th Tank Brigade. Night-time was often the busiest time for tank crewmen, as one recalled: 'We soon found that the tank was the master and we were its slaves. It had to be filled with fuel, oil, water, the batteries had to be checked and charged, and the guns cleaned at the end of each day's fighting. All this had to be done before attending to oneself . . . Every night we would run our charger motor for an hour or so in order to charge up the tired batteries. This small two-stroke engine is tucked away in some corner of the turret and the din it kicks up is devastating as it rocks and quivers on its rubber mountings, buzzing and backfiring and filling the place with fumes.' On 24 May, Vokes wrote to Brigadier Tetley to express his gratitude: 'Well done. We have won a resounding victory. This victory is the fruit of your magnificent courage, endurance and the will to win . . . I am the proudest man in the world.' He concluded by asking if all ranks of the British 25 Tank Brigade 'would wear a Maple Leaf emblem in token of the part played by the brigade in assisting 1st Canadian Infantry Division to breach the Adolf Hitler Line', which they did.

Vokes could take some comfort from the fact that most of Baade's defenders were either in captivity or dead; the number of prisoners – 700 – almost equalled his own casualties – 879, but more importantly, the Hitler Line had been breached, and much to Vietinghoff's surprise his defences were fast crumbling, like sandcastles before an incoming tide.

But Tenth Army's retreat up the valley was not quite the disorganised rout that some imagined. An order issued by the commanding officer of II Battalion, 29th PanzerGrenadier Regiment, which had been stalling the Allies since Salerno, illustrates the rigour and discipline the Wehrmacht still expected: 'Experience has shown that only the firmness of officers can counter this disadvantage. Every company commander must tell his men again and again that the survival of the whole company depends on the vigilance of each single soldier. Every day we must expect more dirty tricks on the part of the enemy. I do not want to hear the soldiers complaining that they have not eaten, slept or drunk for two days and that the situation is impossible. The word "impossible" does not exist in the soldier's dictionary.'

On his way forward, Lieutenant Farley Mowat stopped to examine one of the *Pantherturm* and the debris following the German retreat, remembering the turret of a 'Mark V Panther tank sunk in a steel and concrete emplacement with its gun pointing to three dead Sherman tanks that it had killed.' In the turret, he wrote, 'fly-clouded and stinking, was the body of the German lieutenant who had laid the gun, and who had taken a direct hit from the armour-piercing shell of a fourth Sherman. [Nearby were] the deep bunkers that Dog Company had overrun, complete with underground chicken pens and even with domestic items such as brassieres and women's underpants . . . There was much to see. The unused belts of machine-gun ammunition beside dead German gunners in the slit trenches that had not been deep enough. The pathetic litter of old letters, and photographs of remembered faces scattered about . . . three Lee Enfield rifles, upended on their bayonets in the dirt, with three helmets hanging from their butts.'

Tommy Burns now needed to exploit the breakthrough into a pursuit, and intended to feed in Bert Hoffmeister's 5th Canadian Armoured Division through Vokes's 1st Division, but the onset of heavy rain on the evening of 23 May, combined with exhaustion and traffic-clogged roads, meant the start was delayed until the 24th. Speed was of the essence, for six miles beyond the breached defences lay another geological obstacle, far smaller than the Liri or Rapido, and running at a right angle across the axis of Hoffmeister's advance, the Melfa River. It flowed gently from the hills behind Cassino, past Roccasecca, which had earlier hosted Senger's XIV Panzer Corps HQ in the 'decrepit old Palazzo', across the valley and into the Liri.

Wednesday 24 May was Victoria Day, a public holiday in Canada, a fact that most forgot as they concentrated on the countryside ahead, a 'scrub-tangled region of crisscrossing laneways and near-dry streams', but Burns and Hoffmeister correctly foresaw that Vietinghoff would try to use the Melfa to stem their advance. Chris Vokes devised two battle-groups to rush ahead. Vokes Force, commanded not by him but his younger brother, Fred (with tanks of the British Columbia Dragoons and infantry of the Irish Regiment of Canada), was to establish a firm base halfway, through which Griffin Force (Lord Strathcona's Horse and the Westminster Regiment) would pass and seize the river line itself. While Hoffmeister stuck his neck out for this next advance, elements of 6th Armoured Division, now called forward, were to protect his right flank. The Germans put in a desperate defence of the Melfa, and the lead troop of the British Columbia Dragoons lost all four tanks in minutes to a single well-sited anti-tank gun.

Also advancing in his half-track on the Melfa River position was gun position officer Lieutenant Stan F. Farrow. Having volunteered for the army in Red Deer, Alberta, and been commissioned into the Royal Canadian Artillery, Farrow had landed in Naples with his regiment on Christmas Eve 1943. He was part of Bert Hoffmeister's Division, commanding 'Dog Troop' of four M-7 Priests, with 75mm guns mounted on a Sherman hull. From his half-track, Farrow directed their fire, working with five others. His job was to receive the fire orders, interpret them and pass the order to the four guns. 'As soon as the guns were ready I reported back "Troop ready". The troop commander would then order so many rounds per gun, "Fire" and I would relay that order to the gun sergeants. The commander observed where the shells landed and exploded . . . would then make corrections plus or minus so many yards and so many degrees right or left until we hit the target.' Farrow remembered the top half of his half-track 'was covered by heavy canvas. The driver's and officers' cab at the front was completely covered in armour and a steel plate could be pulled over the windshield leaving just a slit for the driver to see out. There was a roof hatch so I could stand up and observe to direct the driver. We had to be able to follow the tanks with our guns over very rough ground. In the half-track we carried the radio, artillery boards and survey instruments, as well as all our gear and other equipment for setting up the troop command post.'

Private Stan Scislowski of the Perth Regiment was also part of Bert Hoffmeister's Division. He remembered marching 'along a rutted road an inch deep in talcum powder-like dust towards the Melfa in a long single file, with five yards between men, and sections ten yards apart. The rattle of small-arms, ours and the enemy's, grew in volume, and the steady bang of our tanks' 75s, along with the growling crumps of mortars a short distance away, told us that our time to get into the thick of things was almost here.' The friendly armour were from Lord Strathcona's Horse of Griffin Force, which had moved beyond the fordable Melfa River to fight a series of running engagements with a unit of deadly Panther tanks (mobile ones this time, unlike Herbert Fries's turret) – the first Panthers encountered in Italy. Meanwhile, Stan Farrow's troop of Priests were part of the forward artillery supporting the battle, firing at ranges of 1½ miles. 'This was a short range,' he observed, 'as we usually fired at ranges of from 5,000 to 10,000 yards [5½ miles].' At this position they were bombed by several low-flying German fighter-bombers. 'This was our first experience with bombs, and believe me, it scared the dickens out of us! It was at night and we could hear the planes coming low over our positions and then there would be a great blast nearby. Several of us were lying in a shallow ditch and a young gunner about eighteen years old was in front of me. The toes of his boots were beating a tattoo on my helmet from his fright and nerves. From then on we dug slit trenches faster and deeper than ever.'

Scislowski was also under the bombs, recalling: 'some time during the first half of the night two or three German planes flew over the battlefield, and after circling around for a nerve-rattling fifteen or twenty minutes, commenced unloading their bombs on the rear echelons and lines of supply, causing considerable damage and casualties . . . No matter where the Jerry bombardiers chose to drop their bombs, they could hardly miss. From Cassino all the way to the Melfa River, the Liri valley was chock-a-block with troops, vehicles, guns, tanks and supplies.' One of the bombs killed the Perths' regimental provost as he was motorcycling on 'his Norton past an ammo truck parked in a field not far off the road – and at that very moment a bomb hit the truck and it disintegrated in one hell of a blast'.

Because of the very flat valley bottom, Farrow recalled of the Melfa, 'most of our fire was controlled by small observation planes flying low over the battlefield. One of the planes came too low in his endeavour to spot German tanks and sadly was shot down during a salvo from our regiment.' Scislowski remembered the plane incident, too. 'While taking a short breather, sitting on the edge of my trench, I glanced skywards and saw one of our Piper Cub observation planes flying back and forth over the area at an altitude low enough for even riflemen to take potshots at. One minute he was there, and in the next he was gone in a puff of black smoke. Out of the black smoke came a wing and part of the fuse-lage spinning to the ground like maple pods. The two pieces came down less than a hundred yards away . . . I later learned that it had actually flown straight into one of our twenty-five pounder shells on its way to knock down a target on the far side of the Melfa.'

In a desperate bid to increase their apparent strength and slow the Canadian advance, the Germans had constructed a number of fake positions and equipped them with imitation weaponry, such as dummy tanks 'made up of wood framework covered with burlap sacking' that Stan Scislowski encountered. 'From afar, it was supposed to fool us into thinking it was a Tiger tank. To make it look even more realistic, beside it the Jerries had piled up a stack of wooden shell crates. The ruse's value was questionable; it fooled no one.' Scislowski might have reflected that had the fake tank been spotted only from the air, or at night, then intelligence were unlikely to have realised it was a decoy, and couldn't take the chance that it might be; here was the value of the 'aggressive patrolling' undertaken by 3rd Canadian Brigade a few days earlier. By the end of the day, the Strathconas of Griffin force had lost seventeen tanks, but had inflicted losses amounting to twenty of their opponents, an exchange rate the Allies could easily tolerate.

The evening of 24 May saw the landscape surrounding the gently flowing Melfa turn into a scene from Dante's Inferno, as 'the eerie light from burning tanks blended grotesquely with the glow of the setting sun; smoke from burning oil and petrol mingled with the dust that hung over the valley to give the effect of a partial eclipse'. All through the day, the Westminsters had kept the Strathconas company at the Melfa bridge-head, and one of their majors, though thrice wounded, organised the defence against German counterattacks throughout the night; for his leadership Major John Mahoney was awarded a Victoria Cross. Though wide, the Melfa River was shallow, and itself offered little obstacle to the Canadians; its thickly wooded banks helped to conceal the small numbers of Canadians who reached its banks initially, then dashed across.

When alerted that the Canadians had breached the Melfa, Vietinghoff's chief of staff Fritz Wentzell declared: 'We have got to get out of here as fast as we can or we shall lose the whole XIV Panzer Corps.' As the Germans slipped back, they cratered roads, demolished bridges, left verges mined and houses booby-trapped. All road junctions, and likely sites for headquarters and leaguers, were covered by observed or pre-registered artillery fire, or mortars, including their beastly six-barrelled variety the *Nebelwerfers*.' An officer of 2/Lancashire Fusiliers regarded them as 'a typically Germanic terror machine. The barrels discharge their rockets . . . with a sound that is hard to put into words. It is like someone sitting violently on the base notes of a piano, accompanied by the grating squeak of a diamond on glass. Then the clutch of canisters sail through the air with a fluttering chromatic whine, like jet-propelled Valkyries.' The odd Luftwaffe aircraft still roamed at night, all of which provided friction to slow what would otherwise have been a swifter advance.

With the last of the organised German defences broken, Oliver Leese, who had a huge amount of combat power available, was determined to push as much of it as possible up the valley, notwithstanding the poor road network, the cratering, demolitions and booby-traps. Eighth Indian Division had been brought back into line on 20 May, and by the 25th were advancing on the right of Route 6, from Piedmonte San Germano towards the site of Senger's long-gone HQ at Roccasecca. Sixth Armoured and 78th Battleaxe Divisions advanced on the Indians' left; the former had been called forward and on 26 May reached Monte Piccolo and Monte Grande, a pair of ridges that dominated the left-hand edge of Route 6 by the town of Arce, about sixteen miles up the valley. The following day, 'S' Company of 2/Coldstream Guards (of 6th Armoured) had a sharp fight taking Monte Piccolo, losing many casualties, including all its officers. The hill was finally taken by Company Sergeant Major Brown, assisted by Lance Sergeant Jones who seized the barrel of a German machine gun *while the crew were firing it*, 'pulling it towards him and turning it upon its own crew, killing them in one heroic act'.

As 6th Armoured Division moved forward, Alex Bowlby, a Radley-educated private soldier within its 2/Rifle Brigade, remembered, as he jolted up to the front at the tail of a long traffic jam, the outskirts of Cassino: 'tanks and carriers lay around like burnt tins on a rubbish heap. A row of black crosses, topped with coal scuttle helmets, snatched our pity. The smell – the sour-sweet stench of rotting flesh – cut it short. Instinctively I realised I was smelling my own kind, and not animals. I understood what they must feel in a slaughter house. These dead were under the rubble. If we could have seen their bodies it would have helped. The unseen, unconsecrated dead assumed a most terrifying power. Their protest filled the truck. We avoided one another's eyes.'

The same day, towards the head of the same traffic jam, the Canadians had pushed on to Ceprano, astride Route 6, a mass of 'tangled streets, piled here and there with the rubble of buildings blown down by our shellfire', where Stan Scislowski found 'two grey horses lying dead in the scrub and torn-up trees . . . harnessed to a large wagon loaded with ammunition boxes. Big-bodied, majestic animals, perhaps a couple of Clydesdales. What a shame that these two innocent beautiful beasts should die this way,' he wrote. Each day the weather was improving, which brought problems of its own for the infantry. On 26 May, Scislowski remembered 'by mid-morning the heat and humidity rose to an unbearable level. Not a cloud in the sky. Not a tree to give shade. Nothing but heat, sweat, dust, thirst, and sore, burning feet. We kept moving in some semblance of an arrowhead formation, sweat running down our cheeks, hungry as jackals and godawful thirsty.'

Oliver Leese's challenge was to push up the Liri quick enough to trap the German Tenth Army at the top, where US VI Corps were due to be waiting at Valmonte; but his force also had to be strong enough to overcome the delaying tactics of Vietinghoff's men as they withdrew. Leese's solution was to insert every available formation into the Liri to ensure he achieved both. In fact, his solution endangered Eighth Army from achieving either. In the last days of May, the two divisions of

Burns's Canadian Corps were competing for road space with 4th and 78th British, 8th Indian and 6th Armoured Divisions, plus assorted independent brigades, a few Polish units, Corps and Army troops. This also had the unforeseen disadvantage of increasing the likelihood of friendly fire incidents as neighbouring Allies forces clashed in error; Canadian units of 5th Armoured experienced this on 26 May as they moved towards Ceprano.

The traffic began to create logistical problems, as those units at the front ran short of fuel, ammunition, water, rations or medical supplies, and their rear echelons could not get forward. The 8th Princess Louise's Hussars actually had to stop and wait for fuel. Yet another problem also began to manifest itself as the sheer weight of traffic began to degrade some of the Bailey bridges that had been hastily assembled, and several failed, or buckled. 'We have attempted to feed the absolute maximum number of vehicles onto our system,' stated one Canadian report. 'As a result, roads have given way at various points and it has been necessary to lower the classification of a number of weakened bridges. Chaotic conditions have arisen from provost personnel not having a thorough understanding of the current traffic plan; drivers thought only of themselves, and continually blocked roads by breaking out of line, only to find themselves halted by oncoming vehicles, and with the gap in their own traffic closed behind them.'

On 28 May, Leese ordered forward yet another formation, his seventh. The 6th South African Armoured Division, commanded by the South African Major General Evered Poole, had arrived at Taranto in April, and been held back as the Eighth Army reserve between Foggia and Caseta. Its 12th South African Motorised Brigade had already seen some action, being sent immediately on landing to relieve 11th Canadian Brigade, then under the New Zealand Division. Although this division was new, Poole was a safe and trusted pair of hands, having served operationally in Eighth Army since June 1941: and he had slipped over to Cassino for a reconnaissance of the front and witnessed the 15 March air raid with Leese, Kirkman and Keightley. Poole was also given 24th Guards Brigade comprising 1/Scots Guards, 3 Coldstreams and 5/Grenadiers, partly, no doubt, enabled by his attachment to them nine years earlier.

Poole's South Africans were intended to relieve Hoffmeister's 5th Armoured and placed in Tommy Burns's Canadian Corps, but since they could not get forward, they merely added to the traffic on the Canadian's cross-country axis. Burns understandably gave their passage low priority, and required them, following in his wake, to bury any dead Canadians they found. In early June, for example, the South Africans buried a Canadian found in the rubble of Pontecorvo, where he had lain in the heat for at least four days. The South Africans – new to Italy – had to adapt quickly to operating on a narrow front (as opposed to the expanses of the North African desert), with its infinitely varying and difficult terrain. Poole embraced Montgomery's model of a small, highly mobile tactical headquarters 'with frequent face-to-face discussions with his brigadiers, resulting in speedy on-the-spot decisions', wrote one of his staff officers. He was 'continuously in touch with Main Div HQ through one of the two wireless sets installed in both his Tac[tical] HQ jeep and in his command tank. There is no doubt that the sight of the GOC's pennant fluttering from his two-star jeep here, there and every-where, well forward of the Main Div HQ, had a significant effect on the fighting morale of his troops.'

Competition developed between Kirkman's XIII Corps and that of Burns for the best roads down the Liri, exacerbated by the fact that Leese had reserved the only decent road, Route 6, for XIII Corps, forcing the Canadians across a maze of dirt roads which were little more than animal tracks in close country. This began to cause bad blood between form-ations and made Leese's army headquarters unpopular. On 28 May, Hoffmeister's 5th Canadian Division were diverted off Route 6, in favour of the 78th Battleaxe, just when the former were poised to leap beyond Ceprano. Writing his semi-official history six years after the events, Eric Linklater, who served in Italy, observed of this time: 'All our divisions lay locked in stupid conflict for the right of way. Traffic in the narrow, overcrowded and cratered valley had been difficult from the moment after our dogged infantry had broken the bloody door and entered. Now traffic became impossible, it almost ceased to move, and crowded vehicles and guns stood nose to petrol-sniffing tail in helpless confusion, while officers of all degrees swore horribly in impotent wrath and weary huddled soldiers gave their fatigue an aspect of philosophy by sleeping while they could.' A Canadian historian echoed this precisely, noting how this build-up of traffic 'crossed and re-crossed the battlefield in every direction; they tangled in hour-long traffic jams at bottlenecks; they created a maze of misleading tracks; they often coagulated in such great clots as to hinder the movement of troops on foot'.

A South African on Poole's divisional staff, Major A. B. Theunissen, wrote: 'at first, senior commanders in Italy were (without authority) ordering their units on the road in order to get them in the right place at the right time. The resulting traffic jams and confusion were indescribable. On more than one occasion General Poole had to go forward on the pillion of his provost escort's motorcycle, leaving me to bring the Tac HQ jeep forward when possible.' Vehicles were 'merely fed onto the road at a rate of twenty-five vehicles every fifteen minutes'. Soldiers made do with what supplies and rations they carried in their trucks, usually supplemented by cherries plucked from passing trees. 'Meals were erratic while the division was in pursuit mode with mobile kitchens caught up in the traffic.' John Smallwood of the South African Imperial Light Horse noted the chaos in his diary: 'Just completed one leg of the nightmare journey . . . through narrow side roads alongside the modern Route 6 on the road to Rome. Tanks, guns, half-tracks and ambulances were mixed up with 3-ton lorries, carriers and more tanks. An endless column, nose to tail, either waiting with engines running in the overpowering heat and dust or tearing through narrow lanes trying to catch the vehicle in front. Civilians in ragged clothes stand in small groups staring pathetically at the never-ending stream . . . Enemy equipment is everywhere. Broken trucks, burned-out tanks, guns upside down are scattered about . . . above all hangs a thick, nauseating blanket of dust and the stench of the dead.'

While General Alexander held overall responsibility for the traffic foul-up, which contributed to Eighth Army being slow to reach Rome and failing to trap the Tenth Army at Valmonte, the source of the problem lay with Eighth Army's culture. Although commanded by Oliver Leese from the end of December 1943, it was very much Montgomery's creation and still bore his stamp, not least in its dress, but also its doctrine. Monty was very good at set-piece battles (what came to be known as his 'colossal cracks'), but was less proficient in executing an effective pursuit.

Eighth Army's contribution to Operation Diadem, itself devised by a Monty acolyte, John Harding, bore all the hallmarks of Monty in its opening phase: many compared the opening barrage to that of El Alamein on which it was undoubtedly modelled. But Leese, like Monty, proved less good at managing the fluid battle that then developed. He was also fortunate that the Luftwaffe had no means of commanding of the air in daylight hours – otherwise he would have been in severe trouble.

Just as criticisms are often made of Montgomery for not exploiting his opportunities after Alamein to surround and destroy the Afrika Korps, in effect letting Rommel escape to fight another day, the same trait can be observed in Leese's handling of the pursuit of Vietinghoff and Senger's forces up the Liri valley. There was no point in inserting 6th South African Armoured Division at this stage, just as there had been no reason earlier to make two corps – Burns's Canadians and Kirkman's XIII Corps – compete for elbow room in the valley. Leese, who was commanding his Eighth Army from a huddle of caravans at Venafro, fifteen miles away, down Route 6, had sufficient combat power to advance on a single corps front, in three generous tactical bounds. First a break-in, with 4th and 8th Indian Divisions; second an exploitation with Burns's two divisions, 1st Infantry and 5th Armoured; and third, the subsequent passage through and beyond of 78th Battleaxe and 6th Armoured. He would still have had substantial reserves of armour in Brigadier William Murphy's 1st Canadian Armoured Brigade (who never fought in their own corps) and the Churchill tanks of Brigadier James Tetley's 25 Armoured Brigade, to assist the infantry in their battles, plus the South Africans.

In England there was no knowledge of traffic jams. 'Enemy in Flight from Hitler Line. Rearguards Throw Down Their Arms' read the banner headlines of the *Daily Herald* on 25 May, featuring a large picture of the ruined monastery on its front page. 'The battle for the Liri valley, which began with such bloody fighting, developed today into a pursuit . . . Badly chopped-up enemy units have been moving back all day to the Melfa River, harassed by advancing Canadian tanks', the paper informed its readers. Although this news was days old, it seemed at times as though Oliver Leese was taking his own optimistic understanding of the evolving battle from the newspapers, rather than his own intelligence reports. In assessing the Diadem plan, Alexander's chief administrative officer at

Caserta, Major General Sir Brian Robertson, stated that for the pursuit phase it was 'essential to reduce all transport on the roads to a minimum . . . that reserves and non-essential units would be held back'. Although some have laid the blame for Leese's slow progress up the Liri at the feet of Alexander, the latter was also coordinating the breakout from Anzio with Mark Clark, plus dealing with issues relating to the future capture of Rome. The Liri valley traffic problem was definitely one of Eighth Army's making, and it was up to Leese, not Alex, to provide a solution. None was forthcoming, and the traffic was left to sort itself out.

The Germans were amazed at the incompetence of the Liri valley pursuit. Senger – Leese's chief adversary in the Liri – commanding XIV Panzer Corps, was dismissive of the operation, merely noting: 'I saw to it that units rushing back were sent in a general northerly direction, while offering occasional resistance here and there, and I formed an assembly point at Frosinone. Meanwhile, I had to maintain communication with LI Corps on the left until such time as all the troops fighting in the Liri valley had again been put under my unified control. Since the British corps attacking there was not exerting any great pressure the task was relatively easy . . . It was far more difficult to repel the French corps.'

14

Roads to Rome

S ENGER WAS RIGHT. Juin's French Expeditionary Corps were a greater menace to him in the Liri valley than Leese's Eighth Army. Much of the ultimate success of Diadem would, in fact, be owed to Juin personally: it was his vision that enabled Diadem to work so splendidly, and his Corps who had over-delivered in spectacular fashion. The expertise of the FEC, felt Oliver Leese, in a mid-campaign letter to his old boss, Montgomery (then busy in Normandy), was a vital ingredient for success; 'we were handicapped by the lack of mountain troops to operate on our northern flank . . . you will see how much easier our task would have been if we had also had mountain troops . . . on our right'.

Juin's FEC was the longest-serving in the campaign: of all the Allied formations involved in Fourth Cassino, only Juin's could claim to have been present in January for the first assaults – indeed the FEC were in the area before the Cassino campaign began. It was Juin who had first suggested to Clark on 4 April 1944 that his troops were best suited to fighting in difficult terrain such as the Aurunci Mountains. He felt the German defenders would never expect a major assault in such challenging terrain and identified the dominating 3,084ft peak of Monte Maio as the main objective. It was, he felt, probably only lightly defended (if at all), and possession would give the Allies control of the Aurunci range.

Clark and Alexander and their respective chiefs of staff, Gruenther and Harding, readily accepted Juin's advice and recast their plans, though expectations of the Frenchman's claim to be able to fight through the Aurunci were not high. In the event, the boldness and sheer aggression shown by his men would prove to be the decisive factor in turning the whole front and breaking the Gustav Line.

By May, Juin commanded the largest corps in Italy, possessing the equivalent of five divisions, including the 1st and 4th Moroccans, 3rd Algerians and three brigade-sized groups of Berber Tabors, effectively another division. Juin also possessed the 1er Division *Française Libre* (1st Free French Division), comprising a variety of units from the Foreign Legion, colonial naval troops, black Senegalese infantry and battalions formed from French settlers in North Africa; this had a higher proportion of white French soldiers and was organised along British lines. To Juin's left, Keyes's US II Corps were to advance along the coast, using the *Via Appia* – Route 7 – as their axis. On 29 March, the Americans had taken over the bridgehead across the Garigliano gained by 5th British Division (of McCreery's British X Corps) back in January. As the Red Bulls and Texans rotated out of II Corps for Anzio, they were replaced by two new units, John B. Coulter's 85th Custer Division and John E. Sloan's 88th Cloverleafs, otherwise known as the Blue Devils. Both divisions, of draftees rather than volunteers, had left the USA in 1943, trained in North Africa and arrived in Italy in February–March 1944.

Opposite II Corps and the French lay scattered battalions of different German divisions, under Senger's XIV Panzer Corps command, whose defences consisted of bunkers built of logs and boulders, sometimes strengthened with concrete, surrounded by barbed wire obstacles and a scattering of anti-personnel mines. All across the front to be attacked was steep terrain, with plenty of dead ground, offering covered approaches that could not be seen by the German fixed defences. Defending such a long distance (from the Liri valley to the sea was twenty miles) with limited resources meant the Germans lacked depth to their positions. They were gambling that, having held the British 5th and 56th Divisions in this sector over January, no other Allied units would attempt a second assault. Unfortunately for them, this was just the kind of terrain the Expeditionary Corps' mountain-trained warriors were used to. It was to

Général Dody's 2nd Morrocan Division that Juin entrusted the main task of capturing Monte Maio; to his right the 1st Free French would launch into the hills, and to the left the 3rd Algerians and Tabors would attack the high ground as far south as Castelforte.

As with the attacks by British XIII Corps in the Liri valley and the Poles on Monte Cassino, events opened with a massive preliminary barrage all along the front, starting at 11 p.m. on 11 May. The bombardment was well planned, silencing gun batteries, assembly areas for reserves, supply dumps, headquarters and communications outposts. It rapidly threw the Germans into confusion, though Steinmetz's 94th Division, opposite Dody, continued to resist all through 12 May, they committed their last reserves. However, some of Dody's *Tirailleurs* had managed to take the summit of Monte Faito, an important milestone on the way to Monte Maio, by midnight. Throughout 13 May, Dody's Moroccans had worked they way forward to seize Monte Feuci, when a patrol discovered that the divisional objective, Monte Maio, was, in fact, unoccupied. Despite local, half-hearted counterattacks, Monte Maio was taken at 3 p.m. Juin's claims to be able to seize the Aurunci had started to yield results.

With mortars and mountain artillery, the French started to bring down fire on any German artillery positions they could see, who were unaware they were being watched. Such a deep penetration began to unhinge the Germans in this central mountain sector, six miles behind the Gustav Line, where no depth defensive positions had been built, or were thought necessary.

Further south, in the American sector, twenty-eight-year-old Klaus H. Huebner, a surgeon with 349th Regiment of the 88th Cloverleaf Division, was waiting with his medics for H-Hour. A German speaker, Huebner was born in Bavaria but grew up in the United States. Now, he was going into battle against his former countrymen. He remembered 11 May as 'huge, leaping bright flashes which illuminate the entire Garigliano. The roar of the guns is so deafening that you can shout at the man standing next to you and still not be heard. The murderous sound of our atillery is so loud I can't possibly tell if the Germans are shooting back. I see sheets of flame spring from behind every bush. The hills to our north are spattered with phosphorus bursts that illuminate the entire horizon.' Along the coast, the 85th Custermen found the going tough and by the end of 12 May had made only limited progress, while the 88th Cloverleafs had taken Tufo and attacked Santa Maria Infante, a small, elevated town north of Minturno, and considered a major strongpoint in the Gustav Line. The stone buildings sat on a series of terraces, with terrain that dropped steeply away on all sides. Early morning fog on 12 May and challenging ground, which limited the Cloverleafs to a single battalion attack (of Colonel Arthur S. Champney's 351st Infantry Regiment), added to the difficulties caused by anti-tank guns and machine-gun nests. Several Shermans of the supporting 760th Tank Battalion ran onto mines placed along the only access road, but eliminating the town was vital in order for II Corps to progress further into the mountains.

There was not much left of Santa Maria Infante by the time the 3rd Battalion/351st Infantry had cleared out the few German rearguards on the morning of 14 May, but the birds had effectively flown. Because of French successes further north, General Steinmetz had already pulled back his division in an effort to stabilise his front and link up with 71st Infantry Division, under pressure and being pushed by the Moroccans and Algerians to his north.

Very quickly, the right wing of Senger's front was beginning to fall back, threatening to cave in on itself. Many of these isolated mountain towns and villages now revealed their inhabitants, who had had nowhere to escape; the urban scenery was well described by a French Légionnaire. 'Every now and again, I would come face to face with local peasants, ravaged by hunger and poverty, trying to salvage what they could from the wreckage of their homes . . . Numbed by war, shattered by the political turmoil their country had endured for the last few years, these people had lost the light in their eyes. Their bambini would stare blankly at me, their dirt-stained mouths a testament to their foraging. Even the few scrawny dogs I came across seemed to have lost the ability to wag their tails.'

The 14th of May also witnessed the defenders from German 94th Division finally driven out of Casteforte by the Algerian Division, who then started moving on the major town of Ausonia. The terrain was such that even a local withdrawal by one small German unit might result in another being outflanked, so if a breach occurred with no reserves available to counterattack, military logic dictated the whole line fell back slightly, in order to maintain a continuous front. Whenever this happened, Juin ensured that his units were hard on the Germans' tail. The roads through the mountains were good, if unpaved, wide enough for two-way traffic, but where they could, the Germans left mines, craters and demolished bridges. Huebner observed that the craters were usually mined, the lead scouts being the most frequent casualties. 'The shoe-mine casualties are heavy and demoralising,' he wrote. 'A man's foot is usually blown loose at the ankle, leaving the mangled foot dangling on shredded tendons; dirt and rocks imbed themselves into the splintered stump. Additional puncture wounds of both legs and groin make the agony worse. I have no time to clean the wounds. All I can do is administer morphine for the pain and add a thickly padded dressing; splints are useless, since the foot cannot be saved anyway – it has lost its blood supply.'

Juin's FEC was lavishly equipped with American vehicles, and had no worries about supplies of fuel, or command of the skies. They made the most of their mobility, frequently outpacing the German rearguards, who had neither fuel, nor vehicles, let alone air cover. Nevertheless, French progress could be agonisingly slow, as units trundled along behind engineers clearing mines and bulldozers repairing roads. By 15 May, the French had cleared much of the main road running from Castelforte, through Ausonia and Esperia, and had scattered many of the smaller battlegroups of General Raapke's 71st and Steinmetz's 94th Divisions. The lightly armed Goumiers moved along the hilltops, flashing their knives and taking no prisoners, while columns of armour and half-tracked infantry pushed along the roads below. The sudden appearance of the Berbers caused panic in German ranks, which often had a far greater impact on their morale than actual fighting.

Working on the border between his own 88th Division and the extreme left wing of the FEC, Klaus Huebner came across the Goumiers and marvelled at what he saw: 'They are the boys who are expert at knife work. For the first time I have a chance to get a close view of these fellows I have heard so much about. They are a fascinating lot. The native warriors wear dirty grey robes, and their long hair is braided in pigtails. They sing, chatter and howl. Many carry chickens under their arms, and some herd goats before them. All are armed with huge machete knives. We are told they receive fifty cents per enemy ear. I would like to keep mine.'

Never far behind were batteries of French-manned US 105mm guns ready to bring down fire on any likely target identified by the L-4 Piper Cub spotter planes (known as 'Grasshoppers') with which each division was equipped. One much-photographed column of nearly fifty destroyed tanks, guns, half-tracks and trucks was caught in exactly this fashion just north of Esperia on 17 May. The Fifth Army commander Mark Clark later recalled visiting the scene with General Juin: 'Dead Germans, trucks, tanks, guns and personnel carriers were demolished and scattered everywhere . . . the result was so disastrous that the French had to bull-doze vehicles and bodies over the side of the hill in order to permit their troops to pass along the road.'

The American 88th Cloverleaf Division ploughed on through the mountains, towards the Monte Aurunci Ridge, accompanied by surgeon Klaus Huebner. 'The climb is tremendous. We follow a goat trail and at times must clamber on all fours. One of our mules carrying cartons of plasma and litters [stretchers] falls down the slope when halfway up. Our only solution is to hand-carry all our plasma, litters and dressings. On these high slopes we see all the deserted Jerry foxholes – dug into rocks and all over four feet deep. In their hurry to retreat they have left their packs, mess gear, helmets, letters, guns, and first-aid kits behind.'

The 88th were orientated towards Itri, greatly aided by the progress of the FEC on their right, while the 85th Custermen pushed along the coast, capturing Maranola on 17 May and entering the coastal resort of Formia, astride Route 7, on the 18th. The town, which had been a major logistics depot to forward positions of the Gustav Line, had been targeted beforehand by air raids and naval bombardment; by the time the 338th Infantry Regiment entered, huge quarters of the town had literally been reduced to rubble, on a scale similar to Cassino.

It was only at this stage, 17 May, that Senger returned to take over command of XIV Panzer Corps, and was horrified to find that the front of 71st and 94th Divisions had imploded and was in complete disarray, with neither formation able to conjure up any reserves to patch the many holes in their lines. Kesselring, who had hitherto been under the spell of Operation Nunton (which among other things had created false wireless traffic, giving the impression of three divisions at Naples preparing to make another amphibious assault up the coast), now agreed to release his reserves, allocating to Senger part of 15th PanzerGrenadier and 26th Panzer Divisions, to shore up his defences. Furthermore, he, Vietinghoff and Kesselring agreed to pull back their entire front level with the Hitler Line. At this stage, British XIII Corps and the Canadians were groping their way through the Liri valley, nowhere near level the FEC's progress, while the Poles were on the verge of taking Cassino monastery, and would do so on 18 May. Alphonse Juin with his plan offered up in April had certainly delivered in style, and his progress now influenced both Leese's advance and the German reaction to it. Clark later wrote that: 'The Eighth Army's delay made Juin's task more difficult, because he was moving forward so rapidly that his right flank – adjacent to the British – constantly was exposed to counterattacks.'

Allied progress through the Aurunci Mountains was not a story of unmitigated success, however. On 17 May, American war correspondent Will Lang was with a French column that was caught on a narrow mountain road by a German roadside ambush. 'Screams pierced through clouds of smoke as the Germans poured their fire into the exposed men and machines. The tank exploded with a roar and belched a mass of flame and smoke as the ammunition inside caught fire. Other vehicles were catching fire as their frantic, crazed occupants scrambled out, running up the road toward the shelter of thick-walled old buildings in the village.'

Both the French and Americans operating in the Aurunci were reliant on mules as well as wheels. The French had centralised their beasts into a *Groupe Muletier*, which operated ten mule companies, each of 300 animals, allocated as necessary. US II Corps had mule companies attached to each division, served by Italian muleteers working to American officers. The Germans, too, relied not only on mules, but 71st and 94th Divisions routinely used horses for much of their mobility needs, including towing guns, ammunition, field kitchens; keeping them supplied with fodder and water in the summer heat proved a challenge for both sides.

By 18 May, a week into Diadem, both armies, US Fifth and British Eighth, had smashed their way through the Gustav Line and were approaching the Hitler Line. While the defences were formidable across the Liri valley, they were less developed on Fifth Army's front, petering out almost completely south of Pico. Whereas the Canadian Corps had a stiff fight to break through with Operation Chesterfield on 23 May, the Hitler presented no real obstacle to the FEC or the 88th Cloverleafs when they attacked.

However, the town of Itri, on Route 7, was expected to be a different matter, considered (like Santa Maria Infante) a major bastion of the Hitler Line. Yet when 349th and 351st Infantry Regiments entered the town on the morning of 19 May, they found that XIV Panzer Corps had withdrawn yet again, this time as far back as Terracina, in another effort the create a continuous front. With the pace of advance quickening, General Keyes at II Corps urged the Cloverleafs on at top speed, and by mid-afternoon they had entered Fondi, a further ten miles along Route 7. Along the coast the 85th Custermen had taken the port of Gaeta the same day.

Juin's Frenchmen, meanwhile, reached Pico on the Hitler Line by 21 May, though the *Tabor* of Berbers which had seized the high ground overlooking Pico were rapidly counterattacked and pushed back by a company of Panther tanks and PanzerGrenadiers from 26th Panzer Division, proving the Germans still had plenty of fight left in them. The battle for Pico raged until 23 May, which left the 3rd Algerian Division in control of the town. Labouring through the hills, a medical colleague of Klaus Huebner's, another doctor, asked him to check his heart which felt abnormal. 'His heart is fibrillating and he is on the verge of heart failure. I write out his emergency medical tag with great remorse. He has been a fine and brave companion and excellent medical officer, but a man over thirty-five is already too old for rugged mountain warfare.'

Charging up from Cassino on the other main Roman highway, Route 6, were the 6th South African Armoured Division, whose war up until now had been one of sitting in traffic jams in the Liri valley. However, they started to see their first Germans, whom artilleryman Stephen Bourhill of 1/6th Field Regiment contemptuously described as 'grey rodents scurrying away over the hills'. They later noted that 'the retreating Germans had left inferior *Volkdeutsch* troops as a rearguard', many of whom deserted without putting up a fight.

The collapse of Senger's right wing on the coast was by now obvious to Fifth Army's headquarters, as II Corps was making the most rapid progress of all, using good roads, but all the while enabled by the activities of Juin's FEC on the Americans' right. This prompted Clark to urge Keyes on to link up with the forces at Anzio, due in any case to launch their own breakout on 23 May. After an unsuccessful attempt to land infantry at the coastal town of Terracina, by amphibious DUKW, outflanking any landward defences (rough sea forced the amphibious trucks ashore, short of their objective), the 85th Custermen sent a mobile task force down Route 7, which reached the coastal resort on 22 May, where they came up against fierce opposition from the newly arrived 29th PanzerGrenadiers. After two days, the PanzerGrenadiers departed, in danger of being outflanked by another part of the 85th Division.

Far more significant was the move, early on 25 May, of the US 91st Reconnaissance Squadron with a detachment of the 48th Combat Engineer Battalion along the coast to the hamlet of Borgo Grappa. Just after 7.30 in the morning, this motorised column met up with another, comprising the 1/Reconnaissance Regiment of 1st British Division and 1st Battalion of the US 36th Combat Engineer Regiment. The latter task force had emerged from the Anzio perimeter. The link-up between the Cassino and Anzio fronts had at last happened, Alexander's and Clark's nightmare was over, 124 days after the first landings on 22 January.

Unable to resist the lure of a good photo opportunity, Mark Clark (with photographers in tow) left straight away by jeep for Borgo Grappa, and insisted the link-up be restaged, this time for the camera, with his own, very personal appearance. Among others, Captain Alan Whicker of the British Army Film and Photographic Unit was on hand to record the moment. It was at this stage that the Canadians were battling their way across the Melfa River and a traffic jam of epic proportions was building in the Liri valley.

Lucian Truscott, commanding US VI Corps at Anzio, had previously been ordered by Alexander to strike out, when able, from his perimeter towards Valmonte, some thirty miles due north, astride Route 6, thus trapping any of Vietinghoff's Tenth Army withdrawing from the Hitler Line and Melfa River positions, as well as those pulling back from the French across the Aurunci hills. Called Operation Buffalo, this was the genius of Harding's plan: to use the Anzio garrison as the 'gunline' to shoot the 'pheasants' of Vietinghoff retreating forces. In full understanding and compliance of his mission, from the date of his breakout, 23 May, Truscott sent his 3rd US Infantry and 1st US Armoured Divisions in that direction, but both initially came up against massive opposition from two German divisions at Cisterna (roughly halfway to Valmonte), and lost 1,600 men and 100 tanks. Keselring, Vietinghoff and Senger were fully aware of what Truscott was trying to do, and were equally determined to prevent it. The battle raged through 24 May, before Cisterna fell early on the 25th.

Yet, while Clark was busy being photographed at Borgo Grappa, and the battle for Cisterna was ebbing, the American general had already ordered Truscott to reorient his attack away from Valmonte and towards Rome. Major generals John W. O'Daniel of 3rd Infantry and Ernest N. Harmon were 'furious', while Truscott himself was 'dumbfounded', and tried to contact Clark without success throughout the day to query the change. Kesselring couldn't believe his luck when he realised what was happening. In the end, O'Daniel and Harmon continued their advance towards Valmonte, but their formations were stripped of men and equipment for the thrust to Rome. Truscott was highly critical of Clark's decision, recording: 'This was no time to drive to the north-west where the enemy was still strong; we should pour our maximum power into the Valmont Gap to ensure the destruction of the retreating German Army . . . such was the order that turned the main effort of the beachhead forces from the Valmont Gap and prevented destruction of the German Tenth Army. There has never been any doubt in my mind that had General Clark held loyally to General Alexander's instructions, had he not changed the direction of my attack to the north-west on 26 May, the strategic objectives of Anzio would have been accomplished in full. To be first in Rome was a poor compensation for this lost opportunity.'

Initially assisted by Fred Walker's 36th Texans who arrived on the scene shortly afterwards, until diverted to Rome, the result was that a denuded and exhausted US 3rd Division was left to battle it out with elements of four aggressive German divisions determined to prevent the entrapment of Tenth Army's formations. The two forces locked horns until 30 May, by which time seven of Vietinghoff"s divisions had escaped up Route 6 to Rome, causing Kesselring to declare the capital an 'open city'. Truscott's remaining US divisions (34th, 36th, 45th and 1st Armoured) were forced to backtrack and head for the capital up Route 7, while his two British divisions (1st and 5th) were not to participate, but left to hold Anzio's left flank. For four days, Truscott's VI Corps and Keyes's II Corps tried to break through the last German defences on Route 7, before managing to do so on 4 June.

Reactions to Clark's change of plan (a change he was not authorised to make without the consent of Alexander) ranged from a view of 'gross insubordination', to 'a complex balance of personal and professional motives'. One distinguished historian labelled it 'as militarily stupid as it was insubordinate . . . one of the most misguided blunders made by any Allied commander during World War II'. In Clark's defence, although the opportunity to destroy Tenth Army undoubtedly existed, there was every danger that Truscott's blocking force might itself become trapped between Fourteenth Army around Anzio and Tenth Army moving back. A glimpse of the potential ferocity of any German defence was seen in the casualties suffered by 3rd US Infantry and 1st US Armoured Divisions over 23–25 May. These would surely have been greatly magnified, with no guarantee of success, if Clark had pursued the original strategy of seizing Valmonte, given the number of intact German units retiring in good order under Senger's watchful eye. Alexander never publicly criticised Clark's actions, whatever he may have felt privately. Perhaps Clark was too ambitious, or Alexander too gentlemanly; the whole episode neatly illustrates the difficulties inherent in coalition warfare.

Clark's friendship with Juin never suffered, as the former observed: 'For his performance, which was to be a key to the success of the entire drive on Rome, I shall always be a grateful admirer of General Juin and his magnificent FEC.' The French and British eventually bypassed the

Eternal City, although Clark later invited selected French units back to parade through on 18 June. When the FEC eventually left Fifth Army for Operation Dragoon, he acknowledged their professionalism in a formal farewell letter to Juin. 'During these long months, I have had the real privilege of seeing for myself the evidence of the outstanding calibre of the French soldiers, heirs of the noblest traditions of the French Army. Not satisfied with this, you and all your people have added a new epic chapter to the history of France; you have gladdened the hearts of your compatriots, giving them comfort and hope as they languish under the heavy and humiliating yoke of a hated invader. The energy and utter disregard for danger consistently shown by all, along with the outstanding professional skills of the French army officer, have aroused admiration in your Allies and fear in the enemy.'

Despite the inevitable explosion of joy at liberation, Rome had been a tense city since members of the Patriotic Action Group resistance movement had exploded a bomb in the Via Rasella on 23 March. The explosion killed forty-two SS policemen; in reprisals ordered personally by Hitler, 335 Italian civilians were executed at the Ardeatine caves outside the city. The end result of Clark's defiance of Alexander's wishes saw the former visiting a liberated Rome in a convoy of jeeps on 5 June, accompanied by Captain Alan Whicker, while Kesselring's forces were scampering northwards, free to fight another day. Whicker's view? 'If General Mark Clark had been in the German army, Adolf Hitler would have had him shot!'

Klaus Huebner, now attached to 3rd US Division, followed in Clark's wake and found the welcome 'tremendous. The streets are jammed with civilians cheering our convoy. Our vehicles barely have room to pass, and we ride at a snail's pace. Civilians mill around our vehicles throwing flowers and shaking our hands. For the first time in six months we see splendid buildings, well-paved streets, clean-looking children, and beautiful girls wearing lipstick, silk stockings, and for a change, also shoes. Our trip through Rome is fantastic and feels like a dream.'

On 5 June, a flying column from the South African Division, comprising tanks of the Natal Mounted Rifles and a company of the Witwatersrand Rifles, was ordered up Highway 6 into Rome. South

African Trooper John Hodgson described how his truck became 'a mass of beautiful fresh flowers – these were the first fresh flowers I had handled and smelt since leaving the Union. They were really beautiful – we were also given bottles of wine and baskets full of cherries. All the people seemed in very good condition. This is the first place in Italy where I have seen anyone decently dressed or any pretty girls.' Another soldier was met by the same scene as 'millions of people with flags and roses clapped and cheered us for miles through the streets . . . I sat on top of the Quad and was smothered in roses. At first I put them in my tin hat and then took that off and stuck them in my hair. We went in fits and starts through Rome, some places crawling along, when lovely things had the chance to get fags off me for a very quick shy kiss!'

The following morning, Tuesday 6 June 1944, Mark Clark was woken at 6 a.m. to be told of the Normandy landings. For many subordinates, the final piece of the jigsaw puzzle suddenly slid into place in trying to understand why their boss had very suddenly ordered the thrust towards Rome. Unlike them, he was part of the big secret; he *knew* that his friend and mentor Dwight David Eisenhower was about to invade northern France, and realised that whatever his Fifth Army achieved in Italy would take second place to the news from Normandy. Accordingly, when fortune beckoned, Clark chose to take her hand and with it the fleeting opportunity of fame for twenty-four hours in newspapers around the world, as the liberator of Rome. Nothing else in his life would ever match that moment.

Looking back as they passed through the city and on to war, the lipstick-splattered, helmeted soldiers of Fifth and Eighth Armies saw the dome of St Peter's Basilica, seat of the papacy, and the Colosseum, the heart of ancient Rome. These old buildings had witnessed the comings and goings of countless popes and generals through the upheavals of Italian history; some arrived as conquerors, others as liberators. General Mark Clark was merely the latest in a long line of foreign visitors who would be rendered insignificant by the antiquity of the city and its noble monuments. It was the great old amphitheatre that beckoned to Charles Dickens, one night on his grand tour, a hundred years earlier. 'I had seen it by moonlight before (I could never get through a day without going back to it), but its tremendous solitude that night is past all telling.

The ghostly pillars in the Forum; the Triumphal Arches of Old Emperors; these enormous masses of ruins which were once their palaces; the grass-grown mounds that mark the graves of ruined temples; the stones of the Via Sacra, smooth with the tread of feet in ancient Rome; even these were dimmed, in their transcendent melancholy, by the dark ghost of its bloody holidays, erect and grim; haunting the old scene; despoiled by pillaging Popes and fighting Princes.'

15

Roads from Rome

If Allied soldiers had visions of emulating Charles Dickens' exploration of Rome, they were denied the chance to linger. The Germans were haring back to their next defensive line—the Gothic, running from Pisa to Rimini—and Alexander was determined to trip them up before they were able to occupy it; the troops were moved north as quickly as possible. After waging a largely static war for over seven months, Clark's Fifth and Leese's Eighth Armies were now required to race at top speed in pursuit, to rescue what they could from the broken promise of Operation Diadem. Units had to recover their mobility and relearn the art of fighting from the Line of March, whilst retaining an impressive momentum.

But Diadem—an incomplete masterpiece, as it turned out to be—was the last opportunity for an outright victory in Italy. Since the beginning of the year, senior British and American commanders had been engaged in fierce debate about the merits of Operation Anvil, the plan to assault the French Riviera (named to complement Operation Sledgehammer, the initial code name for the Normandy invasion).

Originally timed to coincide with D-Day in Northern France, Anvil's timing slipped to 15 August, partly because the invading American and French forces (together forming the US 6th Army Group, under

Lieutenant General Jacob L. Devers) were themselves to be drawn largely from those forces fighting in Italy.

Failure to deliver Diadem as promised meant postponement of the Allied landings along the French Côte d'Azur. Fundamentally the Americans were never as committed to their Mediterranean strategy as the British, and used the pressure of Anvil to draw down their troops in Italy. As soon as Rome had fallen, they withdrew Truscott's US VI Corps and Juin's FEC (a total of six divisions, with their vital artillery, engineer and logistic support) in preparation for southern France. Churchill, on the other hand, was fully supportive of the Italian campaign (as its main author), and unenthused about southern France. Eventually he had the code name of 'Anvil' changed to 'Dragoon,' in protest at being 'dragooned' into a military operation he did not want.

Thereafter, Italy was inevitably relegated to a secondary front; the twin invasions of Normandy and the French Riviera were designed to be interdependent and eventually met on 10 September, when contact was made between Patch's US Seventh Army, advancing fast from the south, and Patton's US Third Army, near Dijon. Before Rome, therefore, Alexander had the strength and opportunity for a deep, mobile envelopment of the kind practiced by the German and Soviet armies on the Eastern Front. Afterwards, the Allies were never as strong again, and Kesselring never presented them with another option.

The failure to complete Diadem was only partly due to Clark's decision to swing his Fifth Army towards Rome, rather than cut off the German retreat from Cassino. The true fault lies with the collective Allied generalship, for no senior commander realised the fleeting nature of the golden opportunity presented to them in Italy. Certainly none grasped it. That Clark was able to disobey his orders, and Alexander let him get away with the insubordination, underlines that neither was really able to shed their habitual caution and command with aplomb at the operational level. Perhaps this was a particularly German skill, but Clark, Leese and Alexander all fought a series of tactical battles, partly motivated by national rivalries.

This rivalry continued, and contributed to the Allies' slow progress thereafter. Alexander's chief of staff, John Harding, recalled that Oliver Leese remained indescribably jealous of Mark Clark's capture of Rome, which echoed the Patton-Montgomery rivalry in the 1943 battle for Sicily. Leese thereafter persuaded Alexander to let his British Eighth Army operate along the Adriatic coast, far away from Clark's US Fifth Army in the west, rather than in central Italy, where the two forces would have to cooperate more fully. 'He wanted to make quite certain that credit for the next Allied success would go to him alone.'

Sadly, what is striking about the Allied attempts to break through the Gothic line when they reached it in late August are the piecemeal attacks launched by Eighth and Fifth Armies. Instead of administering two-handed punches as an army group under the firm grip of Alexander, the Allies spent the autumn of 1944 (until the weather broke) acting as two separate armies, engaged in different operations, with little attempt to coordinate their activities. In September, Leese launched Operation Olive against the German front at Rimini, using three armoured and seven infantry divisions, against Kesselring's three weak infantry divisions, outnumbering the Wehrmacht by six-to-one in tanks. Yet, it took him three weeks to break through, despite dominance in the air and some brave combat by the newly-arrived 3rd Greek Mountain Brigade.

There is no better place to appreciate the strength of the German Gothic Line defensive positions, and the over-optimism of Leese and Alexander, than to visit the hilltop village of Gemmano, from where the coastal plain and Rimini beckon in the distance. Resolutely defended by the 100th Mountain Regiment of the 5th Gebirgsjäger Division, it took four British attacks between 4 to 15 September to clear the area, causing the diminutive settlement to be dubbed the 'Cassino of the Adriatic' by those who fought there. The German regimental commander wrote a fitting epitaph for the stronghold: 'How much blood this unhappy heap of ruins has drunk! Even if the waste of men had not the proportions of Cassino, the fighting here had the same obstinacy. With the same rage we fought for every house, for every ruin. And as Cassino was the tomb of the 1st Fallschirmjäger Division, so Gemmano was the tomb of my Regiment.' His words echo in my ears whenever I visit, and the little mountain pastures there are still full of shrapnel and cartridges.

The Germans proved to remain as vicious and powerful in the autumn of 1944 as they had been a year earlier; they were not yet ready to yield, and any commander who perceived they were close to collapse was out of touch. Elsewhere in the same week, German troops were giving the Allies a bloody nose at Arnhem and would do so again in the Ardennes that winter.

Although the British broke through to the Coriano Ridge, where Lt. Donald Hunt (whom we last met in the Liri Valley with the North Irish Horse) was wounded, the failure of Operation Olive seemed to confirm what the Americans had suspected all along, that Italy could only ever be a sideshow to the main purpose of defeating Germany. One of the main arguments for launching, then maintaining, operations on the Italian mainland, was that it would draw valuable German reinforcements away from both the Eastern Front, and subsequently, Normandy. In fact, by the winter of 1944–45, it was debateable as to who was distracting whom.

At the time of the first battle for Cassino in January 1944, there were eighteen Allied divisions battling fifteen German ones in Italy. For Operation Diadem, the number rose to a total of twenty-five Allied versus eighteen German. Yet by the late autumn of 1944, Kesselring still managed to hold at bay nineteen Allied divisions (the other six had redeployed to southern France) with twenty of his own. The numbers were broadly similar in May 1945, when the Germans surrendered (actually, seventeen Allied to nineteen German divisions). The 'tying down' argument is sadly demolished by the facts. The eventual Allied casualty bill for Italy (killed, wounded, prisoner or missing, from September 1943 to May 1945) at 312,000, though admittedly less than the German total of 435,000, would certainly have deterred the Americans—possibly even Churchill—had they had a glimmer beforehand that the campaign would be so costly. It was a decidedly expensive way to distract the Germans away from northern France, yet impossible not to have conducted some form of military activity on the Italian mainland.

The Allies achieved their greatest successes in Italy when they learned to work together. Whilst interaction with other nationalities, races, and cultures is commonplace today, in the 1940s it was a novelty. When he first arrived at Cassino, the newly-promoted commander of 2nd New Zealand Division, Major-General Howard Kippenberger, wryly summed up the bizarre, multinational world of Italy. 'Running up Highway Six we were nearly put in the ditch by American negro drivers. An Indian military policeman warned us to waste no time at the San Vittore corner, beyond which we overtook an Algerian battalion with French officers. We passed through an English field regiment's area, several hundred American infantry working on the roads, and reached Corps headquarters immediately behind two Brazilian generals. In the first room I was astounded and mystified to hear that the Japanese had taken the castle.'

Apart from Alexander's nine armies, many other national elements fought elsewhere in Italy, or arrived after the Cassino battles to take part in the last year of the campaign. Most notable amongst these was a divisional-sized formation from Brazil (the *Força Expedicionária Brasileira*, or FEB), which arrived in July 1944 and fought under US command; it included an air observation squadron with Piper Cubs, and a fighter squadron operating Republic P-47 Thunderbolts. Though no Australian or Rhodesian ground forces fought in Italy, squadrons of the Royal Australian Air Force (RAAF) and from Rhodesia, flew overhead supporting land operations.

The 3rd Greek Mountain Brigade fought under I Canadian Corps and the Jewish Brigade Group (hand-picked from soldiers of the Palestine Regiment) served under British Command. Throughout, No. 4 (Belgian) Troop of No. 10 (Inter-Allied) Commando fought with the British 2nd Special Service Brigade; No. 6 (Polish) Troop did likewise before transferring to the Polish Corps, whilst No. 3 Troop of the same unit included Jewish refugees from Germany, Austria and Eastern Europe, attached to 40 and 41 Royal Marine Commandos who also operated in the Italian theatre.

The North Irish Horse—a tank regiment of the British Army—served in Italy, and contained many soldiers who actually lived in the Irish Republic, a neutral country in World War Two. Five mule pack companies from The Cyprus Regiment, some of whom fought at Cassino, served alongside them. Also with the Allied forces in the campaign, troops from Botswana (then the Bechuanaland Protectorate), serving in the African Pioneer Corps, supported the Eighth Army by mule handling and portering for Royal Artillery units or road and bridge-building with Royal Engineer companies. At various times, other volunteers from Lesotho, Swaziland, the Seychelles, Mauritius, Sri Lanka, Lebanon and the West Indies also served and died with British Commonwealth Pioneer Corps units in the Italian campaign.

Apart from this subliminal collection of other nationalities, Harold Alexander's triumph is that he presided over nine of the ten armies at Cassino—and won. Albert Kesselring's triumph in commanding over a force that, if mostly German, also included a wide range of sycophants, is that he did not lose. Both sides drew in the hell that was Cassino. In terms of fighting skill, Alexander (once a commander of German troops in the Baltic) would later compliment the Fallschirmjäger on performance, 'No other troops in the world but German paratroops could have stood up to such an ordeal and then gone on fighting with such ferocity.' Kesselring's men managed to hold on until the last minute, when, wraith-like, they melted away.

Alexander kept his coalition together, with its vastly differing aims and challenging subordinate commanders. The Allies had first arrived in Italy determined to tie down as many German divisions as possible; this aim was both vague, and almost impossible to use as a motivator for his troops. It was easier for Kesselring on the other hand; all he had to do was delay the Allies for as long as possible. This he delivered beyond all expectation, and in spades.

When the Allied polyglot armies arrived on the mainland in 1943, they determined to be the octopus, keeping the Germans busy, everywhere. The fourth battle of Cassino proved they needed to be the great white shark; supreme, unstoppable, and deadly; in this, they failed. Kesselring's force had started off shark-like, but four battles at Cassino robbed it of many teeth, and ultimately it would be the larger, most efficient killing machine that prevailed. Yet the campaign left a sense of disappointment. Some Americans felt, as their official history put it, that 'It is difficult to justify the heavy investment of Allied troops and material into the Mediterranean theatre during 1944.'

Monte Cassino soon became shorthand for the midpoint of the Italian campaign, and eventually—as memories faded—of the whole Italian theatre. Why was this? Firstly, the sheer number of Allied and German troops fighting at some time in the four battles. True, many soldiers never even saw the famed abbey or what was left of the town, let alone fought through it, but many drove through it afterwards, pushing up Highway Six to Rome; it was a name on a map, or a roadsign, that many servicemen saw, whilst passing through a smashed country, full of unnamed, broken villages. 'Cassino' neatly summed up the misery of the whole theatre, from its snow-capped freezing peaks of winter to the dust-blown, parched valleys of summer.

Secondly, Cassino was known back on the Home Fronts because of the prolonged nature of the fighting in a single spot, and the controversy caused in the world's media over the bombing of the abbey on 15 February 1944. In wartime letters home, or indeed from the lips of post-war veterans, the phrase 'I was on the Cassino Front' came to convey far more information than its six words. Thirdly, Cassino was a hill with an easily pronounceable name, and thus represented all the other name-less or unintelligible mountains over which the various combatants had fought.

And finally, once the fighting was over, Cassino became the guardian of many of the campaign's war dead: the 1052 Poles in their imposing cemetery up by the abbey, accompanied by General Wladyslaw Anders who joined his warriors at rest in 1970. Over 8,000 Commonwealth dead and missing (British, Canadians, Indians, Gurkhas, Africans and New Zealanders) are commemorated below it on the western edge of the town; 20,000 Germans lie over at Caira, 975 Italians down the road at Monte Lungo and 6,000 Frenchmen and women at nearby Venafro. Only the Americans elected to take their boys away and bury them in a great concentration cemetery at Nettuno; although 7861 plus 3095 missing are commemorated there, federal policy permitted well over half of the US dead to be taken home and interred nearer their kin.

For several groups of veterans, it was equally poignant that they were unable to celebrate their wartime achievements at Cassino. Juin's FEC, comprising few who actually hailed from France—the majority were technically Moroccans, Algerians and Tunisians—were withdrawn from Italy in the summer of 1944 and landed in southern France as follow-on forces for Operation Dragoon, the US-led landings which began on 15 August. Although the 112,000-strong FEC had fought hard in the first battle and were responsible for a major breakthrough during the fourth, there was a sense of relief when they left. A few lusty Berbers amongst their number had committed shocking and bestial crimes against defenceless Italian civilians, to the extent that even the Pope called for their removal. The victims were described as *Marocchinate*, literally 'Moroccaned,' and dark memories linger still.

General Alphonse Juin's North African contingents found they were less welcome when liberating Metropolitan France as part of Jean de Lattre de Tassigny's French First Army. Some native units were sent home and replaced by white battalions of hastily-recruited resistance fighters, others were sidelined; few appeared in victory parades and most were awarded reduced pensions, enduring racial prejudice for their efforts in fighting for France. This no doubt contributed to the bids for independence of both Tunisia and Morocco (granted in 1956), and the drawn out revolution against France by the Algerian independence movements from 1954 to 1962, which also led to statehood. A sad conclusion to the blood spilt for France of these brave colonial troops, not only in Italy, but during the German blitzkrieg into northern France itself in May-June 1940.

The *Regio Esercito* (Italian Royal Army) who fought so bravely at Monte Lungo, Cassino, and later along the Gothic Line, under Generals Dapino and Utili, disappeared in 1946 with the dissolution of the Italian monarchy. Although the June 1946 referendum on the monarchy was won narrowly by the Republicans (54-46), left-leaning, popular, post-war Italian historians declared that Italy's liberation was 'built on the Partisans,' and so disowned the regular military units that had once worn their King's uniform. Victor Emmanuel's co-operation with Mussolini in the Fascist era had irreversibly tainted the monarchy, and through it, the Royal Army. Thus it is that former Resistance fighters, and their modern day political successors, are the guests of honour at commemorative events, rather than veteran soldiers.

Perhaps the saddest story is that of the Poles. If any nation had a raw deal in the Second World War, it was Poland. Invaded by both Germany and Russia in September 1939, with its people subjugated and systematically slaughtered, its capital, Warsaw, razed to the ground after an uprising in 1944, the nightmare of the Poles continued after 1945 with successive Soviet-dominated repressive governments, until the sudden demise in 1989 of Communism and the Warsaw Pact.

Those Poles who were fit enough and could not reach Iran with Anders in 1942 fought eventually under Soviet command. By the end of the war they had become the First and Second Polish Armies totalling 396,000 in 1945, including ten infantry divisions (with another four in training), five artillery divisions, a cavalry brigade, an armoured corps and a Polish air corps of fighters and bombers. Poles made up 13 per cent of the infantry and 25 per cent of the armoured corps in Zhukov's and Koniev's forces that captured Berlin. Yet only these—good Communist troops—were allowed to celebrate their wartime achievements. The Polish troops who fought at Cassino under Allied command were shunned by successive hardline post-war Communist governments.

Earlier in the war, after the French defeat, some 35,000 Polish airmen, soldiers and sailors had arrived in Britain, making up the largest foreign military force in the country. Two Polish submarines and four destroyers had earlier escaped; British ships manned by the Polish Navy, including two cruisers, six destroyers, and three submarines, served with distinction throughout the war. In April 1940, the Polish Independent Carpathian Rifle Brigade was raised in Syria, then deployed to Libya, and fought at Mersa Matruh and Tobruk with the Eighth Army. In July 1940, two fighter squadrons, 302 and 303, were formed with Polish pilots and ground crews, fighting in the Battle of Britain.

Polish troops evacuated to Britain in 1940 formed I Polish Corps, based in Scotland, which eventually sent 1st Polish Armoured Division to Normandy in 1944 whilst the 1st Polish Parachute Brigade was dropped at Arnhem in September the same year. Three important civilians had also escaped in 1939, just before the invasion, and had eventually made their way to Britain; they were mathematicians of the Polish intelligence service, who had started to unpick the secrets of the German Enigma enciphering machine; their work immeasurably assisted the Bletchley Park code breakers and contributed to Allied victory.

The Polish contribution—perhaps as many as 500,000 serving under British command—was thus huge, yet even in post-World War Two Britain, where many thousands of Poles had chosen exile, their cause was not championed by Atlee's left-wing Labour government, still labouring under the massive misapprehension that Stalin was a great man. Amazingly, the gallant Poles were denied British or Polish citizenship, refused military pensions, and despite their wartime achievements or status, generally managed to secure only poorly-paid jobs.

As late as 1972, a central London local authority, under pressure from the Foreign Office, denied permission for a monument to the Polish victims of Katyñ. This unforgiveable and rather spiteful attitude persisted into 1976; when a private memorial was eventually unveiled, all UK government representation, or armed forces presence, was explicitly forbidden by another Labour administration, although the USA sent a deputation. As a fifteen year-old at the time I remember feeling uneasy about the controversy and penned my first ever letter to *The Times* about it. I am not Polish, nor do I have any connection with the Poles, but I still feel shifty and uncomfortable when discussing Poland in the context of World War Two, with an abiding sense that Britain let down a gallant nation.

At Cassino, with most of the artwork safe at the Vatican, and the architectural plans preserved, the decision was taken immediately to rebuild. It is now almost complete. Although the main buildings have all been standing for a generation, there are still bare patches inside the replacement basilica, awaiting more gentle brushwork. One might be forgiven for thinking this is the original abbey; so huge are the blocks of stone, so extensive and lofty the buildings, but then, the stone is unweathered and has yet to blend in with the surviving masonry of its predecessor. It is uncompromisingly beautiful and no visit to the battlefield is complete without ascending the twisting road to the abbey gates.

There are fewer monks these days, but they are unfailingly courteous to German guests, and even German soldiers who come to study the battles of their forebears. Yes, Cassino is one of the few World War Two battle sites where Bundeswehr troops *in uniform* are welcome, for fond memories remain of General Fridolin von Senger und Etterlin, of Hauptmann Maximilian Becker and Oberstleutnant Julius Schlegel, who saved the treasures. Sometimes less well received are the Allied soldiers (or their offspring) who, after all, levelled the place in 1944. Notable exceptions are the fervently Catholic Poles, who arrive on pilgrimages to visit both the abbey and the Polish war cemetery behind. During the Communist era, this was a hugely important focus of commemoration for 'Free' Poles from outside the Communist state.

Another remarkable aspect of the Cassino battles is how many of those who fought there returned to it in literary form, which also served to keep the campaign in the public eye. Amongst the more significant contributions, as soon as the war had ended, Major Fred Majdalany of the Lancashire Fusiliers battled into print with *The Monastery* (1945), which he extended into a useful, oft-reprinted campaign history a decade later. Still raw after the Communist takeover of his homeland, the Polish commander, General Wladyslaw Anders published his moving but politically charged *An Army in Exile* in 1949. Fifteen years later, in 1964, Harold L. Bond, who had served as a young officer in the 36th Texan Division at the Rapido River Crossing and afterwards, published his *Return to Cassino*, which constituted a remarkably honest attempt to make sense of his war and the deaths or break-downs of friends.

The young Gurkha officer and future brigadier, E.D. 'Birdie' Smith, published an equally humbling account of his war at Cassino in 1978 (*Even the Brave Falter*), whilst the same year saw Colonel John Coldwell-Horsfall, (writing as John Horsfall) produce a trio of erudite observations of war in the Mediterranean, including *Fling our Banners to the Wind*, his highly personal account of the Irish Brigade at Cassino.

On the other side of the hill, General Fridolin von Senger und Etterlin felt the time was right to publish his memoirs in Germany in 1960, translated into English three years later as *Neither Fear nor Hope*. His anti-Nazi sentiments coupled with admiration for the sheer professionalism of his own men was echoed by one of his Fallschirmjäger battalion commanders at Cassino, Major Rudolf Böhmler, whose account of the battles appeared in English in 1964. Understandable, but particularly sad, is the fact that few Indian or French North African soldiers ever went into print with their memories of Cassino. The complete ignorance in those countries today that any of their forebears fought so nobly at Cassino is indeed regrettable.

Remarkably, this key milestone of World War Two has never attracted the attention of a major movie maker. That may be about to be remedied; as I write, the distinguished British director John Irvin (who has a host of films to his credit, including a convincing portrayal of another battle up another mountain, *Hamburger Hill*) has declared his intention to produce a definitive account of Monte Cassino in time for its 70th anniversary. He says he will shoot it in Poland, which closely resembles pre-war Italy: an entirely appropriate location for the project, if he succeeds.

One of the treasures whisked off to the supposed safety of Cassino abbey in 1943 were locks of hair once belonging to the romantic poet John Keats, who died in Rome of tuberculosis in 1821. His devoted admirer, the equally talented Percy Bysshe Shelley, penned the following elegy, written by one English resident in Rome for another. Shelley's words for a man of promise who died aged only twenty-five, reverberate as suitable to the whole company of the young fallen at Cassino:

They borrow not
Glory from those who made the world their prey;
And they are gathered to the Kings of thought
Who waged contention with their time's decay,
And of the past are all that cannot pass away.
(*Adonais: An Elegy on the Death of John Keats*, Stanza XLVIII)

Notes

xv *The D-Day Dodgers.* The term was commonly associated with the reactionary and eccentric Conservative backbench MP Lady (Nancy) Astor, who was inclined to speak out rashly on a wide range of topics. In October 1944 she visited Italy as part of an all-party parliamentary delegation to study British soldiers' living conditions. Unimpressed by the servicemen, she described them as drunken and dissolute, observing that as many appeared to spend their time in brothels, the incidence of VD among them must be extremely high; that when home on leave they should wear yellow armbands so that 'British womanhood could identify them for what they were, and be warned'. Subsequently, by her own account, on 12 December 1944 she received an airgraph letter from some soldiers, signed, in the humour of the day, 'D-Day Dodgers'. Since the American-born Astor did not know her correspondents' names, and thinking they had nicknamed their particular unit with the title, she rather unwisely addressed her reply to the 'D-Day Dodgers' in Italy; her letter apparently travelled its way around many Eighth Army Post Offices in Italy, and was much commented on. At any rate, this was her personal explanation, perhaps by way of apology, that appeared in the pages of the *Daily Mirror* on 27 February 1945. At some stage before Astor's visit, the 'D-Day Dodger' label had already been invented by English-speaking servicemen in Italy, reflecting pride (rather like the 'Desert Rats' of Tobruk, or General Bill Slim's Fourteenth 'Forgotten Army' in Burma). The term evolved probably after 6 June 1944, the best-known of all military D-Days. Eventually a Scottish balladeer-turned-intelligence officer, Major Hamish Henderson, put some lyrics to the popular tune of 'Lili Marlene'. Henderson was not the originator of the lyrics, but embellished what he heard already, and several different versions have emerged, all with the same theme. See Dr David E. Martin, 'Nancy Astor and Hamish Henderson's 'The Ballad of the D-Day Dodgers', *History Teaching Review Yearbook, Vol. 22* (2008), pp. 60–8, and Timothy Neat, *Hamish Henderson: A Biography, Vol. 1: The Making of the Poet* (Polygon, 2007).

Preface

4   *Mr Charles Dickens.* Dickens, *Pictures from Italy* (Bradbury and Evans, 1846), p. 173. At the time of Dickens's visit, Italy was not one state, but many. Although under the sovereignty of the Vatican and less than a hundred miles from the wealth of Rome, in those days Monte Cassino was surrounded by a different kingdom – that of the Two Sicilies, ruled by a Bourbon monarch from Naples. Between 1806 and 1808 the Emperor Napoleon had even installed his elder brother Joseph as ruler in Naples. London's great Victorian social commentator was astonished by the almost medieval poverty he encountered throughout Italy, but particularly under Church rule, given the wealth of the cities. 'The soldiers are as dirty and rapacious as the dogs,' Dickens wrote. 'The inns are such hobgoblin places, that they are infinitely more attractive and amusing than the best hotels in Paris. Here is one . . . which is approached by a quagmire almost knee-deep.' Charles Dickens would have witnessed the unification of Italy into a single state in his later years, when Monte Cassino abbey lost its independence on the dissolution of the Italian monasteries in 1866. Three years earlier, the town at the foot of Monte Cassino officially changed its name from San Germano (the name Dickens used in *Pictures from Italy*) to Cassino. However, the abbey's buildings and priceless collections of cultural artefacts were preserved as state assets (with the monks as custodians), ironically by British lobbying. See Angus Wilson, *The World of Charles Dickens* (Secker & Warburg, 1970).

6   *'the demoralising effect'.* Frido von Senger und Etterlin, *Neither Hope Nor Fear* (Macdonald, 1963), p. 228.

6   *'Fog in front of the outposts'.* Walter Nardini, *Cassino: Fino all'ultimo uomo* (*Testimonianze fra cronaca e storia*) [Cassino: To the Last Man. Testimonials from events and history] (Mursia, 1975). A trained journalist, Nardini was the first Italian to systematically interview the participants from both sides, publishing the result of his researches in 1975. As most of his interviewees are now dead, his papers have since proved an invaluable archival source to scholars of the campaign.

7   *'We passed a burned-out American tank'.* Martha Gellhorn, *The Face of War* (Sphere Books, 1967), p. 98.

7   *'this guy sitting, or rather lying'.* Bill McLaren, 'BBC rugby legend Bill McLaren: The Wartime Hell that Haunted Me', *Daily Mail*, 21 January 2010.

8   *The Allies suffered 312,000 killed.* Almost every source cites different casualty rates for the 1943–45 Italian campaign. I have used the reliable Ian Gooderson's figures – Gooderson, *A Hard Way to Make a War* (Conway, 2008), p. 326 – and those of John Ellis – *Cassino: The Hollow Victory* (André Deutsch, 1984), p. 469. Ellis

estimates that the Allies lost 105,000 in the Cassino/Anzio/Rome campaign and the Germans at least 80,000. The 129 days of the Cassino campaign are calculated from the start of the British attacks of 17 January to the link-up with US IV Corps from Anzio on 25 May 1944.

1. Roads to Cassino

10   *Oberkommando der Wehrmacht*. In a chain of command that has been described as 'Alice in Wonderland', the OKW was directly subordinate to Hitler as the supreme military policy-making organ of the Third Reich. In practice it directed army operations only in the West, Africa and Italy. Commanded by Hitler, its senior officers were the Chief of Staff from 1938–45, Generalfeldmarschall Wilhelm Keitel, and head of its Operations Staff (*Wehrmachtsfuehrungsstab*, or WFST), Generaloberst Alfred Jodl. Theoretically subordinate to OKW, the Army High Command (OKH – Oberkommando des Heeres) effectively ran army operations on the Eastern Front. As its head was also Hitler, this created some unnecessary duplication and tension between OKH and OKW. The Third Reich never achieved a unified tri-service military command centre, for OKW also competed with Oberkommando der Luftwaffe (OKL), created in 1944 and headed by Hermann Göring, and Oberkommando der Marine (OKM), commanded by the submariner *Großadmiral* Karl Dönitz from 30 January 1943. Until the creation of OKL on 5 February 1944, Göring, as a cabinet minister, received his orders direct from Hitler, and bypassed OKW completely.

11   *King Victor Emmanuel III.* A descendant of the House of Savoy, a dynasty of Sardinian nobles whose lineage dated back twenty-nine generations to Umberto I, first Count of Savoy who died in 1047; it produced Victor Emmanuel II, crowned as first King of Italy when the states were merged into one kingdom. The third king of all Italy was Victor Emmanuel III, born in 1869, who assumed the throne on his father's assassination in 1900. He led Italy into the Great War on the Allied side in 1915, in a quest for territorial gain at Austria-Hungary's expense, an aspiration unmet. In the political turmoil after the First World War, the King invited Benito Mussolini to become Prime Minister in 1922, to the surprise of most, including the Fascist leader, whose power base was then minute. Acutely aware of the fate of the Russian royal family just five years earlier, in 1917, and two years after them, the Hohenzollerns in Germany and the Habsburgs in Austria-Hungary, Victor Emmanuel later claimed in his memoirs that the appointment of Mussolini was necessary to prevent a Communist takeover, but few modern historians accept this, pointing out that the Italian Army, which remained utterly loyal to him, was strong enough to put down any insurrection from the right, or left. Although critics of Victor Emmanuel view him as a puppet of the Fascists, the essential truth was that in 1920s, the monarch, church, political elite, middle classes and much of the electorate, for different reasons, all felt Mussolini provided a counter to the radical left, bringing political and financial stability in difficult times. Their relationship was symbiotic; the King brought Mussolini legitimacy while the Fascist leader made Victor Emmanuel Emperor of Ethiopia (1936) and King of Albania

(1939). The King remained hugely popular throughout the inter-war and early war period; it was noted that his presence in cinema newsreels evoked spontaneous applause and cheering, in contrast to a more muted response to Mussolini. Yet, His Majesty's silence while Mussolini gradually abused the democratic systems of government, withdrew Italy from the League of Nations in 1937 and especially in 1938 when Mussolini introduced racial purity laws, was damning. The Rome-Berlin friendship and encouragement of Il Duce's military ambitions also prompted many to question his judgement. Though Victor Emmanuel had helped engineer Mussolini's removal, which increased his popularity, he actually fled Rome for Egypt (where he would die in exile) when the Germans occupied the city, which inevitably diminished his status. From July 1943 what Italy needed was a strong leader to replace Mussolini, but seventy-four-year-old Victor Emmanuel, tainted with Fascism, was not that man. His son, the popular forty-year-old Prince of Piedmont, later Umberto II, would have been a good alternative, and had the King handed over the throne to his son at this time, it is possible that the House of Savoy would have survived the 1946 referendum on the monarchy's survival. The Italian monarchy formally came to an end after a close referendum on 12 June 1946, some 914 years after Umberto I was made first Count of Savoy in 1032. Victor Emmanuel died in 1947 and Umberto in 1983.

11   *The armistice, signed on 3 September in Sicily.* On 15 August 1943, a brigadier general named Giuseppi Castellano, acting for the new government, secretly contacted the British ambassador in Lisbon to negotiate an armistice and offer military help to any Allied venture on the Italian mainland. Castellano's already challenging mission was not made any easier by the need to offer a guarantee to the Allies that any landing would be unopposed by Italian forces. He returned to Italy on 27 August, briefed Badoglio and then shuttled between Allied-occupied Sicily and Rome while the two sides tried to agree on a formula for cooperation. Wisely, many Italian generals and politicians in the know demanded immediate military action to prevent an anticipated German backlash. Eventually King Victor Emmanuel and his premier agreed terms – as if they had any option – and the surrender document was signed at Cassibile, near Syracuse, on 3 September with an Allied assurance that its existence would not be revealed until just before the planned invasion. The Allied negotiating hand was strengthened considerably by intelligence derived from the interception, decryption and analysis of high-level Japanese diplomatic codes, broken at Bletchley Park. The intercepted communications between their Rome embassy and Tokyo (called MAGIC), containing confidential assessments of the Axis to Japan's warlords, revealed the true state of Italian military capability and intentions, and confirmed what they already knew from ULTRA analysis.

14   *Fritz-X glider bombs against the fleet offshore, achieving notable successes.* On 11, 13 and 16 September 1943, German Fritz-X radio-controlled bombs struck the cruisers *Savannah* (killing 200 of her crew), *Uganda* and battleship *Warspite*; all three were seriously damaged by what was, in effect, an early version of a precision-guided cruise missile.

15   *Salerno mutiny.* See Saul David, *Mutiny at Salerno: An Injustice Exposed* (Conway Maritime Press, 2005).

15 *For a while it seemed as though Avalanche might fail.* See Colonel Winifried Heinemann, 'Salerno – A Defender's View', *US Army History* (Spring, 2008), pp. 6–18. The Germans defending at Salerno were ultimately hampered by a lack of fuel which stalled the arrival of reinforcements, little airborne reconnaissance or other intelligence assets, and Allied ship-based fire support. Historians today assess Salerno as an operational draw: the Allies succeeded in their invasion, yet the Germans managed to conduct a successful delaying action. Mark Clark's plans for evacuation were drawn up under the codename Operation Sealion.

15 *Eighth Army, led initially by Monty and subsequently by Oliver Leese.* Montgomery handed over Eighth Army to General Sir Oliver Leese on 29 December 1943 and departed to command 21st Army Group, and oversee preparations for the invasion of Normandy.

16 *vital airfields around Foggia.* The Allies built about two dozen temporary airstrips around Foggia in southern Italy. They had been bombed before capture and 300 German aircraft wrecks lay on the ground amidst old bomb craters.

17 *The Organisation Todt . . .* was named after its founder, Fritz Todt, an engineer and senior Nazi, who died in a 1942 plane crash and was succeeded by Albert Speer. By 1943, the OT was part of Speer's Ministry for Armaments and War Production (*Reichsministerium für Rüstung und Kriegsproduktion*), using an estimated 1.4 million slave labourers from defeated nations in its construction and engineering projects. The Slovak Engineers were formerly 2nd Slovak Infantry Division, degraded from combat in the Ukraine and Belarus, who were redesignated as a fortress construction unit and deployed to build the Gustav, Hitler and Dora Lines from December 1943 to May 1944, and attached to 90th PanzerGrenadier Division.

17 *'destroying village water supplies, electricity'.* Miles Hildyard, *It Is Bliss Here: Letters Home 1939–1945* (Bloomsbury, 2005), p. 250; also see obituary for Hildyard, *Daily Telegraph*, 26 August 2005.

17 *Fries was to 'no longer to pull back . . .'* Frank Kurowski, *Battleground Italy* (Fedorowicz, 2003), p. 66.

18 *'fighting for the comrade on our right. . . .'* Oberst Gerhard Muhm (15th PanzerGrenadier Regiment of 29th Panzer Division), 'German Tactics in the Italian Campaign', trans. from 'La Tattica tedesca nella Campagna d'Italia', chapter in Amedeo Montemaggi (ed.), *Linea Gotica avamposto dei Balcani* (Edizioni Civitas, Roma, 1993).

18 *'This was a true test'* Author's interview with Monsignor Hermann Volk, 1st Fallschirmjäger Division, in Crete, May 2007.

19 *Friedrich Franek's 44th Hoch und Deutschmeister Division.* Named after an order of knights established in 1530, this was the senior regiment in the old Imperial Austrian army, and was founded in 1696.

19 *As many as 300,000 Volkdeutsch 'ethnic Germans'.* See Matthew Bennett and Paul Latawski (eds.), *Exile Armies* (Palgrave, 2005).

20 *'The entire kitchen help was Hiwis.* Valdis O. Lumans, *Latvia in World War II* (Fordham University Press, 2006), p. 292. My thanks to a former Italian front German soldier for allowing me access to his memoirs. See: www.feldgrau.net/forum/viewtopic.php?f=43&t=1806&start=0.

20   *Generalfeldmarschall Albert Kesselring.* He was an outsider to the Prussian military elite, being the son of a schoolmaster, and born in 1885 Bayreuth, Bavaria – an area later seen as the cradle of Nazism and a town connected with Hitler's musical muse, Wagner. Before the First World War, he trained as a balloon observer with the German Army Air Service, where he encountered Hermann Göring, a future air ace. Kesselring served with artillery regiments on the Western Front, commanding guns in combat, winning both classes of Iron Cross, and reaching the rank of *Hauptmann* (captain). In 1917 he was posted to the General Staff (in German eyes a sure indicator of ability), serving on the Eastern Front with a Bavarian division; his war service hints at his extensive talents, for he served at regimental duty in combat and an almost equal length of time on the staff, and had proved adept in both environments. By 1932 Kesselring had reached the rank of *Generalmajor*, just before Hitler came to power. In 1933, the Third Reich was confident enough to immediately defy Versailles by creating in secret its own military air wing – a force explicitly forbidden by the 1919 treaty. Establishing a new military service from scratch, with Hermann Göring at its head, demanded expertise be robbed from elsewhere and, against his wishes, Kesselring was discharged from the army in October 1933 and appointed *Oberst* (colonel) and head of the department of administration at the Reich Commissariat for Aviation (*Reichskommissariat für die Luftfahrt*), nominally a civilian agency, but in fact the forerunner of the Reich Air Ministry. Promotion came fast within the new and growing air arm: he regained his rank of *Generalmajor* in 1934 and fortune came his way in June 1936 with the sudden death of the Luftwaffe's Chief of Staff, Walther Wever, in an air crash. Kesselring was selected as his successor and advanced to *Generalleutnant*. He took over the most important office – after Göring's – in the new headquarters of the *Reichsluftfahrtministerium* (Reich Air Ministry) at Leipziger Straße 7, in Berlin. From September 1936, he also oversaw the deployment of the all-volunteer Condor Legion to support General Franco's Nationalists in the Spanish Civil War. Although it included land and maritime assets, the Condor's largest component was Luftwaffe; the German contribution slowly escalated until peaking at 7,000 in 1937, but Kesselring rotated through double that number, and eventually 19,000 Germans served in Spain; he also used the opportunity to test every aircraft type in combat before the legion returned in May 1939. This was a hugely important development, which brought Kesselring early insight into the demands of communications, command and logistic sustainment in modern war – an opportunity few of his colleagues received until much later. Although a tactical-sized unit, the Condor had an effect at the operational level of war, and strategically helped confirm Franco's victory in Spain. The lessons of the Condor mission to Spain continue to reverberate, for although it was deployed in an offensive (rather than a post-conflict stabilisation) role, in size (roughly a modern all-arms brigade), scope and duration, it remains an important model for expeditionary warfare operations undertaken by Western armies today. Kesselring took over Luftflotte 2, which he commanded for the invasion of France in May 1940 and subsequent Battle of Britain. His chief of staff at this stage was another ex-soldier, Wilhelm Speidel, whose older

brother, Hans, would later be chief of staff to Rommel. As a former soldier, supported by the insights he gained from Spain, Kesselring fully understood the value of close air support to the land campaigns in France and Belgium (where parachutists and glider troops were used for the first time), but was less sure commanding bombing missions over England. In November 1941, Kesselring was appointed *Oberbefehlshaber Süd* (Commander-in-Chief South) and was transferred to Italy along with his Luftflotte 2 headquarters staff, to coordinate air support for Rommel's North African campaigns with the Italians. He enjoyed Hitler's confidence, which may have stemmed from the fact that his Führer felt more comfortable around those, who like himself, came from humbler back-grounds, and originated from the wilder, southern German regions, far away from the starch and hierarchy of Berlin, Prussia and Brandenburg (Rommel, too, fitted this category). Kesselring is often portrayed as politically naïve in over-trusting the Italians, and more accurately, over-optimistic – a view that his subordinate, von Senger, heartily endorsed. However, Kesselring was one of the few who made enormous strides to engage with the Italians, initially hostile to his presence, and won many over. Kesselring's exculpatory memoirs were published under two different titles in English: *The Memoirs of Field Marshal Kesselring* and *Kesselring: A Soldier's Record* (William Kimber, 1953). Also see Kenneth Macksey, *Kesselring: The Making of the Luftwaffe* and Shelford Bidwell's chapter 'Kesselring' in Corelli Barnett (ed.), *Hitler's Generals*.

20   *the splendid Villa Falconieri overlooking Frascati.* See: *ACTA Dell' Instituto Storico Repubblica Sociale Italiana*, Sep/Nov 2003, p. 4.

21   *General Siegfried Westphal.* Westphal's most important memoir first appeared in German as *Heer in Fesseln – Aus den Papieren des Stabschefs von Rommel, Kesselring und Rundstedt* ('Army in Chains – from the Papers of the Joint Chiefs of Rommel, Rundstedt and Kesselring') in 1950; it was published in English as *The German Army in the West* (Cassell, 1951). Born in 1902, Westphal was too young for the Great War, enlisting on 10 November 1918, the day before it ended, but rose steadily in the inter-war years. He was successively 1a (the German designation for Chief of Operations Staff) of 58th Infantry Division in Poland, XXVI Corps in France, and Rommel's PanzerGruppe Afrika from September 1941. A divisional commander for a short while in Africa, he was invalided out due to sickness and took up the post of running Kesselring's Joint Staff in February 1942, also heading the German operations department at Italian Army HQ (Commando Supremo). He was one of the last Wehrmacht senior staff officers alive when he took part in the 1974 *World at War* television series, speaking in fluent English, and died in 1982.

21   *Of him, Kesselring wrote: 'I could not have wished for a better chief of staff'.* Kesselring, *Memoirs*, p. 260.

21   *Westphal observed of Kesselring that 'he wore the uniform of the Luftwaffe'.* Westphal, *The German Army in the West*, p. 164.

21   *Kesselring recounted in his memoirs.* See Kesselring, *Memoirs*, p. 176.

22   *This functioned as Army Group C's command centre until May 1944.* See 'Italians open Nazi bunker to tourists', *The Times*, 5 August 2003.

22   *Promoted in January 1944 to General der Panzertuppen, Fridolin von Senger und Etterlin.* Born in 1891, Fridolin (Frido) von Senger und Etterlin was two months older than Rommel, and like his former boss the Desert Fox is remembered decades later, more than other colleagues and seniors, for his well-written memoirs. His book *Krieg in Europa* ('War in Europe') was translated into English in 1963 with the more memorable title, *Neither Fear nor Hope: the Wartime Career of General Frido von Senger und Etterlin, Defender of Cassino*, and he rapidly became the post-war German spokesman for the Italian campaign. The key part of his book on Cassino is chapter 5, pp. 179–258. The title *Neither Fear nor Hope* refers to the author's fear of neither his enemies nor the terrors of war, but under the Third Reich no hope of a successful outcome to his campaigning. Seen perhaps as the acceptable face of the German Army, Senger is easier to picture in civilian attire than many top generals; surviving photographs of him in uniform are at odds with the Prussian image of peaked cap and arrogance – he appears always to have worn the less officious *feldmütze* (woollen side hat), even at the front, as if reluctant to demand authority by dress, rather than by personality. According to his son, Ferdinand, his father considered a soldier's loyalty was only thinkable in terms of Christian morality and Christian ethics. His friends and acquaintances tended to be non-Nazi cavalrymen with similar outlooks to his own: one of his pre-war subordinates was the rakish Ernst-Günther Baade (who commanded the air defence during the successful evacuation from Sicily, and would later command 90th PanzerGrenadier Division in Senger's Corps), while a much younger officer in his own regiment was Claus von Stauffenberg, author of the 20 July bomb plot against Hitler. Senger would later write of the shame felt among his fellow cavalry officers at war crimes committed by the SS in Poland. This did not stop him taking his cavalry brigade to France in 1940, where he was attached to Rommel's 7th Panzer Division. He was head of the German delegation to the Franco-Italian armistice commission until late 1942, when he took 17th Panzer Division to southern Russia, where he was involved in the relief attempts on Stalingrad and preparations for Kursk. Subsequently promoted to command German forces in Sicily prior to the Allied invasion (Operation Husky), Senger was an undoubted success when commanding at division and corps level; he put emphasis on a firm knowledge of his enemies' intentions, as might be expected from an officer groomed to the traditional cavalry role of scouting, and would attribute much of his success in holding the Cassino front to the correct placement and deployment of fresh reserves at every level. Hitler, grudgingly (because of Senger's known anti-Nazi sympathies), acknowledged that the outstandingly successful evacuation of Sicily at the end of the Allied campaign was due to his leadership, and Senger later commanded the German garrisons on Sardinia and Corsica, where it was felt the Allies would next land. In October 1943, aged fifty-two, he was given XIV Panzer Corps on mainland Italy, being promoted to General der Panzertuppen in January 1944; Senger was thus the principal German corps commander on the Cassino front through the four battles, commanding a variety of divisions initially from 'a decrepit old Palazzo at Roccasecca', and later from Castell Massimo. There was always tension in Berlin

over Senger's known antipathy to the regime, and he was promoted no further, but to a certain extent Kesselring shielded his talented subordinate, and even conspired with him to disobey Hitler's orders to execute Italian officers stationed on Corsica who had sided with Badoglio after Italy's surrender in September 1943. When meeting Hitler on 22 June 1943, his startling assertion that 'the personal sway that Hitler was alleged to hold over so many people made absolutely no impression on me. It could hardly be otherwise, since I detested him for all the misfortune he had brought upon my country' rings true. A May 1944 photograph of Senger about to receive Oakleaves to his Knight's Cross from Hitler personally depicts a senior officer looking utterly disinterested and slightly embarrassed by the whole proceedings. Senger helped negotiate the early German surrender in May 1945 and after the war became a schoolmaster. He penned several historical monographs for the US Army as well as his memoirs and advised on the establishment of the Bundeswehr in 1955, screening officer candidates to prevent access to former Nazis. General von Senger died, much respected by his comrades and former opponents, in 1963. See: General Ferdinand von Senger und Etterlin, 'Senger', chapter 16 in Corelli Barnet (ed.), *Hitler's Generals* (Weidenfeld & Nicolson, 1989).

23   *'Wandering along the path across this battlefield'*. See Senger, *War Diary of the Italian Campaign* (Historical Division, Headquarters, United States Army, Europe, 1953), pp. 102–3 and 'The Battles of Cassino', *RUSI Journal, Vol. CIII* (May 1958), p. 212.

23   *he mused in his diary: 'I wonder what will be the verdict of history'*. David Hapgood and David Richardson, *Monte Cassino* (Angus & Roberston, 1984), p. 41.

23   *'Auftrag wiederholen' ['repeat the mission'] assigned to him*. See Oberst Gerhard Muhm, (15th PanzerGrenadier Regiment of 29th Panzer Division), 'German Tactics in the Italian Campaign'.

23   *This proven doctrine, called 'mission-tactics' [Auftrags-taktik]*. Stretching back to the Waterloo era, generations of Prussian officers had been taught to lead by stating missions (or 'intentions'), leaving subordinates to fill in the detail – with room for freedom of action to exploit opportunities and adapt to circumstances. This enlightened approach to leadership was seen by many as underlying the Prussian victories against Denmark, Austria and France in 1864–70, and German successes against overwhelming odds throughout 1914–18. Furthermore, officers were trained to issue and receive clear and concise verbal orders, in preference to long-winded written ones. An extreme example of mission tactics was in May 1940, when Oberst Kurt Zeitzler, then Chief of Staff of PanzerGruppe Kleist, briefed his assembled divisional commanders succinctly: 'Gentlemen, your divisions will cross the German border, the Belgian border and the River Meuse; I don't care how you do it – that's completely up to you.' Days later, mission tactics was so thoroughly understood by Generalleutnant Heinz Guderian when his XIX Panzer Corps reached the River Meuse at Sedan that the written orders to his entire command for an opposed river crossing amounted to just a couple of pages.

24   *'Stone bunkers collapsed and had to be rebuilt, foxholes bailed out*. See Frank Kurowski, *Battleground Italy*, p. 69.

24 *'how wrong it is to ignore battle exhaustion when assessing a situation'*. Senger, *Neither Fear*, p. 78.

25 *A German eyewitness in 15th PanzerGrenadier Regiment remembered at San Peitro*. See Kurowski, *Battleground Italy*, p. 68.

25 *'In regard to the quick and accurate appreciation of a situation'*. Senger, *Neither Fear*, p. 219.

25 *General Alexander succinctly summed up the prevailing Allied view of their opponents in a February 1944 letter to his army commanders*. Richard Holmes, *Battlefields of the Second World War* (BBC Books, 2001), p. 94.

26 *Kesselring-Lemelsen conversation deciphered at Bletchley Park*. See *Bletchley Park Monthly Archives* 'November 1943: Slow Progress in Italy'.

26 *seven fortification lines stretching across the Italian peninsula*. See Neil Short, *German Defences in Italy in World War II* (Osprey, 2006). The Allies knew the Viktor Line as the Volturno Line; confusingly, the Germans also called the Bernhardt Line the Reinhard. Technically, the Bernhardt (or Winter) Line stretched from coast to coast; the Gustav Line was only the switchback position behind it, in the Cassino area. The Hitler-Senger's western end was also protected by another planned mini-defence, the Dora Line, which existed more on paper than in reality.

27 *Army Group C's Chief Engineer, Generalmajor Hans Bessel*. See Bessel, Construction of Strategic Field Fortifications in Italy, September 1943–October 1944 (NARA M1035/D-013, Foreign Military Studies Program of the Historical Division, US Army Europe, 1947).

27 *Many settlements around Monte Cassino were built on outcrops of travertine limestone*. See John A. Ciciarelli, 'The Geology of the Battle of Monte Cassino, 1944', chapter in Peter Doyle and Matthew R. Bennett (eds.), *Fields of Battle: Terrain in Military History* (Kluwer Academic, 2002).

28 *'for one does not expect to find a huge building perched high on the top of a steep mountain'*. Harold L. Bond, *Return to Cassino: A Memoir of the Fight for Rome* (J. M. Dent, 1964), pp. 38–9.

28 *The dreaded S-mine*. Schrapnellmine, spring-mine or splitter-mine in German. Variants of this jumping mine are still used today.

28 *'Artillery and mortar fire was deafening, caused frightening damage'*. Paul Fussell, 'The Real War 1939–1945', *Atlantic Monthly, Vol. 264, No. 2* (August, 1989), pp. 32–48.

2. An Italian Winter

31 *'very heavy rain fell in central Italy for fifty days out of seventy-three'*. See Wesley Frank Craven and James Lea Cate (eds.), *The Army Air Forces in World War II, Vol. VII: Services Around the World* (Office of Air Force History, University of Chicago Press, 1958), p. 259.

31 *war diary of US 2nd Chemical Mortar Battalion*. As some of their positions were inaccessible to vehicles, this unit, too, relied on Italian mule teams with improvised saddles for their heavy 4.2-inch mortars and ammunition. See www.4point2.org/hist-2w.htm.

32 *'If we had only known'.* See www.bbc.co.uk/ww2peopleswar/stories/46/a5695446. shtml.

32 *a truck driver of the 2nd New Zealand Division.* Jim Henderson, *The Official History of the New Zealand 4th and 6th Reserve Mechanical Transport Companies* (Historical Publications Branch, Wellington 1954), p. 306.

33 *Artilleryman Sergeant James Murray and his comrades.* See www.bbc.co.uk/ ww2peopleswar/stories/46/a5695446.shtml.

33 *An ambulance driver with the American Field Service.* See *AFS Letters, 1942–1945, No. XXII* (edited and published by AFS Headquarters, New York, 1945, 'under the sponsorship of the ambulanciers' relatives and friends, who contribute the excerpts from the letters').

34 *A need for the lumbering quadrupeds.* See Joseph Bykofsky and Harold Larson, *The Transportation Corps: Overseas Operations* (Office of the Chief of Military History, Washington DC, 1957), p. 228; Martin Blumenson, *Salerno to Cassino* (Washington DC, 1969), pp. 250–51. From October 1943, the US Quartermaster Remount Service based in Naples began to purchase animals, initially at $80 a head, but wartime shortages and cunning Italians soon drove this price up to $250 each, though over 11,000 were purchased.

35 *local animals were accustomed to a mixture of home-grown hay.* Much later in the campaign, when the US 10th Mountain Division (including the youthful future Senator Bob Dole) arrived in Italy, they brought nearly 6,000 of their own American mules with them, but found sustainment (at 750 animals a month) and supplies of fodder a serious challenge.

35 *from widely differing backgrounds who were not trained 'muleskinners' (muleteers).* Muleskinners are professional mule drivers whose job is to keep their animals moving, the term being American slang for someone who might 'skin', or outsmart a mule. Experienced skinners try to form the sort of bond with a mule that jockeys do with horses, and as the animals are characteristically highly intelligent (more so than horses) yet stubborn, outsmarting them requires human skill, wit, and determination. Dependent on the size of the load, a muleskinner might be in charge of a single animal or a team, the driver usually riding one and using a leather line to steer and control the rest.

36 *Both Galli and his sergeant major, thirty-one-year-old Oberto Pellegrini.* Corrado Galli's Bronze Star citation reads: 'For meritorious services in support of combat operations in Italy. During this period of operations in which his unit supported American troops in combat, Captain Galli, as Commanding Officer of the 5th Pack Mule Company, displayed outstanding ability and efficiency in the performance of his duties. By skilfully coordinating the activities of his organisation, engaged in carrying vital supplies and ammunition to forward positions and in the evacuation of casualties, he was of great assistance to American commanders in the accomplishment of their mission and contributed materially to the success of the final Allied offensive in Northern Italy. His untiring efforts and capable leadership reflected the finest traditions of the Italian Army.' I am most grateful to Alberto Turinetti of Priero for this information, and to the administrators of the excellent Da Volturno a Cassino website www.dalvolturnoacassino.it.

36   *Private Jo Kindlarski, a US 3rd Division rifleman.* Jo Kindlarski's (1917–2006) Bronze Star citation is at www.warfoto.com/3rdsocietyphotos2ww2.htm.

36   '*a simple operation on their vocal chords*'. See *The Fifth Army at the Winter Line, 15 November 1943–15 January 1944* (Historical Division, War Department, for the American Forces in Action series, 1945; new edition, Center of Military History, US Army, Washington DC, 1990), p. 89.

36   *with more than 15,000 animals, would support the campaign.* See 'Remount in Italy', *Quartermaster Review*, March/April 1946 (www.qmfound.com/remount_in_italy_wwii.htm).

36   '*I was at the foot of the mule trail the night they brought Captain Waskow's body down*'. See 'At the Front Lines in Italy', by Ernie Pyle, *Washington Daily News*, 10 January 1944. Reprinted in David Nichols (ed.), *Ernie's War: The Best of Ernie Pyle's World War II Dispatches* (Random House, 1986), pp. 195–97. The account of Waskow's death inspired the 1945 movie, *The Story of GI Joe*, Hollywood's tribute to American infantrymen, depicted through the actual despatches of war correspondent Pyle, with Robert Mitcham playing Captain 'Walker' who dies on an Italian mountainside, watched by Pyle. A great wordsmith, who would die in April 1945 on Okinawa during the Pacific campaign, Pyle's wartime reports are preserved in four books: *Ernie Pyle In England*, *Here Is Your War*, *Brave Men*, and *Last Chapter*.

37   *George Groom, serving in the King's Shropshire Light Infantry.* Family of George Groom via the Shropshire Regimental Museum Trust at Shrewsbury Castle, Shropshire. His interview is also at www.bbc.co.uk/ww2peopleswar/stories/71/a4056671.shtml.

37   *One of its officers later recalled how 'we gritted our teeth'.* See *5° Reparto di Salmerie da combattimento "Montecassino"*, Numero Unico, Modena, 1945.

37   *One American doctor described an attack where the entire mule train was destroyed.* See Claus K. Huebner, *Long Walk Through War: A Combat Doctor's Diary* (Texas A&M University Press, 1987), p. 80. Huebner was a medical officer in the US 88th Division.

37   *Meanwhile a British soldier, Victor Donald Delves.* BBC People's War interview at www.bbc.co.uk/ww2peopleswar/stories/47/a4463147.shtml.

38   *remembering that he 'could hang onto the tail of a mule'.* My thanks to Ponteland United Reformed Church for making available the wartime memories of Mr Kenneth Hall.

38   *Without mules our winter campaign in Italy would have been impossible.* See *The Fifth Army at the Winter Line*, p. 89.

38   *The officers in the 5th Salmerie Company.* See *5° Reparto di Salmerie da combattimento "Montecassino"*.

38   *Ernie Pyle observed that 'the Italian method of saying "giddap"'.* See 'Ernie Pyle Reports', *Daytona Beach Morning Journal*, 6 January 1944.

39   '*volunteers were plentiful*'. See Richard Lamb, *War in Italy 1943–45: A Brutal Story* (John Murray 1993), p. 186. Nevertheless, Lamb also recorded that a visit to an Italian unit by Crown Prince Umberto in May 1945 was barracked by 'undisciplined elements' and there was a 'widespread feeling in certain quarters that the

regular [Italian] army was merely a device to keep the Italian monarchy in power', and after the war, the generally conservative, monarchist army was certainly used to quell (mostly Communist-inspired) unrest – so the Italian mood was by no means crystal clear. However, when the 1947 constitution was written, the new Italian Republic declared itself to be 'built on the resistance' (partly because it was partisans who captured and killed Mussolini), so denying any achievements of the Royal Army after 1943. See also Julie Le Gac's 'From Suspicious Observation to Ambiguous Collaboration: The Allies and Italian Partisans, 1943–1944', *Journal of Strategic Studies, Vol. 31/5* (October, 2008).

40   *Livio Messina was a typical example.* John Follain, *Mussolini's Island: The Battle for Sicily 1943 by the People Who Were There* (Hodder & Stoughton, 2005), pp. 8–10, 241–2, 305–6, 318.

41   *the British formed the 120-strong F Reconnaissance Squadron of the SAS.* See Kym Isolani, LVO, CBE, obituary, *Daily Telegraph*, 30 September 2004.

41   *'Wigforce', a small British/Italian partisan unit.* See Sir Denis Forman, *To Reason Why* (Pen and Sword, 1991). Montgomery had taken personal exception to Wigram's practical battlefield tactics and had already demoted him from lieutenant colonel. 'Wigforce' appears to have been created only because Monty left Italy in December 1943. As the Allies pushed further north, the numbers of partisans grew. The figures of partisan membership are much disputed (450,000 had requested certification as partisans by 1947). However, 60–70,000 partisans were killed and more than 33,000 wounded, in addition to 15,000–20,000 civilians who were executed by German units or militant Fascists, for assisting them. After the war, over 75,000 Italian civilians were certified to have sheltered thousands of Allied POWs and downed airmen on the run, throughout the period from the Italian surrender of September 1943 to the conclusion of hostilities in May 1945.

41   *The most significant formation of the Co-Belligerent Army.* See Charles T. O'Reilly, *Forgotten Battles Italy's War of Liberation, 1943–1945* (Lexington Books, 2001), pp. 144–5. The First Italian Motorised Group included the 67th Infantry Regiment (two battalions), 51st *Bersagliere* Battalion, and 11th Field Artillery Regiment (two battalions).

43   *Hill 253.* All hilltop numbers are the height above sea level in metres, taken from pre-war Italian maps.

44   *the tough and resourceful 15th PanzerGrenadier Regiment had taken over the position.* The 15th PanzerGrenadier Regiment belonged to 29th PanzerGrenadier Division. Confusingly their neighbours were elements of the 15th PanzerGrenadier Division.

44   *not the sort of opponents.* See Alex Bowlby, *Countdown to Cassino: The Battle of the Mignano Gap, 1943* (Leo Cooper, 1995), p. 134. Von Heyking's biography is at www.lestweforgetww2.com/Rittmeister_Ernst_Georg_von_Heyking.html.

45   *The Bersaglieri Battalion fared no better.* See Bowlby, *Countdown*, pp. 146–7.

45   *a host of dignitaries at his command post.* See Blumenson, *Salerno to Cassino*, pp. 276–7. This problem of visitors to headquarters during military operations continues to bedevil commanders today.

45 *the Italian attack had ground to a halt.* See *Fifth Army*, p. 47.

46 *Had Dapino talked to German eyewitnesses.* See Frank Kurowski, *Battleground Italy 1943–1945: The German Armed Forces and the Battle for the 'Boot'* (Fedorowicz, Canada, 2003), pp. 69–71.

47 *Italy's poor military reputation.* The relevant US Army Official History, Blumenson's *Salerno to Cassino*, is full of explicit criticism against the Italians. For example, on p. 275: 'Overshadowed by Monte Maggiore, which was expected to be in American hands before the Italian attack, Monte Lungo appeared lightly defended. Walker's confidence in the outcome of the attack suffered when Dapino visited Walker's command post to discuss the operation. The Italian commander impressed him less than favourably.' Gregory Blaxland wrote of the Italian repulse on 8 December in *Alexander's Generals* (1979), a well-regarded account of the Italian campaign (in which he served): 'This came as no surprise to the British, who had always regarded the Italian Army as something of a joke and were astonished to find its victors strutting around Southern Italy with the air of victors' (p. 27). Eager to please, the Italian First Motorised Group may not have shone in their first combat, but had fared no better or worse than any of their Allies: they had simply been deployed prematurely for their initial battle, and if the fault was anyone's, the Italians certainly were not to blame. The Americans had short memories, for only ten months earlier they themselves had fought their first major engagement against Rommel in Tunisia. Over 18–23 February 1943, at the Kasserine Pass, the then untested and poorly led US II Corps under Major General Lloyd Fredendall had suffered heavy casualties and been pushed back over fifty miles, and Fredendall was sacked. Monte Lungo was not a setback of the same order, but the Americans should have recalled the effect of committing inadequately prepared troops against a more experienced and dangerous foe. To add insult to injury, the Italian commander's surname, Dapino, was even misspelt as Damiano in US II Corps' War Diary.

47 *'A string of mules accompanied by Cypriot attendants'.* Spike Milligan, *Milligan's War* (Penguin, 1989), pp. 210, 215–16.

47 *'Thousands of men have not been dry . . .'* Ernie Pyle, *Brave Men* (Henry Holt, 1944), p. 98.

48 *Some of 36th Division's battalions were also involved.* In his *Salerno to Cassino*, Blumenson remains grudging towards the second Italian attack, stating that 2nd/142nd and 3rd/143rd US infantry battalions had already reached the top of Monte Lungo by dawn on 16 December. By mid-morning, he says, they 'possessed the greater part of Monte Lungo and were mopping up. To reduce the last remaining ridge in the south-eastern portion of the mountain, the 1st Italian Motorised Group jumped off on the morning of 16 December, moved swiftly, and completed the capture of Monte Lungo that afternoon' (pp. 284–5).

48 *translated through time into an American tactical victory.* A booklet published at the end of the war, for distribution to US soldiers and their families, *The Story of 36th Division* recounted that before the attack on San Pietro, 'In a masterly coordinated night attack, the 142nd [US Regiment] grabbed strategic Mount Longo [sic]'. This helps to demonstrate how the Italians came to be written out

of the campaign. Martin Blumenson in *Bloody River* (Houghton Mifflin Co., 1970), p.45, repeats this oversight: 'The 36th Division performed superbly. During the second week, the troops took Monte Lungo and the extremely difficult village of San Pietro Infine.'

49   *and a disproportionate number of officers.* See Bowlby, *Countdown*, pp. 158–76.

50   *lay at the foot of their first battlefield.* Sited under the shadow of Monte Lungo, the *Museo Storico Sacrario di Monte Lungo*, astride the Via Casilina, repays a visit today. Opposite the small museum housing maps, artefacts and photographs, and the static displays of tanks and guns, lie the graves of Umberto Utili and 975 Italian soldiers who fought on Monte Lungo or were brought from other battlefields. The museum/cemetery complex has rightly become a focus for commemorative activities, where Italy's often forgotten contribution to their own liberation is recalled.

3. France Fights On

55   *Nevertheless Juin's position was not as straightforward.* Juin was Chief of Staff of National Defence from 1944, promoted *Maréchal de France* in 1952 and head of NATO's Central Land Command (COMLANDCENT) from 1952 to 1956. He died in 1967, being buried with France's other military heroes at Les Invalides in Paris.

55   *now commanding Vichy, Maréchal Philippe Pétain.* The politics of Vichy and Free France during 1940–44 were incredibly complex, as nothing was ever as simple as collaboration or resistance. Politically, as head of the Vichy regime, Pétain was genuinely under the illusion that he was 'saving' France from communism, having witnessed the havoc caused by radical left-wing agitation in France in the inter-war years, and seen the destruction caused by modern weaponry in neighbouring Spain during its 1936–39 civil war. Having served in one world war, his primary motivation for the 22 June 1940 Franco-German Armistice was to stop the bloodshed and get the millions of refugees who had taken to the roads home. Aged eighty-three, Pétain hoped to repudiate the 1789 Revolution and recreate a right-wing, aristocratic and church-bound state that was sympathetic to, but not controlled by, Nazi Germany. He expected the 1940 Armistice would permit France to reconstruct herself along these lines, though it must soon have become apparent that all Germany wanted was easy domination, while sucking the wealth out of France. The 1940 Armistice allowed France a fleet, an army and air force of strictly limited size in order to protect her colonies from the marauding British. With an eye to the future, Pétain used this loophole to push a disproportionately high percentage of his best officers and NCOs to North Africa, and hid there huge numbers of weapons, which could serve as the basis of a future army as and when France regained her former status: the region was close to his heart, for in 1925 Pétain had been commander-in-chief of French forces there and subdued the Rif tribes in a successful campaign. Dismayed by France's performance in 1940, Hitler in fact had only eyes for the modern French fleet (much of which had been destroyed by the British in 1940), and was happy to permit the French force in North Africa. Thus the capable Juin wound up in Morocco and

by November 1941 had been made commander of French land forces in North Africa, totalling 137,000 men.

56   *La Coloniale, which included soldiers from France's other territories. La Coloniale* included French African territories which comprise the present-day Chad, Djibouti, Mali, Guinea, Côte d'Ivoire, Burkina Faso, Benin and Senegal, as well as French Indochina, Martinique, Madagascar and Pacific territories. Regardless of origin, the French labelled the Africans collectively as *Tirailleurs Sénégalais*.

56   *Africans would suffer 80 per cent of the casualties.* See Paul Gaujac, *Le Corps Expéditionnaire Français en Italie 1943–1944* (Histoire et Collections, 2004), p. 31.

57   *were reluctant to serve under Juin (because of his previous loyalty to Pétain and Vichy).* The reluctance of Brosset's division to be incorporated into Juin's FEC hinted at the murky politics of the Free French. The original commander of anti-German Free French troops was Général Henri Giraud, captured in 1940, who had escaped to Vichy from a POW camp in 1942, then advised Pétain's government on military affairs, but was decidedly anti-German in stance. In frequent contact with the Allies before Operation Torch (and whisked away by submarine to Gibraltar just before the landings), Giraud – as the Anglo-American preferred candidate – subsequently became commander of all French forces in North Africa. Initially de Gaulle wanted to pursue only his political ambitions, and offered Giraud the position of military commander-in-chief; eventually both became co-presidents of the *Comité Français de la Libération Nationale*, the Allies sensing that Giraud was the better-qualified military commander. However, de Gaulle was never content to share the limelight, and having keener political antennae managed to undermine and depose his rival Giraud in November 1943, becoming sole president thereafter. Only then was his position assured as the undisputed leader of the Free French forces. While de Gaulle appreciated those few who had rallied to him in 1940, when the odds were stacked against Britain and his cause, he also recognised the need to deploy a large enough army that would 'buy' France a place at the post-war conference table. This meant relying on former Vichy troops and their commanders (some of whom, in Syria and North Africa, may even have spilled Allied blood), hence tolerating the amiable Juin.

57   *initially still retaining its North African flavour.* Brook White and others have also noted how the First French Army formations that invaded southern France began to include a much higher percentage of white French soldiers, relieving many of Juin's native African troops; this was a deliberate (and cynical) ploy to persuade the world that metropolitan France was capable of liberating itself, as opposed to relying on the services of colonial soldiers.

62   *'It's pure wishful thinking! It's a crazy gamble!'* René Chambe, *La Bataille Du Belvédère* (Editions J'ai Lu, Paris 1965), p. 25.

63   *'a mission which in other circumstances I would have deemed impossible'.* Alphonse Juin, *La Campagne d'Italie* (G.Victor, Paris, 1962), pp. 62–3.

63   *'in a hollow below the climbing road'.* Gellhorn, *The Face of War*, p. 99.

65   *'fire spat from the mouth of every enemy gun'.* I am most grateful to Karl Gruner himself for access to this information, and to the administrators of the

excellent Da Volturno a Cassino website where his recollections appear: www. dalvolturnoacassino.it. Gruner survived Cassino but was captured by Indian troops on 16 June 1944. His CO, Hauptmann Heger, was posthumously promoted to major and lies buried in the German military cemetery at Caira, in grave 28/362.

69 *'And they are fighting to get home to a country cleansed of Germans'*. Gellhorn, *The Face of War*, p. 100.

69 *is still known as the Ravine Gandoët*. Few French veterans visit the Belvedere these days, and this significant action was in danger of being lost to history, overshadowed as it was by the Normandy invasion of 6 June, where compared to Juin's French Expeditionary Corps of 112,000, a mere 177 French commandos landed on D-Day itself and Leclerc's 2nd Armoured Division of 14,500 (including 3,600 Moroccans and Algerians) fought later in the campaign. However, a recent movie brought the Corp's war to wider public attention: the 2006 film *Indigènes* [*Days of Glory*], directed by Rachid Bouchareb, followed the fortunes of four North African men who joined Juin's Corps and found themselves fighting both the Germans and French racial prejudice. It moved French government figures sufficiently to alter policy and raise the war pensions of former colonial veterans to equate to the pensions of white, metropolitan ex-soldiers.

4. A Very British Way of War

72 *'he developed this method into a remarkable technique'*. Harold Macmillan, *Autobiography, Vol. 2: The Blast of War, 1939–1945* (Macmillan 1967), pp. 303–4.

72 *Lieutenant General John Harding*. This was the future Field Marshal Lord Harding of Petherton (1896–1989), Chief of the Imperial General Staff from 1952 to 1955.

73 *'Events were to prove that I had chosen wisely'*. Alexander of Tunis, *The Memoirs of FM Earl Alexander of Tunis, 1940–45* (Cassel 1962), p. 17.

73 *McCreery's abilities in command*. See Harold Macmillan, *War Diaries: Politics and War in the Mediterranean, January 1943–May 1945* (Macmillan, 1984), p. 739; Richard Doherty, *Ireland's Generals in the Second World War* (Dublin: Four Courts Press, 2004), p. 159. Lieutenant General McCreery was subsequently knighted in the field (July 1944) by King George VI, took over Eighth Army from Oliver Leese on 31 December 1944, and oversaw its peacetime transformation into British Troops Austria. He succeeded Monty as C-in-C of BAOR from 1946 to 1948, then served as British Army Representative on the Military Staff Committee at the UN in 1948–49, was promoted to full general in 1949, retiring to Somerset and dying in 1967.

73 *'the terrain defies description'*. See Harold Nicolson, *Diaries and Letters* (Collins, 1967), pp. 349–50: diary entry for 10 February 1944.

73 *'sinking of my heart'*. Christopher Buckley, *The Road to Rome* (Hodder & Stoughton, 1945), p. 97.

74 *'it was not a prepared offensive against the Gustav Line'*. See Fred Majdalany, *Cassino: Portrait of a Battle* (Longmans, Green, 1957), p. 69.

75 *forty-five-year-old Major General Gerald Templer*. Field Marshal Sir (as he became)

Gerald Templer (1898–1979) was the second Italian campaign commander after John Harding to reach CIGS. He was injured by a land mine in the Liri valley later in the campaign, and spent the rest of the war on intelligence duties in 21st Army Group HQ. During 1952–54, he served as British High Commissioner in Malaya where his tactics against Communist guerrillas are still used as a model for counter-insurgency. He succeeded John Harding as CIGS in 1955–58.

75 *so that at least men could have familiarity.* David Williams, *The Black Cats at War. The Story of the 56th (London) Division TA, 1939–1945* (Imperial War Museum, 1995), p. 73.

76 *The 5th Division's history noted.* See George Aris, *The Fifth British Division 1939–1945* (Fifth Division Benevolent Fund, 1959), p. 202.

76 *Staff Sergeant Bill Quirk.* See www.bbc.co.uk/ww2peopleswar/stories/87/a3320687.shtml

77 *George Pringle, serving in 175th Pioneer Company.* George D. Pringle, 'Remembering Cassino', *Wartime News* (May, 2004).

78 *collapsed and died from exhaustion.* In his honour there is 187 (Tancred) Squadron of 23 Pioneer Regiment in the Royal Logistics Corps. WO 169/12819.

78 *Basuto.* From modern-day Lesotho and South Africa. WO 169/13034.

78 *The Pioneers' work was unglamorous.* I am most grateful to Lieutenant Colonel John Starling (retd) for his assistance in discovering the bravery and activities of the Royal Pioneer Corps at Cassino. Cain's MC citation at WO 373/7, p. 1270.

78 *His superior, Senger, considered it the weakest of all his formations.* Senger, *Neither Fear*, p. 192.

78 *'not the slightest sign that a new landing'.* Blumenson, *Bloody River*, p. 67.

80 *Donald Bailey's genius.* His 1943 OBE and 1946 knighthood recognised his war-winning equipment.

80 *'I never felt so conscious of my regiment'.* Alex Bowlby, *The Recollections of Rifleman Bowlby* (Leo Cooper, 1969), p. 114.

80 *Within 5th Division, odds of five to one.* See Aris, *The Fifth British Division*, pp. 177–8.

81 *'Never 'eard of you,' responded the RN matelot.* Ibid., p. 180.

81 *untie their craft from the river bank.* Ibid., pp. 181–2.

82 *battle-comic style of 'Schweinhunde Englander!'* See Ellis, *Cassino.* p. 79.

84 *'The battle must be fought in a spirit of holy hatred'.* Will Fowler, *Blitzkrieg in North Africa and Italy, 1942–1944* (Ian Allen, 2003), p. 54.

84 *'However, such is the confusion of war'.* Major Hardy Parkhurst, diary entry 20 January 1944, cited in Richard J. Aldrich (ed.), *Witness to War* (Doubleday, 2004), p. 649.

84 *'a less than forceful effort'.* Brigadier C. J. C. Molony et al, *History of the Second World War: The Mediterranean and Middle East, Vol. V* (HMSO, 1973), p. 616.

85 *diverted to Anzio to replace vessels lost at sea.* Blumenson, *Bloody River*, p. 68.

85 *'but you can't count on them for anything but words'.* Ibid.

85 *'The cheeky bastard! I suppose he'll be drawing'.* George Rock, *History of the American Field Service, 1920–55* (AFS/Platen Press, 1956), chapter VII, story by F. B. Cliffe.

85   *'would have been of secondary importance'*. Senger, *Neither Fear*, p. 190.

86   *Radio Berlin was able to announce with more truth than usual*. Janusz Piekalkiewicz, *Cassino: Anatomy of the Battle* (Orbis, 1980), p. 62.

86   *'I am done. The artillery fire is driving me crazy'*. Ellis, *Cassino* (André Deutsch, 1984), p. 86.

86   *due to the solid steel wall of defensive artillery*. Aris, *The Fifth British Division*, p. 186.

87   *'Get that wound dressed'*. Milligan, *Milligan's War*, pp. 243–6.

87   *were a testament to poor discipline*. H. Morus Jones, personal account, Department of Documents, Imperial War Museum (IWM).

88   *'as the bands of deserters in the hills were called'*. Lieutenant Colonel J. C. Watts, *Surgeon at War* (George Allen & Unwin, 1953), pp. 62–3.

88   *'No one except a stretcher-bearer or a wounded man'*. Ellis, *Cassino*, p. 73.

88   *'One bottle per man per month perhaps was pretty accurate*. Bowlby, *Recollections*, p. 62.

89   *'at once surrounded by little boys trying to sell us their mothers'*. See Sir David Cole, *Rough Road to Rome* (William Kimber, 1983), p. 178. A Polish soldier, Edward H. Herzbaum, noted in Campobasso, twenty-five miles behind the lines at Cassino: 'On the streets there are many soldiers of all nationalities, probably more than civilians. A lot of women, but I can't say that they are beautiful; they wear a lot of make-up. The shops are almost empty . . . very narrow streets, people sitting in front of their houses, some girls singing or humming, most of the time terribly out of tune and lots of brats from five years and up, who accost the soldiers with insistent whispers. In fact that's the only reason the soldiers come here. The women are quite brash. They use each other's beds; grandma takes the kid for a few minutes or brings water; the younger brother plays the part of the pimp. At least this way all the money remains in the family. I have the impression that all the women here, without exception, are prostitutes; if not professional then opportunistic.' Edward H. Herzbaum, *Lost Between Worlds* (Matador, 2010), pp. 181–2.

89   *'How are they to live?'* See Norman Lewis, *Naples '44* (William Collins, 1978), p. 115. All units landing at Naples were immediately exposed to the (often VD-ridden) Neapolitan population: large signs greeted the new arrivals with the warning: '"Soldier! If she'll do it,/She's got it!/If you get it, you've had it!" Surgeon-General, US Fifth Army'. Cited in Andrew Gibson-Watt's *An Undistinguished Life* (Book Guild, 1990), p. 133.

89   *'paying for our meals with cigarettes or chocolate'*. Katsugo Miho's interview courtesy of the Center for Oral History, University of Hawaii, at www.nisei. hawaii.edu/object/io_1206615329203.html

89   *'I won't advise when this should be tried'*. WO214/62 Alexander file on Morale, Welfare and Discipline: Alexander/Wilson and Alexander note, 25 February 1944; cited in John Peaty, 'The Desertion Crisis in Italy, 1944', *RUSI Journal*, Vol. *147/3* (June 2002), pp. 76–83.

89   *which was broadly in line with the experience of 1916–18*. John Laffin, *Combat Surgeons* (Sutton, 1970), p. 199.

90   *which were also the highest of any Western Allied army.* See Peaty, 'The Desertion Crisis …'. The desertion figures escalated after the capture of Rome, and reflected the grim nature of the Cassino and Anzio campaigns, and the availability of somewhere nicer to hide.

90   *'the arithmetic was not encouraging'.* Cole, *Rough Road*, p. 179.

90   *The war, he reckoned, taught him two lessons.* Denis Healy, 'Foreign Affairs', *Daily Telegraph*, 18 September 2006; Mark Hookham, 'Denis Healey: The best Prime Minister we never had', *Yorkshire Evening Post*, 3 December 2008.

91   *'I was constantly amazed'.* Denis Healey, *Time of My Life* (Penguin, 1990), pp. 48–9.

91   *'they are ill: ill in the same sense'.* Richard Holmes, *Firing Line* (Jonathan Cape, 1985), p. 254.

91   *varying degrees of this medical problem.* Ryan Flavelle, 'Help or Harm: Battle Exhaustion and the RCAMC During the Second World War', *Journal of Military and Strategic Studies, Vol. 4* (Summer 2007).

91   *which only exacerbated his illness.* Milligan, *Milligan's War*, p. 252.

92   *'Men wear out in battle like clothes'.* Cole, *Rough Road*, p. 179.

92   *or unit R&R was needed.* Laffin, *Combat Surgeons*, pp. 184–205.

92   *for both sides to retrieve their casualties.* Ellis, *Cassino*, p. 83.

92   *'all sat down together for a smoke'.* Bowlby, *Recollections*, p. 109.

93   *'and I am sure he killed him'.* Author's interview with Staff Sergeant John McIntyre (Jack) Dempsey, MM, 78th Field Regiment, RA, Chelsea Hospital In-Pensioner, September 2004.

93   *was awarded a posthumous Victoria Cross.* Mitchell lies buried in Minturno War Cemetery alongside 2,048 other Commonwealth casualties.

94   *'Sunlight by day, the night spent on cold stones'.* Ellis, *Cassino*, p. 86.

94   *'as the flies descended in hundreds from the rafters'.* Ibid., p. 80.

5. Blood and Guts

96   *When mobilised in 1940, the National Guard.* The US Army National Guard, as the oldest component of America's armed forces, traced its origins back to pre-revolutionary settler days, the earliest known militia company originating in 1607 at the English settlement of Jamestown. However, the ancestry of the oldest Guard units in continuous existence dated to legislation of 13 December 1636, the date regarded as their official birthday. A first muster was held on Salem Common, Massachusetts, in April 1637, and ever since, the Guard (like their British Yeomanry and Territorial counterparts, who dated back to legislation of 1794) paraded in uniform on a regular basis, trained with weapons, and formed a pool of soldiers that mirrored the small, professional US Army. Some forty per cent of US combat troops in the First World War were National Guardsmen.

97   *47 billion rounds of small-arms ammunition.* Figures from many different statistical sources; a small percentage of the USA's output were Lend-Lease shipments to the United Kingdom, which included 1.2 million Lee Enfield rifles and over 1.5 million other small-arms weapons. US small-arms annual ammunition

production averaged 12 billion rounds *per year* in 1941–45, while in 1944 Germany's was 5.28 billion and the UK's 2.46 billion.

97 *twelve tons of equipment.* Jean-Pierre Benamou, *10 Million Tons for Victory: The Arsenal of Democracy During the Battle of France in 1944* (OREP, 2003).

98 *nearly a decade older than most US division commanders.* The average age of a US division commander was forty-seven. Lieutenant Colonel Gary Wade, *World War II Division Commanders*, Combat Studies Institute (CSI) Report No.7, 1983. See Walker's obituary, *New York Times*, 8 October 1969, and Robert L. Wagner, *The Texas Army: A History of the 36th Division in the Italian Campaign* (Austin, 1972).

98 *under the patronage of Marshall.* The eight boxes of the Fred L. Walker papers reside at the Hoover Institution of Stanford University. Walker wrote: 'My Story on the Rapido River Crossing' (*Army Magazine*, September 1952); 'The 36th was a Great Fighting Division' *(Southwestern Historical Quarterly*, July 1968) and *From Texas to Rome: A General's Journal* (Taylor Publishing, Dallas, 1969).

98 *where Walker was their instructor.* Judith Hicks Stiehm, *The US Army War College: Military Education in a Democracy* (Temple University Press, 2002).

99 *'one of those romantic generals'.* Robert Murphy, *Diplomat Among Warriors* (Doubleday, 1964), p. 135.

99 *'His vanity was remarkable'.* Alan Whicker, *Whicker's War* (HarperCollins, 2005), p. 184.

99 *'prompted some resentment among his colleagues'.* Blumenson, *Bloody River*, p. 19.

100 *'threatening the rear of German 14 Corps'.* 15th Army Group Operational Instruction No. 32, dated 2 January 1944, cited in Blumenson, *Salerno to Cassino*, p. 301.

100 *the operation to capture Rome.* Clark message to Alexander, 2 January 1944, cited in *Fifth Army History*, Part IV, p. 17.

100 *'it is going to be a success'.* Cited in Blumenson, *Salerno to Cassino*, p. 302.

101 *'literally hundreds of Allied artillery observation posts'.* Buckley, *Road to Rome*, p. 284.

102 *'their existing conditions of hardship'.* Blumenson, *Bloody River*, p. 45.

102 *'ever blow at less than gale force'.* Gellhorn, *The Face of War*, pp. 97–8.

102 *'a numbness and indifference to anything'.* Theresa Deane (ed.), *500 Days of Front Line Combat* (Universe, 2003), p. 104.

103 *lay the village of Sant'Angelo.* Although the Rapido flowed into the Gari River a mile or so upstream, and Italian maps and the locals knew this stretch of water as the *Gari*, in 1944 all US Army reports and post-war histories referred to the current as the Rapido.

103 *'The regimental commanders whom I visited'.* Senger, *Neither Fear*, pp. 182–3; Generalfeldmarschall Albert Kesselring, *Rapido River Crossing Debrief* (ETHINT-71/ European Theater Historical Interrogation, Bad Mondorf, Luxemburg, Office of the Chief of Military History, 6 May 1946).

104 *'it should not, in my opinion, be attempted'.* Lucas Diary, 4 January 1944, cited in Blumenson, *Salerno to Cassino*, p. 354.

104 *'MLR [Main Line of Resistance] of the main German positions'.* Blumenson, *Bloody River*, p. 59.

104 *Then, who will take the blame?* Blumenson, *Salerno to Cassino*, p. 356.

104 *'but am also optimistic'*. Ibid., p. 356.

105 *'if we get some breaks we may succeed'*. Blumenson, *Bloody River*, p. 80.

105 *'a bridge is instantly constructed'*. Book III, 'Passages of Rivers', in Publius Flavius Vegetius Renatus, *Epitoma rei militaris* [*On Roman Military Matters; A Fifth Century Training Manual in Organisation, Weapons and Tactics, As Practised by the Roman Legions*], translated by Lieutenant John Clarke in 1767, (Red and Black Publishers, 2008); see also Christopher Allmand, *The De Re Militari of Vegetius: The Reception, Transmission and Legacy of a Roman Text in the Middle Ages* (Cambridge University Press, 2011).

106 *Colonel Aaron A. Wyatt's*. Major General Howard Kippenberger described Wyatt as 'a very likeable youngish man . . . He told me he was an estate agent from San Antonio, Texas . . . He had been in the Army three years altogether' (Howard Kippenberger, *Infantry Brigadier*, Oxford University Press, 1949, p. 349). Wyatt was killed by shellfire on 12 February in his headquarters.

107 *'were wrecked on the west bank of the Rapido'*. Blumenson, *Bloody River*, p. 110.

108 *'a fine National Guard Division being destroyed'*. Ibid., p. 134.

110 *'he was dissipating his forces'*. Senger, *Neither Fear*, p. 196.

110 *'a thick lentil soup'*. Buckley, *Road to Rome*, p. 289.

111 *fifteen yards of barbed wire*. An American battalion commander commented that the defenders 'had enough barbed wire to fence in all the farms in Iowa and Illinois'.

111 *'none was more noble than Cassino'*. Buckley, *Road to Rome*, p. 288.

112 *'That's how much hell we caught.* I am most grateful to the University of Hawaii Center for Oral History and their Hawaii Nisei website for access to Takashi Kitaoka's interview at www.nisei.hawaii.edu/object/io_1173926403062.html.

113 *ammunition, and even heating*. Buckley, *Road to Rome*, p. 290.

114 *amphibious requirements were also devised*. Most notably the M7 Priest, with a 105mm field gun (when carrying a British 25-pounder this was known as a Sexton), M10 Wolverine, mounting a 3-inch gun (or 'Achilles' when equipped with a British 17-pounder), M36 Jackson (with a 90mm gun), M32 and M74 Recovery vehicles, Sherman V Firefly (17-pounder anti-tank gun), Sherman Crab mine-sweeper and Sherman DD swimming tank.

115 *in order to discuss tactics face to face*. John Sandars, *The Sherman Tank in British Service* (Osprey Vanguard, 1982).

116 *usually burned to death, unable to escape*. Steven J. Zaloga, *The Sherman Tank in US and Allied Service* (Osprey Vanguard, 1982).

116 *fatal explosions, rather than fuel*. Ted J. Hartman, *Tank Driver: With the 11th Armored from the Battle of the Bulge to VE Day* (Indiana University Press, 2003).

116 *'I thanked the good Lord I was not a tanker'*. Deane (ed.), *500 Days*, p. 113.

117 *'That's the way you slept'*. See Parker, *Cassino: The Hardest Fought Battle of World War II* (Headline, 2004), p. 143.

117 *'suspended in a holster from his neck'*. Senger, *Neither Fear*, pp. 207–8.

119 *Japanese-Americans' prowess at baseball*. Ellis, *Cassino*, p. 128.

119 *at this stage of the defence*. Senger, *Neither Fear*, p. 196.

119 'the same in the entire company'. Parker, Cassino, pp. 148–9.

120 'that could still throw a grenade or fire a rifle'. Parker, Cassino, p. 151.

120 were Italian Army volunteers. General C. W. Ryder 'Operations Report 1–31 January', p. 2, cited in Ellis, Cassino, pp. 122–3.

120 deputy chief of staff, Lyman Lemnitzer. Lyman Lemnitzer (1899–1998) would reach full general, serving as chairman of the US Joint Chiefs of Staff under John F Kennedy, 1960–62, then as Supreme Allied Commander of NATO (SACEUR), 1963–69.

120 'disheartened, almost mutinous'. Alexander interview, January 1969, cited in Ellis, Cassino, pp. 130–1.

121 'and if it looks promising I shall reinforce'. See Moloney et al, History of the Second World War, Vol. V, pp. 704–5.

121 'which would be very costly'. The Times, 2 February 1944.

121 'is gradually being prised open'. The Times, 4 February 1944.

121 'is drawing to a close'. The Times, 5 February 1944.

122 'during one violent counterattack'. The Times, 8 February 1944.

122 'The Führer expects the bitterest struggle for every day'. Majdalany, Portrait of a Battle, p. 104.

122 'Krauts push us off the hill'. Deane (ed.), 500 Days, pp. 99–100.

123 'that littered the whole area'. Ibid., p. 101.

123 'the attack failed as almost everyone expected'. Kippenberger, Infantry Brigadier, p. 352.

123 'as often times was the case'. Deane (ed.), 500 Days, p. 104.

124 'nasty battle in a nasty, nasty war'. Parker, Monte Cassino, p. 151.

124 'our first hot meal in two weeks'. Deane (ed.), 500 Days, p. 102.

124 'return to the lives and thoughts they had known'. Margaret Bourke-White, They Called It Purple Heart Valley (Simon & Schuster, 1944), pp. 79–80.

124 'carried out on stretchers'. Kippenberger, Infantry Brigadier, p. 353.

6. How to Destroy a Monastery

126 Premindra Singh Bhagat. His VC was won clearing minefields in Abyssinia (modern Ethiopia) in February 1941.

127 would be casualties. See V. Longer, Red Coats to Olive Green: A History of the Indian Army 1600–1974 (Allied Publishers, New Delhi, 1974), pp. 214–26.

127 'Some chicken . . .'. Winston Churchill, speech to the Canadian Parliament, 30 December 1941, War Speeches, Vol. II: The Unrelenting Struggle (Cassell, 1942), p. 363.

127 Westminster Abbey destroyed by bombs. See Philip Mason, A Matter of Honour (Jonathan Cape, 1974), pp. 477–8.

127 would rely on Muslim effort. Brigadier (Dr) Noor-ul-Haq, The Making of Pakistan: the Military Perspective (NIHCR – National Institute of Historical and Cultural Research, Islamabad, 1993), pp. 51, 258.

127 manpower pool on which he would rely. Sir Winston S. Churchill, The Second World War, Vol. IV (Cassell, 1951), pp. 185–7.

127 *turbans rather than steel helmets*. See Amandeep Singh Madra and Parmjit Singh, *Warrior Saints: Three Centuries of the Sikh Military Tradition* (I. B. Tauris, 1999); F. Yeats-Brown, *Martial India: The Story of Two Million Volunteers* (Eyre & Spottiswoode, 1945); and Kushwant Singh, *A History of the Sikhs* (Princeton University Press, 1966).

128 *vitally important in the trials ahead*. See WO 169/18983: 4/11 Sikhs (Jan–Dec 1944); WO 169/19006: 1/9 Gurkha Rifles (Jan–Dec 1944) and WO 169/18978: 3/10 Baluchs (Jan–Dec 1944).

128 *'unlovely heart of psychological warfare'*. Masters, *Bugles and a Tiger* (Michael Joseph, 1956), pp. 95–6.

129 *'Being very lean, thin and puny'*. See www.mgtrust.org/ind2.htm. Nila Kantan remembered of the desert: 'It was the dust in Libya which left the greatest impression on his earlier soldiering, I have never seen so many tanks going in one go . . . If you want to know the size of two armoured divisions – if the head of the column was in Bangalore, the tail would be in Madras! Numberless tanks passing through, thundering. And their dust clouds – we breathed dust, we ate dust, we drank dust . . . the Sikhs, they suffered the most, with no washing, and all the dust and perspiration caked in their beards. I saw British soldiers shaving with tea.'

129 *reunited with horses and mules*. The old Central India Horse (21st King George V's Own Horse) remains today as the 21st Armoured Regiment (Central India Horse), a tank battalion of the Indian Army.

129 *'sometimes unorthodox mind'*. See Shelford Bidwell and Dominic Graham, *Firepower: British Army Weapons and Theories of War 1904–45* (Allen & Unwin, 1985), p. 242. After the war Tuker would write an outstanding commentary of world conflict, *The Pattern of War* (Cassell, 1948), demonstrating his view that no matter the technology, warfare of all eras, from Alexander to Hitler, follows a definite and unchanging pattern. In 1958 Cassell published his analysis of Eighth Army operations, the thoughtful *Approach to Battle, a Commentary: Eighth Army, November 1941 to May 1943*. Tuker remained bitter that his advice for a wide-flanking movement around Cassino was not taken in 1944, writing in *Approach to Battle*: 'An extraordinary obsession in British commanders' minds is that they must challenge the enemy's strength rather than play on his weakness . . . the waste of hammering at the enemy's strongest point is seen at its most extreme form.'

130 *'with a first-class reputation'*. Donald Haddon, *In Peace and War: A Civilian Soldier's Story* (Fraser Books, New Zealand, 2005), p. 98.

130 *'but none of us envied them'*. Bond, *Return to Cassino*, pp. 100–1.

131 *'like wild animals alive to danger'*. Papers of Signalman B. Smith, Royal Corps of Signals, deposited in Department of Documents, IWM, London.

132 *'killed next to me while I was shaving'*. Author's interview with Colonel John Buckeridge, Royal Sussex Regiment, 1st Signals Brigade Cassino Battlefield Tour, 2002.

132 *'the dead, poor fellows. American dead'*. Papers of Signalman B. Smith.

133 *'safely by showing this paper'*. See Sergeant Major (retd) Herbert A. Friedman's

very useful web article on Axis and Allied Propaganda to Indian Troops, at www.psywarrior.com/AxisPropIndia.html (accessed 10 August 2011).

133 '1/2nd Gurkhas who could read neither'. Lieutenant Colonel G. R. Stevens OBE, *Fourth Indian Division* (McLaren & Son, Toronto, 1948), p. 296.

133 'depressed lower classes of England'. Robin Kay, *New Zealand in the Second World War 1939–45, Official History: Italy Vol. II: From Cassino to Trieste* (Historical Publications Branch, Wellington, 1967), p. 16.

133 *Passierschein [safe conduct pass]*. The example *Passierschein* is in author's possession.

134 *but for latrine purposes, not their literary content*. See Randall L. Bytwerk, *Paper War: Nazi Propaganda in One Battle, on a Single Day: Cassino, Italy, May 11, 1944* (Mark Batty Publisher, 2005).

134 'I sent you a bar of chocolate. Did you get it ok?' Letter, Hansi Rettensteiner, 13 February 1944; translated by Brigitte D'Souza BFLO(G) Linguistic Services, Translation No. 8619, archive material for 1st (UK) Signals Brigade Battlefield Tour to Monte Cassino, 2003.

134 *CRA (Commander, Royal Artillery)*. The American Harold L. Bond became an ADC to the Assistant Divisional Commander of 36th Texan Division, Brigadier General Robert I. Stack, after their attack on Cassino and before they deployed to Anzio, which he describes in chapter 14 (p. 146) onwards of *Return to Cassino*.

135 *for the Red Eagles at Cassino*. Majdalany, *Portrait of a Battle*, p. 139. After handing over to Sandy Galloway on 9 March, Brigadier Dimoline (1903–72) was rested in England as the CRA of 47 (London) Division, then posted to Burma as CRA of 17th Indian Division.

135 *Clark took this badly, as another blow to American prestige*. Alexander's ADC, Rupert Clarke, spends as much time discussing the loss of Colonel William O. Darby's 6615th Ranger Force (a brigade of 1st, 2nd and 4th Rangers), as he does on Lucas's shortcomings and the general setbacks at Anzio. See Rupert Clarke's *With Alex at War: From the Irrawaddy to the Po, 1941–45* (Leo Cooper, 2000), pp. 133–4.

136 *to the prickly and hostile Clark*. I am most grateful to James Holland for our many discussions about Monte Cassino, for his assistance and guidance on the fascinating personality of Lieutenant General Sir (as he became) Francis Tuker, KCIE, CB, DSO, OBE (1894–1967), and the details surrounding the bombing of the abbey. See James Holland's article at www.secondworldwarforum.com/2008/08/05/general-francis-tuker-and-the-bombing-of-monte-cassino/.

136 'cut Route 6 and capture Cassino from the west'. Stevens, *Fourth Indian Division*, p. 279.

136 *These 'were military sins, no less'*. Tuker, *Approach to Battle a Commentary: Eighth Army, November 1941 to May 1943* (Cassell, 1958).

137 *and Compline at nine*. Although established in AD 529, the establishment, if not all the buildings, had survived the tests of war and nature. These included the passage of Rome's last great general, Belisarius, in AD 536, on his way to recapture Rome for the Emperor Justinian, the destructions of AD 583 (by the

Lombards, a warrior tribe from Germany then over-running northern Italy) and AD 883–84 (by the Saracens, when the abbot and his monks were slaughtered). An earthquake had demolished much of the site in 1349, while Spanish and French troops, battling for supremacy over southern Italy, had campaigned through the locale in 1503–4, ushering in 150 years of Spanish rule. Relatively recently, the peaceful settlement had again been plundered by Napoleon's troops on their invasion of the Kingdom of Naples in 1799. In England until the sixteenth century, the black monks of St Benedict had played a key role in every aspect of religious, social and economic life – most of England's oldest cathedrals had begun as Benedictine monasteries, including those at Canterbury, Durham, Ely, Gloucester, Norwich, Winchester – and, of course, Westminster Abbey. Across Europe, it was said that every Benedictine monastery was an agricultural college, clearing land on a large scale and associating preaching with farming. They had been the most influential of all the monastic orders; at their height the Benedictines had established 37,000 monasteries and supplied the Church in Rome with twenty-four popes. Through these times of tranquillity alternating with war, this home of the worldwide Benedictine Order had evolved into a self-contained community.

138 '"Kitty-bomber" missiles'. See Stevens, *Fourth Indian Division*, p. 278.

138 *What Tuker meant by a 'blockbuster'*. Most ordinary bombs (termed medium capacity) contained fifty per cent explosive, the balance being the fragmentation bomb casing. Blockbusters had especially thin casings that allowed them to contain three-quarters of their weight in explosive, so the 4,000-pounder contained around 3,000lb (1,360kg) of amatol.

139 *'position after position on which to fall back'*. Stevens, *Fourth Indian Division*, pp. 277–8.

139 *'fully considered many weeks ago'*. Stevens, *Fourth Indian Division*, p. 277; Majdalany, *Portrait of a Battle*, pp. 126–7.

139 *'there was the monastery watching you'*. Author's interview with Colonel John Buckeridge.

139 *'fifty yards from the abbey walls'*. Hapgood and Richardson, *Monte Cassino*, pp. 185–6.

140 *'telescopes at the windows'*. *The Times*, 10 February 1944.

141 *more at risk than the isolated abbey*. The building in Rome at *Piazza di Spagna 26*, associated with both Keats and Shelly, was felt to be at risk in the German occupation, because of its British connections. It reopened after the liberation as the Keats-Shelly Memorial House.

142 *the remains of St Benedict himself*. The best account of the Becker-Schlegel story is in Hapgood and Richardson, *Monte Cassino*, pp. 1–38. It is also covered in depth by Jeffrey Plowman and Perry Row, *The Battles for Monte Cassino Then and Now* (After the Battle, 2011), pp. 30–5.

142 *salt mine in Austria in 1946*. Other privately looted pieces continued to surface, including the Cassino altar piece, returned only in 1952. Saving the works of art at Monte Cassino may have been an atypical act of the Third Reich, which was already notorious for the looting of cultural artefacts or wanton destruction on

an industrial scale across occupied Europe. This was partly a basic attempt to redefine culture by the Nazis (led by Hitler the anti-Semitic, failed artist), but also a reflection of the greed of senior Nazis, like Göring, to possess major works of art. The very size of the Wehrmacht, on the defensive in 1944 and ordered to wage pernicious war by Hitler, meant that it left a trail of senseless destruction in retreat – defying all the established rules of war and Geneva Protocols – which the Allies had first encountered in Sicily, and later in Naples. Eisenhower's official line for the Mediterranean theatre, from Sicily onwards, and subsequently in north-west Europe, was the protection of art treasures 'to the fullest extent consistent with military operations'. However, as a direct result of the disappearance of such quantities of important art, and the destruction of an internationally recognised architectural gem (although the Allies, in this case, were responsible for the damage), after Cassino the Allied joint chiefs established the Monuments, Fine Arts, and Archives (MFA&A) Section of their AMGOT (Allied Military Government of Occupied Territories) in April 1944. This grew to a task force of over 350 distinguished British, American and Canadian art historians, museum curators, artists, architects and other specialists, put into uniform as officers. They were dubbed the 'Monuments Men' and their primary task after the Cassino debacle was the protection of statues, historic buildings, cultural landmarks, libraries and art collections. Privately, an account of their advanced years, AMGOT soon became known as 'Ancient Military Gentlemen On Tour'. A lively tussle developed within the multi-tiered bureaucracy of Allied HQ as to whether this additional organisation was necessary, but the MFA&A survived to track down and restore countless works of art after the war and its successors remain active in Iraq, Afghanistan and Libya today. While both sides were responsible for cultural rescue, in contrast to Monte Cassino the Wehrmacht was just as capable of wanton vandalism. Today, some twenty miles south-east of Rome, nestling in the Alban Hills, the keen classical scholar may happen upon a purpose-built museum which once housed two special naval artefacts. The exhibits were two enormous wooden boats, 230 feet long, thought to have once belonged to the Emperor Caligula, and salvaged from the bottom of nearby Lake Nemi, where their timbers had lain perfectly intact for 1,900 years. It was one of Mussolini's public works projects which had preserved these unique vessels; the larger of the two appears to have been an elaborate floating palace, which contained marble mosaic floors, heating and baths among its amenities. In terms of importance, modern marine archaeologists today compare the two with the preserved wrecks of the *Marie Rose* in England, lost in 1545, or the *Vasa* in Sweden, which sank in 1628. Although the museum was struck by Allied shells, no great damage was caused. However, shortly after a German flak battery departed the vicinity on 31 May 1944, smoke was seen coming from the display and in a short while the two wooden ships were completely burned to ashes, though the concrete shell of the museum was unharmed. Despite later denials, it is generally acknowledged that the retreating Germans set fire to the ships in what seems to have been nothing more than an act of spite. Today, the almost empty museum provides mute testimony to this wartime vandalism, housing only pathetically diminutive models, rather than the awesome original craft. See Anthony Firth, *Managing Archaeology Underwater: A Theoretical, Historical and Comparative Perspective on Society and its Submerged Past* (British Archaeological Reports, Archaeopress, 2002).

142 *'along the abbey walls'. The Times*, 11 February 1944.

143 *'a target for the Allies' guns or bombers'. The Times*, 14 February 1944.

143 *'with the utmost ferocity'.* Piekalkiewicz, *Anatomy of the Battle*, p. 92.

143 *'they've been looking so long they're seeing things'.* Hapgood and Richardson, *Monte Cassino*, p. 169.

143 *'the slopes of the hill below the wall'.* Majdalaney, *Portrait of a Battle*, p. 133.

143 *'an unsatisfactory fighting position'.* Ibid., pp. 132–3.

143 *'They don't like it'.* 'The Bombing of Monte Cassino', *Time Magazine*, 28 February 1944.

143 *until pressurised by Tuker.* Majdalany, Portrait of a Battle, p. 112.

144 *'knocking down the monastery'.* Luther H. Wolff, MD, *Forward Surgeon: The Diary of Luther H Wolff, MD, Mediterranean Theater, World War II, 1943–45* (New York: Vantage Press, 1985), p. 77.

144 *'nothing was left unsaid'.* Buckley, *Road to Rome*, p. 294. This issue is of major contemporary relevance, as coalition commanders in the Balkans, Iraq, Afghanistan and Libya have been presented routinely with cultural targets of mosques and temples, TV stations and historic buildings, used by, or of potential use to, an opponent. These days, with specific provisions in international law governing such actions, the implications of such targeting are always carefully considered by very senior military commanders, assisted by a POLAD (political adviser), LEGAD (legal expert on international law) and a media adviser, but in 1944, there was none of this.

144 *US Twelfth Air Force.* Twining's Fifteenth Air Force was the Mediterranean 'twin' to Major General James Doolittle's Eighth Air Force, based in England, the two forces forming Lieutenant General Carl Spaatz's US Strategic Air Force (USSTAF). This allowed Spaatz to 'borrow' the Fifteenth in Italy for long-range strategic bombing missions, when poor weather in England prevented the Eighth from flying missions. Thus, heavy bombers could take off from Italy, bomb targets, and land in England. The Eighth did likewise, landing in Italy.

145 *'whip it out like a dead tooth'.* Brigadier E. D. 'Birdie' Smith, *The Battles for Monte Cassino* (Ian Allen, 1975), p. 68.

145 *576 tons of munitions throughout the day.* Wesley Frank Craven and James Lea Cate (eds.), *The Army Air Forces in World War II, Vol. III: Europe: Argument to V-E Day, January 1944 to May 1945* (University of Chicago, 1951), p. 332.

145 *Allied soldiers in the vicinity.* In fact only thirty-five bombs were recorded falling anywhere within the vicinity of the abbey.

146 *'sixteen bombs exploded nearby'.* Whicker, *Whicker's War*, p. 138. Whicker may here be conflating the two raids of 15 February (on the abbey) and 15 March (on the town); several writers and many veterans have accidentally merged the two.

146 *'I'd hie me back to dear old Pittsburgh'.* Stevens, *Fourth Indian Division*, p. 283.

146 *'on Monte Cassino, due west of Cassino'.* Blumenson, *Salerno to Cassino*, p. 397.

146 *'nor houses of worship are to be fired on'*. Ibid., p. 398.

147 *the responsibility for a failure of the attack.* Hapgood and Richardson, *Monte Cassino*, pp. 170–1.

148 *'for they were strangely quiet'*. Bond, *Return to Cassino*, pp. 115–16.

148 *'as they set out upon a sortie'*. Buckley, *Road to Rome*, p. 296.

148 *'the raid was not due for at least another day'*. Author's interview with Colonel John Buckeridge.

148 *'first shower of eggs [bombs] came down'*. Stevens, *Fourth Indian Division*, p. 285.

148 *'first flights struck at the monastery'*. Ibid.

148 *'and dust which concealed the entire hilltop'*. Bond, *Return to Cassino*, pp. 115–16.

149 *of which 224 were serviceable.* Wesley Frank Craven and James Lea Cate (eds.), *The Army Air Forces in World War II, Vol. III: Europe: Argument to V-E Day, January 1944 to May 1945* (University of Chicago, 1951), p. 332; Allies and Luftwaffe strength as at 21 January 1944 (Moloney et al, *History of the Second World War, Vol. V*, pp. 653, 876).

149 *oceans of mud which inhibited flying.* Wing Commander Andrew Brookes, RAF, 'Air Power and the Italian Campaign, 1943–1945', *RUSI Journal*, Vol. 141/6 (December 1996), pp. 55–62.

149 *'Indian troops with turbans are retiring'*. Stevens, *Fourth Indian Division*, p. 286.

149 *'walls of the abbey still stood'*. Bond, *Return to Cassino*, pp. 115–16.

149 *'fall well short of the target'*. See Clarke, *With Alex at War*, pp. 137–8.

149 *'asking questions with some asperity'*. Stevens, *Fourth Indian Division*, pp. 285–6.

149 *'thinning gradually upwards'*. Buckley, *Road to Rome*, p. 296.

150 *'and ruined the monastery'*. See www.mgtrust.org/ind2.htm.

150 *'the battlefield remained relatively quiet'*. Bond, *Return to Cassino*, pp. 115–16.

150 *'whether we had gained anything'*. Kippenberger, *Infantry Brigadier*, p. 356.

150 *'the venerable building could not be saved'*. Piekalkiewicz, *Anatomy of the Battle*, pp. 92–3.

151 *'after fourteen centuries of religious life, buried for ever'*. Iris Origo, *War in the Val D'Orcia* (Jonathan Cape, 1947).

151 *up the Liri valley from Cassino.* Senger's former HQ is now a restaurant, but according to photographs of Senger there in 1944, has changed little in appearance.

151 *signed declarations to the same effect.* Plowman and Rowe, *The Battles for Monte Cassino*, pp. 116–17.

151 *as headquarters and observation posts.* Hapgood and Richardson, *Monte Cassino*, pp. 233–44.

152 *Tragically this discovery was made too late.* See Clarke, *With Alex at War*, pp. 137–8; also John Ezard, 'Error led to bombing of Monte Cassino: Monastery destroyed after translation slip by British intelligence officer', *Guardian*, 4 April 2000.

152 *'no Germans at Cassino before it was bombed'*. The Countess of Ranfurly, *To War With Whitaker: The Wartime Diaries of the Countess of Ranfurly 1939–45* (William Heinemann, 1994), p. 216.

152 *'the protection of historic monuments'*. *The Times*, 16 February 1944.

152 *'to his Catholic electorate'*. Hapgood and Richardson, *Monte Cassino*, pp. 224–5.

153 *'Naturally it created worldwide interest'*. Helen D. Millgate (ed.), *Mr Brown's War. A Diary of the Second World War* (Sutton Publishing, 1998), p. 205.

153 'the position remains unchanged'. *The Times*, 19 February 1944.

7. The Empire Strikes Back

154 *'and we had so far always been successful'*. Smith, *The Battles for Cassino*, p. 82.

155 *'showed where the shells struck'*. Stevens, *Fourth Indian Division*, p. 286.

156 *'in his turban with his special chai'*. For F. S. Simmons, see www.hlf.org.uk/news/Pages/ YoungsterswinlotterygrantformostimportantbattleofWWIIresearch.aspx.

156 *badly smashing up four good battalions*. As well as the losses to 1/Royal Sussex, these attacks cost the Rajputanas 196 officers and men, the 1/9th Gurkhas 149 and the 1/2nd Gurkhas 96.

161 *best cadet going into the Indian Army*. Lieutenant Colonel George Nangle, DSO, OBE, obituary, *Daily Telegraph*, 7 October 1994.

161 *'seemed to be nearest to the castle'*. Majdalany, *Portrait of a Battle*, p. 191.

162 *'It led to my taking command of B Company'*. Plowman and Rowe, *The Battles for Monte Cassino*, p. 165.

163 *but were unable to return in daylight*. War Diary 4/6 Rajputana Rifle Regiment (WO 169/18970).

163 *'marking a route up to the castle'*. Parker, *Cassino*, pp. 236–7.

163 *'the walls and ground alike'*. Ibid., p. 237.

165 *'guns and small arms was brought to bear'*. Colonel T. A. Martin, MBE, *The Essex Regiment 1929–1950* (Brentwood: The Essex Regimental Association, 1952), p. 314; Plowman and Rowe, *The Battles for Monte Cassino*, p. 178.

165 *'we talked a bit and then he died'*, *recalled Beckett*. See Parker, *Cassino*, p. 241.

165 *'gauntlets as a trophy of the occasion'*. Stevens, *Fourth Indian Division*, p. 305; another version of Major D. A. Beckett's experiences is contained in his papers at the IWM, London.

166 *'all unburied'*. Philip Brutton, *Ensign in Italy* (Leo Cooper, 1992), p. 35.

166 *nicknamed 'Birdie' on account of his beaky nose*. Brigadier E. D. 'Birdie' Smith, CBE, DSO, obituary, the *Herald* (Scotland), 24 March 1998.

166 *'strength of purpose that saved us'*. See E. D. 'Birdie' Smith, *Even the Brave Falter* (Robert Hale, 1978), pp. 16–17.

167 *'battalion reached their transport'*. Ibid., p. 26.

167 *'Now do them yourself'*. Ibid., p. 18.

167 *'wet patch down my trouser legs'*. Ibid., p. 19.

167 *before the end of the third battle*. Brigadier (as he became) Birdie Smith would often recount this very personal tale, with great humility, to young officers at Sandhurst, and it was from Birdie that I first heard of the terrible struggles at Cassino.

167 *'and four other chaps were hit also'*. Colonel T. A. Martin, MBE, *The Essex Regiment*, p. 318.

168 *muddy, snowy and exhausted halt*. Galloway himself found Third Cassino so

shattering that he saw no further action, he handed command to Richard Hull and eventually returned to the UK to recuperate.

8. Man Versus Nature

169 *'for the capture of Rome'*. See www.28bn.homestead.com/history14.html.

170 *'Victoria Cross in World War One'*. Raleigh Trevelyan, *Rome '44: The Battle for the Eternal City* (Secker & Warburg, 1981), pp. 83–4.

170 *'either as leader or as a tactician'*. Courtesy of Matthew Wright, *Freyberg's War*, blog at www.matthewwright.net/commentaries.htm. The subordinate was Major General Sir Howard Kippenberger.

170 *'newly raised 63rd (Royal Naval) Division'*. Freyberg letter to Churchill, 23 February 1949: CHUR 4/217/26–29.

170 *'though much wounded – British general officers'*. Laurie Barber and John Tonkin-Covell, *Freyberg: Churchill's Salamander* (Hutchinson, 1990), pp. 1–6. His VC citation appeared in the *London Gazette* on 15 December 1916; that for his first DSO had appeared in the *London Gazette* on 3 June 1915 ('In recognition of his services with the Mediterranean Expeditionary Force. For most conspicuous gallantry and devotion to duty during the landing on the Peninsula the night of 24–25 April 1915, when he swam ashore at night, alone, and lit flares on the beach to distract attention from the landing operations which were happening elsewhere; he was several hours in the water, before being picked up.') His first DSO Bar citation read: 'For most conspicuous bravery and devotion to duty in the attacks which led up to the capture of Gheluvelt on 28 September 1918, where the success of the operations was greatly due to his dash and leading power. Wherever the fighting was thickest he was always to be found leading and encouraging his troops,' *London Gazette*, 1 February 1919. His second DSO Bar citation read: 'For marked gallantry and initiative on 11 November 1918 at Lessines. He personally led the cavalry, and though at the time he only had nine men with him, he rushed the town, capturing 100 of the enemy and preventing the blowing up of important road bridges over the Dendre,' *London Gazette*, 8 March 1919. His third and final DSO Bar citation read: 'In recognition of gallant and distinguished services in Italy, as General Officer Commanding the 2nd New Zealand Expeditionary Force,' *London Gazette*, 5 July 1945.

171 *'But we'll have no more Passchendaeles'*. Major General W. G. Stevens, *Freyberg, VC: The Man 1939–45* (Herbert Jenkins, 1965), p. 92.

171 *'in the Second World War, another three'*. See 'General Lord Freyberg VC: A Born Fighter and an Inspiring Leader', obituary, *The Times*, 6 July 1963. The reference is to Winston S. Churchill, *The Second World War, Vol. III* (Cassell, 1952), p. 242. When corresponding with Churchill about the Crete campaign, Freyberg would suggest in a letter of 23 February 1949 that Winston's count of his wounds was exaggerated (letter at CHUR 4/217/26–29).

171 *on the outbreak of war*. After leaving Gallipoli, Freyberg transferred from the Royal Naval Division to the British Army, and served on the Western Front with

the Royal West Surreys. He then commanded 173 Brigade (58th Division) and 88 Brigade (29th Division), 1917–19. After the war Freyberg transferred to Grenadier Guards, then served as CO of 1st Battalion, the Manchester Regiment, 1929–31, was appointed Assistant Quartermaster General (AQMG) of Southern Command, 1931–33, and served as General Staff Officer, Grade 1 (GSO1) in the War Office, 1934; promoted to major general in July 1934.

171 *seaborne invasion of the island.* Churchill sought the advice of his CIGS, Sir John Dill, who recommended Freyberg.

172 *'All good wishes to you and them'.* CHAR 20/77/62 cited in Churchill, *The Second World War, Vol. IV*; and Rudolf Böhmler, *Monte Cassino* (Cassell, 1964), p. 156. Freyberg's love of danger had exposed him to a further wound from a German shell at Mersa Matruh in June 1942, causing Churchill on a visit to the division of 4 February 1943 to describe him as 'the salamander of the British Empire' – after the lizard which could allegedly live in fire and survive. Today 'on either side a Salamander Proper' supports the heraldic arms of the Barons Freyberg. Winston Churchill would also have known that his ancestor John Churchill, Duke of Marlborough, nicknamed one of his foremost commanders, Lieutenant General John Cutts (1661–1707), 'the Salamander' because of his indifference to fire at and after the Siege of Namur in 1695. Freyberg was frequently in the vanguard of the advance in North Africa, to the extent that the engine of his command tank was fitted with a governor to limit its speed, without his knowledge. In this sense he appears to have been remarkably similar to one of his desert opponents – the danger-loving and also highly decorated Rommel. This stretch of road, an easy target for enemy artillery, was within range – and observation – of mortars sited on Cassino hill; the usual custom was to cross it at full speed and hope for the best. 'It was one of the many "mad miles" in the Division's career . . . the General sat alongside his driver Cpl. Norris, with the CRA Steve Weir and ADC Murray Sidey in the back. All was quiet; then just as they slowed down to cross the bridge the General said: "Pull up, Norris," and after a few seconds: "I'm sure I heard a nightingale. Let's wait and listen for it." Three people in the jeep were listening for only one thing, the sound of mortar rounds leaving the barrel. After . . . an agonised pause, Sidey said firmly: "I think it was only a thrush, sir." The General was not convinced, and even got Norris to turn off the engine . . . but in the end after further discussion he agreed to go on, albeit reluctantly.' (Stevens, *Freyberg*, pp. 96–7).

172 *'prison camp instead of still facing us'.* B. H. Liddell Hart (ed.), *The Rommel Papers* (Collins, 1953), p. 240; this book comprises Rommel's letters to his wife, with commentary by General Fritz Bayerlein, who is certainly echoing Rommel's sentiments about Freyberg.

172 *a pursuit in the event of a break-out.* Christopher Pugsley, 'New Zealand: From the Ends of the Earth', in John Bourne, Peter Liddle and Ian Whitehead (eds.), *The Great World War 1914–45, Vol. 2: Who Won? Who Lost?* (Collins, 2001), p. 214.

172 *three brigades of his division.* Throughout the war, 3,600 men served in the

Maori battalion; of these, 649 were killed or died of wounds while another 1,712 were wounded; in total, the Maori Battalion would receive more individual bravery decorations than any other New Zealand unit, including one Victoria Cross and a recommendation for a second (which was upheld only in 2005).

173 '*as they refused to surrender*'. Lieutenant General Sir Edward Puttick, *The Official History of New Zealand in the Second World War 1939–1945: History of the 25 Battalion* (Historical Publications Branch, Wellington 1960), p. 418.

173 '*to the Pacific – going home*'. Henderson, *The Official History of New Zealand*, p. 303.

173 '*biding its terrible time*'. Dickens, *Pictures from Italy*, pp. 158–61.

173 '*fall back again inside the cone*'. Hildyard, *It Is Bliss Here*, p. 254.

173 '*while the tanks withdrew*'. W. A. Glue and D. J. C. Pringle, *The Official History of New Zealand in the Second World War 1939–1945: History of the 20th Battalion and Armoured Regiment* (Historical Publications Branch, Wellington 1957), p. 365.

174 '*the traffic stream of a metropolis*'. N. C. Phillips, *The Official History of New Zealand in the Second World War 1939–1945: Italy Vol. I: The Sangro to Cassino* (Historical Publications Branch, Wellington, 1957), p. 185.

174 '*especially around meal times*'. A. L. Kidson, *The Official History of New Zealand in the Second World War 1939–1945: Petrol Company* (Historical Publications Branch, Wellington 1961), p. 301. Feist was misspelled 'Feisst' in the original work.

174 '*it had to be neutralised*'. Interview with Stuart Hayton; courtesy of Patrick Bronte of Nga Toa (his excellent website, dedicated to the collection of oral histories from New Zealand's war veterans www.kiwiveterans.co.nz/times-produce-events-and-events-produce-the-men).

175 '*No one would talk*'. Selwyn Manning, 'Back to Cassino', *New Zealand Listener*, 5 June 2004 (issue 3343).

175 '*reach out and touch it*'. W. E. Murphy, *The Official History of New Zealand in the Second World War 1939–1945: History of the 2nd New Zealand Divisional Artillery* (Historical Publications Branch, Wellington 1966), p. 553.

175 '*there were many refugees to be seen*'. Ibid., p. 554.

175 *99th Light Anti-Aircraft Regiment, Royal Artillery*. See WO 170/1246, Light Anti-Aircraft Regiments: 99 Regt. (Jan–Aug 1944).

176 '*as the guns opened up on our front*'. Courtesy of the American documentary film-makers Grand Island Films; see www.mindspring.com/~gif212/jwdiary.htm.

176 '*employing sets of microphones, was used*'. Murphy, *History of the 2nd New Zealand Divisional Artillery*, p. 578.

176 '*Stonk*'. Standard (artillery or mortar) concentration; known as a 'hate' in 1914–18.

176 '*identified by its centre point*'. Staff Sergeant Tim Rowe, *Steve Weir: New Zealand's Master Gunner* (New Zealand Military Studies Institute Occasional Paper No. 4, 2004) and unpublished MA Thesis, Massey University, New Zealand, 2003.

176 '*bastion of their Winter Line*'. Ian Stuart, NZPA, 'Cassino 2004: Ex Padre "Bloody

Glad" Abbey was Bombed', *Royal New Zealand Returned Servicemen's Association (RNZRSA) Review*, August 2004.

177 *'I had fired a shot whilst away'*. Jimmy Ellington, 'A Reluctant Hero', *Manawatu Standard* (NZ), 24 April 2009.

177 *'Bugger that thing,' he said*. Manning, 'Back to Cassino'.

178 *'filling with water when it rained'*. 'Remembering Monte Cassino', *Marlborough Express* (New Zealand), 25 March 2009.

178 *'capitalising on their success'*. Plowman and Rowe, *The Battles for Monte Cassino*, p. 130.

179 *'recommend the local commander for the Knight's Cross'*. J. F. Cody, *The Official History of New Zealand in the Second World War 1939–1945: History of the 28th Maori Battalion* (Historical Publications Branch, Wellington 1956), p. 363. In 1994, a plaque was placed on the wall of the railway station to commemorate the Maori's exploits in the area fifty years earlier.

179 *of 300 dead and 1800 captured*. See 1st Fallschirmjäger Division 1944 Order of Battle in Bruce Quarrie, *German Airborne Divisions: Mediterranean Theatre 1942–45* (Osprey, 2005), pp. 39–43.

180 *Freyberg was also under personal strain*. Freyberg's wife was also in Italy, visiting hospitals and raising the morale of the wounded. On the other side of the fence, Anzio also claimed the life of Hauptmann Friedrich Paulus, whose father had surrendered Stalingrad a year earlier. See Barber and Tonkin-Covell, *Churchill's Salamander*, p. 211; Peter Singleton-Gates, *General Lord Freyberg VC: An Unofficial Biography* (Michael Joseph, 1963), pp. 282–3.

180 *the Indian Division about the same*. Majdalaney, *Portrait of a Battle*, p. 178.

180 *'ammunition boxes and shell cases'*. Glue and Pringle, *History of the 20th Battalion and Armoured Regiment*, p. 373.

181 *'the dead soldier's foot'*. Ken Ford, *Battleaxe Division, From Africa to Italy with the 78th Division 1942–45* (Sutton Publishing 1999), p. 144.

181 *'he associated with dead Germans'*. Ellington, 'A Reluctant Hero'.

181 *'Graves were quite out of the question'*. Ford, *Battleaxe Division*, p. 154.

181 *'over a thousand [propaganda] leaflet shells'*. Henderson, *The Official History of New Zealand*, p. 311.

181 *'and thumb ripped up. Frank slightly hurt'*. Kippenberger, *Infantry Brigadier*, p. 360.

181 *'He is irreplaceable'*. Majdalaney, *Portrait of a Battle*, p. 180.

182 *'the inferno seemed endless'*. Böhmler, *Monte Cassino*, p. 210.

182 *'Bostons and Mitchells'*. Buckley, *Road to Rome*, p. 303.

182 *'a mass of drifting smoke'*. Hardy Parkhurst, *Diary of a Soldier* (Pentland Press, 1993), p. 84.

182 *'cloud cover from making their attack'*. Plowman and Rowe, *The Battles for Monte Cassino*, p. 145.

183 *'if he decides to hold to the last man'*. See Molony et al., *History of the Second World War*, p. 779.

183 *'silenced half-way through the morning'*. Phillips, *Italy, Vol. I: The Sangro to Cassino*, p. 268.

183 *'shook the ground under our feet'*. Ibid., p. 267; Gregory Blaxland, *Alexander's Generals* (William Kimber, 1979), p. 59.

183 *'blew me over backwards about ten yards'*. Parker, *Cassino*, p. 225.

183 *'disappear shortly before midday'*. D. W. Sinclair, *History of the 19th Battalion and Armoured Regiment, The Official History of New Zealand in the Second World War 1939–1945* (Historical Publications Branch, Wellington 1954), p. 374.

183 *'as though hurled by some giant hand'*. Böhmler, *Monte Cassino*, p. 210–11.

184 *'we waited for the pitiless hail to end'*. Ibid.

184 *'glowing iron and burnt powder'*. Senger, *Neither Fear*, p. 215.

184 *added to the firepower*. How many guns took part is not clear; Brigadier Weir (acting CRA of the NZ Corps) gives the figure of 890 guns, but does not specify whether this includes anti-tank and anti-aircraft artillery. Another careful estimate is 610 guns, which several New Zealand unit histories quote. Both of these figures may include guns far from the Cassino battlefield, either deep in the mountains to the north or among the Aurunci Mountains to the south-west.

184 *'with fragments flung into the air'*. Murphy, *History of the 2nd New Zealand Divisional Artillery*, pp. 568–9. Redolent with hindsight, the history went on to explain that: 'The violence of the bombardment was frightening to behold even from a safe distance and, as events were soon to prove, it was too much and the damage it did was more hindrance than help to the 6th NZ Brigade infantry fighting their arduous way through the ruins. To the tanks that were supposed to be with them it was altogether too much, and most of them ended up facing impassable mountains of rubble or vast uncrossable chasms. The whole thing was grossly overdone.'

185 *'a festive look to the distant mountains'*. Cole, *Rough Road*, p. 173.

185 *'forty civilians and wounding 250'*. Plowman and Rowe, *The Battles for Monte Cassino*, pp. 145–6.

185 *8 per cent were within 1,000 yards*. See Holmes, *Battlefields of the Second World War*, p. 116.

186 *'when the fourth battle for Cassino began'*. Luftwaffe General Wenninger (1890–1945) was a brilliant administrator on Kesselring's staff, who had won a *Pour le Mérite* as a U-boat captain in 1918. See Frederick M. Sallagar, *Operation Strangle, Italy, Spring 1944: A Case Study of Tactical Air Interdiction* (USAF & RAND Corporation, 1972); Milan N. Vego, *Joint Operational Warfare: Theory and Practice* (Naval War College Press, 2009), *Part V*, p. 105; and the excellent chapter 5 in Eduard Mark, *Aerial Interdiction: Air Power and the Land Battle in Three American Wars* (Center for Air Force History, Washington DC, 1994), pp. 141–78.

187 *'shooting into the sky for thousands of feet'*. Courtesy of the excellent website with eyewitness accounts about the 1944 eruption, www.warwingsart.com/12thAirForce/Vesuvius.html

187 *'the volcano's fluctuating light'*. Milligan, *Milligan's War*, pp. 259–62.

187 *Plexiglass and control wires*. See Daniel Setzer, *Historical Sources for the Events in Joseph Heller's Novel, Catch-22*, at www.home.comcast.net/~dhsetzer/heller/JHeller.pdf.

187 *'sprinkled holy water in the direction of the cinders'*. Norman Lewis, *Naples '44*, p. 104.

188 *'We can but admire this gesture of the Gods'*. Winston S. Churchill, *The Second World War, Vol. V* (Cassell, 1952), p. 444.

9. Kiwis at Cassino

190 *'attributable to the bombing'*. Majdalany, *Portrait of a Battle*, p. 214.

190 *'scabbard of the man in front'*. Ibid., p. 189.

191 *'and hence could not harm them'*. Plowman and Rowe, *The Battles for Monte Cassino*, p. 202. Also, interviews with author.

192 *'every fortress where he elects to make a stand'*. Ibid., p. 144.

192 *'and down into the alleyway'*. Ibid., pp. 405–6.

193 *'any building that looked suspicious'*. Sinclair, *History of the 19th Battalion and Armoured Regiment*, pp. 380–1.

193 *'finally doing a good deal of damage to it'*. Murphy, *History of the 2nd New Zealand Divisional Artillery*, pp. 575–6.

194 *'each one of which has become a sniper's post'*. See *The Times*, 18 March 1944.

194 *'After the war, every time I dropped a dead ewe down the offal pit, the sound reminded me of that night'*. Manning, 'Back to Cassino'.

195 *'more important than Nigel's [his son] life or mine'*. Harold Nicolson (ed. Nigel Nicolson), *Diaries and Letters 1939–45* (Collins, 1967), p. 358.

196 *'had to take over its heavy load by himself'*. Böhmler, *Monte Cassino*, pp. 240–1.

196 *A total of forty-seven tracked armoured vehicles from three different national forces.* They comprised three M-4 Shermans and five turretless M-5 Honey tanks from the 7th Indian Brigade Recce Squadron, seventeen Stuarts from Company 'D' of the US 760th Tank Battalion, three M-7 Sherman Priests from the US 760th Assault Gun Platoon, sixteen Shermans of 'C' Squadron, 20th NZ Armoured Regiment and three bulldozers of 12th Indian Field Company. The NZ Regiment was formerly the 20th Infantry Battalion, commanded by Kippenberger, it had also contained Captain Charles Upham, VC and bar, and Sergeant Jack Hinton VC.

197 *'the Germans bravely firing away at us until the end'*. Glue and Pringle, *History of the 20th Battalion and Armoured Regiment*, pp. 389–90.

197 *'over the air from Buck Renall'*. Ibid., p. 391.

197 *'Germans running across and down a steep hill'*. Plowman and Rowe, *The Battles for Monte Cassino*, p. 190.

198 *'rattling along a narrow mountain path'*. Böhmler, *Monte Cassino*, p. 236.

198 *'drove towards the monastery'*. Ibid.

198 *'their position and surrendered'*. Ibid. Rudolf Böhmler's account goes on to describe the destruction in combat by intrepid Fallschirmjäger of no less than fourteen tanks with Teller mines. However, the usually accurate Böhmler was perhaps getting carried away with his prose; all the American, New Zealander and Indian Army accounts agree that perhaps no more than three tanks were actually destroyed in combat, the others had to be abandoned when bogged down or from shedding tracks and subsequently were blown up by Oberleutnant Raimund

Eckel and his comrades, and far from capture or death, most of the crews were, in fact, rescued. Perhaps it does not matter who destroyed which tank or how; the point is that on 19 March, using the best weapon of all – surprise – the Allies came to within an ace of unhingeing the German defences and taking the abbey.

199 *'immense mounds of rubble caused by our bombing'*. The Times, 20 March 1944.

200 *'the after-effects of their own smoke'*. Murphy, *History of the 2nd New Zealand Divisional Artillery*, p. 577.

200 *'to suffer the severest losses'*. 'In dem Krater Bereichen Cassino' [in the crater fields of Cassino], *Völkischer Beobachter*, 21 March 1944.

202 *'the Pommies are English'*. Plowman and Rowe, *The Battles for Monte Cassino*, pp. 222–3.

202 *'the only sort of battle in which General Freyberg'*. Kippenberger was writing in 1956; courtesy of Matthew Wright's blog *Freyberg's War*, www.matthewwright.net/commentaries.htm.

203 *'humiliatingly out of Crete in May 1941'*. Holmes, *Battlefields of the Second World War*, pp. 115–16.

203 *'and huge bomb craters that would challenge infantry'*. Plowman and Rowe, *The Battles for Monte Cassino*, p. 137.

204 *'why no flanking movements can be made'*. Churchill, *The Second World War*, Vol. V, p. 448.

204 *'I cannot stick any more meetings like it!'* Field Marshal Lord Alanbrooke (ed. Alex Danchev and Daniel Todman), *War Diaries 1939–1945* (Weidenfeld & Nicolson, 2001), p. 533.

204 *'The war weighs very heavy on us all just now'*. Churchill, *The Second World War*, Vol. V, p. 450.

10. Poland the Brave

206 *'deciding which they wanted to fight the most'*. George S. Patton, Jr., The Patton Papers (Houghton Mifflin, 1974), pp. 80–81.

206 *as many as 1.7 million were rounded up and sent to Siberian gulags*. There were three major waves of deportations to various regions of eastern and northern Russia, but no accurate records were kept by Soviet officials who were intent on the extermination, rather than survival of their charges. A useful indication of the attrition was that of 10,000 Poles known to have been deported to the Kolymskaya (far north-east Russia) goldfields in 1940–41, only 583 returned alive. Polish authorities today estimate that at least one-third to a half of all Polish deportees and prisoners in Russian hands had died by the time of the German invasion of 22 June 1941. Anders wrote in his memoirs: 'I tried to assess the real figure of Polish citizens deported in 1939–41, but it was extremely difficult. After many months of research and enquiries among our people who were pouring from thousands of prisons and concentrations camps spread all over Russia, we were able to put the numbers at 1,500,000–1,600,000 people. Statistics obtained afterward from Poland confirmed these figures. But unfortunately, it was clear that most of these poor people were no longer alive. God only knows

how many of them were murdered, and how many died under the terrible conditions of the prisons and forced labour camps.'

206 *mass graves uncovered in the Katyñ Forest, near Smolensk.* In early 1943, the Nazis announced to the world the discovery of mass graves of 4,321 Poles executed in the Katyñ forest, near Smolensk. The Soviet Union immediately denied responsibility suggesting they were in fact victims of German war crimes, carried out after the June 1941 invasion. Despite misgivings (and vociferous objections from the Free Poles – who sensed, rather than knew the truth), the Allies found it convenient to accept this version of history until 1990, when the Soviet Union officially acknowledged and condemned the mass killings of the NKVD. In November 2010, the Russian State Duma approved a declaration blaming Stalin and other Soviet officials for having personally ordered the massacre. Found recently in the Russian State Archives was a secret memo to Krushchev, dated 3 March 1959, from Aleksandr Shelepin, head of the KGB, which gave full details of the numbers executed in accordance with Stalin's written order. We now know that the mass grave discovered in 1943 was but one of several resting places of 21,857 later known to have been executed and buried. Elsewhere, 3,820 died at the Starobelsk camp (near Kharkov), 6,311 in Ostashkovo camp (Kalinin), and 7,305 in other camps and prisons throughout western Ukraine and western Belorussia. Although the Soviets executed fourteen Polish generals in April–May 1940, those who died at Katyñ included an admiral, two generals, 24 colonels, 79 lieutenant colonels, 258 majors, 654 captains, 17 naval captains, 3,420 NCOs, seven chaplains, three landowners, a prince, 43 officials, 85 privates, 131 refugees, 20 university professors, 300 physicians, several hundred lawyers, engineers, and teachers, and more than a hundred writers and journalists as well as about 200 pilots – for no other reason it seems than for being Polish. In all, the NKVD murdered almost half the Polish officer corps on Stalin's direct orders.

207 *to the nominated concentration area of Buzuluk.* A small town literally in the middle of nowhere, 620 miles south-east of Moscow and 435 miles north-east of Stalingrad.

208 *'For a long time ten to twenty people died each day'.* General Klemens S. Rudnicki, DSO, *The Last of the War-Horses* (Bachman & Turner, 1974), p. 241.

208 *but it is thought to be between 114,000 and 300,000.* According to a note from Beria (head of the NKVD) to Stalin dated 15 January 1943, over 389,000 Poles were freed as a result of the 1941 'amnesty', though not all will have survived the journey to Persia. Some of those Poles who could not reach safety would eventually fight under Soviet command; by July 1944 they numbered 100,000, and at the end of the war, by forcibly conscripting liberated Poles, they had grown to the First and Second Polish People's Armies, totalling 400,000. This tragic, mass migration via Siberia is all but unknown outside the expatriate Polish community (now several million around the world), yet is the dominant narrative in most Polish émigré family histories. In the 2001 Canadian Census, nearly one million Canadians claimed Polish ancestry, nearly all arriving after the Second World War. Australian estimates that 200,000 citizens are descended from post-1945 settlers and in South Africa there are about 30,000 Poles descendants of the

12,000 Polish soldiers and 500 Polish orphans who settled there after the Second World War. In the US Population Census of 2000, 9 million Americans claimed Polish ancestry (3.2 per cent of the population), though many of these will have arrived before the Second World War. By comparison, 42.8 million claimed German ancestry (15.2 per cent) making them the largest ancestral group. (See www.census.gov/prod/2004pubs/c2kbr-35.pdf.)

209 *in circumstances that have never been properly explained*. While Sikorski's death was undoubtedly convenient, for different reasons, to the British and the Russians, it has never been established whether the crash on 4 July 1943 that killed the Prime Minister of Poland's government in exile and commander-in-chief of her armed force, was suspicious or merely an unfortunate accident. See David Irving, *Accident: The Death of General Sikorski* (Focal Point, 1967).

209 *3rd Carpathian Rifle Division*. The Polish General Staff's original plan was to fall back to the mountainous SE border with Romania and use it as a redoubt from which to carry on the fight. This hope was destroyed by Russia's invasion on 17 September, so surviving Polish units were ordered to escape through Romania towards French-held Syria, the nearest Allied territory.

210 *Private Wojtek would eventually accompany his unit to Italy*. Wojtek's story is probably the only romantic aspect of the Poles' very harsh journey from their homeland to Italy, and consequently has become a popular folk tale with several Polish generations, but is nonetheless an incredible footnote of recent war. The subject of at least two books, one would be hard put to pen a better tale than the true story of Wojtek. Motherless at about eight weeks old, the cub was rescued by a young Iranian boy who spotted him, emaciated and lost, whimpering near the entrance of a cave. The boy was in the act of carrying home the small bear in a sack when the Polish 22nd (Artillery Supply) Transport Company thundered past en route for Palestine in a column of trucks. One of the lorries stopped, intrigued by the small, hungry-looking boy and his bulky sack. Throughout history soldiers and children – who are no threat to them – have formed instant friendships across the barriers of language and culture; kids are a reminder of home, of another world, and with a smile, they usually manage to beg sweets and rations from willing troops. This occasion was no exception, but as the boy wolfed down his food, the sack beside him began to move and the head of a honey-coloured bear cub emerged sleepily into the sunlight. The orphaned cub was in poor condition and unlikely to survive, but was bought by the Poles for a bar of chocolate, a tin of corned beef and an army penknife 'that opened up like a flower'. Christened 'Wojtek' the cub was fed with condensed milk diluted with water, and curled up on the lap of Lance Corporal Piotr Prendys, who became his guardian. In the way that troops often adopt stray dogs, the bear was hugely popular with the Poles, for he seems to have represented a long-lost domestic life, with a hint of the Carpathian Mountains. He grew to be almost six feet tall, was treated as a fellow soldier, never as a pet; fed food, beer and cigarettes, he was taught to march on two legs. Well known throughout the Polish Corps, his army life was well documented and adorable film footage shows him wrestling and playing with his soldier comrades.

210 *the first Polish unit to be bloodied in a raid on German positions.* A couple of inter-connected factors united Anders's men: one was a hatred of the Germans. One British officer noticed: 'We got along very well together, though they [the Poles] could never wholly conceal their slight impatience with our attitudes. They hated the Germans, and their military outlook was dominated by their hate. Their one idea was to find out where the nearest Germans were and go after them. It was praiseworthy, but often impractical' (Majdalany, *Portrait of a Battle*, p. 168). The other unifier was deeper: clearly the Polish Corps needed something to sustain them mentally and spiritually, and this is perhaps why Poles across the world have such a strong cultural identity. Far from wiping out a sense of who they were, the continued repressions over the generations left their mark, and the Polish community seems to have been incredibly tightly knit as a means of sharing adversity. Eyewitnesses told of classes in Catholicism, Polish history and language being set up in gulags by the internees, despite the threat of further punishment for so doing, while in the forthcoming battles, Polishness expressed itself when a forward company of the 5th Kresowa Division had run out of ammunition in the face of a German counterattack: 'the men actually began hurling stones at the enemy and kept up their spirits by singing the national anthem' (see Charles Connell, *Monte Cassino, The Historic Battle*, Elek Books, 1963, p. 143). More important even than this was their faith. I have spoken to combat leaders of different faiths and creeds over the years; many have hinted that religious conviction on a battlefield is a crucial, yet often unspoken, factor when the soul is tortured, and the individual has to dig deep to be able to carry on and overcome fear or fatigue. Poland is a country united by Catholicism like no other, and I am sure the very adversity its people suffered gave its soldiers an extra resource with which to carry on: perhaps this is why a few Jews were allowed to quietly slip away in Palestine; the silent nod between the utterly committed, which the British would never have understood.

210 *Colonel Casimir Wisniowski and interpreter Prince Eugene Lubomirski.* Later promoted to brigadier general, Casimir Winiowski (1896–1964) was Anders's chief of staff from November 1943 and had likewise endured prison and the gulags. He was another senior Polish officer who chose exile and died in London. Prince Eugene Lubomirski was arrested as a landowner when the Soviets invaded in 1939; after three years in ten different prisons, he was released to serve under General Anders.

210 *'I answered that I would undertake the task'.* General Anders, *An Army In Exile* (Macmillan 1949), pp. 163–4.

211 *'Germans are never far removed from his thoughts'.* Harold Macmillan, diary for 24 April 1944, Department of Western Manuscripts, Bodleian Library, Oxford.

211 *imitate the Blitzkrieg-type war at operational level.* Diadem is taught at many NATO defence colleges today as the most perfect example of a modern high-tempo, multinational, all-arms military operation.

213 *General der Gebirgstruppen Valentin Feuerstein's LI Mountain Corps.* General Valentin Feuerstein (1885–1970) was an Austrian officer who served on the Imperial Staff in the First World War and had risen to Generalmajor at the time

of the Anschluss in 1938. He commanded 2nd Mountain Division in 1940, then LXX Corps in Russia until 1943, when he was sent to Italy to command LI Mountain Corps from August 1943.

213 *'A series of explosions shook the ground'.* Bowlby, *Recollections*, p. 57.

214 *'overlapping and interlocking arcs of fire'.* Particularly challenging was the MG-42, the standard German lightweight, mass-produced infantry machine gun, often known as a Spandau, after its Berlin manufacturing plant. However, its unusually high rate of fire (1,200–1,500 rounds per minute) generated large amounts of heat, necessitating frequent changes of the air-cooled barrel every 200 rounds. This could take a trained gunner only five seconds, but was an agonisingly long and frequent silence for defenders during combat. Importantly, each barrel only had a life of 5,000 rounds, which meant carrying many spare barrels as well as endless ammunition belts to feed its high rate of fire. With a sturdy tripod, the 7.92mm MG-42 was especially useful in Italy as a heavy machine gun – reaching across the valleys with its excellent Zeiss optics, to ranges of nearly two miles. At more than double the rate of fire of the British 0.303-inch Bren, US BAR (Browning Automatic Rifle), or Browning 0.30-inch calibre machine guns, the MG-42 was well ahead of its time. The slower Allied guns, though, had their supporters: 'I realised that such a tremendous rate of fire [of the MG-42] must make the gun difficult to control, and really accurate shooting was impossible. As a scatter-gun, at night, at long range, or for continuous fire – here the Spandau, belt-fed, scored heavily over the Bren – the Spandau was supreme. But for accuracy it was the Bren every time,' wrote one British rifleman frequently on the receiving end (Bowlby, *Recollections*, p. 125).

214 *'One of them was the monastery'.* Romuald E. Lipinski's *Memoir* is courtesy of the Polish Combatants Association, at www.kpk-london.org/spk/EN-SPK04.htm.

216 *'Tired, hungry, thirsty and surrounded by rotting corpses'.* Connell, *Monte Cassino*, p. 163.

216 *painted onto the unit's vehicles.* Wojtek survived the war, moving to Scotland with his unit after service in Italy. In 1947 when the Polish army in Scotland was demobilised, he was found a home in Edinburgh Zoo, where his old army friends used to visit, leaping over barriers to wrestle and play with him. In many ways his journey from Iran to Scotland was just as improbable as that of the Poles who first adopted him, and Wojtek was probably the most famous bear in the world at his death, aged twenty-two, in 1963.

216 *Operation Nunton.* The amphibious left-hook was to imply a seabourne invasion at Civitavecchia, forty miles north of Rome, similar to that of Anzio in January and destroyers were actually despatched to bombard the town. Fake radio traffic was carefully scripted and broadcast to imply that both divisions of I Canadian Corps, in Eighth Army reserve, and the US 36th Infantry Division, in Fifth Army reserve, were engaged in amphibious training in the Naples-Salerno area, while road signs bearing the tactical badges of totally spurious units signs were placed where intrepid German patrols might find them. All real troop movements were made only at night, and in strictly controlled penny packets. As late as the second day of the final Cassino battle

(12 May), Kesselring was recorded as estimating the Allies had six divisions facing his four at Cassino, whereas the reality was sixteen (the US 85th and 88th; four French divisions; 4th British, 8th Indian, 78th British, 6th Armoured and 6th South African; the two Canadian divisions, and three Polish). See Ralph Bennett, 'Ultra and Some Command Decisions' (*Journal of Contemporary History*, Vol. 16/1, Jan., 1981).

217 '*It was praiseworthy, but often impractical*'. Majdalany, *Portrait of a Battle*, p. 168.

217 '*in my case my rifle, and ammo*'. See Lipinski *Memoir*.

218 '*The entire history of the battle could be read from these corpses*'. Ibid.

218 '*after which we had gone on leave*'. Senger, *Neither Fear*, p. 244.

219 '*reminded me of the aurora borealis*'. Connell, *Monte Cassino*, p. 160.

11. Winning Cassino

221 '*do nothing to rid ourselves of it*'. Connell, *Monte Cassino*, p. 179.

221 '*drive off the Germans in the same manner*'. See Lipinski *Memoir*.

222 '*with rocks and made small shelters*'. Connell, *Monte Cassino*, p. 161.

222 '*was intolerable in the hot May sun*'. Böhmler, *Monte Cassino*, p. 266. Kurt Veth was awarded the Knight's Cross for leading his battalion at Cassino. Later in the Italian campaign he was awarded the rarer Oakleaves to his cross for delaying the Allied advance over the River Po in 1945.

223 '*That was all that was left*'. James Holland, *Heroes: the Greatest Generation and the Second World War* (Harper Perennial, 2007), pp. 267–85.

223 '*we could occasionally hear nightingales singing*'. Connell, *Monte Cassino*, p. 162.

224 '*clearing approximately a hundred mines*'. Ibid., p. 169. One of these tanks, a Sherman of 4th Troop/3rd Squadron of the Skorpion Armoured Regiment commanded by Lieutenant Bialecki, went up violently on a string of mines, which blew off its turret. It is one of the most evocative relics of any Second World War battlefield, and remains in situ, exactly as it was left on 12 May 1944, with the addition of tank tracks being welded into a giant calvary cross poking out of the turret ring.

224 '*corpse of a man killed some time beforehand*'. Stanislaw Bierkieta Memoir courtesy of the Polish Institute and Sikorski Museum, 20 Prince's Gate, London SW7 1PT.

226 '*we must have looked a hell of a sight*'. Several different interviews with the sprightly Robert Frettlöhr have appeared on television documentaries, but this is based on an interview courtesy of The Second World War Experience Centre, at www. war-experience.org/collections/land/axis/frettlohr/pagetwo.asp.

226 *Krakow Heynal trumpet call*. According to legend, during the Mongol invasion of Poland in 1241, Tatar warriors approaching Krakow were spotted by a guard in the Mariacki (St Mary's) church tower, who sounded the alarm by playing the Heynal, saving his city. The bugler, however, was shot in the throat and did not complete the tune, which is why it ends abruptly. Rather like the 'Last Post' played nightly by the Ypres Fire Brigade in Belgium, the Krakow Heynal gradually became an iconic melody representing the whole Polish nation, and is still played daily from the Mariacki church tower and broadcast live at noon on Polish national radio.

227 *'The Poles have achieved almost impossible feats'*. Daily Telegraph, 17 May 1944.

228 *'everything they could lay their hands on'*. Böhmler, *Monte Cassino*, p. 299.

228 *'but we have not forgotten those days'*. Major Colonel A. P. de T. 'Tony' Daniell, OBE, MC, TD, *Mediterranean Safari, March 1943–October 1944* (Buckland Publications, 1990), pp. 121–2.

228 *'Sir, I'm killed!'* Connell, *Monte Cassino*, p. 162; CSM Franciszek Sochacki lies in Plot 2–A-13 of the Polish Cassino War Cemetery.

228 *'dust and broken plaster'*. Anders, *Army in Exile*, p. 179.

229 *'life returning to the battlefields were poppies'*. Feliks Konarski, a II Corps soldier and Polish composer, wrote a song still well known among the expatriate community, 'The Red Poppies of Monte Cassino'; its most evocative verse reads: 'The red poppies on Monte Cassino/Drank Polish blood instead of dew . . ./O'er the poppies the soldiers did go/Mid death, and to their anger stayed true/Years will come and ages will go,/Enshrining their strivings and their toil/And the poppies on Monte Cassino/Will be redder for Poles' blood in their soil.'

229 *'we had shown everyone what we were capable of'*. Holland, *Heroes*, pp. 267–85.

229 *'were ever able to force the Germans back'*. Daily Herald, 19 May 1944.

230 *'frightening blast that followed his imprudence'*. Connell, *Monte Cassino*, p. 174.

230 *was to be buried with his men at Cassino*. Despite the noted award of a CB (Companion of the Bath) by the British after Cassino, in 1946 the Soviet-run Communist government in Poland deprived Lieutenant General Anders of Polish citizenship and of his military rank. Realising that prison and probably execution awaited him in Poland, he chose to live out the life of an exile in Britain, the spiritual head of over a hundred thousand Poles similarly displaced through no fault of their own (the Polish community in Britain grew from 44,642 at the 1931 census to 162,339 in the 1951 census). Prominent in the Polish government in exile in London, Anders died in 1970 almost on the twenty-sixth anniversary of his great victory at Monte Cassino. General Anders's wife, Irena, died while this book was being written in November 2010, aged ninety. Born Irena Jarosiewicz, she was a singer and actress who toured with the Polish Second Corps Parade Band. Her ashes were buried in her husband's grave at Monte Cassino in May 2011. I frequently encounter Polish Benedictine pilgrims, who have driven all the way from their homeland, paying their respects to their fellow countrymen in this much-visited cemetery, where the nature of its amphitheatre-like design echoes the delightful hymns and prayers they offer. Beyond the Polish cemetery the climb to Point 593 is a heart-thumping affair. The freshwater spring at the rebuilt Doctor's House provides a welcome pause in the climb, and it is difficult to relate the carnage of rats, dead bodies and foxholes of 1944 to the present domestic setting. Pressing on to the peak of Point 593, however, one is rewarded by spectacular views in every direction and a reminder of the hill's significance in 1944 – indeed it is impossible to understand the success of the German defence without making the climb. Around the base of the peak are a series of caves, artificially enlarged, full of the rusting metal junk of war, where Poles and Germans sheltered from artillery and mortar concentrations. The vegetation hides most of the rocky scree, though it is still possible to see

stone-built defensive sangars, used at different times by both sides, and sharp eyes will detect the odd rifle cartridge, bullet-head or piece of shrapnel still nestling among the pebbles; but what really draws the attention is the obelisk erected on the peak after the battle. It bears the unforgettably moving inscription: We Polish soldiers/For our freedom and yours/Have given our souls to God/Our bodies to the soil of Italy/And our hearts to Poland.

230 *'The British government wished to see a Poland strong and friendly to Russia'.* United States Department of State, Foreign Relations of the United States (FRUS) diplomatic papers, *The Conferences at Cairo and Tehran, 1943* (US Government Printing Office, 1943), pp. 594–604.

230 *Alex, who greatly admired the Polish Corps.* Ironically Alexander and Anders shared a common loathing of the Soviets, for in 1919–20, as Lieutenant Colonel Alexander, the former had commanded Baltic German troops against Russian Bolsheviks in Latvia. Alexander was very loyal to Anders, and after attending the Yalta summit conference in February 1945, felt sufficiently responsible to drive two hours in appalling weather by jeep to tell Anders that 'I'm afraid I have bad news for you, General; your country has been given away to the Russians.' Anders replied: 'In that case how can you expect my men to go on fighting in this awful place?' Alex said quietly, 'General, you and I are both soldiers; we are obliged to go on fighting until the end, whatever the end may be . . .'. When he left, the Pole and his HQ staff were actually in tears (Clarke, *With Alex at War*, pp. 203–4).

230 *'I pay my tribute to you'.* The full citation read: 'By conferring on General Anders the Order of the Bath, my Sovereign has decorated the Commander of the II Army Corps for his excellent leadership, and also by it expressed his appreciation for the extreme gallantry and great spirit of self-sacrifice shown by the Polish soldiers during the battle of Monte Cassino. It was a day of great glory for Poland, when you took this stronghold the Germans themselves considered to be impregnable. It was the first stage of a major battle that you went through for the European fortress. It is not merely a brilliant beginning: it is a signpost showing the way to the future. Today I can sincerely and frankly tell you that. Soldiers of the II Polish Corps, if it had been given to me to choose the soldiers I would like to command, I would have chosen the Poles. I pay my tribute to you.' Anders's CB citation courtesy of the Polish Institute and Sikorski Museum.

12. Trouble in the Liri

232 *'prone to sudden explosion'.* Gregory Blaxland, *Alexander's Generals* (William Kimber, 1979), pp. 21–2; Blaxland (1919–1986) would write fourteen books on military history, several on the North African and Italian campaigns. Blaxland thought that Leese 'lacked Montgomery's flair for making rapport with the troops, which would never come easily to a Guards officer'. He 'rarely made much progress beyond a genial wave of the hand and a strange custom inherited from Montgomery, the distribution of cigarettes in the manner of Father Christmas'. The impression left by Leese's visits, as made on Blaxland at the time and confirmed by others, was of 'a funny old duffer'.

233 *commanded by Major Ernst Frömming*. See Joseph Klein's self-published book, *Pioniere der 1. Fallschirmjägerdivision im Italienkrieg 1943–45* (1st German Parachute Engineer Battalion and the Italian War 1943–45), informal English translation in author's possession and interviews with Herr Klein, 2004, 2009 and 2010, and interview with Monsignor Volk, 2006.

234 '*in the strongpoint we were to capture*'. Courtesy of Brigadier E. H. Cubitt-Smith DSO, OBE, *Yadgari, Memoirs of the Raj* (self-published, 1987) p. 90.

234 '*even through the heaviest artillery*'. Lieutenant Colonel R. L. V. Ffrench-Blake DSO, *A History of the 17/21st Lancers 1922–1959* (Macmillan, 1962), p. 167.

234 '*falling into huge shell holes and craters*'. Cubitt-Smith, *Memoirs*, p. 92.

236 '*The Spandau did not fire again*'. Daniell, *Mediterranean Safari*, p. 117; also see his obituary, *Daily Telegraph*, 4 January 2012. Parry is buried at Azizio Beach head War cemetery.

237 '*without a moment's hesitation the driver agreed*'. Ibid., p. 118.

238 '*the landslides of rubble, the torn roofs*'. Gellhorn, *The Face of War*, p. 98.

238 '*It is an awe-inspiring sight at first but in reality horrifying*'. (Anonymous) letter of 11 January 1944, *AFS Letters, 1942–1945, No. XXII*, (ed. and pub. by AFS Headquarters, New York, 1945, 'under the sponsorship of the ambulanciers' relatives and friends, who contribute the excerpts from the letters').

238 '*a pervading odour of damp and good thick walls*'. Gellhorn, *The Face of War*, p. 101.

238 '*They were as good as central heating*'. See www.bbc.co.uk/ww2peopleswar/ stories/91/a8737491.shtml.

240 '*placed a couple of sticky bombs on the turret*'. See WO 170/918 RHA & HAC: 12 HAC Regt (Jan–Dec 1944); and Brigadier RF Johnson, *Regimental Fire! The Honourable Artillery Company in World War II 1939–1945* (HAC, 1958).

240 '*This is real war, and makes Africa seem a picnic*'. Ffrench-Blake, *A History of the 17/21st Lancers*, pp. 165, 167.

240 '*swelling in the scorching heat of the sun*'. 'Extract from the Memoirs of William Lawrie, MBE, MM, 1939–1945: Through Mud and Blood to Green Fields Beyond', chapter in James Colquhoun, *The Honourable Artillery Company at Cassino May 1944* (HAC, no date).

241 '*thirteen anti-tank guns destroyed*'. Cubitt-Smith, *Memoirs*, p. 97.

241 '*soon made aimed fire impossible to both sides*'. John Horsfall, *Fling Our Banners to the Wind* (Roundwood Press, 1978), pp. 46–7.

242 '*only resorting to a steel helmet when actually leading an attack*'. Horsfall obituary in *Daily Telegraph*, 22 January 2007.

242 '*the next lot of hummocks*'. Horsfall, *Fling Our Banners*, p. 56.

242 '*outlined against the backdrop of the barrage*'. Ibid.

243 '*and motored slowly back to the village*'. Ibid., pp. 56–7, 62.

243 '*charred remains of the men who manned them*'. Ibid., pp. 62–3.

243 '*impartially to both sides in both languages*'. Ibid., p. 60.

244 *evacuated out of the combat zone*. Major General 'Bala' Bredin (1916–2005), obituary in *Daily Telegraph*, 3 March 2005; Bredin would go on to win two further DSOs in 1945 and on Cyprus in 1957, and was also twice mentioned in despatches.

244 '*we knew they were prime candidates for death*'. Klein, *1st German Parachute*

Engineer Battalion and the Italian War 1943–45: informal English translation in author's possession and interviews with Herr Klein, 2004, 2009 and 2010.

245 '*and close to our small fortress*'. Ibid.

246 '*I don't have anyone else available*'. Ibid.

13. Pursuit from Cassino

248 '*it would be taken as a reflection on their ability*'. W.R Feasby, *Official History of the Canadian Medical Services 1939–45, Vol. 2* (Ottawa 1956), p. 58.

248 '*and give him my loyal support*'. See chapter 5, 'Tommy Burns: Problems of Personality', in J. L. Granatstein, *The Generals, The Canadian Army's Senior Commanders in the Second World War* (Stoddart/University of Calgary Press 1993), pp. 116–44; and J. P. Johnston, 'E. L. M. Burns – A Crisis of Command', *Canadian Military Journal, Vol. 7/1*, Spring 2006. For an alternate view, see Will Lofgren, 'In Defence of "Tommy" Burns', *Canadian Military Journal*, Vol. 7/4, Winter 2006–07.

249 '*Its citizens had long since scattered to the four winds*'. Stanley Scislowski, *Not All Of Us Were Brave* (Dundurn Press, Toronto, 1997), p. 168.

249 '*their white bodies reddening in the welcome heat*'. Farley Mowat, *The Regiment* (McClelland and Stewart, 1955), p. 178. One of Canada's foremost and prolific authors, Farley Mowat served as a platoon commander, and later as intelligence officer in the Hastings and Prince Edward Regiment from Sicily, through Italy and into Europe. One of his first works was about his war service, *The Regiment*, and launched Mowat on a successful literary career.

249 '*All troops will ensure that faces are covered with soil after each person has defecated*'. Ibid.

249 '*God's Gift to Hungry Girls*', or '*Good God, How Gorgeous*'. Daniel G. Dancocks, *The D-Day Dodgers, The Canadians in Italy, 1943–45* (McClelland & Stewart 1991), p. 265.

250 '*the area practically guaranteed success*'. See Scislowski, *Not All Of Us Were Brave*, pp. 187–8.

250 '*overlaid with the autumnal wreckage of war*'. Mowat, *The Regiment*, p. 184.

251 '*Curious smells came from their cooking fires*'. Gibson-Watt, *An Undistinguished Life*, p. 153.

251 '*rain-slicked meadow, speckled thickly with poppies*'. Scislowski, *Not All Of Us Were Brave*, p. 192. Scislowski mused immediately: 'How could any of us not have the words to John McCrae's 'In Flanders Fields' come to memory?' John McCrae was a field surgeon, who composed the famous 'In Flanders Fields' memorial poem on 3 May 1915 during the Second Battle of Ypres. Poignantly for these soldiers, McCrae was a Canadian medical officer, and failed to survive the war, dying in January 1918.

251 '*a determined advance should be made tomorrow*'. See Dancocks, *D-Day Dodgers*, p. 242.

252 '*when word spread of the Polish flag fluttering over the abbey*'. Ford, *Battleaxe Division*, p. 171.

252 *Van Doos (22ème) Regiment*. Then part of 3rd Canadian Infantry Brigade, the Royal 22nd Regiment (Royal 22ème Régiment) is Canada's most famous francophone unit, and nicknamed the 'Van Doos', an anglicised mispronunciation of their number in French, *vingt-deuxième*.

252 *'supposed to be abandoned shortly anyway'*. Eric McGeer and Matthew Symes, *The Canadian Battlefields in Italy* (Canadian Battlefields Foundation, 2007), p. 74.

252 *'contained in that succinct sentence'*. Mowat, *The Regiment*, p. 184.

253 *'quietly withdrawing by night'*. Interview with Herbert Fries in 2004. Herbert Fries was shortly afterwards made *Fähnrich* (officer cadet), attended officer school in early 1945 and promoted to *Leutnant* (second lieutenant), on 20 April, just before the German surrender in Italy. He is one of about twenty-five Knight's Cross winners still alive at the time of writing.

255 *'was a surreal affair'*. Interview with Donald Hunt in 2002.

255 *'carry on until the next bend'*. Donald F. Hunt, *To the Green Fields Beyond* (Pentland Press, 1993), p. 91.

255 *'in the middle of a very dark night'*. Ibid., p. 95.

255 *'His sniper's rifle had six notches in it'*. Dancocks, *D-Day Dodgers*, p. 271.

256 *'the minefield on the extreme right'*. Hunt, *Green Fields Beyond*, p. 95.

256 *'in the space of a few seconds in my life'*. Ibid.

257 *'lost collectively sixteen tanks by mid-afternoon – a squadron's worth'*. Bryan Perrett, *The Churchill* (Ian Allen, 1974), pp. 59–63.

257 *'because the town must have been pretty'* McGeer and Symes, *The Canadian Battlefields in Italy*, p. 97.

258 *'even though we suffered so heavily'*. See 'The Valley of Death', chapter 5 in Dancocks, *D-Day Dodgers*, pp. 252–64.

258 *'filling the place with fumes'*. 'Extract from the Memoirs of William Lawrie'.

258 *'to breach the Adolf Hitler Line, which they did'*. Perrett, *The Churchill*, p. 63.

259 *'was not quite the disorganised rout that some imagined'*. Dominick Graham and Shelford Bidwell, *Tug of War: The Battle for Italy 1943 –45* (Hodder & Stoughton, 1986), p. 337.

259 *'does not exist in the soldier's dictionary'*. Cited in Ellis, *Cassino*, p. 443.

259 *'with three helmets hanging from their butts'*. Mowat, *The Regiment*, pp. 192–3.

261 *'for setting up the troop command post'*. Lieutenant Stan F. Farrow's memoirs courtesy of www.spiritofcanada.com/veterans/stories/open.php?type=rca&target=ddayDodger.

261 *'to get into the thick of things was almost here'*. Scislowski, *Not All Of Us Were Brave*, pp. 199–200.

261 *'we dug slit trenches faster and deeper than ever'*. Stan F. Farrow's memoirs.

262 *'it disintegrated in one hell of a blast'*. Scislowski, *Not All Of Us Were Brave*, pp. 201–2.

262 *'during a salvo from our regiment'*. Stan F. Farrow's memoirs.

262 *'on the far side of the Melfa'*. Scislowski, *Not All Of Us Were Brave*, pp. 201–2.

262 *'The ruse's value was questionable; it fooled no one'*. Ibid., p. 200.

263 *'to give the effect of a partial eclipse'*. J. M. McAvity, *Lord Strathcona's Horse* (Bridgens, 1947), p. 77; cited in Dancocks, *D-Day Dodgers*, p. 267.

263 'beastly six-barrelled variety, the Nebelwerfers'. See Horsfall, *Fling Our Banners*, p. 56.

263 'fluttering chromatic whine, like jet-propelled Valkyries'. Fred Majdalanay, *The Monastery* (The Bodley Head, 1948), p. 105.

264 'killing them in one heroic act'. Michael Curtis, *A Pilgrimage of Remembrance* (privately published, 2004), p. 24.

264 'We avoided one another's eyes'. Bowlby, *Recollections*, p. 20.

264 'two innocent beautiful beasts should die this way'. Scislowski, *Not All Of Us Were Brave*, p. 204.

264 'hungry as jackals and godawful thirsty'. Ibid., p. 206.

265 'the gap in their own traffic closed behind them'. G. W. L. Nicholson, *Official History of the Canadian Army in the Second World War: The Canadians in Italy, 1943–1945, Vol. II* (Cloutier, Ottawa 1956), p. 446.

265 'witnessed the 15 March air raid with Leese, Kirkman and Keightley'. Lieutenant General Geo. E. Brink, 'Tribute to late Major General W. H. Evered Poole, CB, CBE, DSO', in *Military History Journal of the South African Military History Society*, Vol. 1/4 (June, 1969).

266 'where he had lain in the heat for at least four days'. James Bourhill, *Come Back to Portefino. Through Italy with the 6th South African Armoured Division* (30° South Publishers, 2011), p. 131.

266 'the fighting morale of his troops'. Major A. B. Theunissen, 'Major General W. H. Evered Poole, CB, CBE, DSO: 1902–69: Personal Retrospects', in *Military History Journal of the South African Military History Society*, Vol. 9/5 (June, 1994).

266 'an aspect of philosophy by sleeping while they could'. Eric Linklater, *The Campaign in Italy* (HMSO 1951), p. 267.

267 'in such great clots as to hinder the movement of troops on foot'. Dancocks, *D-Day Dodgers*, pp. 270–1.

267 'bring the Tac HQ jeep forward when possible'. Theunissen, 'Major General W.H. Evered Poole'. Mark Clark would later describe Poole as 'a most competent leader', and his division as 'a battle-wise outfit, bold and aggressive against the enemy and willing to do whatever job was necessary . . . Their attacks against strongly organised German positions were made with great élan and without regard for casualties. Despite their comparatively small numbers, they never complained about losses,' Mark Clark, *Calculated Risk* (Harrap 1951), p. 379. During the Italian campaign, the 6th South African Division suffered 3,543 casualties – 711 killed, 2,675 wounded and 157 missing.

267 'with mobile kitchens caught up in the traffic'. Bourhill, *Come Back to Portefino*, p. 132.

267 'above all hangs a thick, nauseating blanket of dust and the stench of the dead'. Ibid., p. 129.

268 'the paper informed its readers'. *Daily Herald*, 25 May 1944.

269 'and non-essential units would be held back'. Major General W. G. F. Jackson, *The Battle For Rome* (Batsford, 1969), p. 32.

269 'It was far more difficult to repel the French corps'. Senger, *Neither Fear*, p. 259.

14. Roads to Rome

270 '*if we had also had mountain troops . . . on our right*'. Leese papers, IWM.

272 '*with phosphorus bursts that illuminate the entire horizon*'. Klaus H. Huebner, *Long Walk Through War*, p. 62.

273 '*Even the few scrawny dogs I came across seemed to have lost the ability to wag their tails*'. Wendy Holden and Susan Travers, *Tomorrow to Be Brave: A Memoir of the Only Woman Ever to Serve in the French Foreign Legion* (Simon and Schuster, 2007), p. 230. Susan Travers, who died in 2003, joined de Gaulle's Free French and was attached to the 13th Demi-Brigade of the Legion Etrangere (Foreign Legion), which sailed for North Africa. There, she drove the brigade's senior officers, who affectionately dubbed her 'La Miss', and later Colonel Marie-Pierre Koenig, commander of the Free French-held Bir Hakeim fort in Libya. They became lovers; refusing to leave his side she stayed on when Bir Hakeim was besieged by the Afrika Korps, the only woman among 3,500 men, she then led a break-out, driving Koenig's car. Under heavy machine-gun fire, she burst through enemy lines, later noting eleven bullet holes in her vehicle. Travers stayed on with the Legion, which is how she ended up driving ambulances to and from the front line in Juin's Corps in Italy, though, as she later admitted, she preferred towing anti-tank guns into and out of combat. By the end of the war she had achieved the distinction of being the only woman ever to have served in the French Foreign Legion and had been awarded the Legion d'Honneur, Medaille Militaire and the Croix de Guerre.

274 '*it has lost its blood supply*'. Huebner, *Long Walk Through War*, p. 73.

275 '*I would like to keep mine*'. Ibid., p. 81.

275 '*in order to permit their troops to pass along the road*'. Plowman and Rowe, *The Battles for Monte Cassino*, p. 276.

275 '*mess gear, helmets, letters, guns, and first-aid kits behind*'. Huebner, *Long Walk Through War*, p. 69.

276 '*crazed occupants scrambled out, running up the road toward the shelter of thick-walled old buildings in the village*'. Plowman and Rowe, *The Battles for Monte Cassino*, p. 277.

277 '*but a man over thirty-five is already too old for rugged mountain warfare*'. Huebner, *Long Walk Through War*, p. 79.

278 '*left inferior Volkdeutsch troops as a rearguard*'. Bourhill, *Come Back to Portefino*, p. 135.

279 '*To be first in Rome was a poor compensation for this lost opportunity*'. Majdalany, *Portrait of a Battle*, pp. 256–9. Mark Clark's decision to strike for Rome dominates the end of the Cassino campaign, as no other, and has never been satisfactorily explained. In effect, Clark is usually blamed for allowing the Germans to escape, thus prolonging the war in Italy for a further year. It goes without saying that he personally felt himself in competition with the British and wanted to reserve some American glory. He undoubtedly felt himself in competition with his friend Eisenhower; he may, indeed, have harboured secret presidential ambitions himself, and felt a reputation as the

liberator of Rome would help. The popular view is to lambast Clark – and Alexander for not controlling him more readily. However, his failure to close the trap at Valmonte may be down to other factors. We have seen how tough German leadership and strict orders ensured the withdrawing formations were combat-ready, and dangerous. At Valmonte, astride Route 6, the Germans would have met the Americans on equal terms in numbers of well-motivated and efficient combat troops, and there is no guarantee the battle would have ended in Allied success. The prospect of an Allied defeat at Valmonte, and German success, or even a 'draw', on the eve of the Normandy invasion would have been crippling to Allied morale and a fantastic shot in the arm for the Third Reich. Two and a half months later at Falaise, similar numbers of Germans were surrounded by far superior numbers of Allied divisions, with complete air superiority: yet, substantial numbers of German soldiers still escaped. All of the Allied units, as well as the German ones in late May 1944 were tired, but the terrain from Velletri to Valmonte (a distance of about fifteen miles) certainly favoured the Germans defending it. Even had Valmonte been blocked, Route 6 was not the only escape path, and other more minor routes would have served the German units' needs instead. Operation Strangle also proved how the Germans were able to overcome Allied air interdiction and continue to move troops and materiel, especially at night. Even when Clark switched direction, he still had a tough four-day battle to break out towards Rome along Route 7. A balanced reassessment may well conclude that while Clark, therefore, made a controversial decision, it is by no means certain he made the wrong one.

280 'one of the most misguided blunders made by any Allied commander during World War II'. Carlo D'Este, *Fatal Decision: Anzio and the Battle for Rome* (HarperCollins, 1991), pp. 365–6.

281 'Our trip through Rome is fantastic and feels like a dream'. Huebner, *Long Walk Through War*, p. 97.

282 'seen anyone decently dressed or any pretty girls'. Bourhill, *Come Back to Portefino*, p. 138.

282 'when lovely things had the chance to get fags off me for a very quick shy kiss!' Ibid., p. 137.

283 'erect and grim; haunting the old scene; despoiled by pillaging Popes and fighting Princes'. Dickens, *Pictures from Italy*, p. 85.

Bibliography

Unpublished Sources

Archives

Bodleian Library, Oxford: Department of Western Manuscripts: Harold Macmillan, diary for 24 Apr 1944

Bundesarchiv-Militärarchiv, Freiburg: Ktb (*Kriegstagebücher* – War Diaries) of the Tenth Army and of the XIV Panzer Corps

Churchill Archives Centre, Churchill College, Cambridge: CHUR 4/217/26–29, Freyberg letter to Churchill, 23 Feb 1949; CHAR 20/77/62, Churchill telegram to Freyberg, 3 Jul 1942

Directorate of History, National Defence Headquarters, Ottawa: Canadian Military Headquarters Report No. 165, Operations of 1 Cdn Inf Div and 1 Cdn Armd Bde in Italy, 25 Nov 1943–4 Jan 1944; Report No. 175, Operations of 1 Cdn Armd Bde in Italy, May 1944–Feb

Imperial War Museum, London: Department of Documents: personal account of Dr H. Morus Jones, RAMC; papers of Signalman B. Smith, Royal Corps of Signals; papers of Major D. A. Beckett, 1/4th Essex; papers of Lieutenant-General Sir Oliver Leese

Joint Services Combined Staff College Library, Defence Academy, Shrivenham, Wiltshire: Air Historical Branch: 'RAF Narrative – The Italian Campaign 1943–1945, Vol. II'; 'Notes From the Theatre of War: No. 14, Italy'; 'Translation of Captured German Documents: the Luftwaffe in Italy, the German Supply Situation by Colonel Ernst Faehndrich'

National Archives and Records Administration, USA: Generalmajor Hans Bessel, 'Construction of Strategic Field Fortifications in Italy, Sep 1943–Oct 1944' (NARA

M1035/D-013, Foreign Military Studies Program of the Historical Division, US Army Europe, 1947); Generalfeldmarschall Albert Kesselring, 'Rapido River Crossing Debrief' (ETHINT-71/ European Theater Historical Interrogation, Office of the Chief of Military History, 6 May 1946)

The National Archives, Kew, London: AIR 23/8567 Reports, summaries, photographs, maps, etc., May 1944; AIR 8/1358 Bombing of Cassino; FO 371/37330 Vatican/ Foreign Office telegrams about Monte Cassino; FO 371/60797 Vatican booklet about Monte Cassino abbey; FO 371/43817 Preservation of the abbey/Reports of German Military activity in abbey area; WO 204/985 G-2 Intelligence Notes, 11 Jan–11 Apr 1944; WO 204/986 G-2 Intelligence Notes, 12 Apr–27 Jun 1944; WO 204/1096 Report by G-3 Training Section on visits to Units, Jul 1943–Apr 1945; WO 204/1454–1456 Operations in Italy, Jan–Jun 1944; WO 204/4354 Lessons from the Cassino Operation; WO 204/6724 Status of Infantry Soldiers Jul–Nov 1944; WO 204/10388 G-3 Plans: Operational Policy (Italy), Aug 1943–Apr 1944; WO 204/10413 G(Ops): papers relating to Sicilian and Italian Campaigns; WO 204/6832 AA1/43/G/Ops Operational Instructions, Aug 1943–Aug 1944; WO 204/6835 AA1/48/G/Ops: Operation Diadem reports; WO 204/1096 North African and Italian campaigns, Nov 1942–Feb 1944; WO 204/4365 34 US Division: Nov 1942–Sep 1944; WO 204/6809 Fifth Army: Operational Memoranda, Dec 1943–Aug 1944; WO 204/7566 Fifth Army: Cassino Operation: lessons learnt 15–24 Mar 1944; WO 204/7564 HQ NAF Theatre Ops: lessons learnt from the Italian Campaign; WO 204/8221 Operations 11 Polish Corps against Monte Cassino; WO 204/7275 Operations of New Zealand Corps, 3 Feb–26 Mar 1944; WO 204/8287 Historical notes on Operation Dickens, 15–23 Mar 1944; WO 204/8289 2 NZEF: Operations report, Nov 1943–Nov 1944; WO 204/8202 1 Canadian Division in the Liri Valley, 15–28 May 1944; WO 204/8207 5 Canadian Armoured Division: reports on Operations; WO 204/10425 The Irish Brigade in Italy, Mar 1944–Mar 1945 by Brigadier T. P. D. Scott; WO 169/18983: 4/11 Sikhs (Jan–Dec, 1944); WO 169/18978: 3/10 Baluchs (Jan–Dec 1944); WO 169/19006: 1/9 Gurkha Rifles (Jan–Dec 1944); WO 169/18970: 4/6 Rajputana Rifle Regiment (Jan–Dec 1944); WO 170/918 RHA & HAC: 12 HAC Regt (Jan– Dec, 1944); WO 170/1246, Light Anti-Aircraft Regiments: 99 Regt (Jan–Aug 1944)

US Army Military History Institute Library, Carlisle Barracks, USA: 'Lessons Learned in Combat, 8 Nov 1942–Sep 1944', Headquarters 34th Infantry Division, US Army (Charles L. Bolte papers, Box 6)

Research Papers

Allen, Major Gregory A., 'Third Infantry Division at the Battle of Anzio-Nettuno' (MA Thesis, US Army Command and General Staff College, Fort Leavenworth, 1995)

Allin, Major, George R., and thirteen other officers, 'Cassino: The Second, Third, and Fourth Battles, 13 Feb–18 May 1944' (Battle Analysis Program Student Paper, Combat Studies Institute, US Army Command and General Staff College, Fort Leavenworth, 1984)

Bailey, Major Don W., 'Operational Defense: Covering all the Bases' (Monograph,

School of Advanced Military Studies, US Army Command and General Staff College, Fort Leavenworth, 1993)

Bielecki, Christine Ann, 'British Infantry Morale during the Italian Campaign' (PhD Thesis, University College, London, 2006)

Bitner, Captain Teddy D., 'Kesselring: An Analysis of the German Commander at Anzio' (MA Thesis, US Army Command and General Staff College, Fort Leavenworth, 1983)

Bliss, Major James C., 'The Fall of Crete 1941: Was Freyberg Culpable?' (MA Thesis, US Army Command and General Staff College, Fort Leavenworth, 2006)

Botters, Major Robert J. Jr, 'Operational Liaison in Combined Operations: Considerations and Procedures' (Monograph, School of Advanced Military Studies, US Army Command and General Staff College, Fort Leavenworth, 1996)

Browne, Joseph Edward, 'Deception and the Mediterranean Campaigns of 1943–1944' (Military Study Project, US Army War College, Carlisle, 1986)

Clark, Lt Comd., W. J., 'Operational Analysis: Anzio' (Paper for US Naval War College, Newport, RI, 1994)

Clement, Major John G., 'The Necessity for the Destruction of the Abbey of Monte Cassino' (MA Thesis, US Army Command and General Staff College, Fort Leavenworth, 2002)

Cote, Lt Col. Stephen R., USMC, 'Operation Husky: A Critical Analysis' (Paper for US Naval War College, Newport, RI, 2001)

Daskevich, Col. Anthony F., 'Insights into Modularity: 753rd Tank Battalion in World War II' (Masters Thesis, US Army War College, Carlisle, 2008)

Donaldson, Keith L. G., 'Thunder in the Mountains: 1st Canadian Armoured Brigade in Italy, 1943–1944' (MA Thesis, University of Calgary, 2008)

Dumas, Commander John, 'Learning Lessons from Operation Shingle' (Paper for US Naval War College, Newport, RI, 2006)

Evans, Lt Col. David L., MG (Retd) 'Benjamin J. Butler: A Historical Perspective of Leadership on the Battlefield' (Strategy Research Project, US Army War College, Carlisle, 1988)

Gerbara, Lt Col. Andrew J., USAF, 'Damage Control: Leveraging Crisis Communications for Operational Effect' (Paper for US Naval War College, Newport, RI, 2008)

Gober, Major Donald F., and fourteen other officers, 'Battle Analysis: Cassino. The Second, Third and Fourth Battles, 13 Feb–18 May 1944' (Battle Analysis Program Student Paper, Combat Studies Institute, US Army Command and General Staff College, Fort Leavenworth, 1984)

Gray, Captain Stephen P., USAF, 'Anzio (Operational Shingle): An Operational Perspective' (Paper for US Naval War College, Newport, RI, 1994)

Griebling, Erik Karl, 'Broken Fasces: Historical Perceptions on the Failure of Fascist Italy' (MA Thesis, Hawaii Pacific University, 2009)

Hunter, Wilson, 'Where Have All the Nazis Gone? A Study of German Memoirs from the Second World War' (BA Thesis, Vanderbilt University, 2007)

King, Major Glenn L., 'From Salerno to Rome: General Mark W. Clark and the Challenges of Coalition Warfare' (MA Thesis, US Army Command and General Staff College, Fort Leavenworth, 2007)

Knorr, Major Mathias and fourteen other officers, 'Battle Analysis of the River Rapido Crossing' (Battle Analysis Program Student Paper, Combat Studies Institute, US Army Command and General Staff College, Fort Leavenworth, 1984)

Krueger, Major Daniel W., 'Calculated Risk? Military Theory and the Allies' Campaign in Italy, 1943–44' (Monograph, School of Advanced Military Studies, US Army Command and General Staff College, Fort Leavenworth, 1988)

Maclean, Major French L., 'German General Officer Casualties in World War II – Harbinger for US Army General Officer Casualties in Airland Battle?' (Study Paper for School of Advanced Military Studies, US Army Command and General Staff College, Fort Leavenworth, Kansas, 1988)

———— 'The Unknown Generals – German Corps Commanders in World War Two: A Leadership Analysis' (MA Thesis, US Army Command and General Staff College, Fort Leavenworth, 1988)

Mason, Chris, 'Falling From Grace: The German Airborne in World War II' (MA Thesis, Marine Corps University, Quantico, Virginia, 2002)

Mikolashek, Jon, 'Flawed, But Essential: Mark W. Clark and the Italian Campaign in World War II' (PhD Dissertation, Florida State University, 2007)

Miller, Major Christopher D., and Porter, Major Dennis C., 'Terror from the Skies: Exploiting the Psychological Impact of the Heavy Bomber' (Paper for US Naval War College, Newport, RI, 1991)

Penteado, Lt Col. Carlos José Russo Assumpçaõ, 'The Brazilian Participation in World War II' (MA Thesis, US Army Command and General Staff College, Fort Leavenworth, 2006)

Prescott, Lt Col. James E., 'What Operational Level of War Lesson Can Be Learned From the Allied Invasion of Sicily?' (Paper for US Naval War College, Newport, RI, 1994)

Santala, Major Russell D., 'Fads and Hobbies or Lessons Learned? An Analysis of the US Army Wartime Lessons Learned Program' (Monograph, School of Advanced Military Studies, US Army Command and General Staff College, Fort Leavenworth, 1993)

Sassman, Commander Roger W., USNR, 'Operation Shingle and Major General John P. Lucas' (Strategy Research Project, US Army War College, Carlisle, 1999)

Saxon, Timothy D., 'The German Side of the Hill: Nazi Conquest and Exploitation of Italy, 1943–45' (PhD Thesis, University of Virginia, 1999)

Scudieri, Major James D., 'The Indian Army in Africa and Asia, 1940–42: Implications for the Planning and Execution of Two Nearly-Simultaneous Campaigns' (Monograph, School of Advanced Military Studies, US Army Command and General Staff College, Fort Leavenworth, 1995)

Sheffield, Major Clayton Odie, 'The War Film: Historical Perspective or Simple Entertainment' (MA Thesis, US Army Command and General Staff College, Fort Leavenworth, 2001)

Smith, Major Phillip A., 'Bombing to Surrender: The Contribution of Air Power to the Collapse of Italy, 1943' (MA Thesis, School of Advanced Air Power Studies, Air University, Maxwell Air Force Base, 1997)

St Clair, Major Matthew G., USMC, 'The Twelfth US Air Force: Tactical and

Operational Innovations in the Mediterranean Theater of Operations, 1943–44' (MA Thesis, School of Advanced Air Power Studies, Air University, Maxwell Air Force Base, 2007)

Stewart, Major Jeff R., 'The Ranger Force at the Battle of Cisterna' (MA Thesis, US Army Command and General Staff College, Fort Leavenworth, 2004)

Tracy, Mary, 'Operation Avalanche: Prelude to Stalemate. A Case Study in Operational Art' (Paper for US Naval War College, Newport, RI, 1995)

White, Brook, 'Another Forgotten Army: the French Expeditionary Corps in Italy, 1943–44' (MA Thesis, University of Central Florida, 2008)

White, Major S. L., and fourteen other officers, 'Battle Analysis: The Battle of Monte La Difensa. Deliberate Assault, Mountains, Winter, 2–8 Dec 1943' (Battle Analysis Program Student Paper, Combat Studies Institute, US Army Command and General Staff College, Fort Leavenworth, 1984)

Wilbeck, Maj. Christopher W., 'Swinging the Sledgehammer: the Combat Effectiveness of German Heavy Tank Battalions in World War II' (MA Thesis, US Army Command and General Staff College, Fort Leavenworth, 2002)

Published Sources

Absalom, Roger, 'Hiding history: the Allies, the Resistance and the others in Occupied Italy 1943–1945', *Historical Journal, Vol. 38* (1995), pp. 111–31

Adleman, Robert H, *The Devils' Brigade* (Chilton Books, 1966)

Adleman, Robert H., and Walton, Col. George, *Rome Fell Today* (Little, Brown, & Co., 1968)

Agarossi, Elena, *A Nation Collapses: The Italian Surrender of September 1943* (Cambridge University Press, 2000)

Ahmed, Rafiuddin, *History of the Baloch Regiment, 1939–56* (Naval & Military Press, 2004)

Aldrich, Richard J. (ed.), *Witness to War* (Doubleday, 2004)

Alexander of Tunis, Field Marshal the Viscount, *Report by the Supreme Allied Commander, Mediterranean, to the Combined Chiefs of Staff on the Italian Campaign,* 12 Dec 1944 to 2 May 1945 (HMSO, 1951)

————*The Alexander Memoirs 1940–1945* (Cassell, 1962)

Alper, Benedict S., *Love and Politics in Wartime: Letters to My Wife, 1943–45*; selected and edited by Scott, Joan Wallach (University of Illinois Press, 1992)

Anders, Lt General Wladyslaw, *An Army in Exile: The Story of Second Polish Corps* (Macmillan, 1949)

Ankrum, Homer R., *Dogfaces Who Smiled Through Tears in World War II* (Graphic Publishing Company, 1988)

Anon., 'The Desertion Crisis in Italy: Some Views from an Eighth Army Infantry Platoon Commander', *RUSI Journal, Vol. 147/5* (Oct, 2002)

Arris, G., *The Fifth British Division 1939 to 1945* (Fifth Division Benevolent Fund, 1959)

Atkinson, Rick, *The Day of Battle: The War in Sicily and Italy, 1943–44* (Henry Holt, 2007)

Ball, Major Edmund F., *A Staff Officer in the Fifth Army: Sicily, Salerno, Anzio* (Exposition Press, 1958)

Barber, Laurie and Tonkin-Covell, John, *Freyberg: Churchill's Salamander* (Century Hutchinson, 1989)

Barclay, Brigadier C. N., *The History of the Duke of Wellington's Regiment, 1919–52* (William Clowes, 1953)

Baris, Tommaso, 'Le Corps Expéditionnaire Français en Italie: Violences des libérateurs durant l'été 1944', *Vingtième Siècle Revue d'Histoire*, 93

Barkawi, Tarak, 'Culture and Combat in the Colonies: The Indian Army in the Second World War', *Journal of Contemporary History* (2006), 41/2, pp. 325–55

Barnett, Correlli (ed.), *Hitler's Generals* (Weidenfeld & Nicolson, 1989)

Batty, Peter, *Paper War: Nazi Propaganda in One Battle, on a Single Day, Cassino, Italy, 11 May 1944* (Mark Batty Publishing, 2005)

Bayley, C. A., 'The Nation Within: British India at War 1939–1947', chapter in Prof. P. J. Marshall (ed.), *Proceedings of the British Academy, 2003 Lectures* (British Academy, 2004)

Beale, Nick, *Ghost Bombers, the Moonlight War of NSG 9: Luftwaffe Night Attack Operations from Anzio to the Alps* (Classic Publications Ltd, 2001)

Beale, Nick, D'Amico, Ferdinando, and Valentini, Gabriele, *Air War Italy 1944–45, the Axis Air Forces from the Liberation of Rome to the Surrender* (Airlife, 1996)

Behan, Tom, *The Italian Resistance: Fascists, Guerrillas and the Allies* (Pluto Press, 2009)

Belote, Lt Col. Howard D., USAF, *Once in a Blue Moon: Airmen in Theater Command: Lauris Norstad, Albrecht Kesselring, and Their Relevance to the Twenty-First Century Air Force* (CADRE Paper No.7, Maxwell Air Force Base, Air University Press, 2000)

Benamou, Jean-Pierre, *10 Million Tons for Victory: The Arsenal of Democracy During the Battle of France in 1944* (OREP, 2003)

Ben-Arie, Katriel, *Die Schlacht bei Monte Cassino 1944* (Rombach Verlag, 1985)

Bimberg, Edward L., *The Moroccan Goums: Tribal Warriors in a Modern War* (Greenwood Press, 1999)

Blaxland, Gregory, *Alexander's Generals: The Italian Campaign, 1944–45* (William Kimber, 1979)

Bloch, Herbert, *The Bombardment of Monte Cassino, February 14–16, 1944* (Montecassino, Tipografia Italo-Orientale, 1979)

Blumenson, Martin, *Bloody River: The Real Tragedy of the Rapido* (Houghton Mifflin Co., 1970)

———*Mark Clark: The Last of the Great World War Commanders* (Congdon & Weed, 1984)

———*Salerno to Cassino* (United States Army in World War II series. Mediterranean Theatre of Operations, Center of Military History, United States Army, Washington DC, 1969)

Blumenson, Martin, Garland, Lt Col. Albert N., and Smyth, Howard McGaw, *Sicily and the Surrender of Italy* (United States Army in World War II series. Mediterranean Theatre of Operations, Center of Military History, United States Army, Washington DC, 1965)

Böhmler, Rudolf, *Monte Cassino. A German View* (Cassell, 1964)

Bond, Harold L., *Return to Cassino: A Memoir of the Fight for Rome* (Doubleday, 1964)

Bonomi, Giovanni, *Dal Volturno al Po con le truppe cobelligeranti in Italia, Vol.1: Il I Raggruppamento Motorizzato* (Milano: Nuovo Edizione, 1974)

Boog, Horst, Krebs, Gerhard and Vogel, Detlef, *Germany and the Second World War: VII: The Strategic Air War in Europe and the War in the West and East Asia, 1943–1944/5* [Militärgeschichtliches Forschungsamt, Potsdam] (English trans., Oxford University Press, 2006)

Bosworth, R. J. B., *Mussolini s Italy: Life Under the Fascist Dictatorship, 1915–1945* (Allen Lane, 2005)

Botjer, George F., *Sideshow War: The Italian Campaign, 1943–1945* (Texas A&M University Press, 1996)

Boulle, Lt Col. Georges, *Le Corps Expeditionnaire Français en Italie, 1943–44: Vols 1 and 2* (Paris: Imprimerie Nationale, 1971)

Bourhill, James, *Come Back to Portofino: Through Italy with the 6th South African Armoured Division* (30 Degrees South Publishers (South Africa) 2011)

Bowlby, Alex, *Countdown to Cassino: The Battle of Mignano Gap 1943* (Leo Cooper, 1994)

————*The Recollections of Rifleman Bowlby* (Leo Cooper, 1969)

Brager, Bruce L., *The Texas 36th Division: A History* (Eakin Press, 2002)

Brett-Smith, Richard, *Hitler's Generals* (Osprey, 1976)

Breuer, William B., *Agony at Anzio: The Allies' Most Controversial and Bizarre Operation of World War II* (Zeus Publishers, 1985)

Brey, Ilaria Dagnini, *The Venus Fixers: The Remarkable Story of the Allied Soldiers who Saved Italy's Art during World War II* (Farrar, Straus and Giroux, 2009)

Brigety, Rueben E., II, 'Moral Ambiguities on the Bombing of Monte Cassino', *Journal of Military Ethics, Vol. 4/2* (2005)

Brookes, Wing Cdr. Andrew, *Air War over Italy* (Ian Allan, 2000)

———— 'Air Power and the Italian Campaign, 1943–1945', *RUSI Journal, Vol. 141/6* (Dec 1996)

Brooks, Thomas R., *The War North of Rome June 1944–May 1945* (Sarpedon, 1996)

Brown, Brig. Gen. John Sloan, *Draftee Division; The 88th Infantry Division in WW2* (University Press of Kentucky, 1986)

Brutton, Philip, *Ensign in Italy: A Platoon Commander's Story* (Pen and Sword, 1992)

Buckley, Christopher, *Road to Rome* (Hodder and Stoughton, 1945)

Buffetaut, Yves, 'Les Quatres Batailles de Cassino', *39–45 Magazine* (Nov, 1988)

Bulteel, Capt. Christopher, *Something About a Soldier: Wartime Memoirs* (Airlife, 2000)

Burrell, Kathy, 'Migrant Memories, Migrant Lives: Polish National Identity in Leicester since 1945', *Transactions of the Leicester Archaeology and History Society 76* (2002)

Bykofsky, Joseph and Larson, Harold, *The Transportation Corps: Overseas Operations* (Office of the Chief of Military History, Washington DC, 1957)

Cancelli, Diego, *Aprilia 1944: Immagini Quotidiane di una Guerra* (Poligraf, 1994)

Capps, Robert S., *Flying Colt: Liberator pilot in Italy: diary and history, 456th Bombardment Group (Heavy), 15th Air Force* (Manor House Publications, 1997)

Carloni, Fabrizio, *San Pietro Infine 8–17 dicembre 1943: la battaglia prima di Cassino* (Milano: Mursia, 2003)

Carpentier, Gen. Marcel, *Les Forces Alliées en Italie: la Campagne d Italie* (Paris: Berger-Levrault, 1949)

Carver, Field Marshal Lord, *Imperial War Museum Book of the War in Italy: A Vital Contribution to Victory in Europe 1943–1945* (Sidgwick & Jackson, 2001)

————— 'The War in Italy 1943–45', *RUSI Journal, Vol. 146/5* (2005)

Cavallaro, Livio, *Cassino. Le battaglie per la Linea Gustav. 12 gennaio–18 maggio 1944* (Mursia Gruppo Editoriale, 2004)

Chambe, Général, *L'epopee francaise d'Italie* (Paris: Flammarion, 1952)

Chant, Christopher (ed.), *Hitler's Generals and Their Battles* (Salamander Books, 1977)

Chaplin, Lt Col. H. D., *The Queen's Own Royal West Kent Regiment, 1920–50* (Michael Joseph, 1954)

Chartrand, Réné, *Canadian Forces in World War II* (Osprey, 2001)

Cheetham, A. M., *Ubique* (privately printed, Formby, 1987)

Churchill, Brig. T. B. L., 'The Commandos in Action at Salerno', *Army Quarterly, Vol. LI*, No. 2 (Jan, 1946)

Ciciarelli, John A., 'The Geology of the Battle of Monte Cassino, 1944', chapter in Peter Doyle and Matthew R. Bennett (eds.), *Fields of Battle: Terrain in Military History* (Kluwer Academic, 2002)

Clark, Gen. Mark W., *Calculated Risk: His Personal Story of the War in North Africa and Italy* (Harper & Brothers, 1950)

Clark, Lloyd, *Anzio, The Friction of War, Italy and the Battle for Rome 1944* (Headline, 2006)

Clark, Martin, *Modern Italy, 1871–1995* (Longman, 1996)

Clarke, Rupert, *With Alex at War: From the Irrawaddy to the Po, 1941–1945* (Leo Cooper, 2000)

Coakley, Robert W., and Leighton, Richard M., *Global Logistics and Strategy: 1943–45* (US Army in World War II Series, Washington DC, 1968)

Cole, Sir David, *Rough Road to Rome, A Foot-Soldier in Sicily and Italy, 1943–44* (William Kimber, 1983)

Condon, W. E. H., *The Frontier Force Regiment* (Gale & Polden, 1962)

Connell, Charles, *Monte Cassino: The Historic Battle* (Elek Books, 1963)

Conti, Giuseppe, *Il Primo Raggruppamento Motorizzato* (Rome: Ufficio Storico, 1984)

Copp, Terry, and McAndrew, Bill, 'Closing Out the Italian Campaign: Part 89', *Legion Magazine* (Canada), 11/8/2010

Copp, Terry, and McAndrew, Bill, *Battle Exhaustion: Soldiers and Psychiatrists in the Canadian Army, 1939–45* (McGill-Queen's University Press, 1990)

Cornwell, John, *Hitler's Pope; The Secret History of Pius XII* (Penguin Putnam, 1999)

Corti, Eugenio, *The Last Soldiers of the King: Wartime Italy, 1943–45* (University of Missouri Press, 2003)

Corvo, Max, *The OSS in Italy, 1942–45: A Personal Memoir* (Praeger, 1990)

Cox, Sir Geoffrey, *The Race for Trieste* (William Kimber, 1977)

Crang, Jeremy A., *The British Army and the People's War* (Manchester University Press, 2000)

Crapanzano, Salvatore Ernesto, *I Gruppi di Combattimento Cremona, Friuli, Folgore,*

Legnano, Mantova, Piceno, 1944–45 (Ministero della Difesa, Rome: Ufficio Storico, 1951)

Craven, Wesley Frank, and Cate, James Lea, (eds.), *The Army Air Forces in World War II, Vol. II, Europe: TORCH to POINTBLANK* (The University of Chicago Press, 1949); *Vol. III, Europe: ARGUMENT to VE Day* (Chicago, 1951); *Vol. VII, Services Around the World* (Chicago, 1958)

Crawford, John, *North from Taranto: New Zealand and the Liberation of Italy, 1943–45* (New Zealand Defence Force, 1994)

Crew, Francis A. E., *The Army Medical Services, Campaigns, Vol. 3: Sicily, Italy, Greece, 1944–45* (HMSO, 1959)

Curtis, Michael, *A Pilgrimage of Remembrance: An Anthology of the History of a Scots Guards Company in the Italian Campaign 1944–45* (Published by the author, 2004)

D'Este, Carlo, *Bitter Victory: The Battle for Sicily, 1943* (Collins, 1988)

———*Fatal Decision: Anzio and the Battle for Rome* (HarperCollins, 1991)

Daddis, Major Gregory A., 'Understanding Fear's Effect on Unit Effectiveness', *Military Review*, Jul–Aug 2004, pp. 22–27

Danchev, Alex, and Todman, Dan, *War Diaries of Field Marshal Lord Alanbrooke, 1939–45* (Weidenfeld & Nicolson, 2001)

Dancocks, Daniel. *D-Day Dodgers: The Canadians in Italy, 1943–45* (McClelland and Stewart, 1991)

Daniell, A. P. de T, *Mediterranean Safari – Five Nine Field Company, Royal Engineers, Mar 1943 to Oct 1944* (Buckland, 1990)

Darlington, Albert F., *The D-Day Dodger* (Laundry Cottage Books, 2006)

David, Saul, *Mutiny at Salerno* (Conway, 2005)

Davies, Norman, *Heart of Europe: A Short History of Poland* (Oxford University Press, 1986)

Davis, Melton S., *Who Defends Rome?* (Dial Press, 1972)

de Guingand, Major Gen. Sir Francis, *Operation Victory* (Hodder & Stoughton, 1947)

Deakin, Frederick William, *The Brutal Friendship: Mussolini, Hitler and the Fall of Italian Fascism* (Weidenfeld & Nicolson, 1962)

Deane, Theresa, *500 Days of Front Line Combat: The WWII Memoir of Ralph B. Schaps* (Universe, 2003)

Deayton-Groom, Major C.W., 'Cassino and Anzio – A Sketch of the Battles with Some Personal Experiences, Parts 1–3', *British Army Review*, Nos. 87, 88 & 89

Delaney, John, *The Blue Devils in Italy; A History of the 88th Infantry Division in World War II* (Infantry Journal, 1947, reprinted Battery Press, 2002)

De Lee, Nigel, 'Moral Ambiguities in the Bombing of Monte Cassino', *Journal of Military Ethics*, Vol. 4/2 (Jun, 2005)

Dethick, Janet, *The Arezzo Massacres, A Tuscan Tragedy, Apr –Sep 1944* (Duca Della Corgna, 2005)

Dettmer, Friedrich, Jaus, Otto, and Tolkmitt, Helmut, *Die 44. ID and Reichs-Grenadier-Division Hoch und Deutschmeister 1938–1945 Bildband* (Podzun-Pallas-Verlag, 1979)

Dickens, Charles, *Pictures From Italy* (Bradbury and Evans, 1846), especially Chapter Eleven: 'A Rapid Diorama'.

Didmon, Tom, *Lucky Guy: Memoirs of a World War II Canadian Soldier* (Trafford Publishing, Canada, 2000)

Ditner, Elmar, *Hero or Coward: Pressures Facing the Soldier in Battle* (Frank Cass, 1985)

Doherty, Richard, *Clear The Way!* (Irish Academic Press 1993)

————*Eighth Army in Italy 1943–45: The Long Hard Slog* (Pen and Sword, 2007)

————*The North Irish Horse: A Hundred Years of Service* (Spellmount, 2002)

Dulles, Allen. *The Secret Surrender* (Harper, 1966)

Dupuy, Col. T. N. (ed.). *Tactical Air Interdiction by USAAF in WWII in Italy* (NOVA, 1972)

Eager For Duty: Unit history of the 157th Infantry Regiment of the 45th Division from 6 June 1943 to 8 May 1945 (Army and Navy Publishing, 1946)

Edsel, Robert M., *The Monuments Men: Allied Heroes, Nazi Thieves, and the Greatest Treasure Hunt in History* (Preface Random House, 2009)

Eisenhower, John S. D., *They Fought at Anzio* (University of Missouri Press, 2007)

Ellis, John, *Cassino: The Hollow Victory: The Battle for Rome, Jan–Jun 1944* (André Deutsch, 1984)

Ellwood, David, *Italy 1943–1945* (Leicester University Press, 1985)

English, Ian, MC and Bar, *Assisted Passage: Walking to Freedom Italy 1943* (Ian English, 1994)

Faber, Harold (ed.), *Luftwaffe: an Analysis by Former Luftwaffe Generals* (Sidgwick & Jackson, 1979)

Farish, Greggs, *Algiers to Anzio with 72 and 111 Squadrons: An RAF Engineer Officer's Experiences in North Africa and Italy with 239 Wing, DAF, during World War II* (Woodfield Publishing, 2001)

Farwell, Byron, *The Gurkhas* (Allen Lane, 1984)

Ffrench Blake, Lt Col. R.L.V., *A History of the 17th/21st Lancers 1922–1959* (Macmillan, 1962)

Fielding, W. L., *With the 6th Division: An Account of the Activities of the 6th South African Armoured Division in WWII* (Pietermaritzburg: Shuter and Shooter, 1946)

Fiftieth Anniversary of the Cyprus Regiment, 1939–1945 (Cyprus Info. Office, 1990)

Filose, A. A., *King George V's Own Central India Horse* (Blackwood, 1950)

Fisher, Ernest F., Jr, *Cassino to the Alps* (United States Army in World War II series. Mediterranean Theatre of Operations, Center of Military History, United States Army, Washington DC, 1977)

Flavelle, Ryan, 'Help or Harm: Battle Exhaustion and the RCAMC during the Second World War', *Journal of Military and Strategic Studies, Vol. 9/4* (Summer, 2007)

Ford, Ken, *Battleaxe Division: From Africa to Italy with the 78th Division, 1942–45* (Sutton Publishing, 2003)

————*Cassino 1944: Breaking the Gustav Line* (Osprey, 2004)

Forman, Sir Denis, *To Reason Why* (Abacus Press, 1991)

Forty, George, *The Battle for Monte Cassino* (Ian Allan, 2004)

Fowler, Will, *Blitzkrieg in North Africa and Italy, 1942–44* (Ian Allen, 2003)

Franklin, Robert J., *Medic!: How I Fought World War II with Morphine, Sulfa and Iodine Swabs* (University of Nebraska Press, 2006)

Fraser, Gen. Sir David, *And We Shall Shock Them: The British Army in the Second World War* (Hodder & Stoughton, 1983)

French, David, *Raising Churchill's Army: The British Army and the War Against Germany 1919–45* (Oxford University Press, 2001)

———— 'Colonel Blimp and the British Army: British Divisional Commanders in the War Against Germany, 1939–45', *English Historical Review*, Vol. CXI (Nov, 1996)

———— 'Discipline at the Death Penalty in the British Army in the War Against Germany in the Second World War', *Journal of Contemporary History*, Vol. 33/4

Freyberg, Paul, *Bernard Freyberg VC: Soldier of Two Nations* (Hodder & Stoughton, 1991)

Frost, C. Sydney, *Once a Patricia: Memoirs of a Junior Infantry Officer in World War II* (Vanwell, 1988)

Gaujac, Paul, *Le Corps Expeditionnaire Français en Italie, 1943–44* (Paris: Histoire and Collections, 2004)

Gellhorn, Martha, *The Face of War* (Sphere Books, 1967)

George Rock, *History of the American Field Service, 1920–1955* (AFS/Platen Press, 1956)

Die Geschichte der 94: ID, Erinnerungsbuch der 94. ID an die Kriegsjahre 1939–1945 (published by Unit Association, Podzun Pallas, 1975)

Gibson-Watt, Andrew, *An Undistinguished Life* (Book Guild, 1990)

Goddard, Lance, *Hell and High Water: Canada and the Italian Campaign* (Dundurn, 2007)

Golla, Karl-Heinz, *Zwischen Reggio und Cassino: Das Kriegsgeschehen in Italien im zweiten Halbjahr 1943* (Bernard and Graefe, 2004)

Gooderson, Ian, *A Hard Way to Make a War: The Allied Campaign in Italy in the Second World War* (Conway, 2008)

————*Cassino* (Brassey's, 2003)

Goodyear, Harry J., *History of the 3rd Battalion, 338th Infantry Regiment, 85th Infantry Division* (Campus Publishing, 1946)

Graham, Dominick and Bidwell, Shelford, *Tug of War: The Battle for Italy 1943–45* (Hodder & Stoughton, 1986)

Granatstein, J. L., *The Generals: The Canadian Army's Senior Commanders in the Second World War* (University of Calgary Press, 2005)

———— 'Hoffmeister in Italy', *Canadian Military History*, Vol. 2/2 (1993), pp. 57–64

Graver, B. D., and Hoile, K. J. T., *English Studies Series, Vol. 5: Military Texts* (Oxford University Press, 1967)

Green, Colonel J. H., 'The Destruction of the Abbey of Monte Cassino', *British Army Review*, No. 90

Greenfield, Kent Roberts (ed.), *Command Decisions* (Harcourt, Brace, 1959)

Greiner, Gen. Heinz, *Kampf um Rom Inferno am Po: Der Weg der 362 Infanterie-Division 1944/45* (Kurt Vowinckel-Verlag, 1968)

Grif, Henry, *The Mules of Monte Cassino* (e-book, published by Brown Fedora, 2010)

Gropman, Alan (ed.), *The Big 'L': American Logistics in World War II* (National Defense University Press, 1997)

Guglielmi, Daniel, *26th Panzer Division: Capagna d'Italia 1943–45* (Helion and Co., 2001)

Gunner, Colin, with Foreword by Philip Larkin, *Front of the Line* (Greystone Books, 1991)

Hallion, Richard P., *Strike from the Sky: The History of Battlefield Air Attack, 1911–45* (Smithsonian Institution Press, 1989)

Hapgood, David and Richardson David, *Monte Cassino: The Story of the Most Controversial Battle of World War II* (Angus & Robertson, 1984)

Harris, C.R.S., *History of the Second World War, UK Military Series: Allied Military Administration of Italy, 1943–45* (HMSO, 1957)

Harrison, Mark, *Medicine and Victory: British Military Medicine in the Second World War* (Oxford University Press, 2004)

———— 'Medicine and the Culture of Command: the Case of Malaria Control in the British Army in the British Army in the Two World Wars', *Medical History, Vol. 40* (1996)

Hart, Basil Liddell, *The Other Side of The Hill: Germany's Generals, their Rise and Fall, with their own Account of Military Events 1939–45* (Cassell, 1948)

Hart, Peter, *The Heat of Battle: The 16th Battalion Durham Light Infantry in the Italian Campaign, 1943–45* (Pen and Sword, 1999)

Haupt, Werner, *Kriegsschauplatz Italien 1943–45* [Italy: Theatre of War, 1942–1945] (Motorbuch: Stuttgart, 1977)

Heefner, Wilson Allen, *Dogface Soldier: The Life of General Lucian K. Truscott, Jr.* (University of Missouri Press, 2010)

Heinemann, Dr Winfried, 'Salerno – A Defender's View', *Army History* 67 (Spring, 2008)

Heller, Joseph, *Catch-22* (Simon and Schuster, 1961)

Henderson, Dr Diana M., *The Lion and the Eagle: Polish Second World War Veterans in Scotland* (Cualann Press, 2002)

Hickey, Des, and Smith, Gus, *Operation Avalanche: The Salerno Landings 1943* (Heinemann, 1983)

Higgins, Trumbull, *Soft Underbelly: The Anglo-American Controversy over the Italian Campaign 1939–45* (Macmillan, 1968)

Hildyard, Miles, *It Is Bliss Here: Letters Home 1939–45* (Bloomsbury, 2005)

Hill, Mike, *The 451st Bomb Group of WW2: A Pictorial History* (Schiffer, 2001)

Hill, Robert M., *In the Wake of War: Memoirs of an Alabama Military Government Officer in World War Two Italy* (University of Alabama Press, 1982)

Hinsley, Prof. F. H. et al., *British Intelligence in the Second World War: Its Influence on Strategy and Operations (History of the Second World War) Vol. 3: Part 1* (HMSO, 1984)

Hirlinger, Kurt (ed.), *Combat History of Schwere Panzer-Abteilung 508: In Action in Italy with the Tiger I* (Fedorowicz, 2001)

The History of the 58th, 1939–45 (Gale and Polden, 1947)

Hoffman, Jon T., 'The Legacy and Lessons of the Campaign in Italy', *Marine Corps Gazette* 78 (Jan, 1994)

Holden Reid, Brian, 'The Italian Campaign, 1943–45: A Reappraisal of Allied Generalship', *Journal of Strategic Studies, Vol. 13/1* (Mar, 1990)

Holland, James, *Italy's Sorrow: a Year of War, 1944–45* (HarperCollins, 2009)

Holmes, Richard, 'Five Armies in Italy' in *Time to Kill: The Soldier's Experience of War in the West 1939–45*, ed. Paul Addison and Angus Calder (London, 1997)

———*Battlefields of the Second World War* (BBC Books, 2001)

———*The D-Day Dodgers* (on BBC website: www.bbc.co.uk/history/worldwars/wwtwo/d_day_dodgers_01.shtml

———*World War Two: The Battle of Monte Cassino* (BBC website)

Hood, Stuart, *Pebbles from My Skull* (Hutchinson, 1963)

Hooton, E. R., *Eagle In Flames: The Fall of the Luftwaffe* (Arms and Armour, 1997)

Hoppe, Harry, *Die 278 Infanterie-Division in Italien 1944–45* (Podzun, 1953)

Horsfall, John, *Fling Our Banner to the Wind* (Roundwood Press, 1978)

Howe, George F., *The Battle History of the 1st Armored Division: 'Old Ironsides'* (Combat Forces Press, 1954)

Hoyt, Edwin, *Backwater War: The Allied Campaign in Italy, 1943–5* (Praeger, 2002)

Huebner, Claus K., *Long Walk through War: A Combat Doctor's Diary* (Texas A&M University Press, 1987)

Humble, Richard, *Hitler's Generals* (Arthur Barker, 1973)

Hunt, Donald F., *To the Green Fields Beyond* (Pentland Press, 1993)

Hutching, Megan, *A Fair Sort of Battering: New Zealanders Remember the Italian Campaign* (HarperCollins, 2009)

Il Corpo Italiano di Liberazione, Aprile–Settembre 1944 (Ufficio Storico, 1950)

Il I Raggruppamento Motorizzato Italiano, 1943–44 (Ufficio Storico, 1949)

Infield, Glenn B., *Disaster at Bari* (Macmillan, 1971)

Irving, David, *Hitler's War* (Hodder & Stoughton, 1977)

Iskander, Anthon, 'From Siberia to Italy', *World War Investigator Magazine* (Aug, 1988)

Jackson, Ashley, *The British Empire and the Second World War* (Hambledon Continuum, 2006)

Jackson, General Sir W. G. F., *Alexander of Tunis as Military Commander* (Batsford, 1971)

———*The Battle for Italy* (Batsford, 1967)

———*The Battle for Rome* (Batsford, 1969)

Jackson, General Sir W. G. F. and Gleave, Group Capt. T. P., *The Mediterranean and Middle East, Vol. 6: Victory in the Mediterranean, Part 3: Nov 1944–May 1945* (HMSO, 1988)

———*The Mediterranean and Middle East, Vol. 6: Victory in the Mediterranean, Part 2: Jun to Oct 1944* (HMSO, 1987)

Jars, R., *La Campagne d'Italie 1943–45* (Paris: Payot, 1954)

Jay, Bernard, *The Adventures of a Romantic* (Logaston Press, 1998)

Johnston, Major J.P., 'E.L.M. Burns – A Crisis of Command', *Canadian Military Journal* (Spring, 2006)

Jones, Kevin, *Intelligence, Command and Military Operations: The Eighth Army Campaign in Italy, 1943–45* (Routledge, 2011)

Jones, Matthew, 'Macmillan, Eden, the War in the Mediterranean and Anglo-American Relations', *Twentieth Century British History*, Vol. 8/1 (1997), pp. 27–48

Jowett, Phillip, *The Italian Army 1940–45 (3): Italy 1943–45* (Osprey, 2001)

Joyce, Kenneth H., *Snow Plough and the Jupiter Deception: The True Story of the 1st Special Service Force and the 1st Canadian Special Service Battalion, 1942–45* (Vanwell, 2006)

Juin, Maréchal Alphonse, *La Campagne d'Italie* (Editions Guy Victor, coll. 'Moments de l'Histoire', 1962)

Katz, Robert, *Death in Rome* (Macmillan, 1967)

——*The Battle for Rome; the Germans, the Allies, the Partisans, and the Pope* (Simon & Schuster, 2003)

Kay, Robin, *The Official History of New Zealand in the Second World War 1939–45, Italy, Vol. II: From Cassino to Trieste* (Historical Publications Branch, Wellington, 1967)

Kazamias, Georgios, 'Military Recruitment and Selection in a British Colony: The Cyprus Regiment 1939–1944', in E. Close, M. Tsianikas and G. Couvalis (eds.) *Greek Research in Australia: Proceedings of the Sixth Biennial International Conference of Greek*

Keegan, John (ed.), *Churchill's Generals* (Weidenfeld & Nicolson, 1991)

Kelly, Matthew, *Finding Poland* (Vintage, 2010)

Kelly, Michael, 'The Italian Resistance in Historical Transition: Class War, Patriotic War or Civil War?' *Eras Journal 4* (2008), Monash University

Kesselring, Albert, *Soldat bis zum letzten Tag* [A Soldier to the Last Day] (Athenäum-Verlag, 1953); translated as *A Soldier's Record* (William Kimber, 1953); later editions retitled *The Memoirs of Field Marshal Kesselring*

Keyter, Barry, *From Wings to Jackboots* (Janus Publishing Co., 1995)

Kingseed, Cole C., 'Review Essay: The Anzio Campaign', *Parameters* (Winter, 2008–09)

Klein, Joseph, *Fallshirmjäger*, Engineer Battalion, 1st *Fallshirmjäger* Division (self-published); also, author's interview with Herr Klein, 2006; and see interview with James Holland at www.secondworldwarforum.com/my-oral-history-archive/pilots-aircrew/joseph-joop-klein-german/

Knox, MacGregor, *Hitler's Italian Allies* (Cambridge University Press, 2000)

Koskodan, Kenneth K., *No Greater Ally* (Osprey, 2009)

Kowalik, Ernest, *Alone and Unarmed* (Glenn Curtis Press, 2005)

Kros, Jack, *War in Italy: With the South Africans from Taranto to the Alps* (Johannesburg: Ashanti, 1992)

Krz stek, Tadeusz, *Battle of Monte Cassino, 1944* (Polish Interpress Agency, 1984)

Kurowski, Franz, *Battleground Italy 1943–45: The German Armed Forces in the Battle for the Boot* (Fedorowicz, 2003)

——*The History of the Fallschrim-PanzerKorps Herman Göring* (Fedorowicz, 1995)

Kurzman, Dan, *The Race For Rome* (Doubleday, 1975)

Lake, Harold L., *Perhaps They Left Us Up There* (Harry Cuff, 1995)

Lamb, Richard, *War in Italy, 1943–1945: A Brutal Story* (John Murray, 1993)

Lanquetot, A., *Le 8e R.T.M.: Un Hiver dans les Abruzzes, 1943–44* (Imprimerie Nationale, 1991)

Le Gac, Julie, 'From Suspicious Observation to Ambiguous Collaboration: The Allies and Italian Partisans, 1943–1944', *Journal of Strategic Studies, Vol. 31/5* (2008)

Le Goyet, Col. Pierre, *La Participation Française à la Campagne d Italie, 1943–44* (Imperimerie Nationale, 1969)

Lee, William Mark, *From the Back Streets to the Front Line: A True Story of Growing Up in Cardiff and Travelling Through Africa, Italy and Austria in the 2nd World War* (AuthorHouse, 2008)

Lemelsen, Gen. Joachim, and Schmidt, Julius, *29 Division, 29 Infanterie-Division (mot.), 29 Panzergrenadier-Division* (Podzun-Pallas-Verlag, Bad Nauheim 1960)

Lewis, Norman, *Naples 44: An Intelligence Officer in the Italian Labyrinth* (Collins, 1978)

Lihou, Maurice G., *Out of the Italian Night: Wellington Bomber Operations 1944–45* (Airlife, 2000)

Lingen, Kerstin von, and Salter, Michael, 'Contrasting Strategies within the War Crimes Trials of Kesselring and Wolff', *Liverpool Law Review, Vol. 26* (2005)

———*Kesselring's Last Battle: War Crimes Trials and Cold War Politics, 1945–60* (University Press of Kansas, 2008)

Linklater, Eric, *The Campaign in Italy* (HMSO, 1951)

———*Private Angelo* (Jonathan Cape, 1946)

Longer, V., *Red Coats to Olive Green: A History of the Indian Army 1600–1974* (Allied Publishers, 1974)

Loud, G. A., *Montecassino and Benevento in the Middle Ages: Essays in South Italian Church History* (Ashgate/Variorum, 2000)

Lucas, James S., *Hitler's Commanders: German Bravery in the Field, 1939–45* (Cassell, 2000)

———*Hitler's Enforcers* (Arms and Armour, 1996)

Lucian K. Truscott Jr, *Command Missions: A Personal Story* (E. P. Dutton, 1954)

Lutter, Horst, *Das war Monte Cassino: Die Schlacht der Grünen Teufel* (Wancura, 1958)

Macdonald, Helen Bajorek, 'Once Upon a War Time', *Canadian Women's Studies, Vol. 19/4*

McAndrew, Bill, 'Fifth Canadian Armoured Division: Introduction to Battle', *Canadian Military History, Vol. 2/2* (1993) pp. 43–56

McAndrew, Bill, *Canadians and the Italian Campaign, 1943–45* (Art Global/Vanwell, 1996)

McCarthy, Michael C., *Air-to-Ground Battle for Italy* (Air University Press, 2004)

McCreery, Lt Gen. Sir Richard (Foreword), *The Story of 46th Division 1939–1945* (Graz, 1945)

McDougall, Robert L., *A Narrative of War: From the Beaches of Sicily to the Hitler Line with the Seaforth Highlanders of Canada, 10 Jul 1943–8 Jun 1944* (Golden Dog Press, 1996)

McGeer, Eric, and Symes, Matthew, *The Canadian Battlefields in Italy: Ortona and the Liri Valley* (Canadian Battlefields Foundation, Wilfrid Laurier University, 2007)

MacIntyre, Eric, *Canadian Armour in the Italian Campaign, Italy 1943–45* (Canadian Tracks Publishing, no date)

Mackay, J. N., *History of the 7th Duke of Edinburgh's Own Gurkha Rifles* (Blackwood, 1962)

Macksey, Kenneth, *Kesselring: German Master Strategist of the Second World War* (Stackpole Books, 1996)

Macmillan, Harold, *Autobiography, Vol. 2: The Blast of War, 1939–45* (Macmillan 1967)

———*War Diaries: Politics and War in the Mediterranean, Jan 1943–May 1945* (Macmillan, 1984)

Madeja, Witold, *The Polish 2nd Corps and the Italian Campaign, 1943–45* (Game Publishing, 1981)

Majdalany, Fred, *Cassino: Portrait of a Battle* (Longmans, Green, 1957)

———*The Monastery (John Lane/The Bodley Head, 1945)*

Marteinson, John, and McNorgan, Michael, *The Royal Canadian Armoured Corps: An Illustrated History* (Robin Brass Studio, 2000)

Mason, Philip, *A Matter of Honour: an Account of the Indian Army, its Officers and Men* (Jonathan Cape, 1974)

Matloff, Maurice, *Strategic Planning for Coalition Warfare: 1943–44* (US Army in World War II Series, Washington DC, 1959)

Mauldin, Bill, *Up Front* (Henry Holt, 1945)

Mavrogordato, Ralph S., 'Hitler's Decision on the Defense of Italy', in Kent Roberts Greenfield, (ed.), *Command Decisions* (Harcourt, Brace, 1959)

Michulec, R., *The Fall of Monte Cassino* (Concord, 2007)

A Military Encyclopedia : Based on Operations in the Italian Campaigns, 1943–45 (G-3 Section, Headquarters 15 Army Group, Italy 1945)

Milligan, Spike, *Milligan's War* (Penguin, 1989)

———*Mussolini: My Part in His Downfall* (Michael Joseph, 1978)

Mitcham, Samuel W. Jr, *Hitler's Field Marshals and Their Battles* (Scarborough House, 1990)

Mitcham, Samuel W. Jr, and Stauffenberg, Friedrich von, *The Battle of Sicily: How the Allies Lost Their Chance for Total Victory* (Orion, 1991)

Molony, Brig. C. J. C., Flynn, Capt. F. C., Davies, Major Gen. H. L., and Gleave, Group Capt., *History of the Second World War: The Mediterranean and Middle East, Vol. 5: The Campaign in Sicily 1943 and the Campaign in Italy, 3rd Sep 1943 to 31st Mar 1944* (HMSO, 1973)

———*The Mediterranean and Middle East, Vol. 6: Victory in the Mediterranean, Part 1: 1st Apr–4th Jun 1944* (HMSO, 1984)

Monte Cassino: Battle of Six Nations (Polish Military Printing Press, 1945)

Montemaggi, Amedeo (ed.), *Linea Gotica avamposto dei Balcani* (Edizioni Civitas, 1993)

Montgomery of Alamein, Field Marshal the Viscount, *El Alamein to the River Sangro* (BAOR, 1946)

Moorhead, Alan, *Eclipse* (Hamish Hamilton, 1946)

Mordal, Jacques, *Cassino* (Amiot-Dumont, 1952)

Mork, Werner, *Aus Meiner Sicht* ('From My View'), translated by Daniel H. Setzer (2006), www.home.comcast.net/~dhsetzer/Mork/

Morris, Eric, *Circles of Hell: The War in Italy 1943–45* (Hutchinson, 1993)

———*Salerno: A Military Fiasco* (Stein and Day, 1983)

Mowat, Farley, *And No Birds Sang* (McClelland and Stewart, 1979)

———*The Regiment* (McClelland and Stewart, 1955)

Muhm, *Oberst* Gerhard (29th Pz.-Gr. Division), *German Tactics in the Italian Campaign*, www.larchivio.org/xoom/gerhardmuhm2.htm

Munro, Ross, *Gauntlet to Overlord: The Story of the Canadian Army* (Macmillan, 1946)

Murphy, Robert, *Diplomat Among Warriors* (Doubleday, 1964)

Murphy, W. E., *The Official History of New Zealand in the Second World War 1939–1945: History of the 2nd New Zealand Divisional Artillery* (Historical Publications Branch, Wellington, 1966)

Nafziger, George, *German Order of Battle World War II, Vol. I, Panzer Divisions* (Stackpole, 1999); *Vol. II, Infantry Divisions* (Greenhill, 2000)

Nardini, Walter, *Cassino: Fino all'ultimo uomo (Testimonianze fra cronaca e storia)* [*Cassino: To the Last Man. Testimonials from events and history*] (Mursia, 1975)

Neillands, Robin, *Eighth Army: From the Western Desert to the Alps, 1939–45* (John Murray, 2004)

Newby, Eric, *Love and War in the Apennines* (Hodder & Stoughton, 1971)

Nichols, David (ed.), *Ernie's War: The Best of Ernie Pyle's World War II Dispatches* (Random House, 1986)

Nicholson, Lt Col. G. W. L., *Official History of the Canadian Army in the Second World War: Vol. II, The Canadians in Italy, 1943–45* (Queen's Printer, 1956)

Nicolson, Harold, (ed. Nigel Nicolson), *Diaries and Letters 1939–45* (Collins, 1967)

Nicolson, Nigel, *Alex: The Life of Field Marshal Earl Alexander of Tunis* (Weidenfeld & Nicolson, 1973)

The North Irish Horse Battle Report: North Africa and Italy (Baird, 1946)

Notes from Theatres of War, No. 20 Italy, 1943/44 (The War Office, 1944)

Notin, Jean-Christophe, *La campagne d Italie 1943–45: Les victoires oubliées de la France* (Perrin, 2007)

O'Reilly, Charles T., *Forgotten Battles Italy's War of Liberation, 1943–45* (Lexington Books, 2001)

Oliver, Kingsley M., *The RAF Regiment 1942–46* (Forces and Corporate, 1997)

Orgill, Douglas, *The Gothic Line* (Heinemann, 1967)

Origo, Iris, *War in Val D'Orcia: An Italian War Diary, 1943–44* (Jonathan Cape, 1947)

Orpen, Neil, *The South African Forces in World War II, Vol. V, Victory in Italy* (Purnell, 1975)

Orr, Aileen, *Wojtek the Bear: Polish War Hero* (Birlinn Ltd, 2010)

Paff, Lucjan, *Kresowa Walczy w Italii* (Kultury i Prasy, 1945)

Pal, Dr Dharm, *Official History of the Indian Armed Forces in the Second World War: The Campaign in Italy, 1943–45* (Combined Inter-Services, 1960)

Palit, Major Gen. D. K., *Italian Campaign, 1943–45: An Analytical Digest* (Natraj Publishers, 1992)

Palmer, Allan, M. D., 'Casualty Survey, Cassino, Italy', in Major James C. Beyer, *Wound Ballistics in World War II, Medical Department, US Army* (Office of the Surgeon General, Department of the Army, Washington, DC, 1962)

Paoletti, Ciro, *A Military History of Italy* (Praeger, 2008)

Parker, John, *The Gurkhas: The Inside Story of the World's Most Feared Soldiers* (Headline, 2005)

Parker, Matthew, *Cassino: The Hardest Fought Battle of World War II* (Headline, 2004)

Patalas, Kazimierz, *Providence Watching: Memories of Polish War Combatants from the Second World War* (University of Manitoba Press, 2003)

Peaty, Dr John, 'The Desertion Crisis in Italy, 1944', *RUSI Journal, Vol. 147/3* (Jun, 2002)

Pesce, Angelo, *Salerno 1943: Operation Avalanche* (Falcon Press, 1993)

Phillips, N. C., *The Official History of New Zealand in the Second World War 1939–45, Italy, Vol. I: The Sangro to Cassino* (Historical Publications Branch, 1957)

Piatkowski, Col. H., 'The Second Polish Corps in the Battle for Monte Cassino and Piedimonte', *Army Quarterly, Vol. LI,* Nos. 1 and 2 (Oct 1945/Jan 1946)

Piekalkiewicz, Janusz, *Cassino: Anatomy of a Battle* (Orbis, 1980)

Place, Dr Timothy Harrison, *Military Training in the British Army, 1940–44: From Dunkirk to D-Day* (Frank Cass, 2000)

Plowman, Jeffrey, and Malcolm, Thomas, *2nd New Zealand Divisional Cavalry Regiment in the Mediterranean* (Plowman, 2002)

——*Rampant Dragons: New Zealanders in Armour in World War II* (Plowman, 2002)

——*4th New Zealand Armoured Brigade in Italy* (Plowman, 2000)

Plowman, Jeffrey, and Rowe, Perry, *The Battles for Monte Cassino: Then and Now* (After the Battle, 2011)

Poems from Italy, with Foreword by Lt Gen. Sir Oliver Leese and Introduction by Siegfried Sassoon (George G. Harrap, 1945)

Pond, Hugh, *Salerno* (William Kimber, 1961)

Porch, Douglas, *Hitler's Mediterranean Gamble: The North African and the Mediterranean Campaigns in World War II* (Weidenfeld & Nicolson, 2004)

——*The Path to Victory: The Mediterranean Theater in World War II* (Farrar, Straus and Giroux, 2004)

Portelli, Alessandro, *The Order Has Been Carried Out: History, Memory and Meaning of a Nazi Massacre in Rome* (Palgrave Macmillan, 2003)

Praval, Major K. C., *Red Eagles: A History of Fourth Division of India* (Vision Books, 1982)

Prieur, Charles, *War Chronicles 1939–45: Three Rivers Regiment* (e-book at: www.12rbc.ca/PDF/Anglais.pdf)

Puddu, Mario, *Tra due invasioni: La campagna d'Italia, 1943–45* (Nardini, 1965)

Pujo, Bernard, *Juin: maréchal de France* (Albin Michel, 1988)

Pyle, Ernie, *Brave Men* (Henry Holt & Co., 1944)

——*Here is Your War* (Henry Holt, 1943)

Quilter, D.C., *No Dishonourable Name: The 2nd and 3rd Battalions Coldstream Guards, 1939–46* (William Clowes, 1947)

Qureshi, Mohammed, *First Punjabis: History of the First Punjab Regiment, 1759–1956* (Gale & Polden, 1958)

Raiber, Richard, *Anatomy of Perjury: Field Marshal Albert Kesserling, Via Rasella, and The Ginny Mission* (University of Delaware Press, 2008)

Ray, Cyril, *Algiers to Austria: The History of the 78th Division 1942–1946* (Eyre & Spottiswoode, 1982)

Ready, J. Lee, *Forgotten Allies: The Military Contribution of the Colonies, Exiled Governments and Lesser Powers to the Allied Victory in World War II. Vol. I: The European Theatre* (McFarland & Co., 1985)

Renner, Major Robert A., USAF, 'Allied Airpower Comes of Age: The Roles and Contributions of Air Power to the Italian Campaign', *US Air and Space Power Journal*, 2003 and in *RAF Air Power Review, Vol. 6/3* (Autumn, 2003)

Ricchezza, Antonio, *Il Corpo Italiano di Liberazione, 1943–45* (Museo del Risorgimento e Raccolte Storiche del Comune di Milano, 1963)

Ringel, Gen. Julius, *Hurra, die Gams! Ein Gedenkbuch für die Soldaten der 5 Gebirgs-Division* (Leopold Stocker Verlag, 1963)

Robbins, Major Robert, *91st Division* (Infantry Journal Press, 1947)

Roberts, Andrew, *The Storm of War: A New History of the Second World War* (Harper, 2011)

Robichon, J., *Le Corps Expeditionnaire Français en Italie 1943–44* (Presses de la Cite, 1981)

Rosignoli, Guido, *The Allied Forces in Italy, 1943–45* (David and Charles, 1989)

Rottman, Gordon, *The Fall of Monte Cassino* (Concord, 2007)

Roy, Edouard, *Les chemins d'Italie* (Editions France-Empire, 1970)

Russell, Edward T., and Johnson, Robert M., *Africa to the Alps: The Army Air Forces in the Mediterranean Theater* (Air Force History and Museums Program, 1999)

Rust, Kurt Albert, *Der Weg der 15. PzGr.-Div. von Sizilien bis Wesermünde, Teil 1: Sizilien - Florenz 1943–44* (self-published, 1990)

Ryder, Rowland, *Oliver Leese* (Hamish Hamilton, 1987)

Sallagar, F. M., *Operation Strangle, Italy, Spring 1944: A Case Study of Tactical Air Interdiction* (Rand, 1972)

Sarner, Harvey, *General Anders and the Soldiers of the Second Polish Corps* (Brunswick Press, 1997)

Saunders, Anne Leslie, *A Travel Guide to World War II Sites in Italy: Museums, Monuments, and Battlegrounds* (Travel Guide Press, 2010)

Saxon, Dr Timothy D., 'Hidden Treasure: The Italian War Economy's Contribution to the German War Effort, 1943–45', *30th Int. Congress of Military History*, Rabat (2004)

Schorer, Avis, *A Half Acre of Hell* (Galde Press Inc., 2000)

Schultz, Duane, *Crossing the Rapido: A Tragedy of World War II* (Westholme, 2010)

Schultz, Paul L., *85th Infantry Division in World War II* (Battery Press 1949, reprinted 1979)

Schwonek, Matthew R., 'Kazimierz Sosnkowski as Commander in Chief: The Government-in-Exile and Polish Strategy, 1943–44', *Journal of Military History, Vol. 70/3* (Jul, 2006)

Scislowski, Stanley, *Not All of Us Were Brave* (Dundurn Press, 1997)

Seago, Edward, *Edward Seago's War Paintings. The Italian Campaign 1944* (The Fine Art Society, 1999)

Second World War 60th Anniversary: The Battles for Monte Cassino, Central Italy, 12 Jan–5 Jun 1944 (Central Office of Information, 2004)

Selwyn, Victor (ed.), *From Oasis into Italy, War Poems and Diaries from Africa and Italy 1940 –46* (Shepheard-Walwyn Publishers, 1983)

Senger und Etterlin, General Fridolin von, 'The Battles of Cassino', *RUSI Journal, Vol. CIII* (May, 1958) pp. 208–14

———*Krieg in Europa* (Kiepenheuer and Witsch, 1960); translated into English as *Neither Fear nor Hope: the Wartime Career of General Frido von Senger und Etterlin, Defender of Cassino* (Macdonald, 1963)

———*War Diary of the Italian Campaign* (Historical Division, Headquarters, USAREUR [US Army Europe], 1953)

Shepperd, Lt Col. G. A., *The Italian Campaign 1943–45: A Political and Military Reassessment* (Arthur Barker, 1968)

Short, Neil, *German Defences in Italy in World War II* (Osprey, 2006)

Siedlecki, Julian, *The Fate of Poles in the USSR, 1939–86* (Gryf Publications, London, 1987)

Singh, Gajendra, *The Anatomy of Dissent in the Military of India During the First and Second World Wars*, Papers in South Asian Studies, No. 20 (University of Edinburgh, 2006)

Singleton-Gates, Peter, *General Lord Freyberg VC: An Unofficial Biography* (Michael Joseph, 1963)

Slaughter, Jane, *Women and the Italian Resistance, 1943–45* (Arden Press, Denver, 1997)

Smith, Brigadier E. D. ('Birdie'), *Even the Brave Falter* (Robert Hale, 1978)

———*The Battles for Monte Cassino* (Ian Allen, 1975)

Smith, Lee Carraway, *A River Swift and Deadly: The 36th Texas Infantry Division at the Rapido River* (Eakin Press, 1989)

Southern, George, *Poisonous Inferno: WWII Tragedy at Bari Harbour* (Airlife, 2002)

Spence, Wing Cdr. F., 'Did Allied Air Interdiction Live up to Expectations in the Italian Campaign 1943–44?', *RAF Air Power Review, Vol. 8/4* (Winter, 2005)

Spooner, Keith, *The Battalion* (London Scottish Regimental Trust, 1997)

Springer, Joseph A., *The Black Devil Brigade: The True Story of the First Special Service Force in World War II* (Motorbooks International, 2001)

Squire, G. L. A., and Hill P. G. E., *The Surreys in Italy* (The Queen's Royal Surrey Regiment Museum, 1992)

Stachura, Peter D., *The Poles in Britain, 1940–2000: From Betrayal to Assimilation* (Routledge, 2004)

Stafford, David, *Mission Accomplished: SOE and Italy 1943–45* (Bodley Head, 2011)

Staiger, Jörg, *Anzio-Nettuno* (Die Wehrmacht im Kampf, No. 32: Neckargemünd 1962)

Starr, Chester, *From Salerno to the Alps: A History of the Fifth Army, 1943–45* (Infantry Journal Press, 1948)

Steinberg, Jonathan, *All or Nothing: The Axis and the Holocaust, 1941–43* (Routledge, 1990)

Steinhoff, Johannes, *The Straits of Messina. The Diary of a Fighter Commander* (André Deutsch, 1971)

Steinmetz, B., *Erinnerungsbuch der 94 Infanterie-Division an die Kriegsjahre 1939–45: Der Einsatz in Italien 1943–45* (Kameradschaft 94 Infanterie-Division, 1973)

Stevens, Lt Col. George Richard, *Fourth Indian Division* (McLaren, 1948)

———*History of the 2nd King Edward VII's Own Goorkha Rifles (The Sirmoor Rifles)* (Gale and Polden, 1952)

Stiehm, Judith Hicks, *The US Army War College: Military Education in a Democracy* (Temple University Press, 2002)

Stille, Alexander, *Benevolence and Betrayal: Five Italian Jewish Families under Fascism* (Summit, 1992)

Stimpel, Hans-Martin, *Die deutsche Fallschirmtruppe 1942–45* (Hamburg, Koehler/Mittler Verlagsgesellschaft, 2006)

Stockfisch, J. A., *Linking Logistics and Operations: A Case Study of World War II Air Power* (Rand, 1991)

The Story of the 34th Infantry Division: Louisiana to Pisa (US Army, Italy, 1945)

Strawson, Major Gen. John, *The Italian Campaign* (Secker & Warburg, 1987)

Sumner, Ian, *The Indian Army 1914–47* (Osprey, 2001)

Sumner, Ian, and Vauvillier, François, *The French Army, 1939–45: Free French, Fighting French and the Army of Liberation* (2) (Osprey, 1998)

Sword, Keith, *Deportation and Exile: Poles in the Soviet Union, 1939–48* (Macmillan, 1994)

Tanaka, Chester, *Go for Broke: A Pictorial History of the Japanese American 100th Infantry Battalion and the 442nd Regimental Combat Team* (Presidio Press, 1997)

Tatham, Bill, *Spitfires Rampant – The SAAF in the Italian Campaign* (Self-published, 2010)

Terlecki, Olgierd, *Poles in the Italian Campaign: 1943–45* (Interpress Publishers, 1972)

Terraine, John, *The Right of the Line: The RAF in the European War 1939–45* (Hodder & Stoughton, 1985)

Thomas, David, 'The Importance of Commando Operations in Modern Warfare, 1939–82', *Journal of Contemporary History* 18/4 (Oct, 1983)

Thomas, Robert Dalzell Dillon, Lt, Grenadier Guards, *The Note-Book of a Lieutenant in the Italian Campaign* (Privately printed, 1946)

Thornton, Martin, 'The Second Polish Corps, 1943–46: Were They a Functional Mixture of Soldiers, Refugees and Social Workers?' *Journal of Slavic Military Studies*, 10/2 (Jun, 1997) pp. 125–37

The Tiger Triumphs: The Story of Three Great Divisions in Italy (HMSO for the Government of India, 1946)

Tobin, James, *Ernie Pyle's War: America's Eyewitness to World War II* (Simon & Schuster, 1997)

Tomblin, Barbara Brooks, *With Utmost Spirit: Allied Naval Operations in the Mediterranean, 1942–45* (University Press of Kentucky, 2004)

Tregaskis, Richard, *Invasion Diary* (Random House, 1944)

Trevelyan, Raleigh, *Rome 1944: The Battle for the Eternal City* (Secker & Warburg, 1981)

———*The Fortress: A Diary of Anzio and After* (Collins, 1956)

Tudor, Malcolm Edward, *Prisoners and Partisans: Escape and Evasion in World War II Italy* (Emilia, 2006)

———*Special Force: SOE and the Italian Resistance 1943–45* (Emilia, 2004)

Tuker, Lt Gen. Sir Francis, *The Pattern of War* (Cassell, 1944)

US Congress Committee on Military Affairs, *The Rapido River Crossings: Hearings* (Government Printing Office, Washington DC, 1946)

Vaughan-Thomas, Wynford, *Anzio* (Longmans, 1961)

Vego, Prof. Milan N., 'Major Combined/Joint Operations', *JFQ* 48 (1st Quarter, 2008)

Vigneras, Marcel, *Rearming the French* (United States Army in World War II series; Special Studies, Center of Military History, United States Army, Washington DC, 1957)

Villari, Luigi, *The Liberation of Italy, 1943–47* (C. C. Nelson, 1959)

Vrba, L., *Kampf am Volturno 1943, der mörderische Weg nach Montecassino* (Rastatt: E. Pabel, 1986)

Wagner, Robert L., *The Texas Army: A History of the 36th Division in the Italian Campaign* (State House Press, 1972)

Wagner, Wilmer 'Bud', *And There Shall Be Wars*: *WW2 Diaries And Memoirs* (Wilmer and Lloyd Wagner Publishing, 2000)

Walker, Gen. Fred L., *From Texas to Rome: A General's Journal* (Taylor Publishing, 1969)

Wallace, John E., *The Blue Devil 'Battle Mountain' Regiment in Italy: A History of the 350th Infantry Regiment, 1944–45* (Battery Press, 1977)

Wallace, Robert, *Italian Campaign* (Time Life Education, 1978)

Wallenda, Wolfgang, *Die Frontsoldaten von Monte Cassino: Ein Soldat wider Willen erzählt von Kameradschaft, Heimatliebe, Gewissenskonflikten, falschem Heldentum* [The soldiers at the Monte Cassino front: A soldier reluctantly tells of comradeship, patriotism, moral conflict, false heroism] (Triga, 2006)

Walters, Major James W. Jr, 'Artillery and Air Support of Ground Attack, Cassino, 1944', *Military Review, Vol. XXVI*, No. 10 (Jan, 1947)

Wakowicz, Melchior, *Bitwa o Monte Cassino* [The Fight for Monte Cassino], 3 Vols (Wydawnicto, 1945–47)

Werner, Bret, *First Special Service Force, 1942–44* (Osprey, 2006)

Westphal, General Siegfried, *The German Army in the West* (Cassell, 1951)

Wheeler, Lt Col. Charles M., 'Control of Typhus in Italy 1943–44 by Use of DDT', *American Journal of Public Health, Vol. 46* (Feb 1946), pp. 119–29

Whicker, Alan, *Whicker's War* (HarperCollins, 2005)

Whitehead, Don, (ed., Romeiser, John B.), *Combat Reporter: Don Whitehead's World War II Diary and Memoirs* (Fordham University Press, 2006)

Whitlock, Flint, *The Rock of Anzio: From Sicily to Dachau: A History of the 45th Infantry Division* (Westview Press, 1998)

Wilhelm, Maria De Blasio, *The Other Italy: The Italian Resistance in World War II* (W. W. Norton & Co., 1988)

Wilhelmsmeyer, Helmut, *Der Krieg in Italian, 1943–45* (Graz: Stocker, 1995)

Wilkinson, Richard F., *The Breakthrough Battalion: Battles of Company C of the 133rd Infantry Regiment, Tunisia and Italy, 1943–45* (R. Wilkinson, 2005)

Williamson, Hugh, *The Fourth Division, 1939 to 1945* (Newman House, 1951)

Wilson, Field Marshal Sir Henry Maitland, *Report by the Supreme Allied Commander, Mediterranean, to the Combined Chiefs of Staff on the Italian Campaign, Part I, 8 Jan 1944–10 May 1944* (HMSO, 1946); *Part II, 10 May 1944–12 Aug 1944* (HMSO, 1948); *Part III, 13 Aug 1944–12 Dec 1944* (HMSO, 1948)

Windsor, Lee, 'Review Essay: The First Special Service Force: Waste of an Elite Unit or Mountain "Rangers" at the Perfect Time?', *Journal of Conflict Studies* (Winter, 2006)

Wolff, Walter, *Bad Times, Good People: A Holocaust Survivor Recounts His Life in Italy During World War II* (Whittier, 1999)

Woods, Thomas E., Jr., *How The Catholic Church Built Western Civilization* (Regnery Publishing, 2005)

Yeats-Brown, F., *Martial India* (Eyre & Spottiswoode, 1945)

Youngdahl, Herbert M., *The Other Side of War* (Robert Reed Publishers, 2000)

Zaloga, Steven J., *Anzio 1944: The Beleaguered Beachhead* (Osprey, 2005)

———*The Polish Army, 1939–45* (Osprey, 1982)

Zimmerman, Joshua D., (ed.) *Jews in Italy under Fascist and Nazi Rule, 1922–45* (Cambridge University Press, 2005)

Zuehlke, Mark, *Ortona: Canada's Epic World War II Battle* (Stoddart, 1999)

———*The Liri Valley, Canada's World War II Breakthrough to Rome* (Douglas & McIntyre, 2001)

List of Illustrations

23. Shellshock. From the author's collection
24. Cavendish Road © US National Archives and Records Administration
25. Propaganda. From the author's collection
26. Canadians © Hulton-Deutsch Collection/Corbis
27. Under fire. From the author's collection.
28. French Expeditionary Corps © US National Archives and Records Administration
29. Goumiers © US National Archives and Records Administration
30. Cassino leaflet. From the author's collection
31. Climbing into hills © US National Archives and Records Administration
32. Wrecked truck © US National Archives and Records Administration
33. Clearing farm © US National Archives and Records Administration
34. AA Gunners © US National Archives and Records Administration
35. Train wreck. From the author's collection
36. Ruined town. From the author's collection
37. Medic with casualty © US National Archives and Records Administration
38. Panther turret © US National Archives and Records Administration
39. Transport © US National Archives and Records Administration
40. Rome © US National Archives and Records Administration

Acknowledgements

The book is the result of over fifteen years of visiting the Monte Cassino battlefields, which has also brought the immense privilege of meeting some of those who fought there in 1943–44. Though many of them are no longer with us, over the years they have lent me their letters, diaries and reminiscences to bear the torch on their behalf. Those warriors of yesteryear represent each of the ten armies in this book, and while they would have nodded to the presence of 'hell' at Cassino in its various forms – they also remembered the happy, comradely times that are the currency of soldiering.

A theme running through this story of ten nations and four battles at Cassino is coalition warfare. The extraordinary rainbow alliance of nations and races fighting on the Italian front was one of the most varied ever to have operated in military history. Field Marshall Alexander thought the national diversity important enough to list in his post-war report on the 1943–45 campaign, where he identified twenty-six nationalities. It provides a pertinent echo to modern multinational military operations seen since the 1990s in the former Yugoslavia, Middle East, Afghanistan, Libya and elsewhere, where coalitions of widely disparate cultures and countries are very much the order of the day. To study the Cassino campaign of 1944 provides a useful window through which to understand the pressures on coalition armies facing lengthy deployments in far-off, inhospitable terrain today.

I am privileged to work in the very multinational, tri-service environment of the UK Defence Academy at Shrivenham, where military colleagues, staff and students continually throw new light on old battles for me. One advantage of life here was the annual visit to past fields of war, studying aspects of military history, technology, leadership, doctrine and logistics, and their relevance to today. One of the most outstanding of these tours was to Monte Cassino in 2007, for which I tip my hat in very overdue fashion to Susan Truesdale, who temporarily forsook her duties as Academic Registrar to glue together an excellent expedition. I learned so much on that tour, particularly from my friend, colleague, mentor and fellow battlefield guide Professor Richard Holmes, who sadly died in April 2011. It is sometimes difficult to express the crucial impact a single individual has on one's professional life, but Richard shaped my career as no other. He was a delightful man who was always ready to drop everything else and help. I doubly miss the unique sparkle he brought with him, for he was twice my boss: as Professor Holmes at Cranfield University and Brigadier Holmes of the Territorial Army.

Another historian to whom I owe a great debt is James Holland, who has written on the last year of the Italian campaign, and unbidden, placed his archives at my disposal. I am grateful as well to my colleagues at Cranfield and across the Defence Academy campus at Shrivenham, especially: Dr Laura Cleary, head of the Centre for International Security and Resilience, for allowing me to invest so much professional time in this project; David Turns, who guided me through the intricacies of international law vis-à-vis the bombing of the monastery; Lieutenant Colonel (retd) John Starling, historian of the Royal Pioneer Corps and curator of the Small Arms Wing, who taught me much about Allied and German weaponry; and Lieutenant Colonel (retd) Tom Hamilton-Baillie and his wife Marina (née von Senger und Etterlin) who helped me on matters of German army history, have been enormously helpful, as has Anne Harbour, my secretary. This book would have taken three times as long to write were it not for the staff of the two libraries here, Iain McKay and Rachel Daniels of the Barrington Library and Chris Hobson and his team at the Joint Services Command and Staff College Library.

Some help was anticipated, but other assistance arrived unexpectedly, such as the day when I discovered Field Marshal Sir John Stanier at the Polish Memorial on Point 593 at Cassino, and received an hour of his erudite thoughts on Cassino; or the moment in the German Military Cemetery at Maleme on Crete when I bumped into the former Fallschirmjäger Leutnant, now Monsignor, Hermann Volk, who had jumped onto the island in 1941 and fought at Cassino. The years fell off him as he instantly recalled the words to the Fallschirmjägerleid paratroopers' song '*Rot scheint die Sonne*' ('*Red Shines the Sun*'). To the Polish Institute and Sikorski Museum in London SW7, and Polish veterans I have met, I owe special thanks. Their moving monument at Point 593 overlooking Cassino says it all: 'We Polish soldiers/For our freedom and yours/Have given our souls to God/Our bodies to the soil of Italy/And our hearts to Poland.'

Three colleagues overseas have been particularly helpful over the years in guiding me around their local battlefields: Michele Di Lonardo who somehow juggles running the excellent *Hotel Ristorante Al Boschetto* in Cassino with being an expert guide; Federico Lamberti, publisher of many books about the campaign, which can be bought in his bookshop in the Piazza De Gasperi, Cassino; and Diego Cancelli at Aprilia, who likewise combines his job as an architect with intimate knowledge of every aspect of the Anzio campaign, thanks to the three of you. My good friend, the classicist and philosopher Dr. Angeliki Vasilopoulou, has also provided valuable insights and much help and support. I must acknowledge also the invaluable assistance of the Commonwealth War Graves Commission, who are responsible for the immaculate

Cassino and Minturno cemeteries; and their counterparts at the Volksbund Deutsche Kriegsgräberfursorge and the American Battlefields Monuments Commission, who administer the 'Sicily-Rome' US War Cemetery at Nettuno. In museums across the world, I have received a great deal of assistance, especially at Cassino's new Museo La Battaglia di Monte Cassino, Il Museo dello Sbarco di Anzio, San Pietro Infine War Museum, the Monte Lungo War Museum and Piana Delle Orme, Latina. The Abbott of Montecassino and various defence attaches on staff of the British Embassy in Rome, including Colonel Tom Huggan, have all been most generous with their time and help.

So, too, have fellow members of the Guild of Battlefield Guides and British Commission for Military History; the staff of the Aerial Reconnaissance Archive, Edinburgh; *After the Battle Magazine*; Bletchley Park; the British Library, the British Library Newspaper Collection at Colindale, north London; the Bundesarchiv, Freiburg; the Canadian War Museum, Ottawa; Churchill Archives Centre, Cambridge; the Gurkha Museum, Winchester; Nigel Steel, Simon Robbins and the staff at the Imperial War Museum, London; the Liddell Hart Centre for Military Archives at King's College, London; Militärgeschichtliches Forschungsamt in Potsdam; Militärshistoriche Museum der Bundeswehr, Dresden; the Military Museums (formerly the Museum of the Regiments), Calgary, Canada; Musée de l'Armée at Les Invalides, Paris; the National Archives, Kew; Michael Ball and colleagues at the National Army Museum, Chelsea, which holds archives of the old British-Indian forces as well; the National Army Museum, Waiouru, New Zealand; professors Chris Bellamy, John Buckley, Ashley Jackson, Gael Miller, Gary Sheffield, Hew Strachan and Trevor Taylor; Drs David Chuter, Dale Clark, Lloyd Clark, Ed Flint, David Hall, Charles Kirke; Patrick Mercer MP and Keith Simpson MP; Peter Macdonald and Toby Macleod, RMAS Library, Sandhurst; the Royal United Services Institute Library at Whitehall; the Second World War Experience Centre, Walton, West Yorkshire; South African Military History Society; the Ditsong National Museum of Military History (formerly the South African National Museum of Military History), Erlswold Way, Saxonwold, Johannesburg; the Tank Museum, Bovington, Dorset; the US Army Command and General Staff College Library at Fort Leavenworth, Kansas; the US Army Center of Military History, Fort Lesley J. McNair, Washington, DC; the US Army Quartermaster Museum, Fort Lee, Virginia; the US Army War College Library, Forbes Avenue, Carlisle, Pennsylvania.

I am enormously fortunate to have a very supportive and patient editor in Kate Johnson, who had been as much an ADC or adjutant, and whose long hours of turning my ramblings into crisp prose I can never repay adequately. I owe much to her guidance and knowledge. To Trevor Dolby and Nicola Taplin, leading the team at Preface Publishing, Random House, my heartfelt thanks for indulging me with this second title for them; like commanding generals on the field of battle, they saw the potential of this project, encouraged me enormously to assemble my troops and advance. When setbacks occurred, they refused to panic, altered their plans, and only when necessary issued threats of a last cigarette, blindfold and execution at dawn, but always with good grace. Ruth Waldram has nimbly cranked the handles of their publicity machine. My agent, Patrick Walsh at Conville and Walsh, assisted by Alex Christofi, has been an excellent guide and mentor, to him I am equally grateful.

My family have been hugely supportive; my thanks to Stefania and Emmanuelle for enduring this next project. As the ink dried on my last book I promised to restore our house to its former condition and tidy away my book skyscrapers from each and every room. Alas, *Monte Cassino* has resulted merely in my reconstructing a passing resemblance to the high walls of that venerable Italian monastery from more volumes distributed evenly throughout the house. Mr Charles Dickens, I feel, would have nodded, and approved.

Index